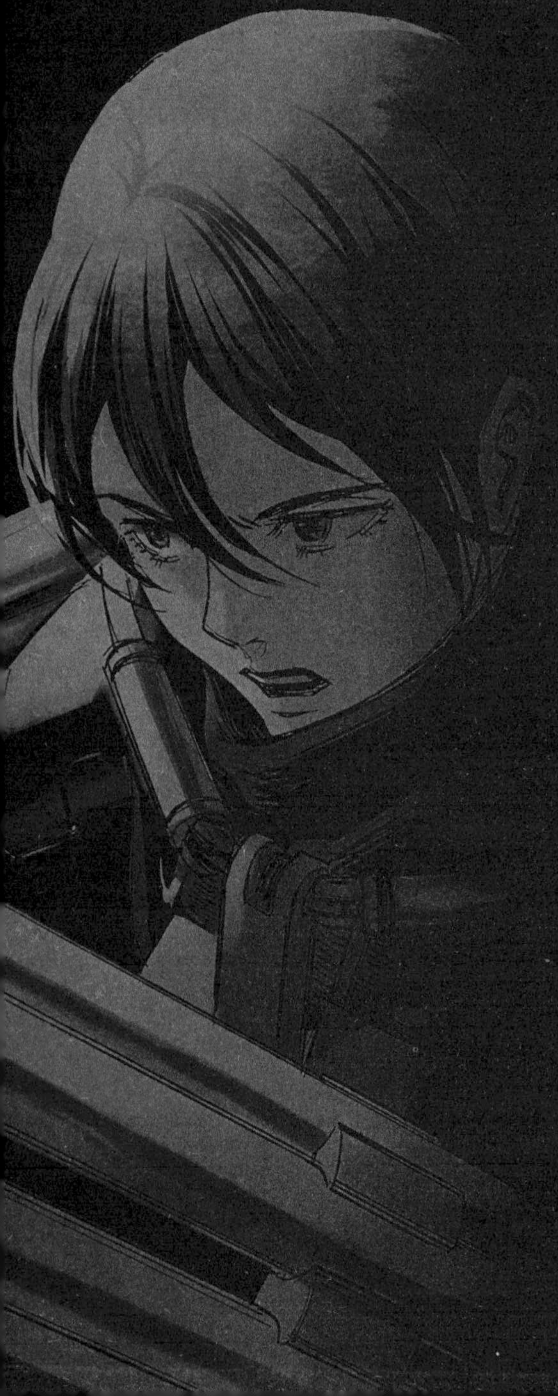

ATTACK ON TITAN
26

HAJIME ISAYAMA

THE ELDIAN WARRIORS IN THE MARLEYAN ARMY

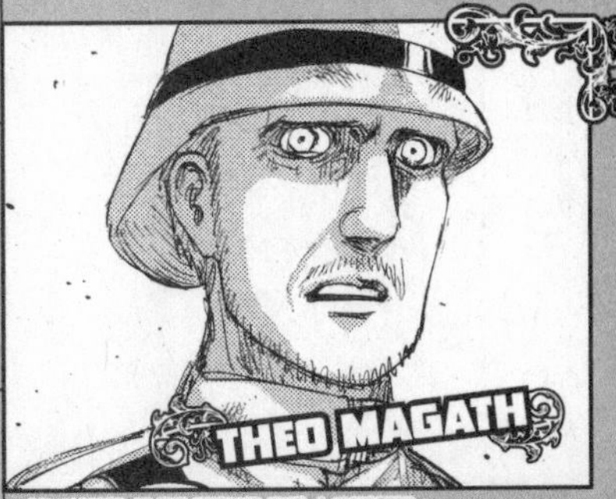
THEO MAGATH

COMMANDER OF THE WARRIOR UNIT. A MARLEYAN WHO LEADS A UNIT OF ELDIANS.

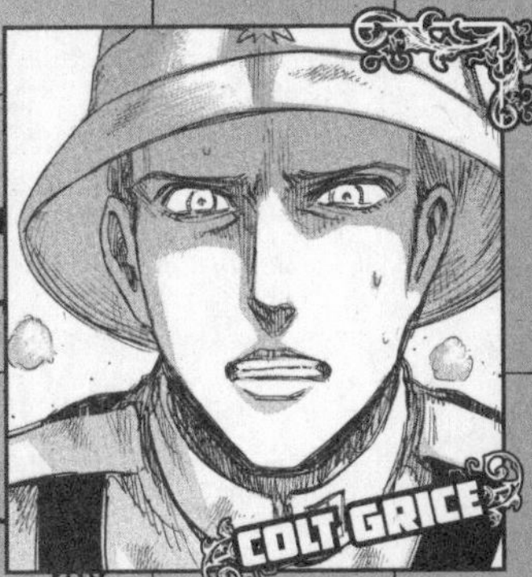
COLT GRICE

ALCO'S OLDER ROTHER WHO, S THE OLDEST OF THE WARRIOR CANDIDATES, CTS AS THEIR EADER. ON THE PATH TO NHERITING THE BEAST TITAN.

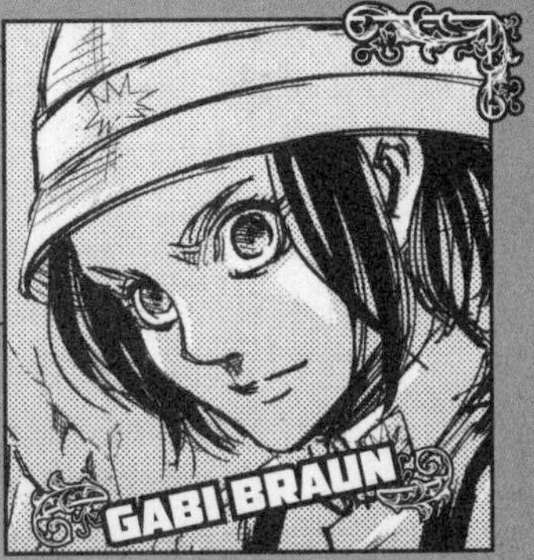
GABI BRAUN

REINER'S COUSIN WHO SEEKS TO INHERIT THE ARMORED TITAN. SIMPLE AND INNOCENT, AS WELL AS BOLD AND BRAVE.

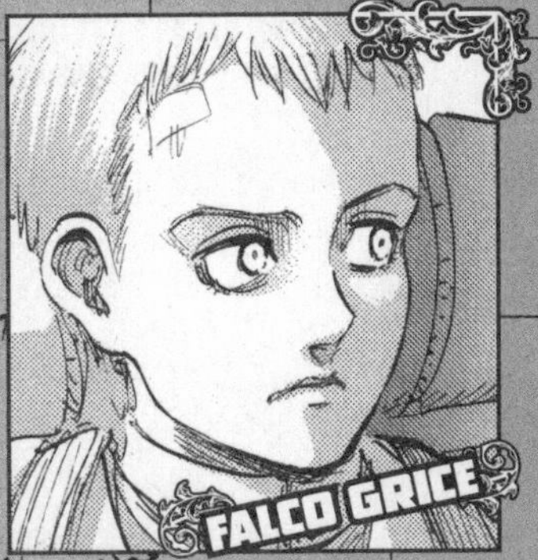
FALCO GRICE

ECAUSE OF THE AFFECTION ALCO HAS FOR GABI, HE TOO ASPIRES TO INHERIT THE RMORED TITAN IN ORDER TO ROTECT HER.

THE BEAST TITAN

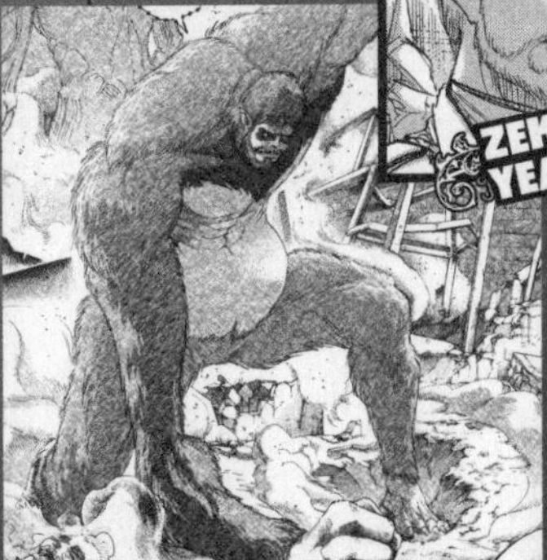
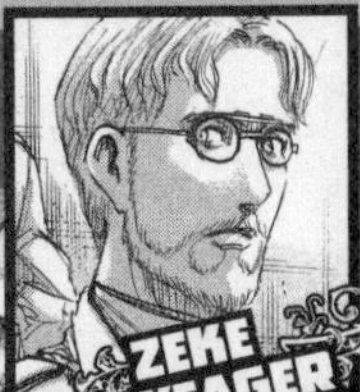
ZEKE YEAGER

CAPTAIN OF THE WARRIORS. GRISHA'S SON AND EREN'S HALF-BROTHER.

HE ARMORED TITAN

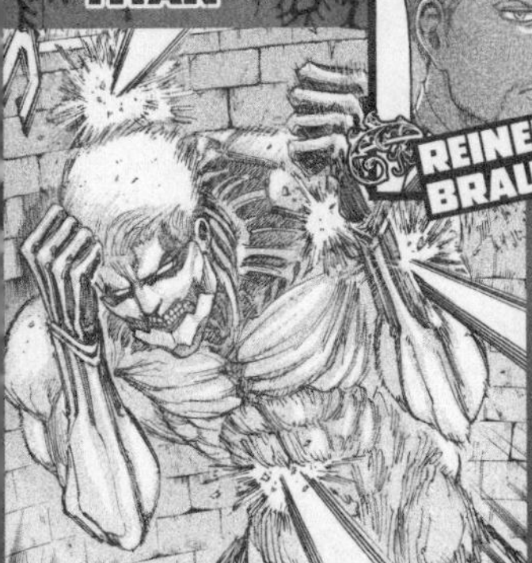
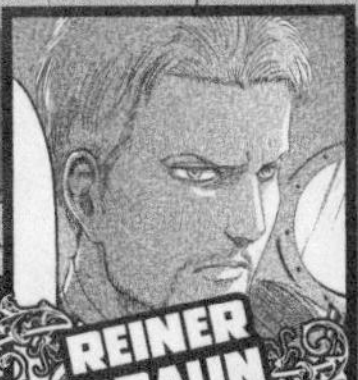
REINER BRAUN

VICE-CAPTAIN OF THE WARRIORS. THE ONLY ONE TO MAKE IT BACK ALIVE AMONG THOSE WHO INFILTRATED PARADIS ISLAND.

ATTACK ON TITAN CHARACTERS: MARLEY AR

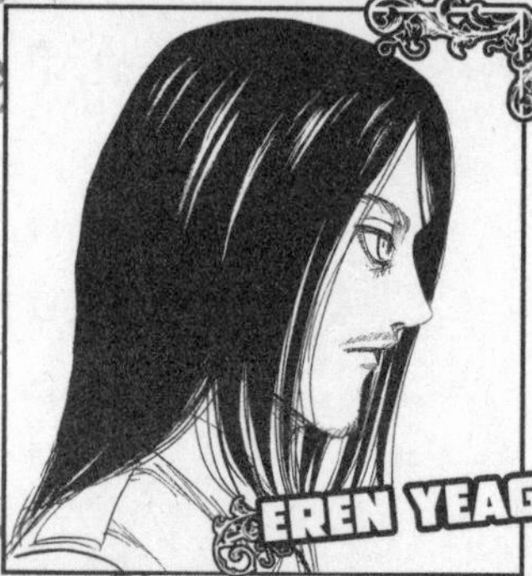

EREN YEAGER

INFILTRATED MARLEY BY HIDING HIMSELF AMONG WOUNDED ELDIAN WARRIORS.

THE WAR HAMMER TITAN

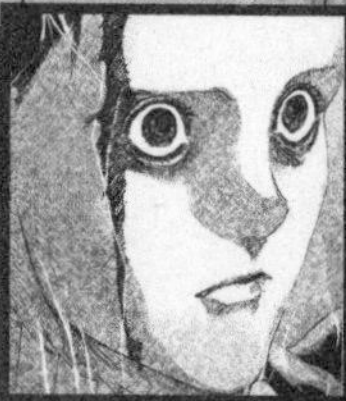

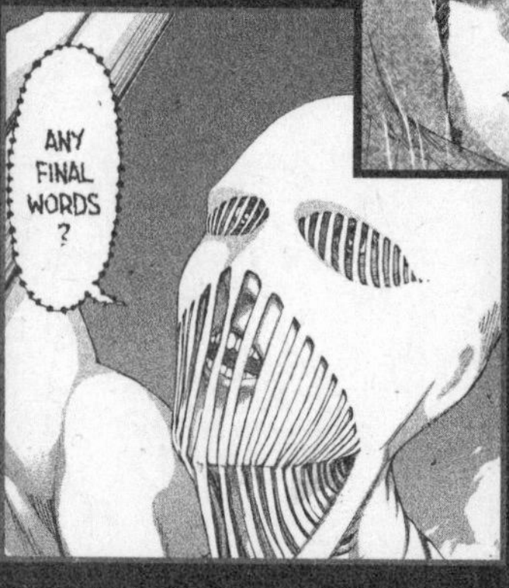
ANY FINAL WORDS?

THE YOUNGER SISTER OF WILLY, THE HEAD OF THE TYBUR FAMILY. THEY HAD CONCEALED THAT SHE WAS THE HEIR TO THE WAR HAMMER.

WARRIOR CANDIDATES

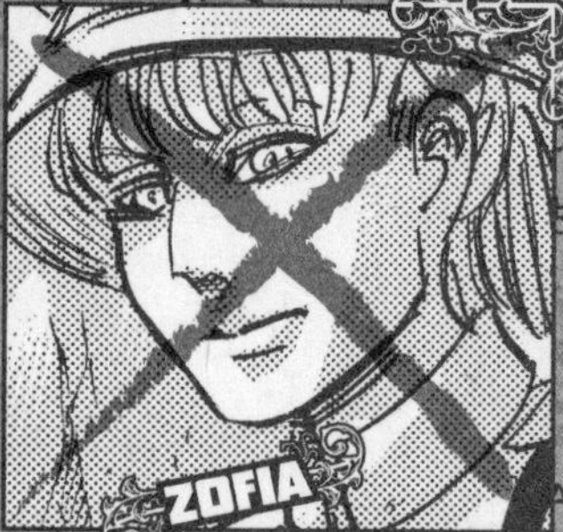

ZOFIA

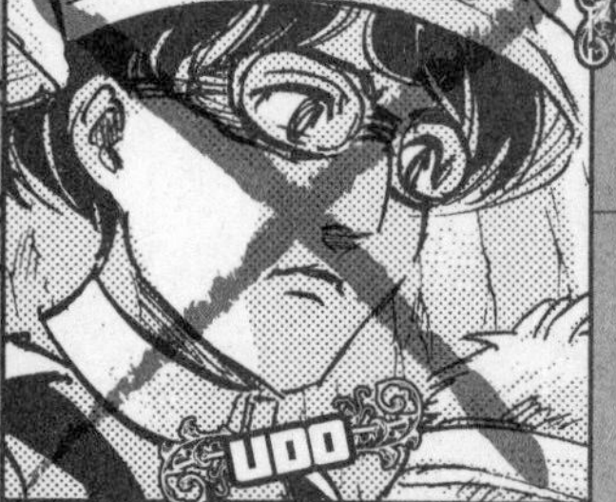

UDO

THE JAW TITAN

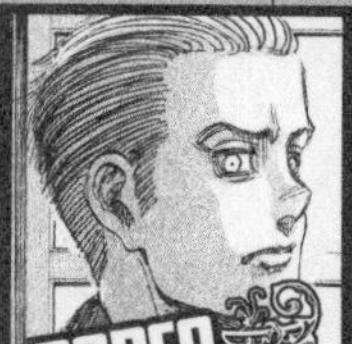

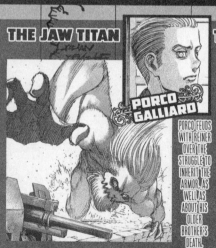

PORCO GALLIARD

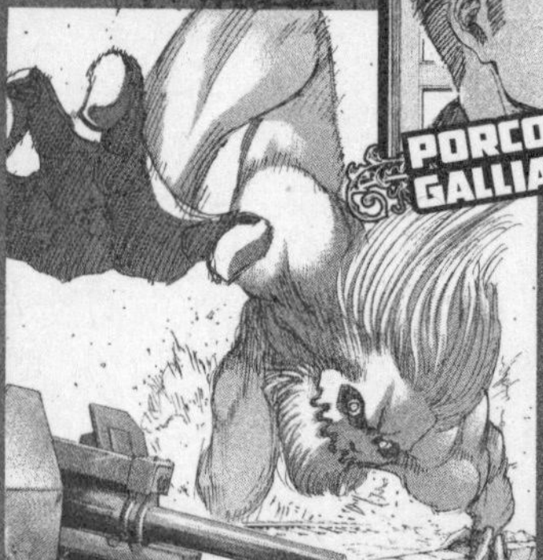

PORCO FEUDS WITH REINER OVER THE STRUGGLE TO INHERIT THE ARMOR, AS WELL AS ABOUT HIS OLDER BROTHER'S DEATH.

THE CART TITAN

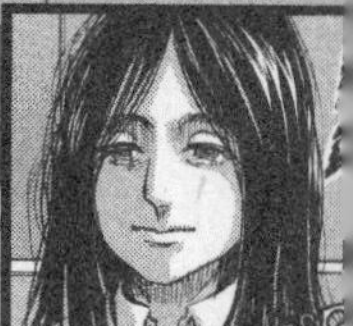

PIECK

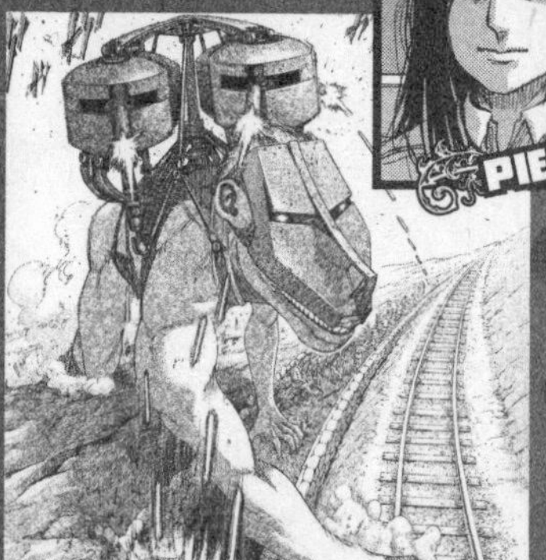

WHILE SHE SEEM LA PERHAPS DU THE EFFECT WALKING ON FOURS FOR EXTENDE PERIODS TIME, SHE RECOGNIZED HER JUDGM

ATTACK on TITAN

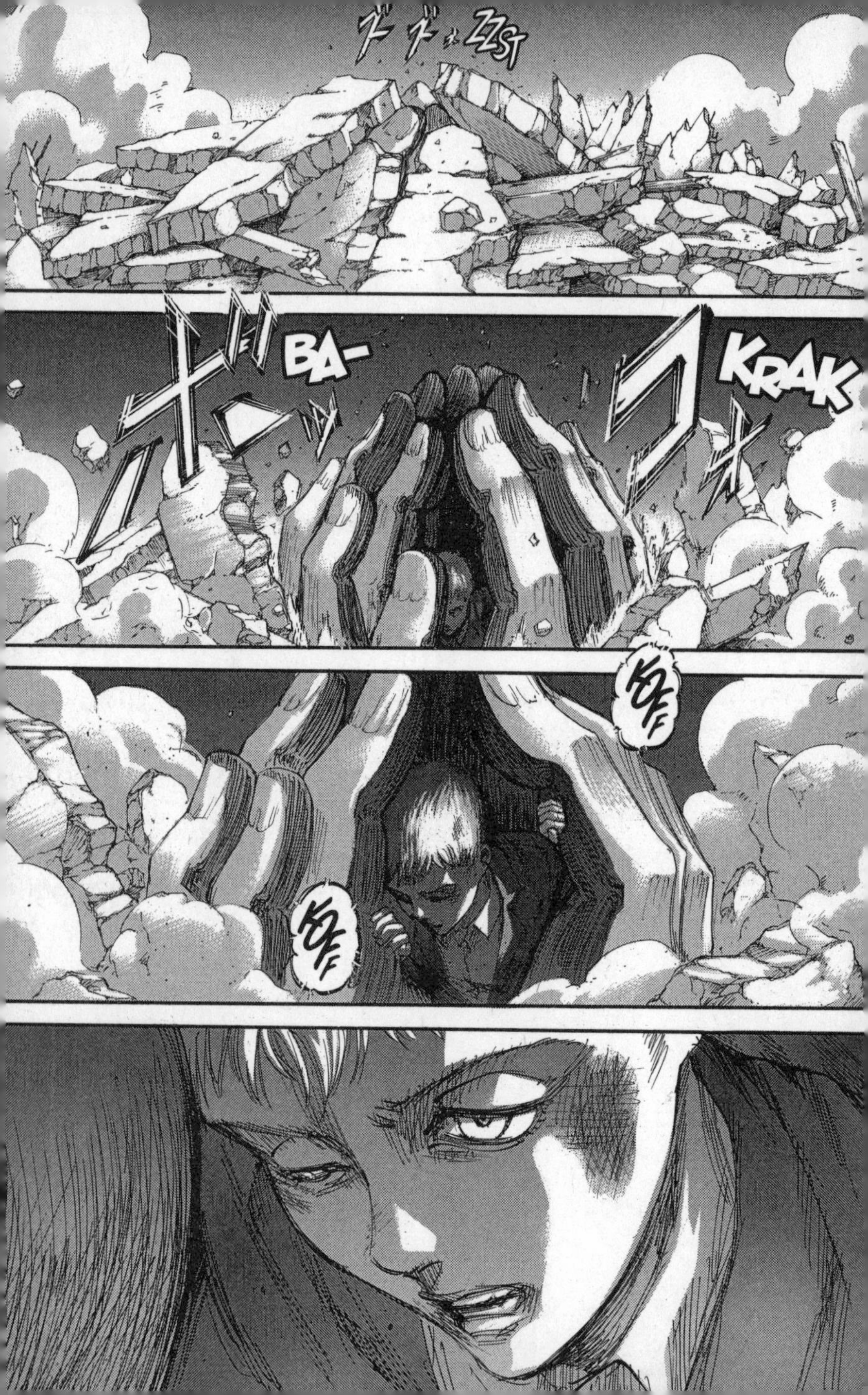
ZZST
KRAK
BA-
KOFF
KOFF

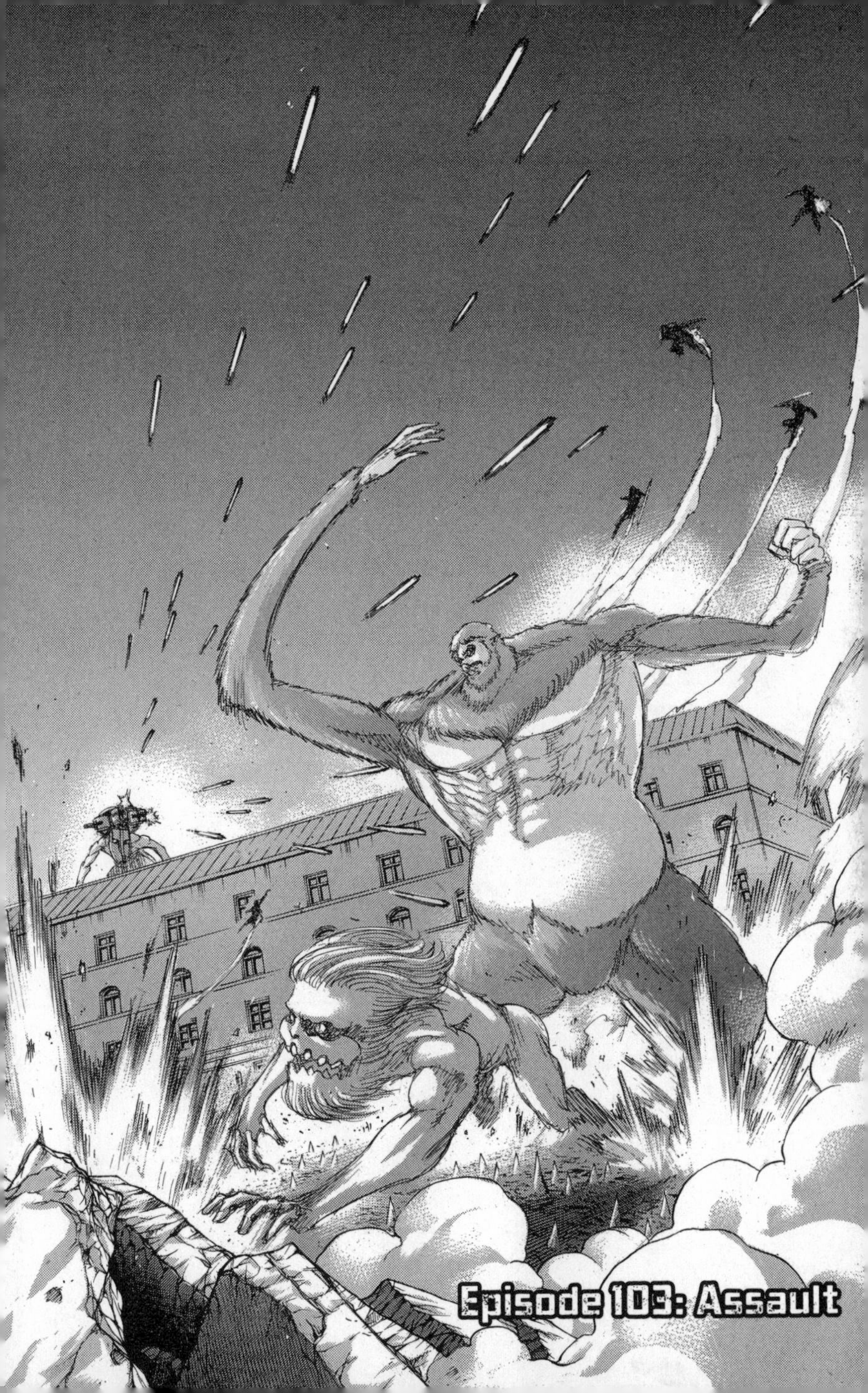
Episode 103: Assault

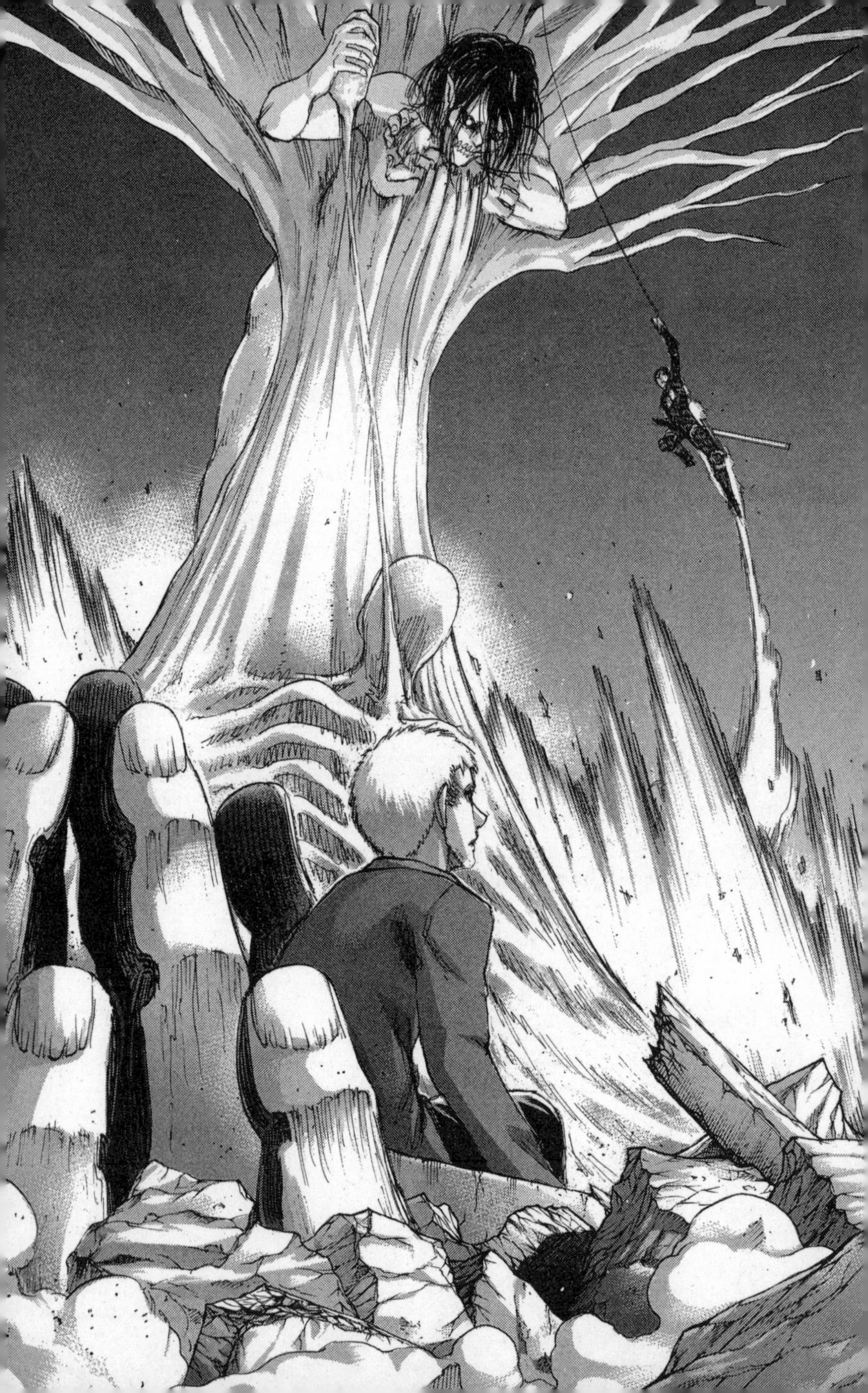

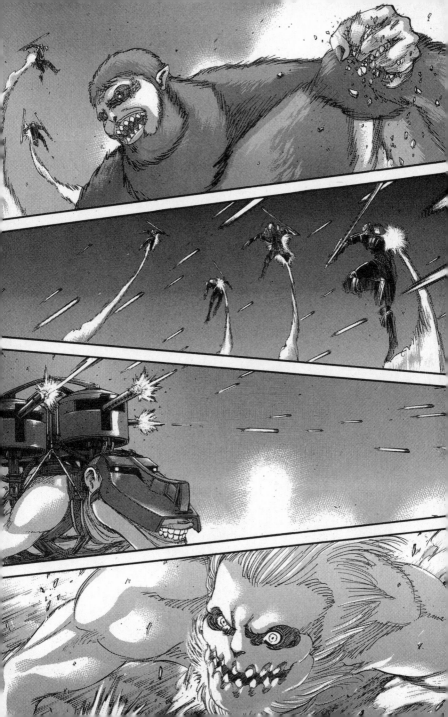

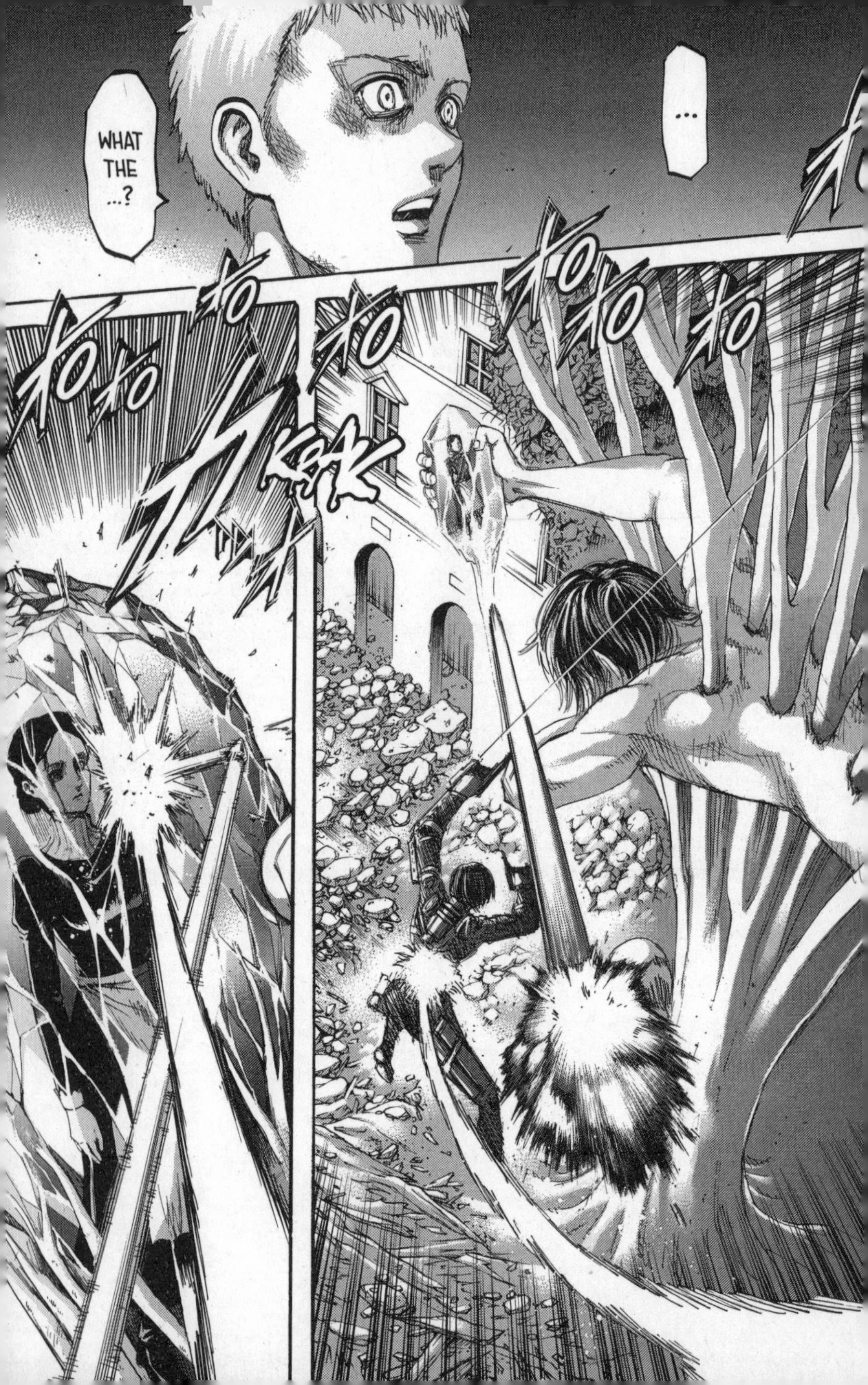
...
WHAT THE ...?
KRAK

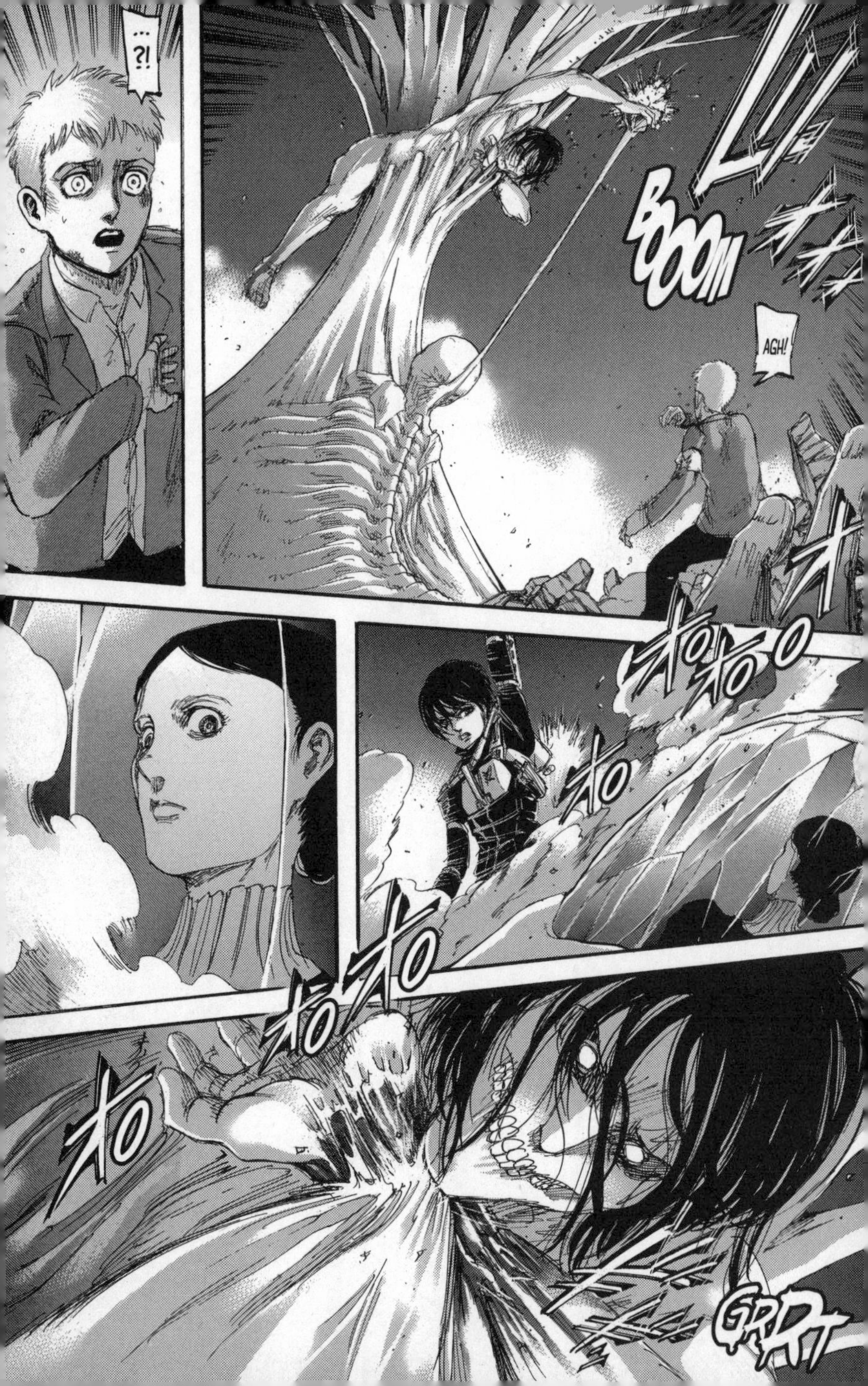
BOOOM
AGH!
...?!
GRRRT

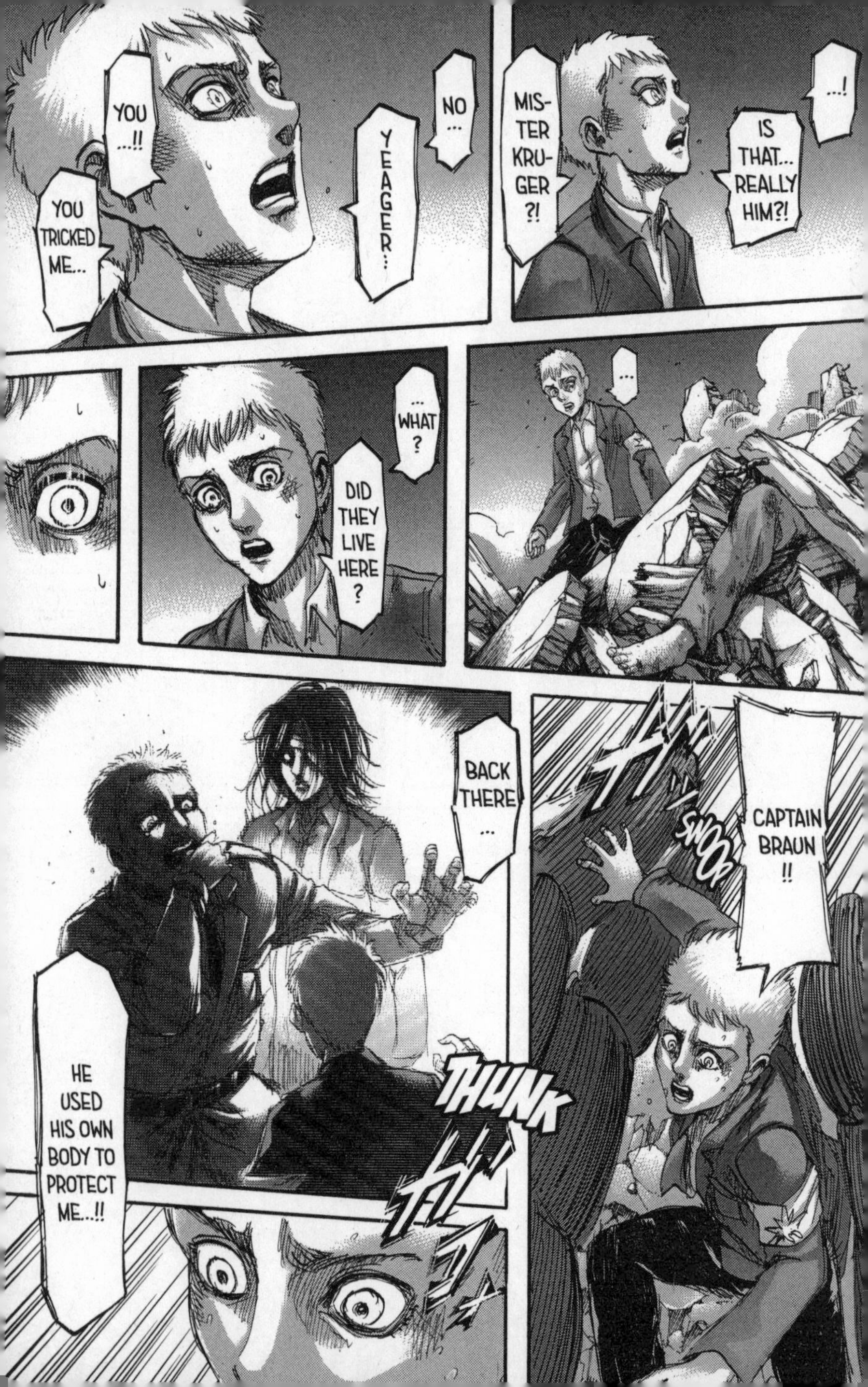
…!
IS THAT… REALLY HIM?!
MISTER KRUGER?!
NO…
YEAGER…
YOU…!!
YOU TRICKED ME…
…
…WHAT?
DID THEY LIVE HERE?
CAPTAIN BRAUN!!
SWOOP
BACK THERE…
THUNK
HE USED HIS OWN BODY TO PROTECT ME…!!

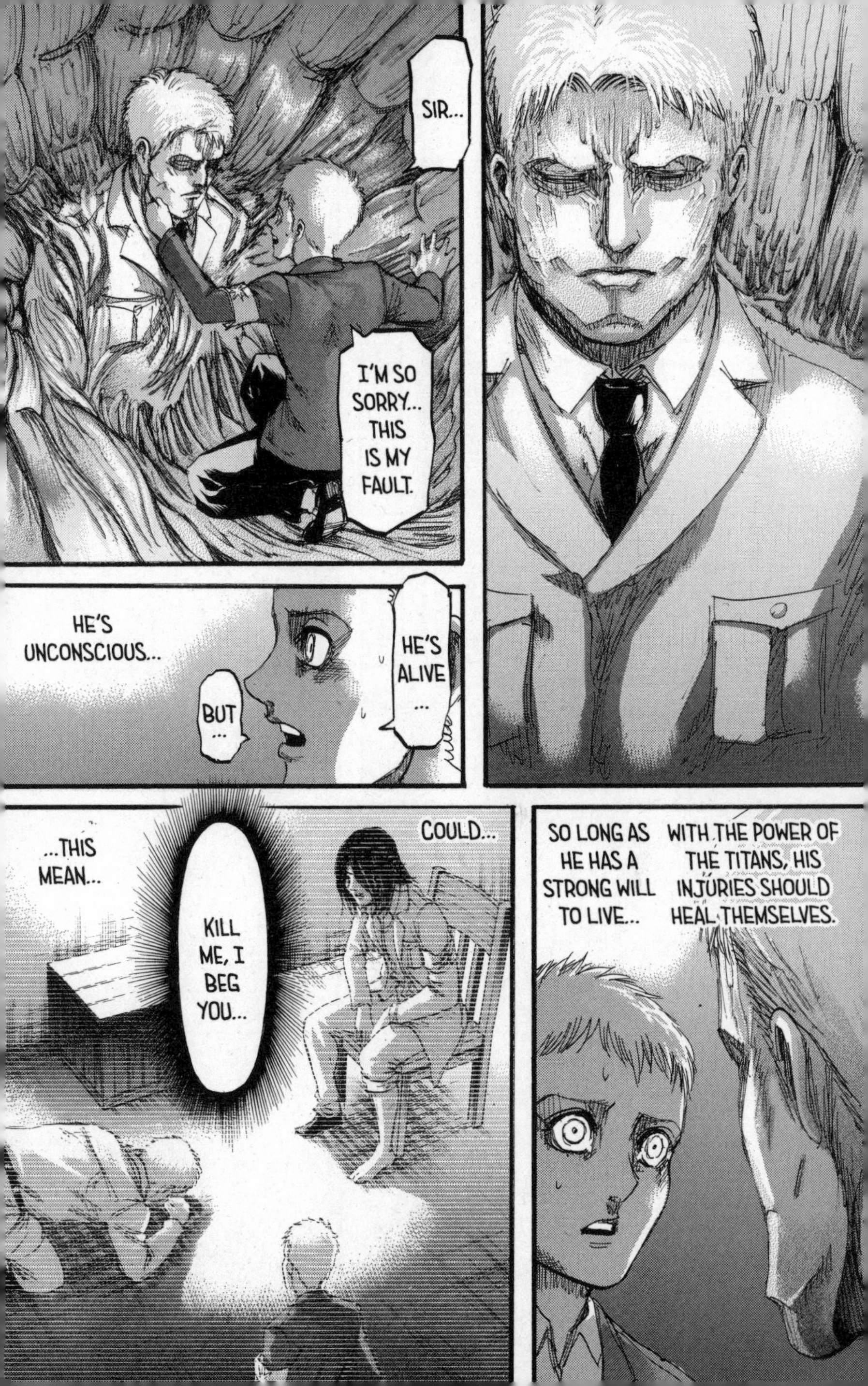
SIR...
I'M SO SORRY... THIS IS MY FAULT.
HE'S ALIVE ...
BUT ...
HE'S UNCONSCIOUS...
WITH THE POWER OF THE TITANS, HIS INJURIES SHOULD HEAL THEMSELVES.
SO LONG AS HE HAS A STRONG WILL TO LIVE...
COULD...
KILL ME, I BEG YOU...
...THIS MEAN...

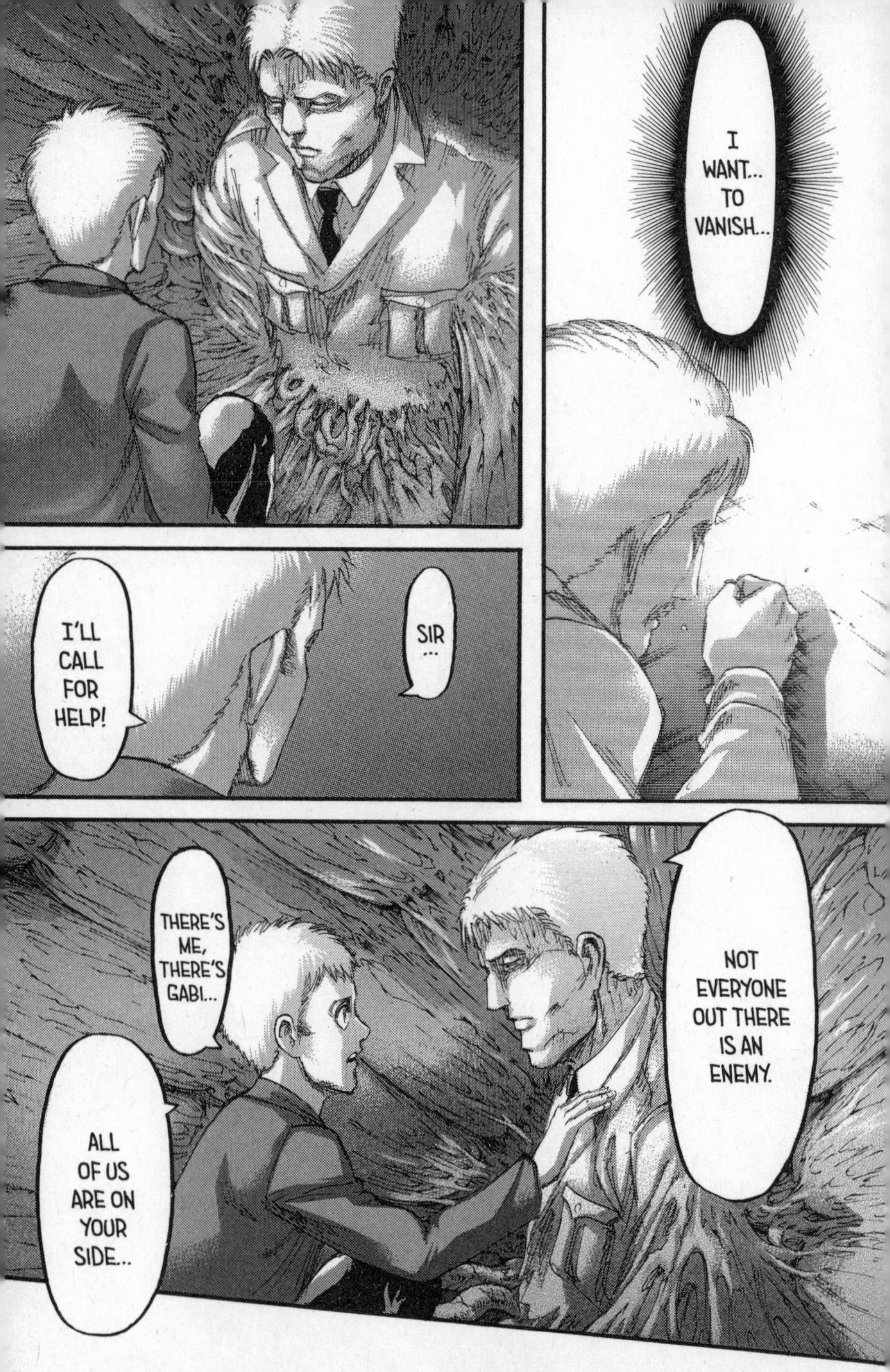
I WANT... TO VANISH...
SIR...
I'LL CALL FOR HELP!
NOT EVERYONE OUT THERE IS AN ENEMY.
THERE'S ME, THERE'S GABI...
ALL OF US ARE ON YOUR SIDE...

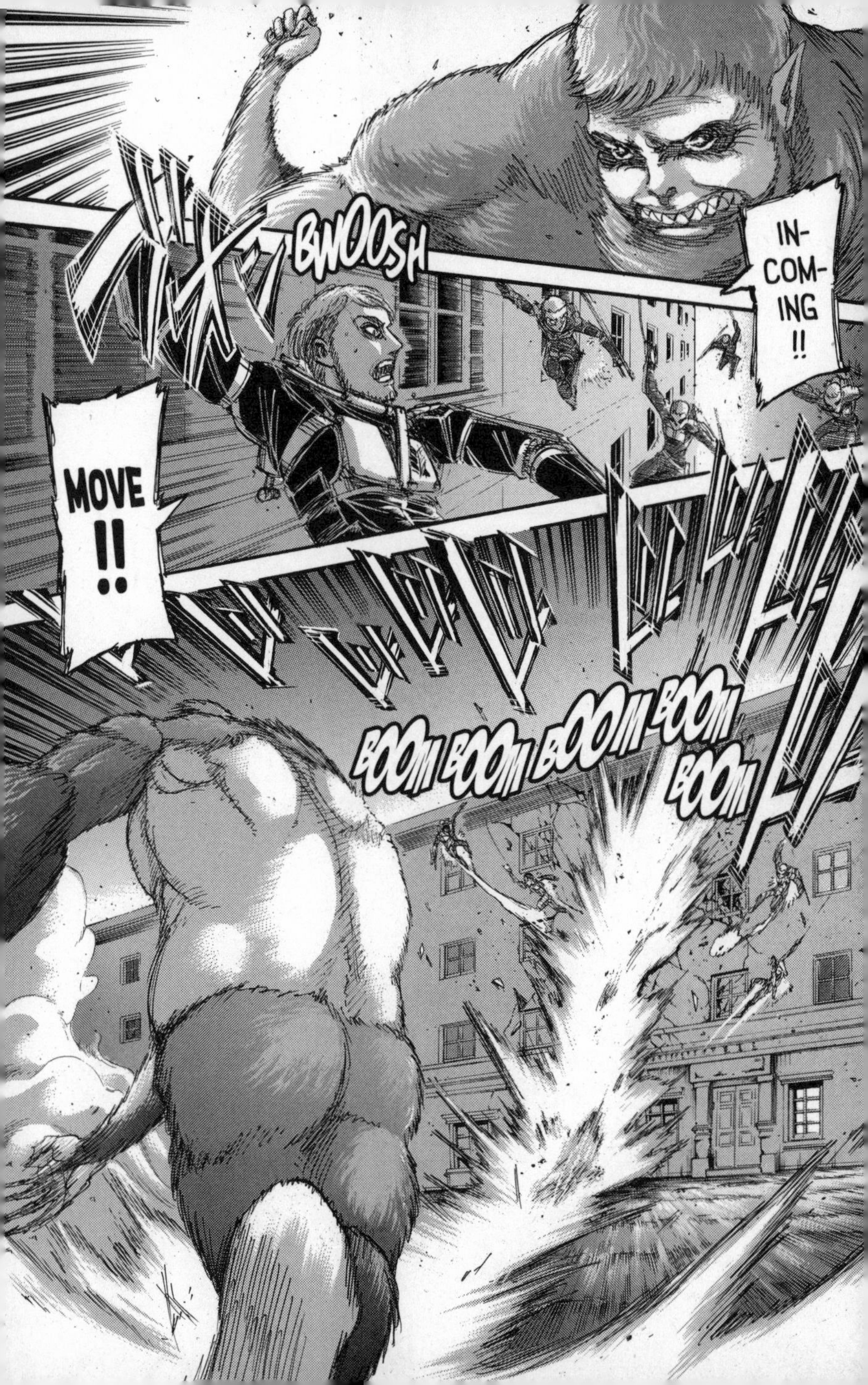

INCOMING!!
BWOOSH
MOVE!!
BOOM BOOM BOOM BOOM BOOM

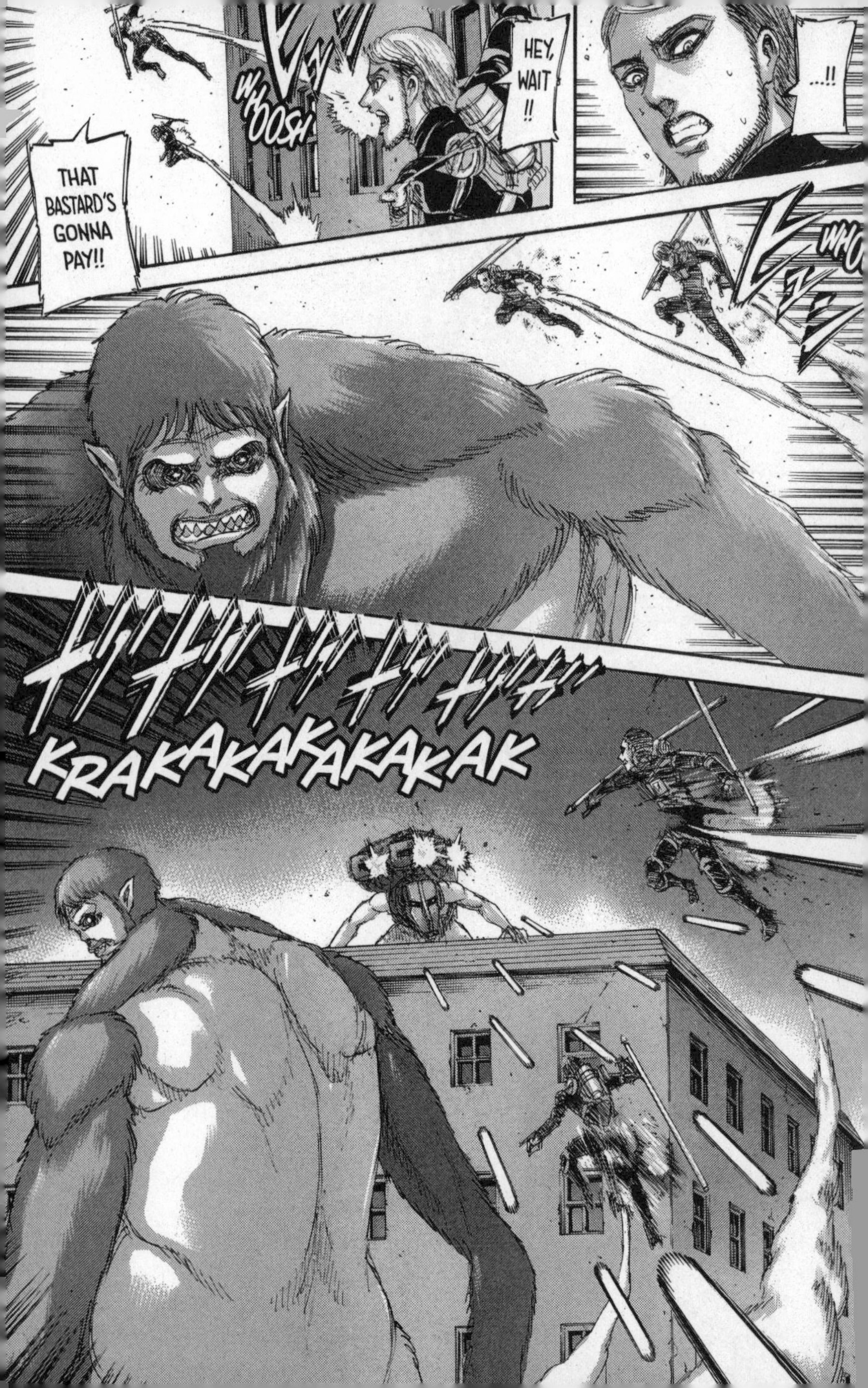
...!!
HEY, WAIT !!
WHOOSH
THAT BASTARD'S GONNA PAY!!
KRAKAKAKAKAKAK

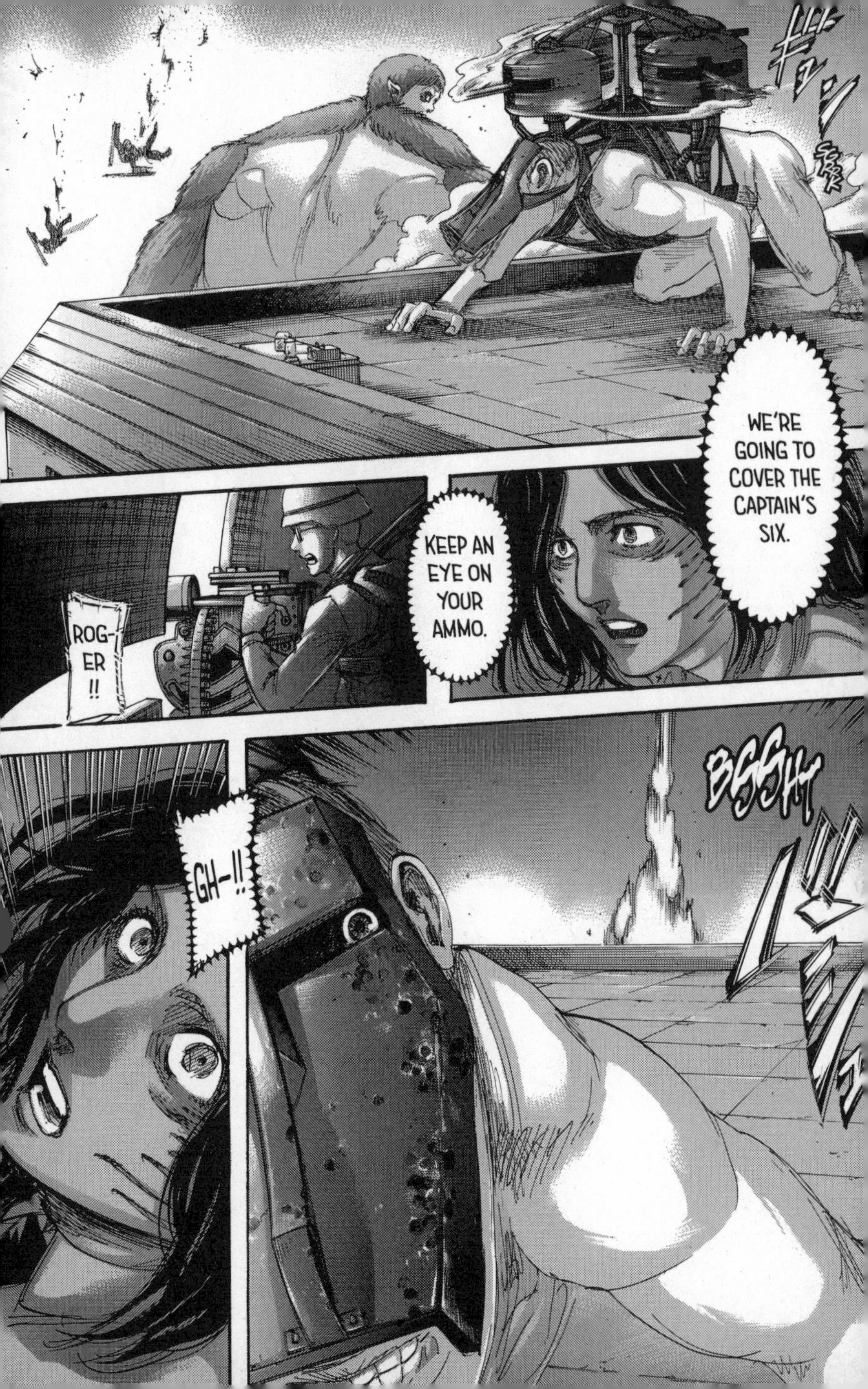
SCRRK
WE'RE GOING TO COVER THE CAPTAIN'S SIX.
KEEP AN EYE ON YOUR AMMO.
ROG-ER !!
BGSH
GH-!!

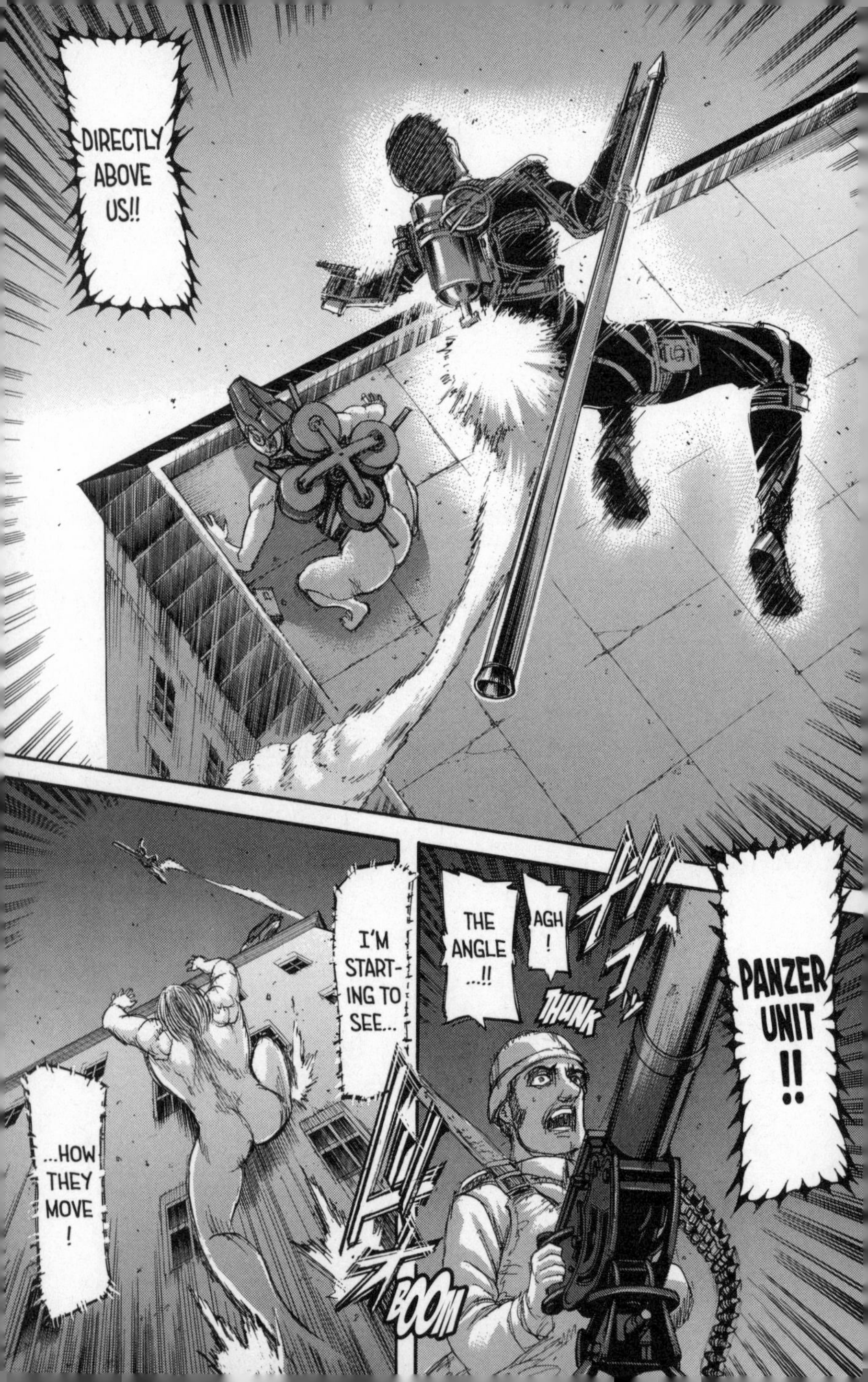
DIRECTLY ABOVE US!!
PANZER UNIT!!
AGH!
THE ANGLE...!!
THUNK
BOOM
I'M STARTING TO SEE...
...HOW THEY MOVE!

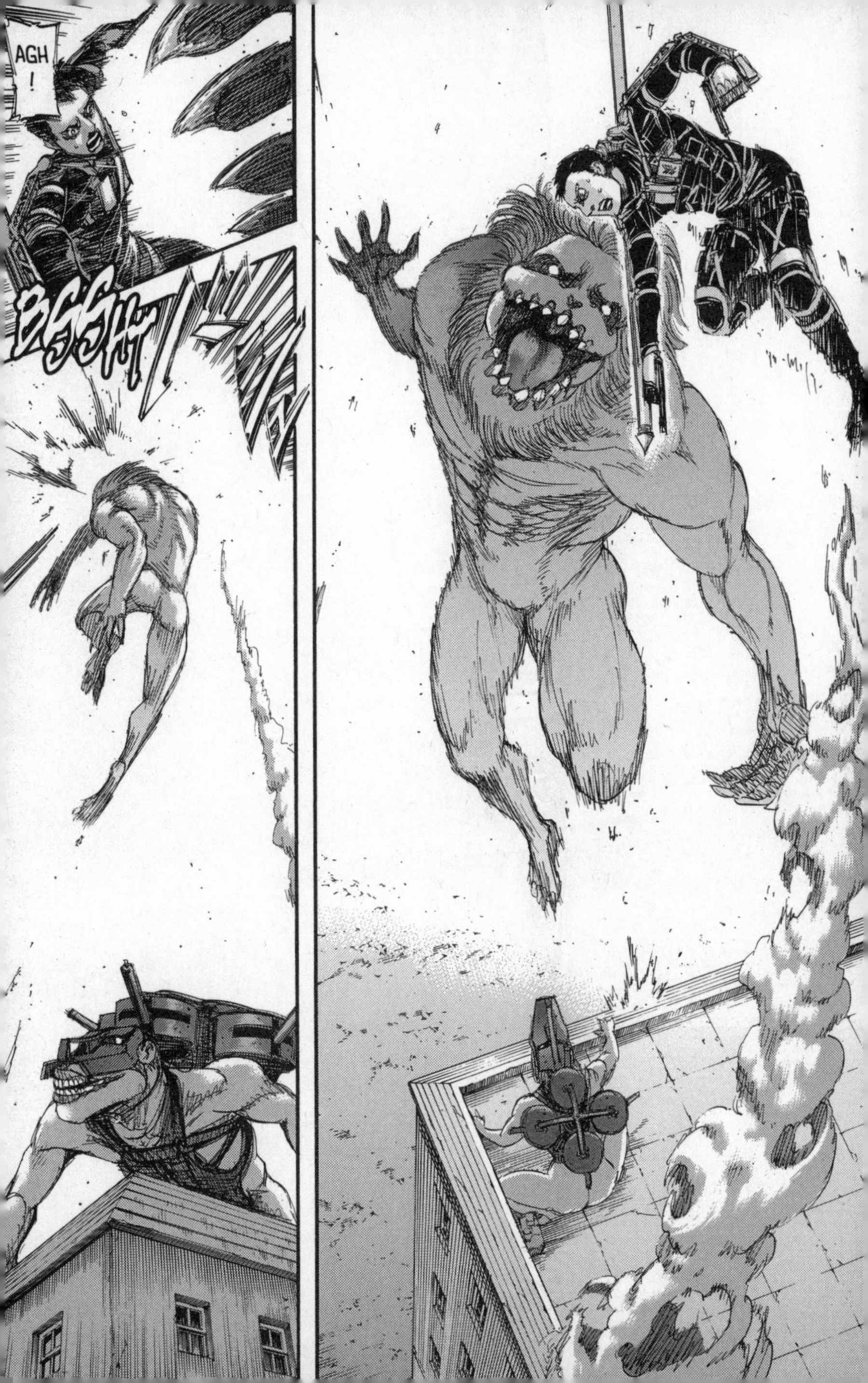
AGH!
BGSH

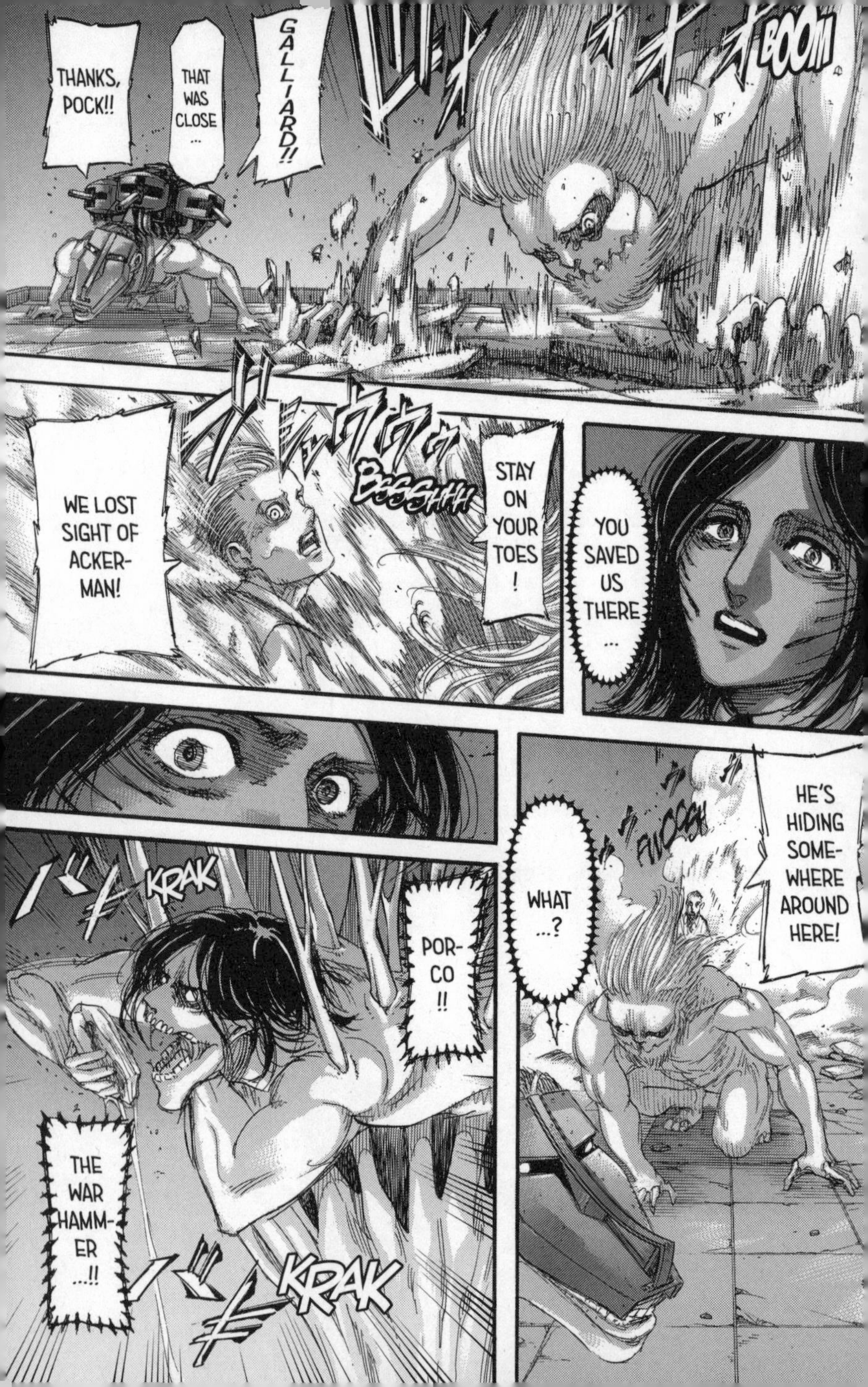
BOOM
GALLIARD!!
THAT WAS CLOSE ...
THANKS, POCK!!
YOU SAVED US THERE ...
STAY ON YOUR TOES!
BSSSHHH
WE LOST SIGHT OF ACKER-MAN!
HE'S HIDING SOME-WHERE AROUND HERE!
FWOOSH
WHAT ...?
PORCO!!
KRAK
THE WAR HAMM-ER ...!!
KRAK

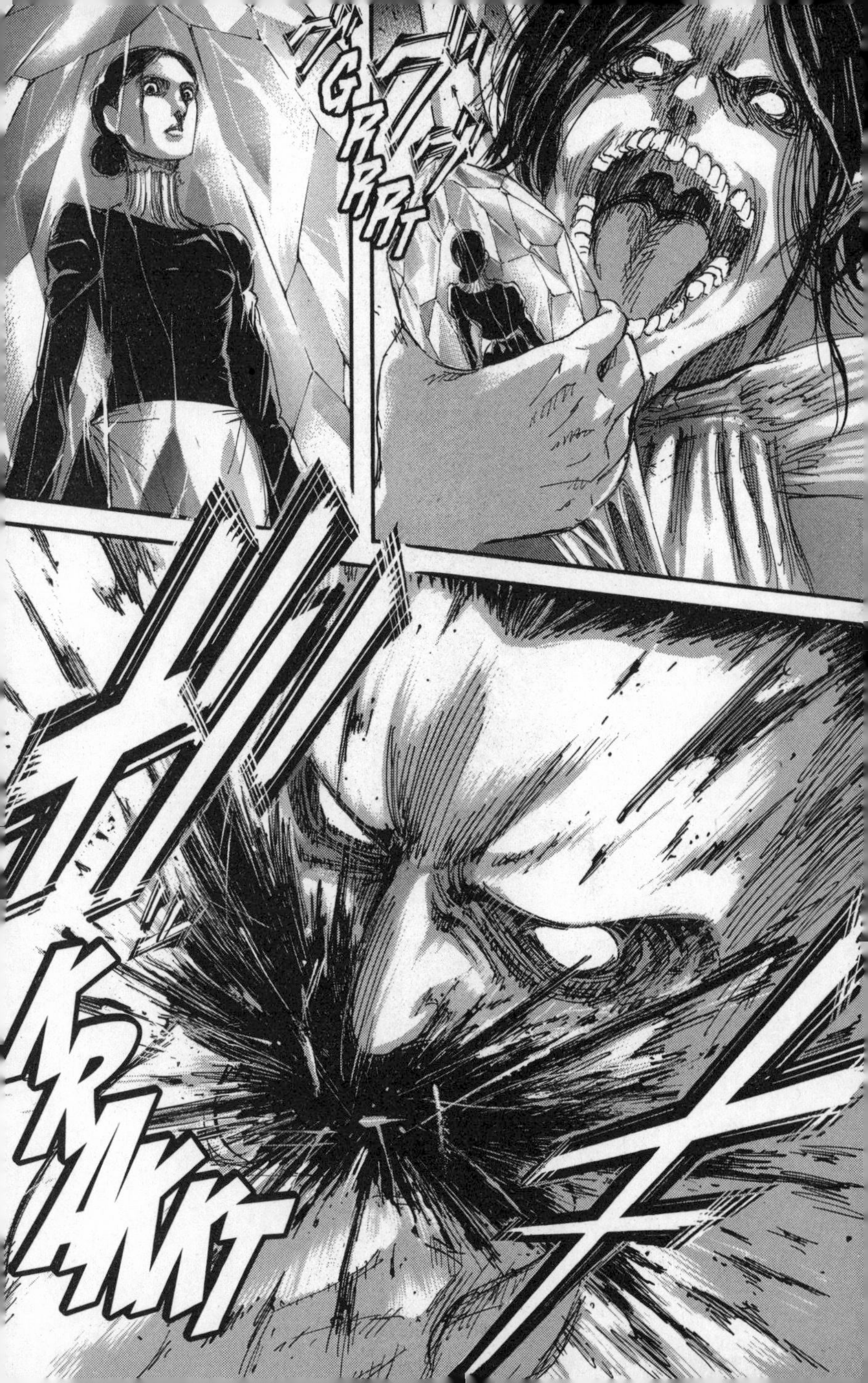
GRRRT
KRAKT

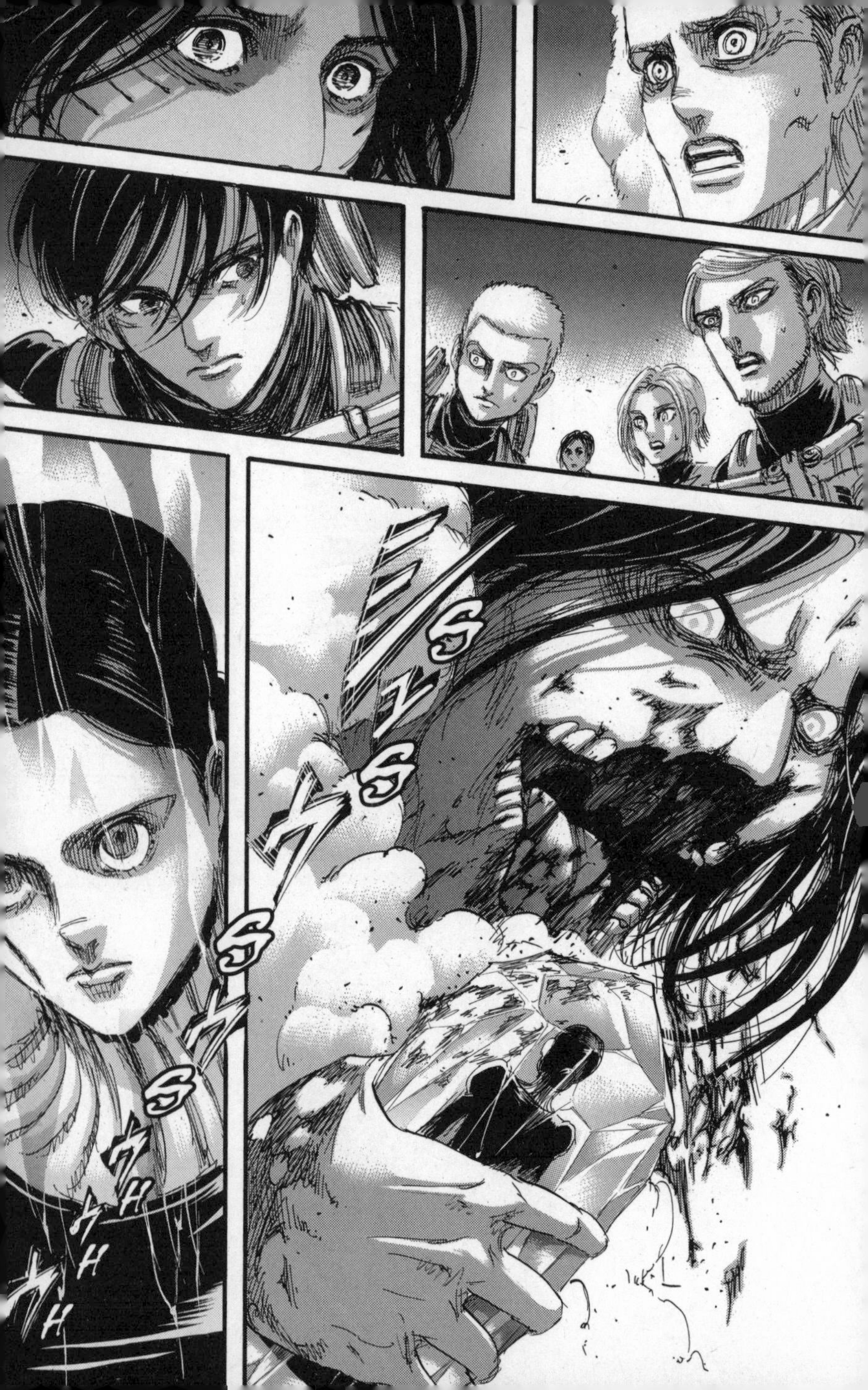
SSSSHHH

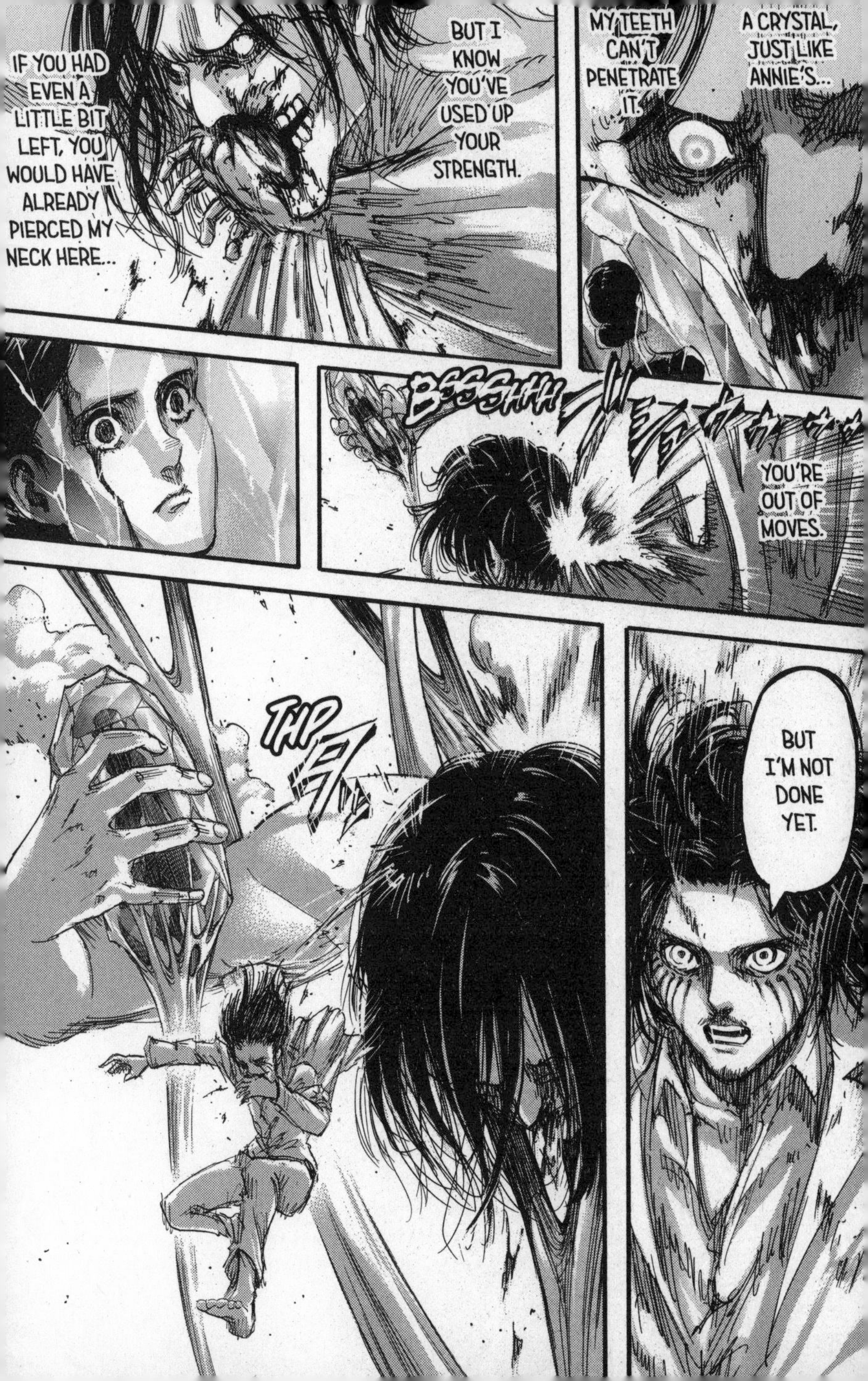
A CRYSTAL, JUST LIKE ANNIE'S...
MY TEETH CAN'T PENETRATE IT.
BUT I KNOW YOU'VE USED UP YOUR STRENGTH.
IF YOU HAD EVEN A LITTLE BIT LEFT, YOU WOULD HAVE ALREADY PIERCED MY NECK HERE...
BSSHHH
YOU'RE OUT OF MOVES.
BUT I'M NOT DONE YET.
THP

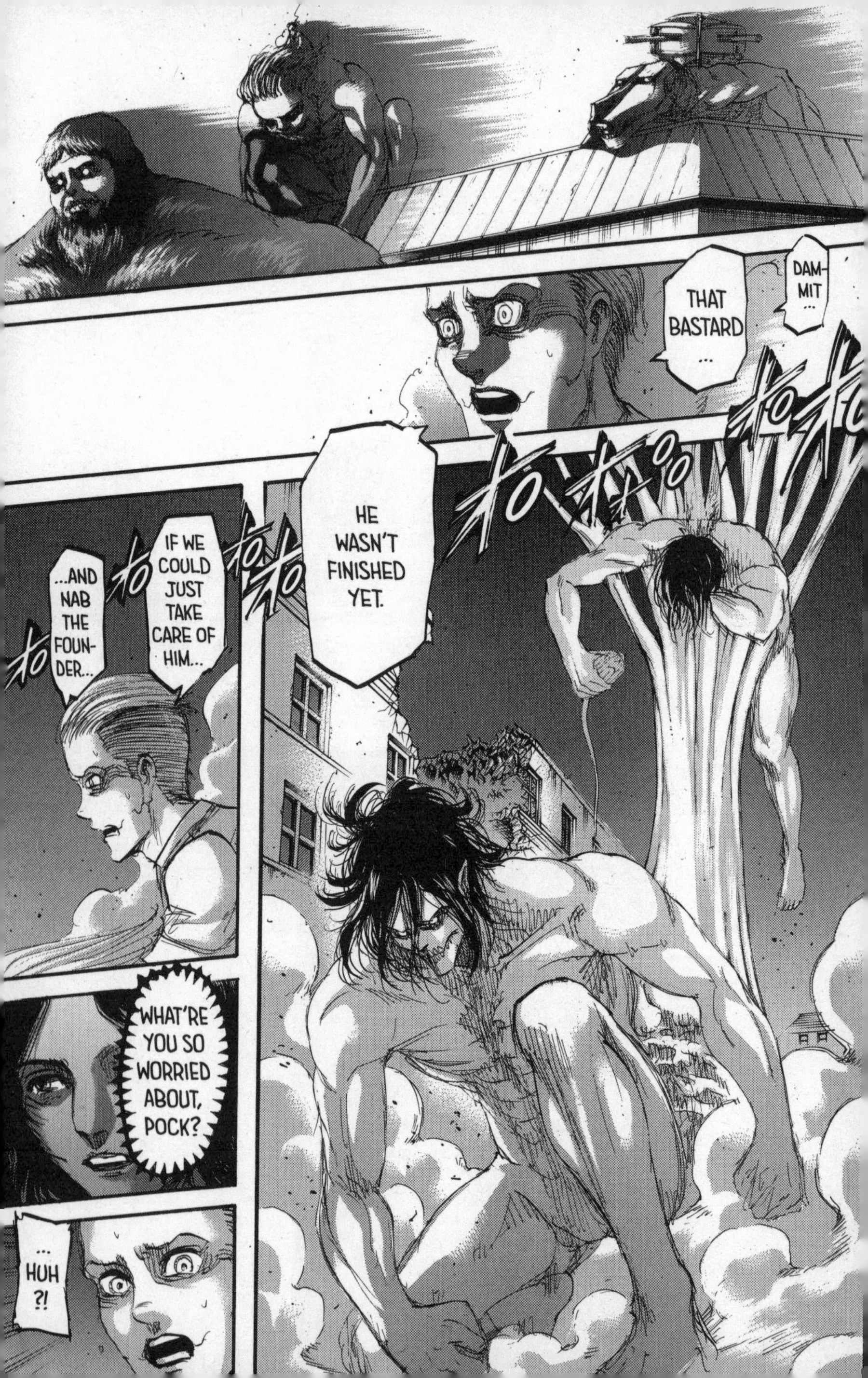
DAM-MIT...
THAT BASTARD...
HE WASN'T FINISHED YET.
IF WE COULD JUST TAKE CARE OF HIM...
...AND NAB THE FOUN-DER...
WHAT'RE YOU SO WORRIED ABOUT, POCK?
...HUH?!

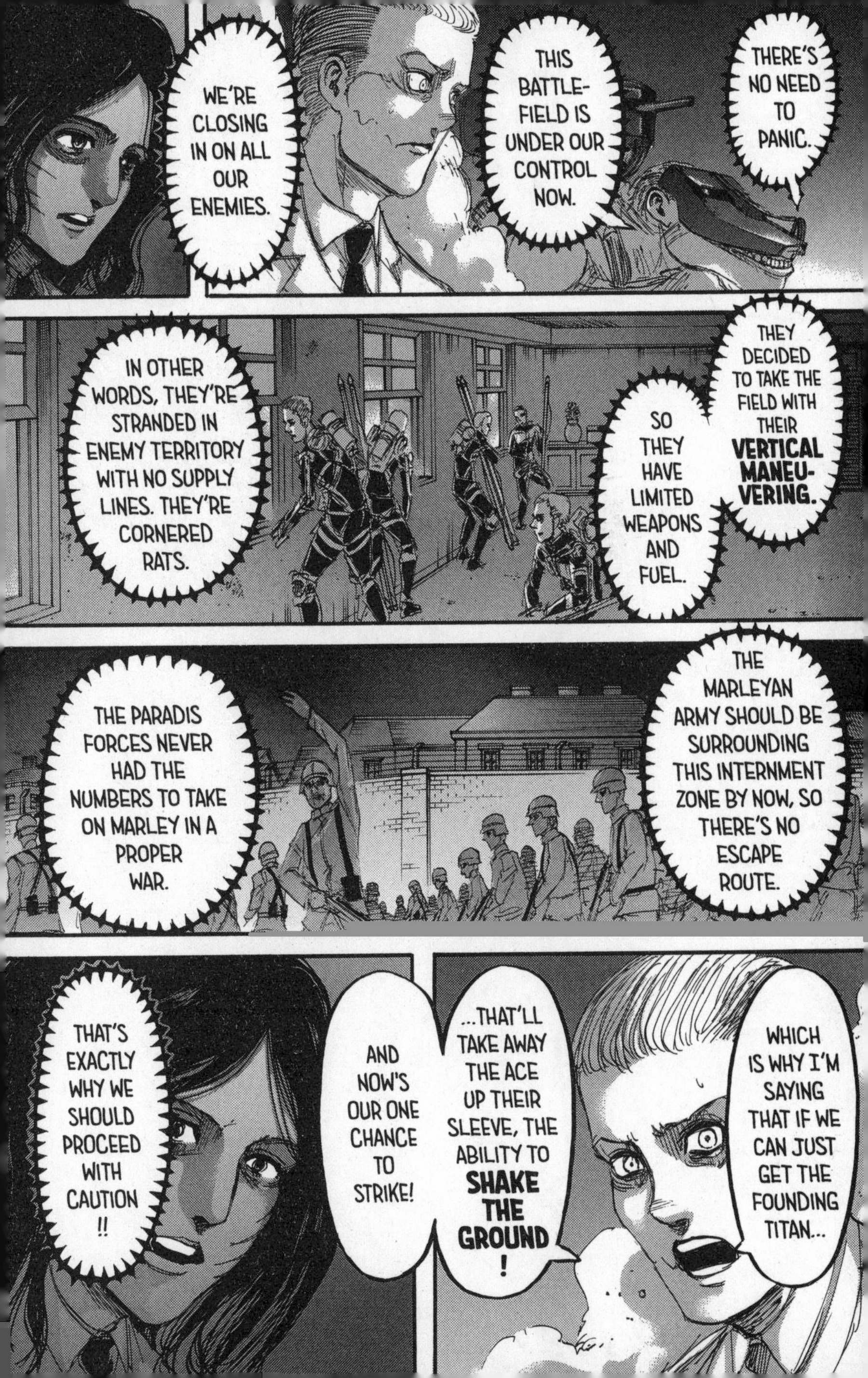
THERE'S NO NEED TO PANIC.
THIS BATTLEFIELD IS UNDER OUR CONTROL NOW.
WE'RE CLOSING IN ON ALL OUR ENEMIES.
THEY DECIDED TO TAKE THE FIELD WITH THEIR **VERTICAL MANEUVERING.**
SO THEY HAVE LIMITED WEAPONS AND FUEL.
IN OTHER WORDS, THEY'RE STRANDED IN ENEMY TERRITORY WITH NO SUPPLY LINES. THEY'RE CORNERED RATS.
THE MARLEYAN ARMY SHOULD BE SURROUNDING THIS INTERNMENT ZONE BY NOW, SO THERE'S NO ESCAPE ROUTE.
THE PARADIS FORCES NEVER HAD THE NUMBERS TO TAKE ON MARLEY IN A PROPER WAR.
WHICH IS WHY I'M SAYING THAT IF WE CAN JUST GET THE FOUNDING TITAN...
...THAT'LL TAKE AWAY THE ACE UP THEIR SLEEVE, THE ABILITY TO **SHAKE THE GROUND** !
AND NOW'S OUR ONE CHANCE TO STRIKE!
THAT'S EXACTLY WHY WE SHOULD PROCEED WITH CAUTION !!

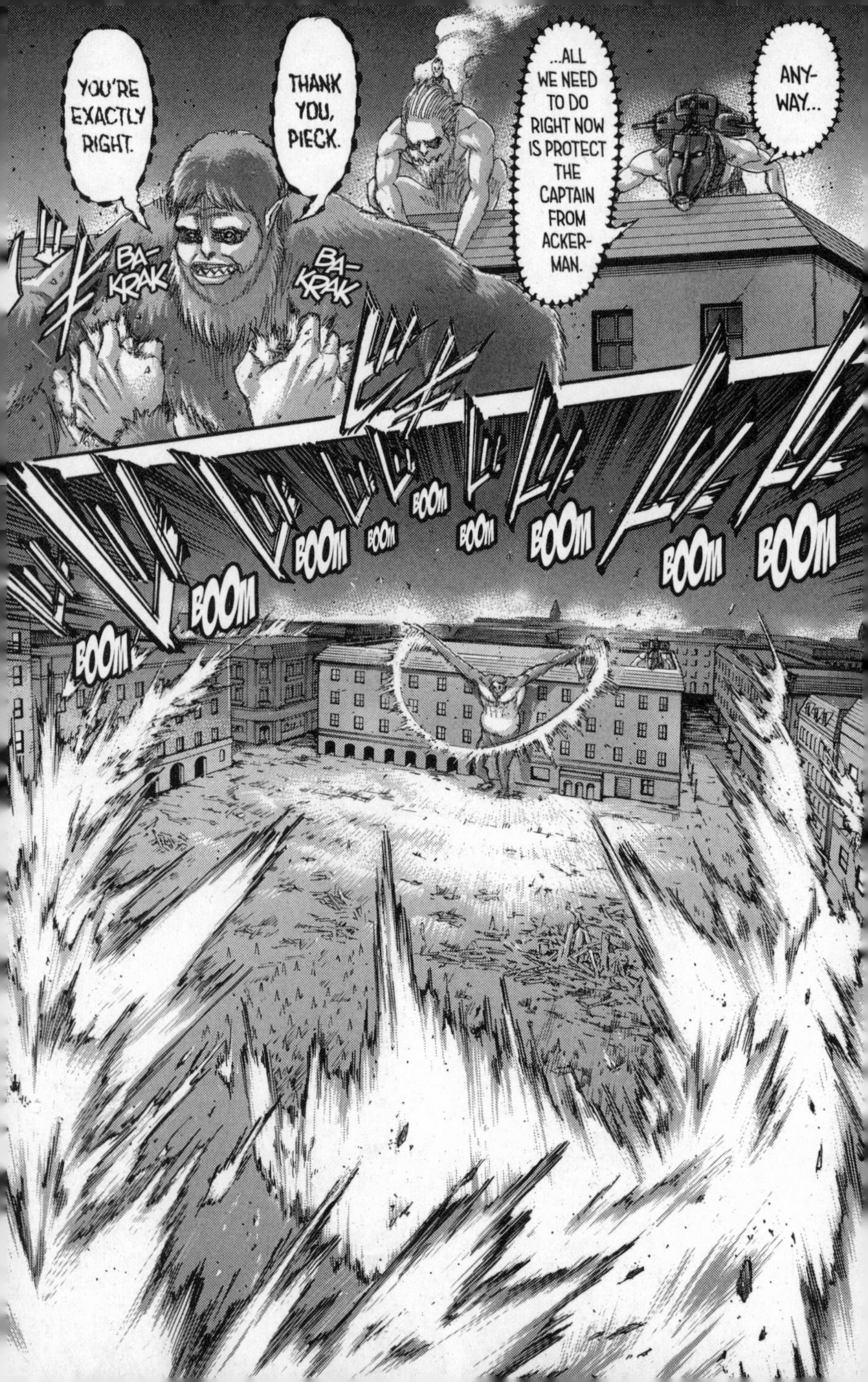
ANY-WAY...
...ALL WE NEED TO DO RIGHT NOW IS PROTECT THE CAPTAIN FROM ACKER-MAN.
THANK YOU, PIECK.
BA-KRAK
YOU'RE EXACTLY RIGHT.
BA-KRAK
BOOM
BOOM
BOOM
BOOM
BOOM
BOOM
BOOM
BOOM
BOOM

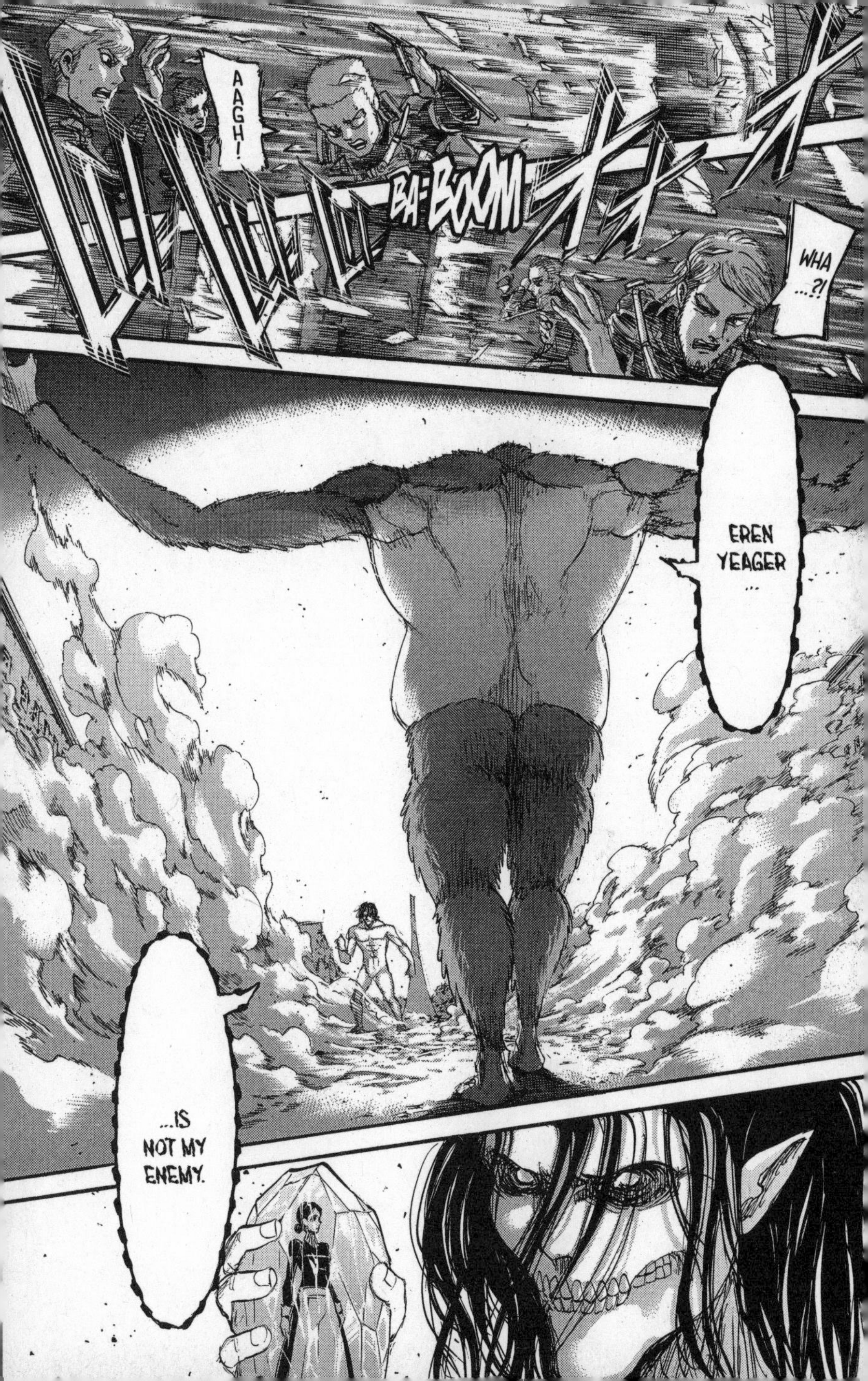
WHA ...?!
BA-BOOM
AAGH!
EREN YEAGER ...
...IS NOT MY ENEMY.

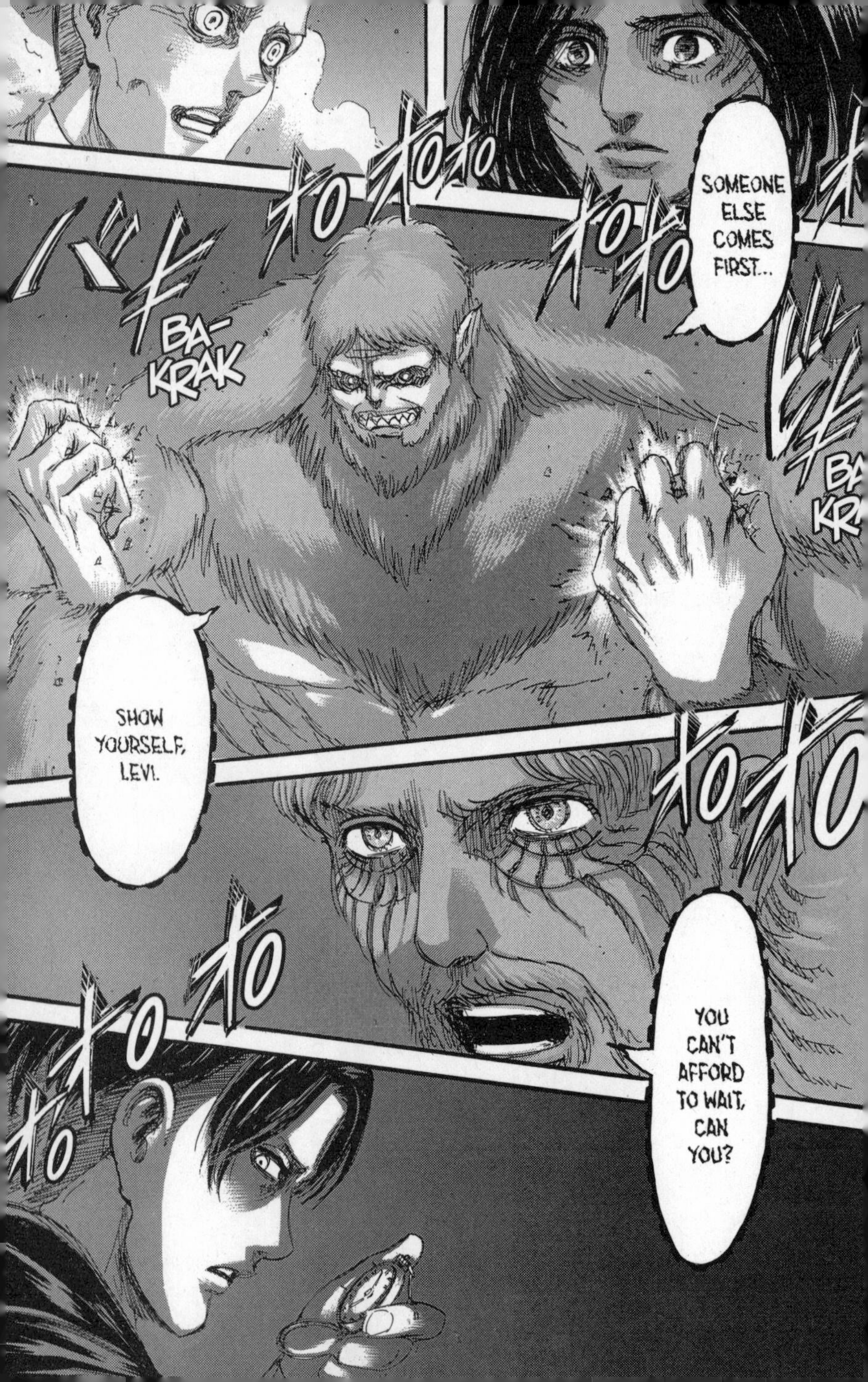
SOMEONE ELSE COMES FIRST...
BA-KRAK
SHOW YOURSELF, LEVI.
YOU CAN'T AFFORD TO WAIT, CAN YOU?

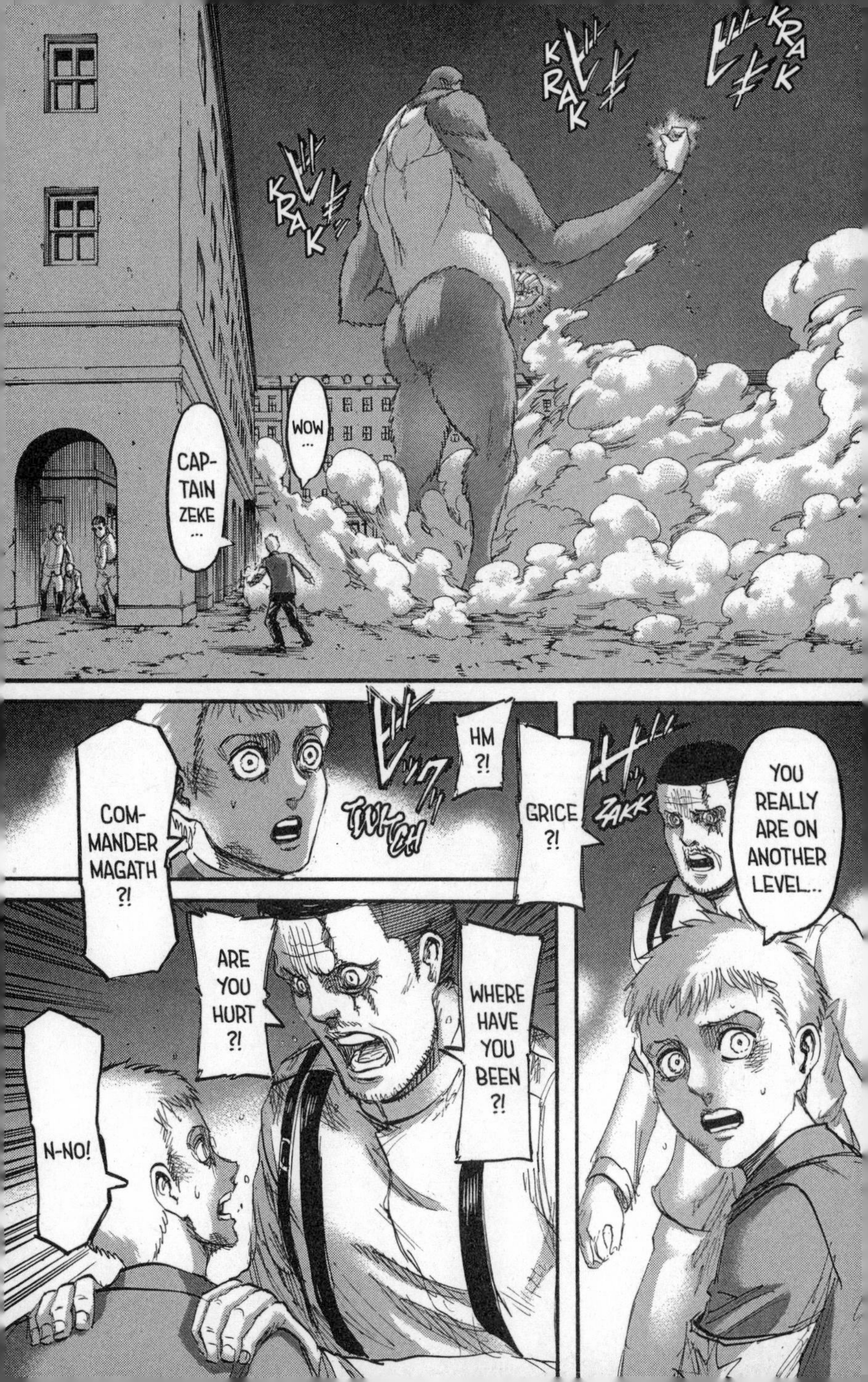
KRAK KRAK
KRAK KRAK
KRAK
WOW ...
CAP-TAIN ZEKE ...
ZAKK
YOU REALLY ARE ON ANOTHER LEVEL...
GRICE ?!
HM ?!
TWITCH
COM-MANDER MAGATH ?!
WHERE HAVE YOU BEEN ?!
ARE YOU HURT ?!
N-NO!

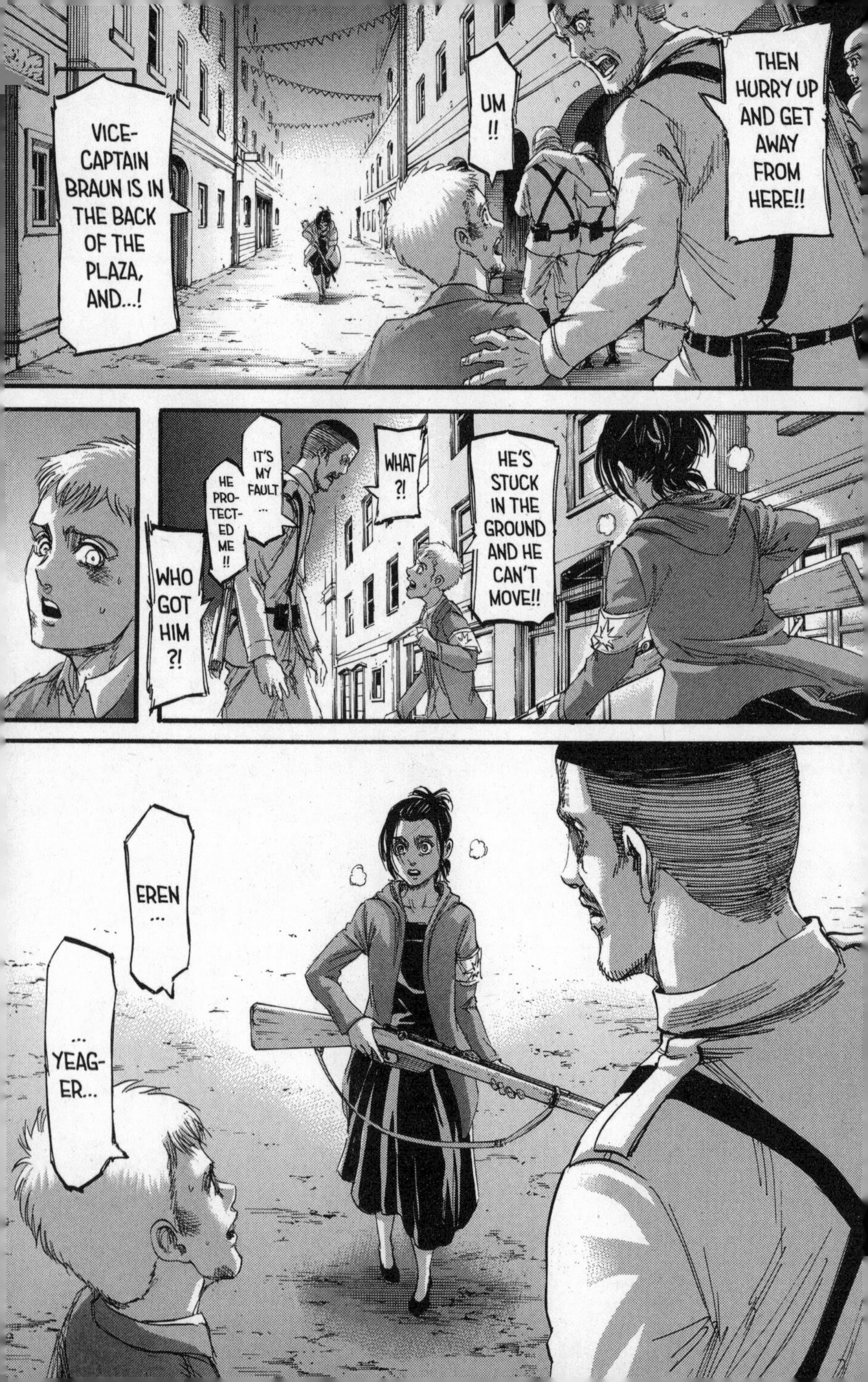
THEN HURRY UP AND GET AWAY FROM HERE!!
UM !!
VICE-CAPTAIN BRAUN IS IN THE BACK OF THE PLAZA, AND...!
HE'S STUCK IN THE GROUND AND HE CAN'T MOVE!!
WHAT ?!
IT'S MY FAULT ...
HE PRO-TECT-ED ME !!
WHO GOT HIM ?!
EREN ...
... YEAG-ER...

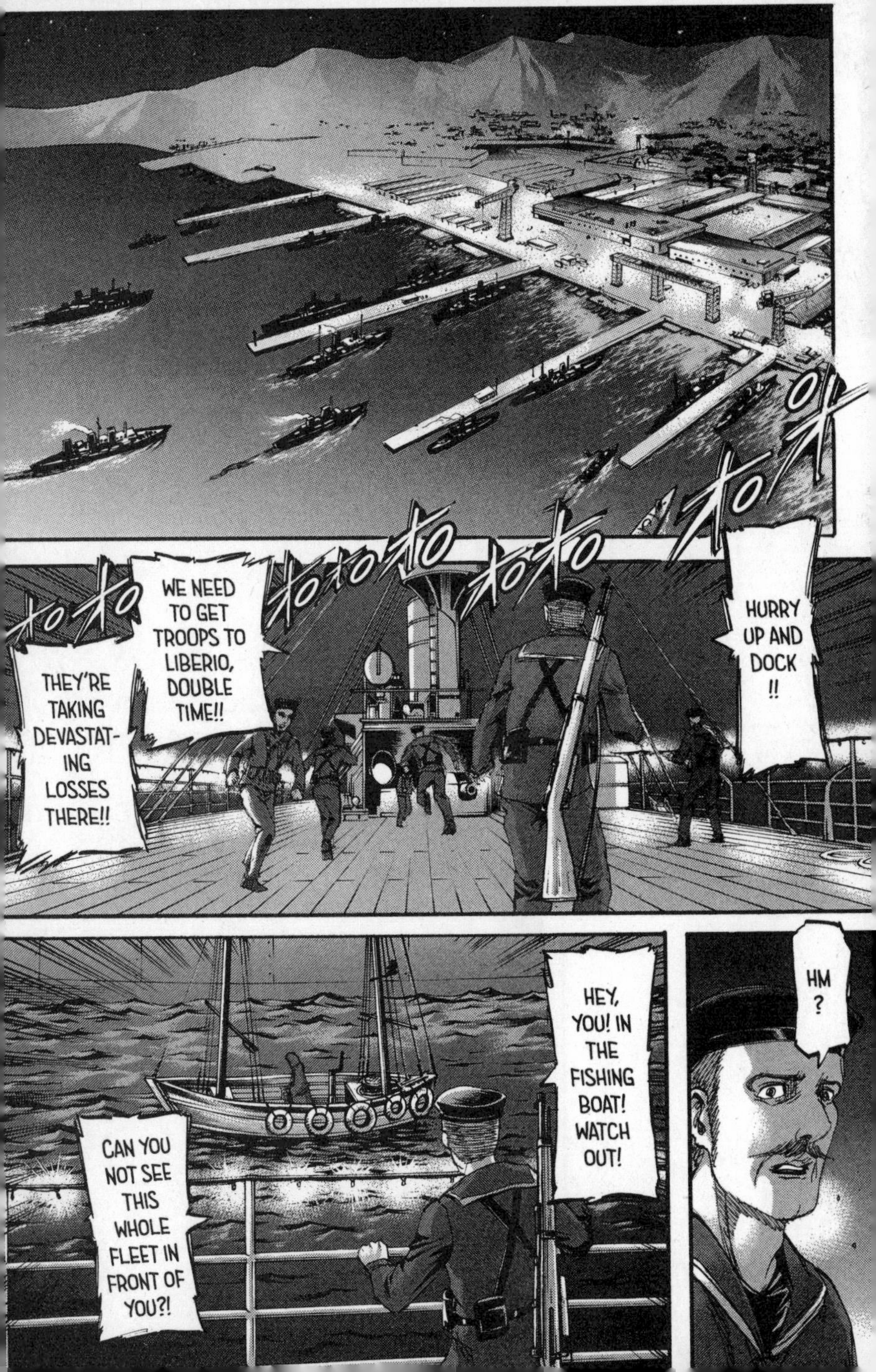
HURRY UP AND DOCK !!
WE NEED TO GET TROOPS TO LIBERIO, DOUBLE TIME!!
THEY'RE TAKING DEVASTAT-ING LOSSES THERE!!
HM ?
HEY, YOU! IN THE FISHING BOAT! WATCH OUT!
CAN YOU NOT SEE THIS WHOLE FLEET IN FRONT OF YOU?!

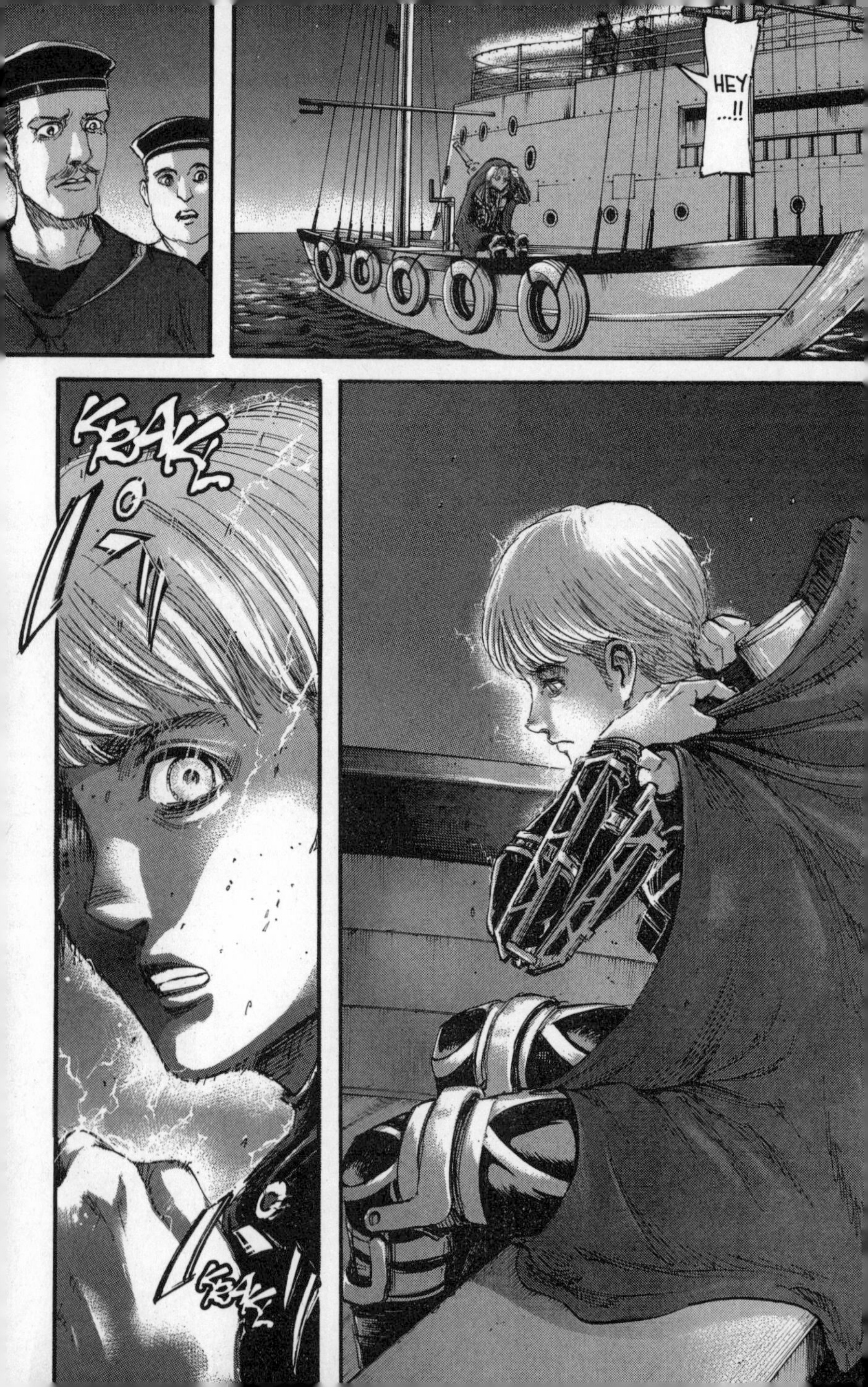
HEY ...!!
KRAK
KRAK

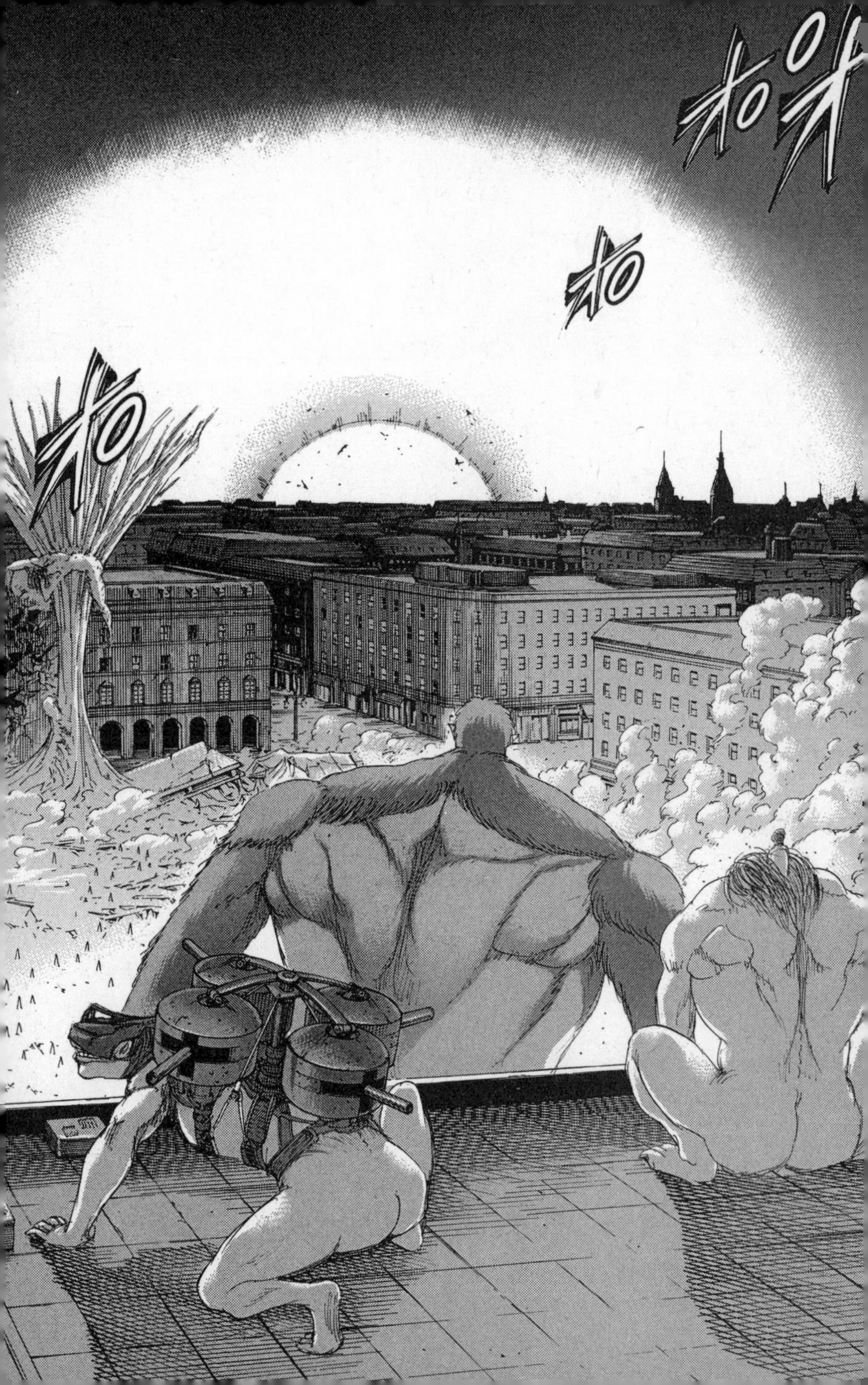

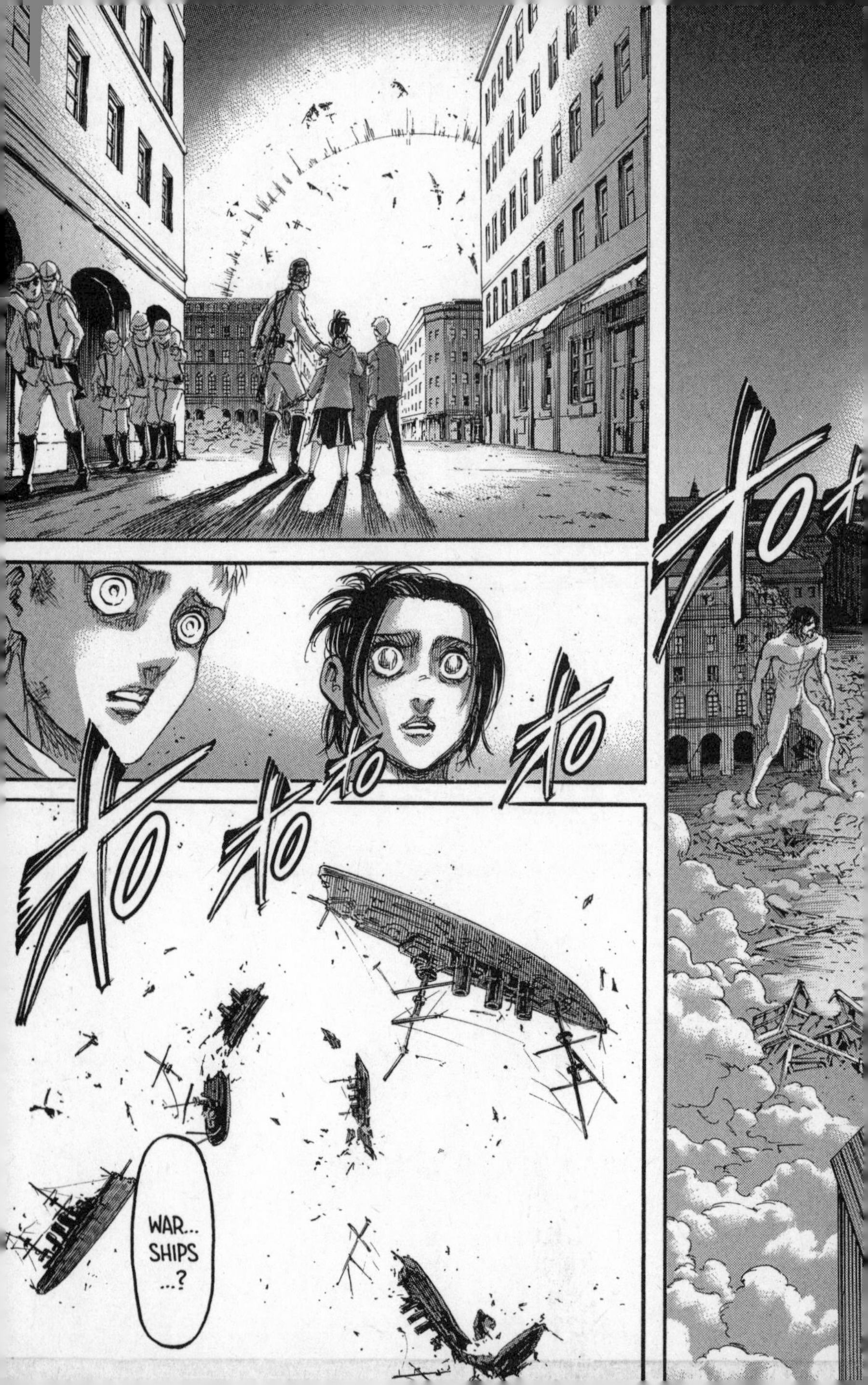
WAR... SHIPS ...?

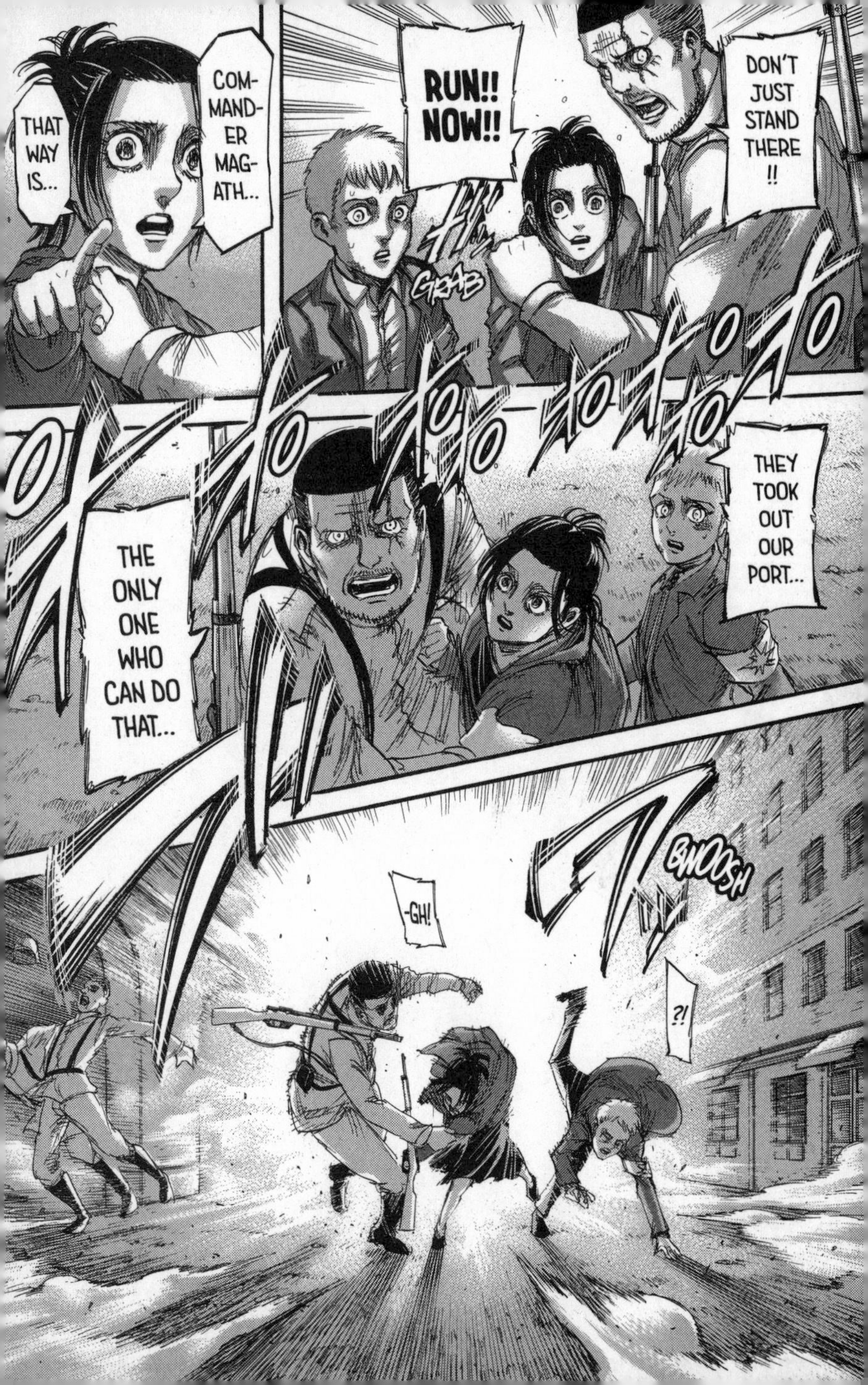
DON'T JUST STAND THERE!!
RUN!! NOW!!
GRAB
COM-MAND-ER MAG-ATH...
THAT WAY IS...
THEY TOOK OUT OUR PORT...
THE ONLY ONE WHO CAN DO THAT...
BWOOSH
-GH!
?!

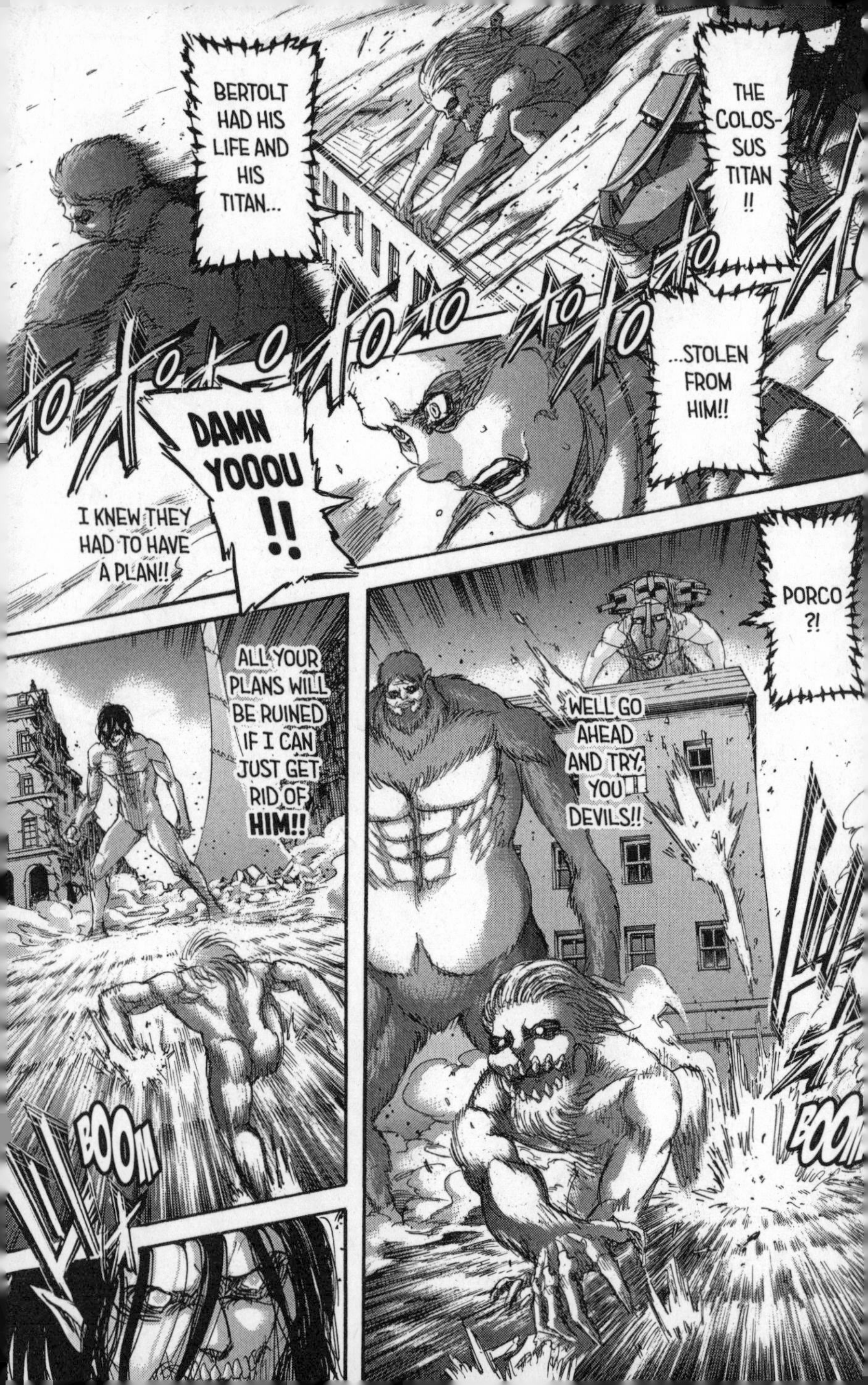
THE COLOSSUS TITAN !!
BERTOLT HAD HIS LIFE AND HIS TITAN...
...STOLEN FROM HIM!!
DAMN YOOOU !!
I KNEW THEY HAD TO HAVE A PLAN!!
PORCO ?!
WELL GO AHEAD AND TRY, YOU DEVILS!!
BOOM
ALL YOUR PLANS WILL BE RUINED IF I CAN JUST GET RID OF HIM!!
BOOM

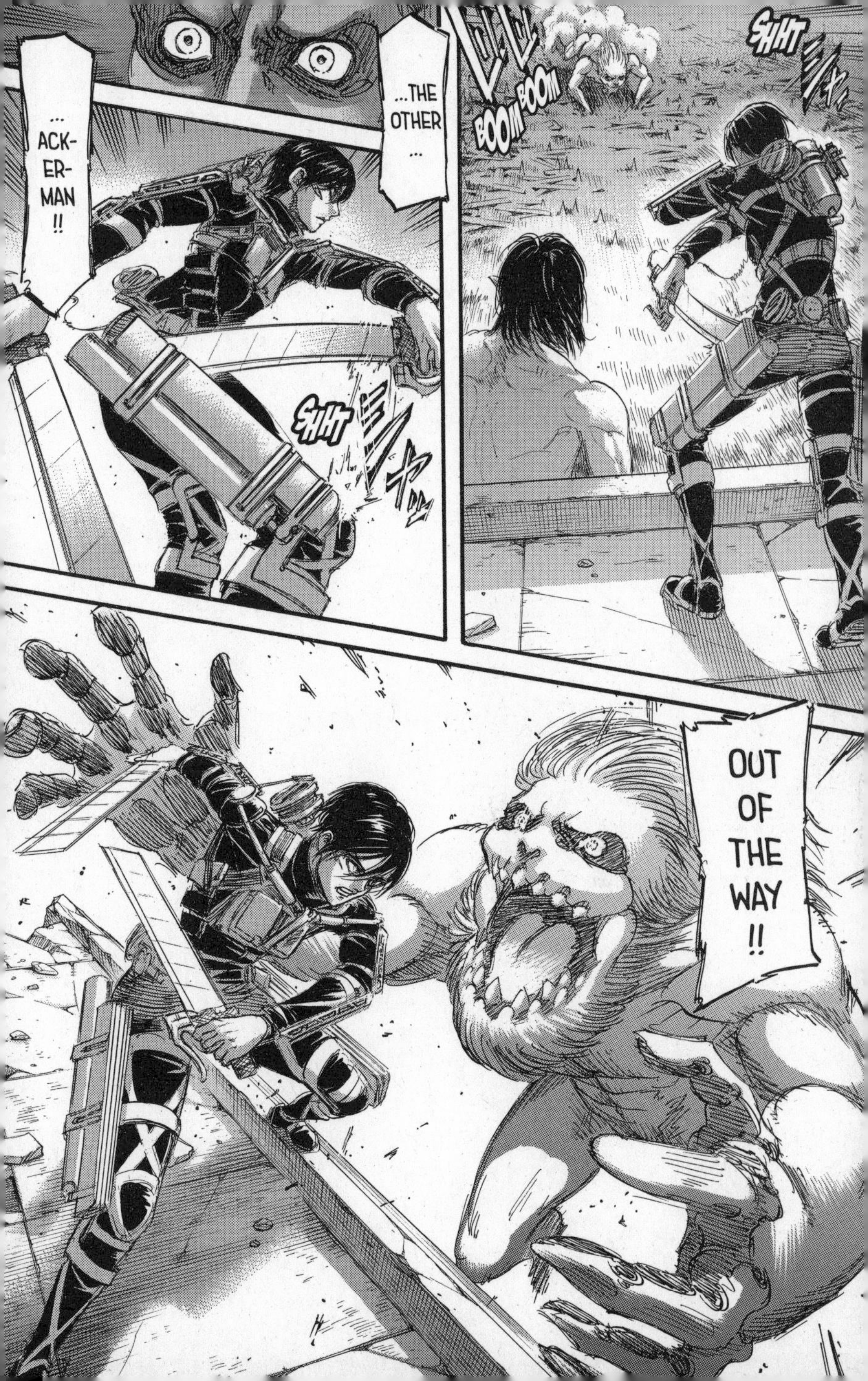
SHHT
BOOM BOOM
...THE OTHER ...
... ACK-ER-MAN !!
SHHT
OUT OF THE WAY !!

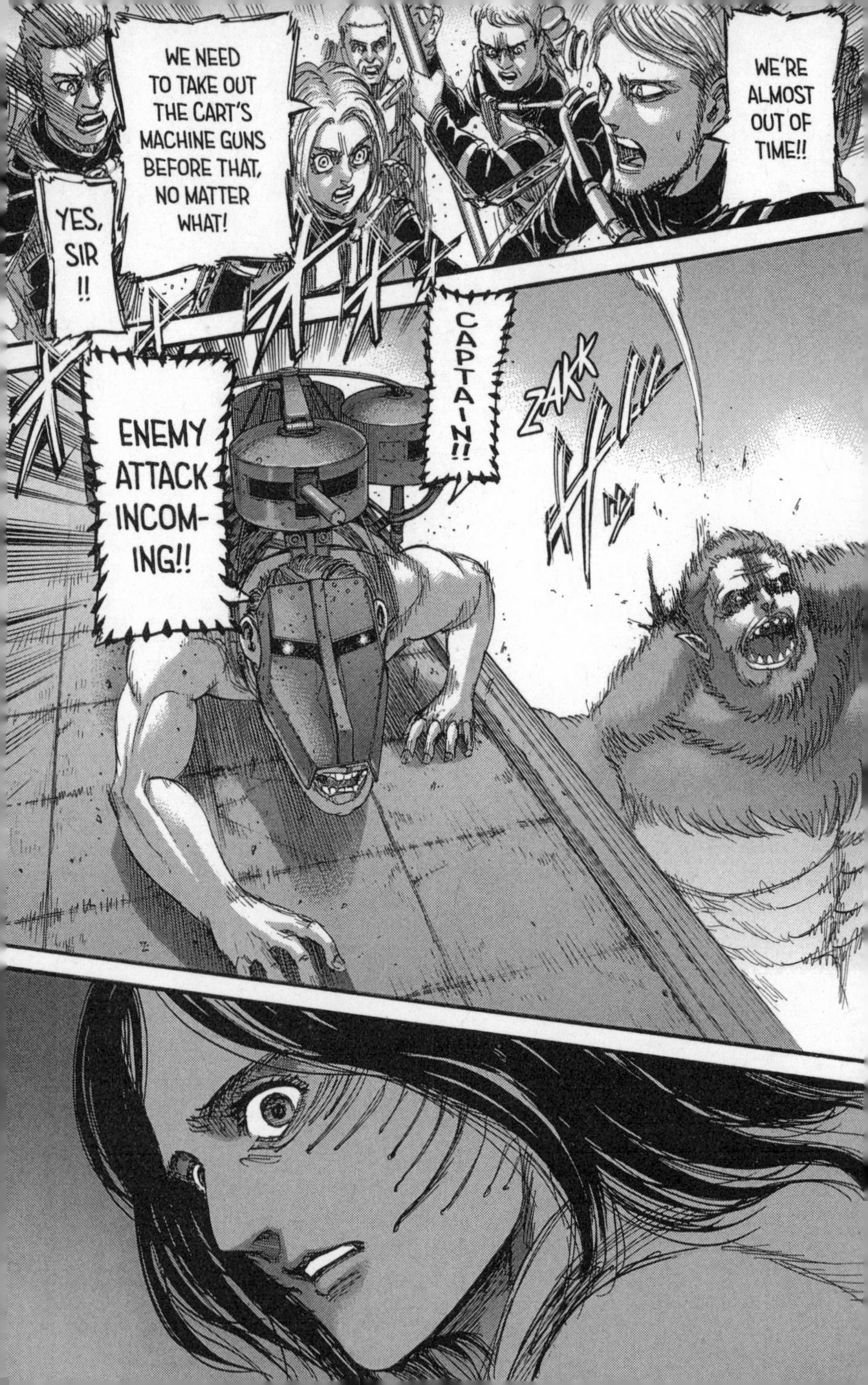
WE'RE ALMOST OUT OF TIME!!
WE NEED TO TAKE OUT THE CART'S MACHINE GUNS BEFORE THAT, NO MATTER WHAT!
YES, SIR!!
ZAKK
CAPTAIN!!
ENEMY ATTACK INCOM-ING!!

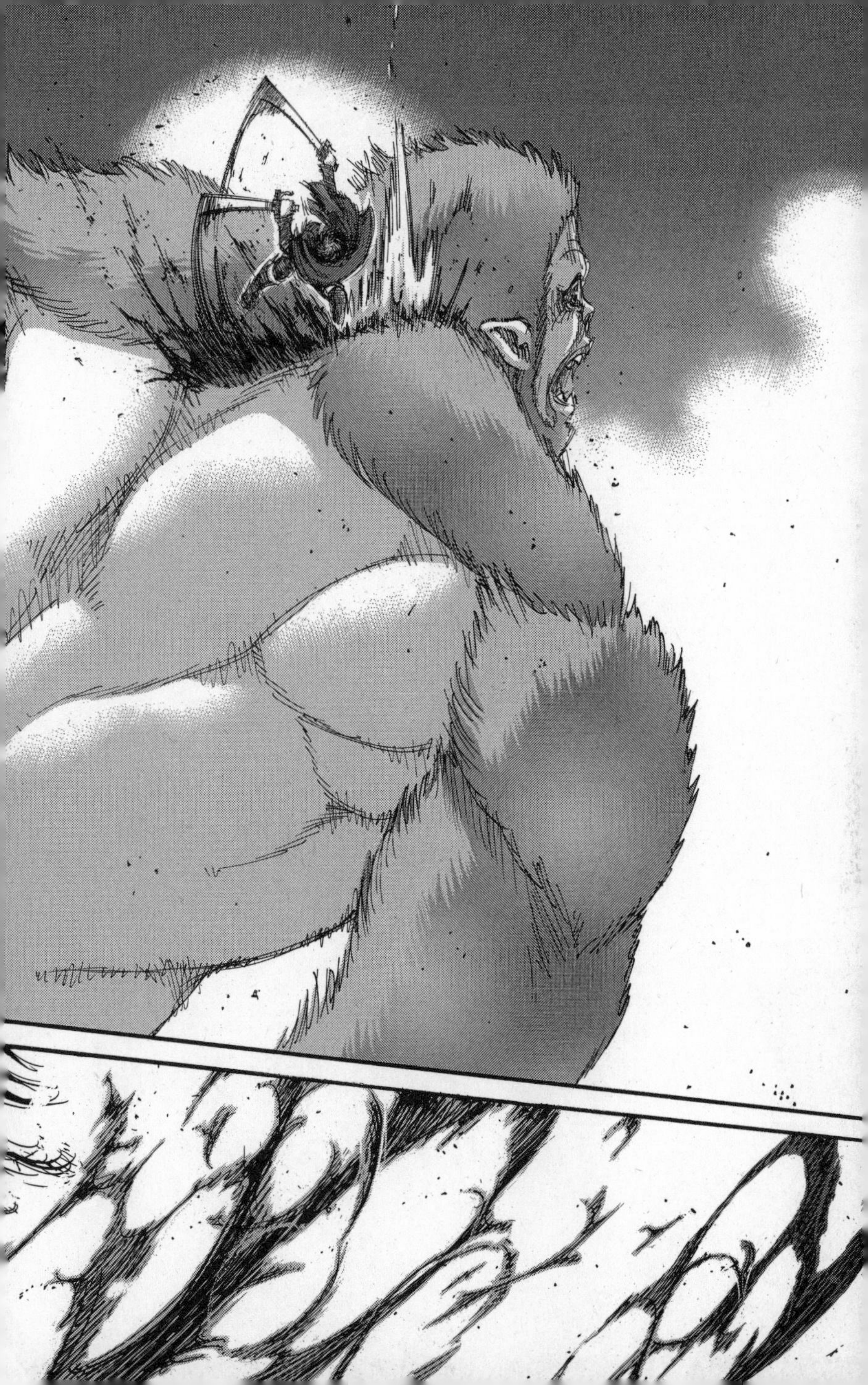

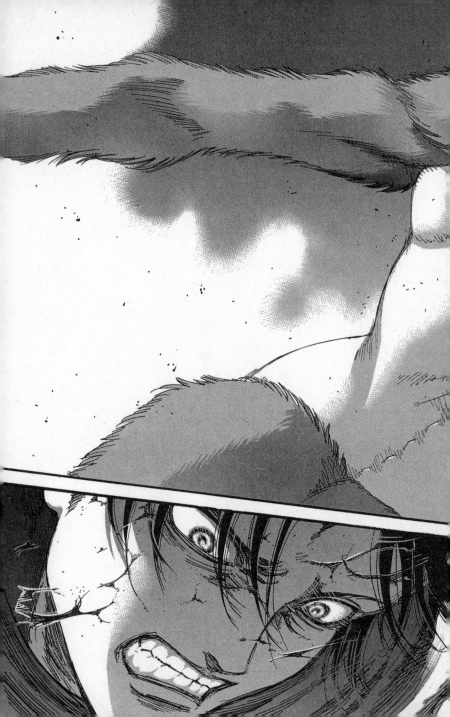

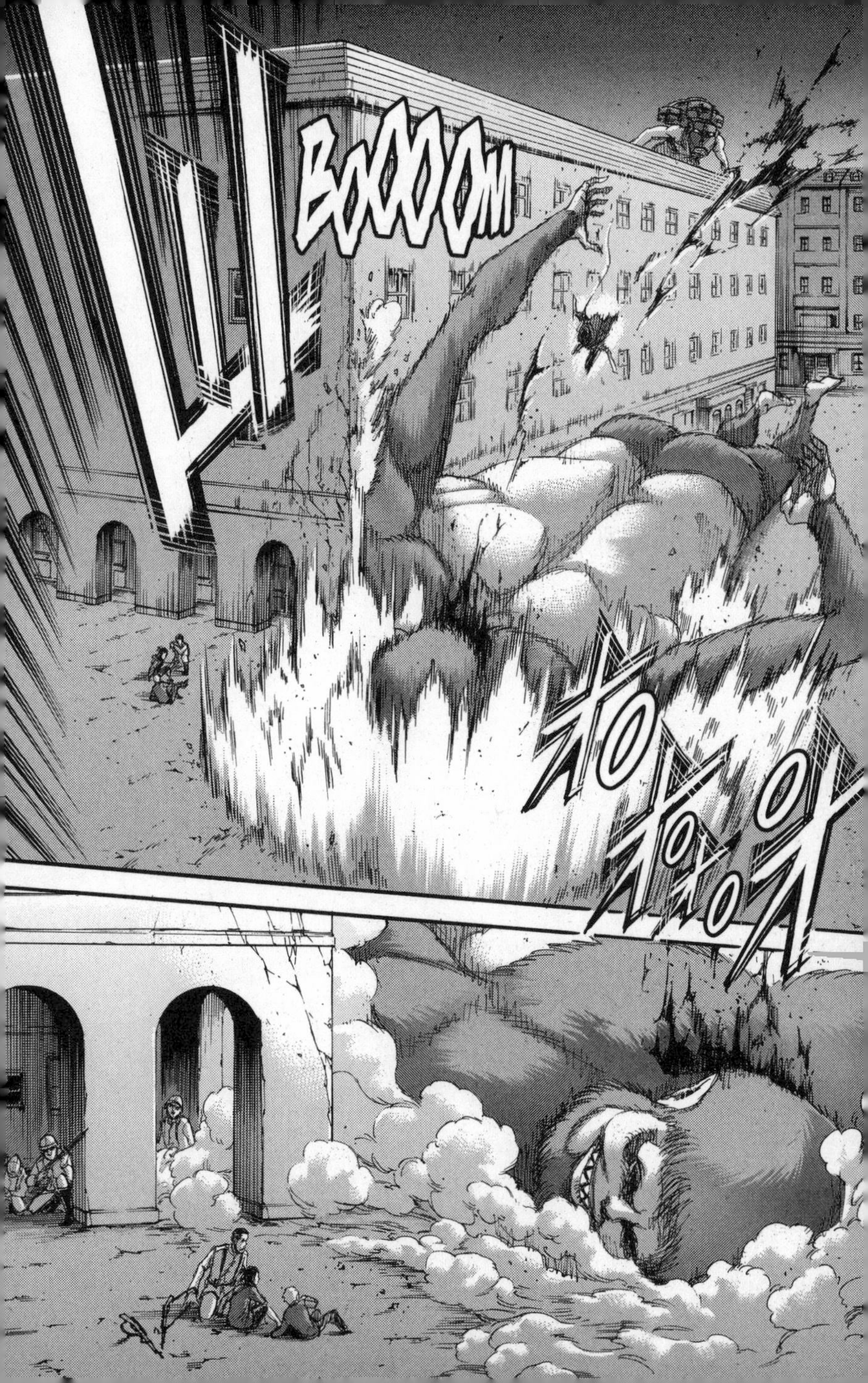
BOOOOM

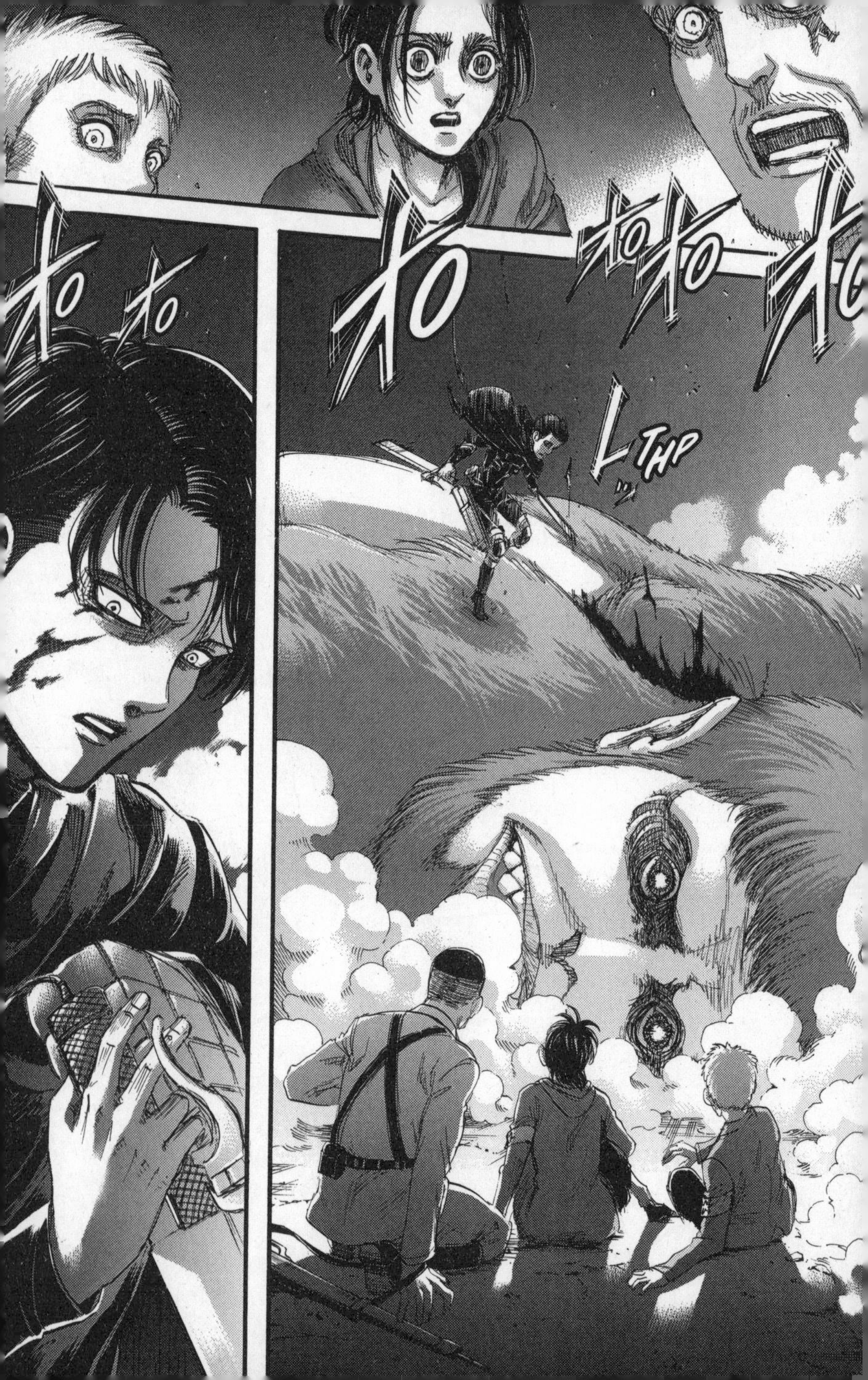
THP

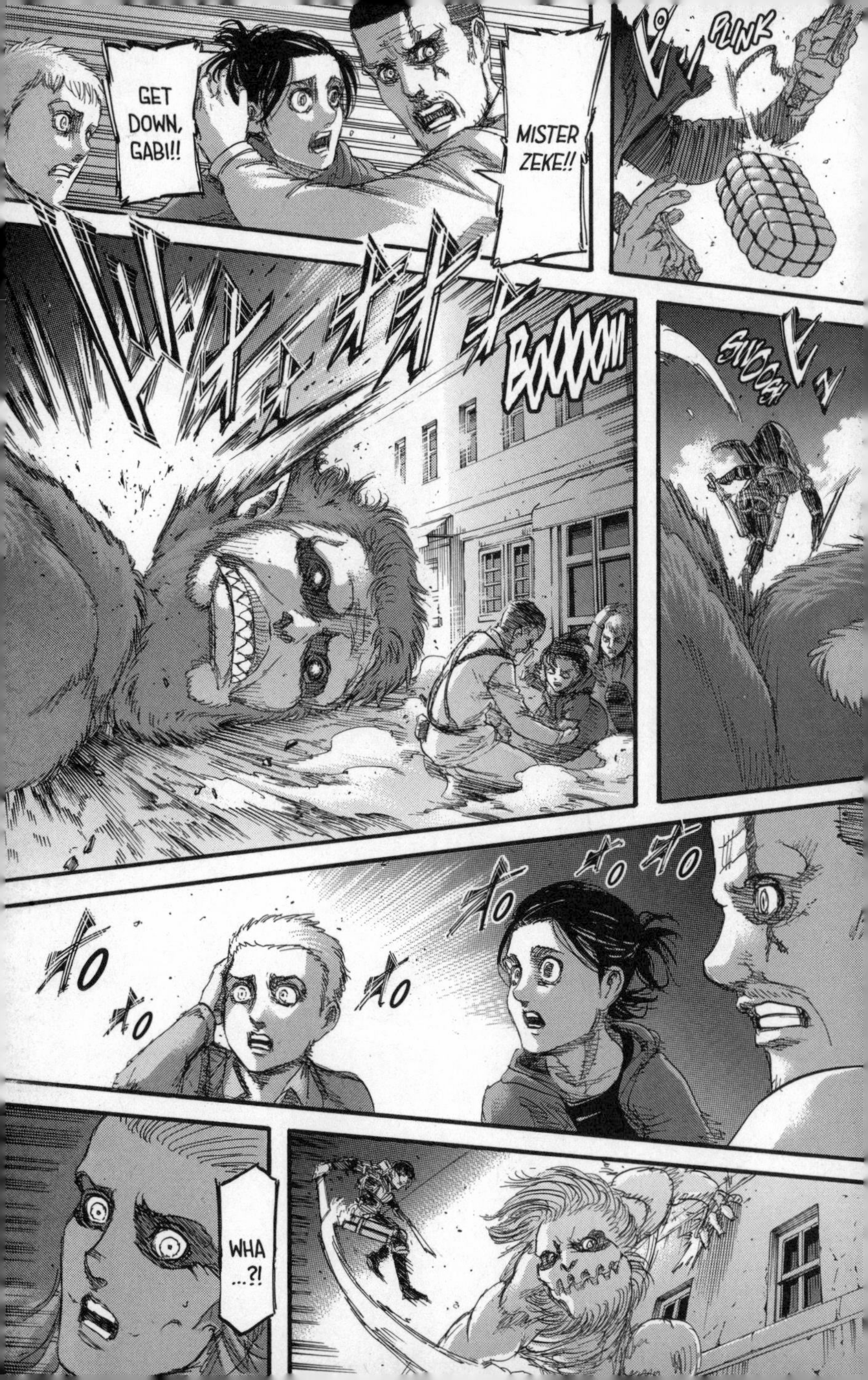
PLINK
MISTER ZEKE!!
GET DOWN, GABI!!
SWOOSH
BOOOOM
WHA ...?!

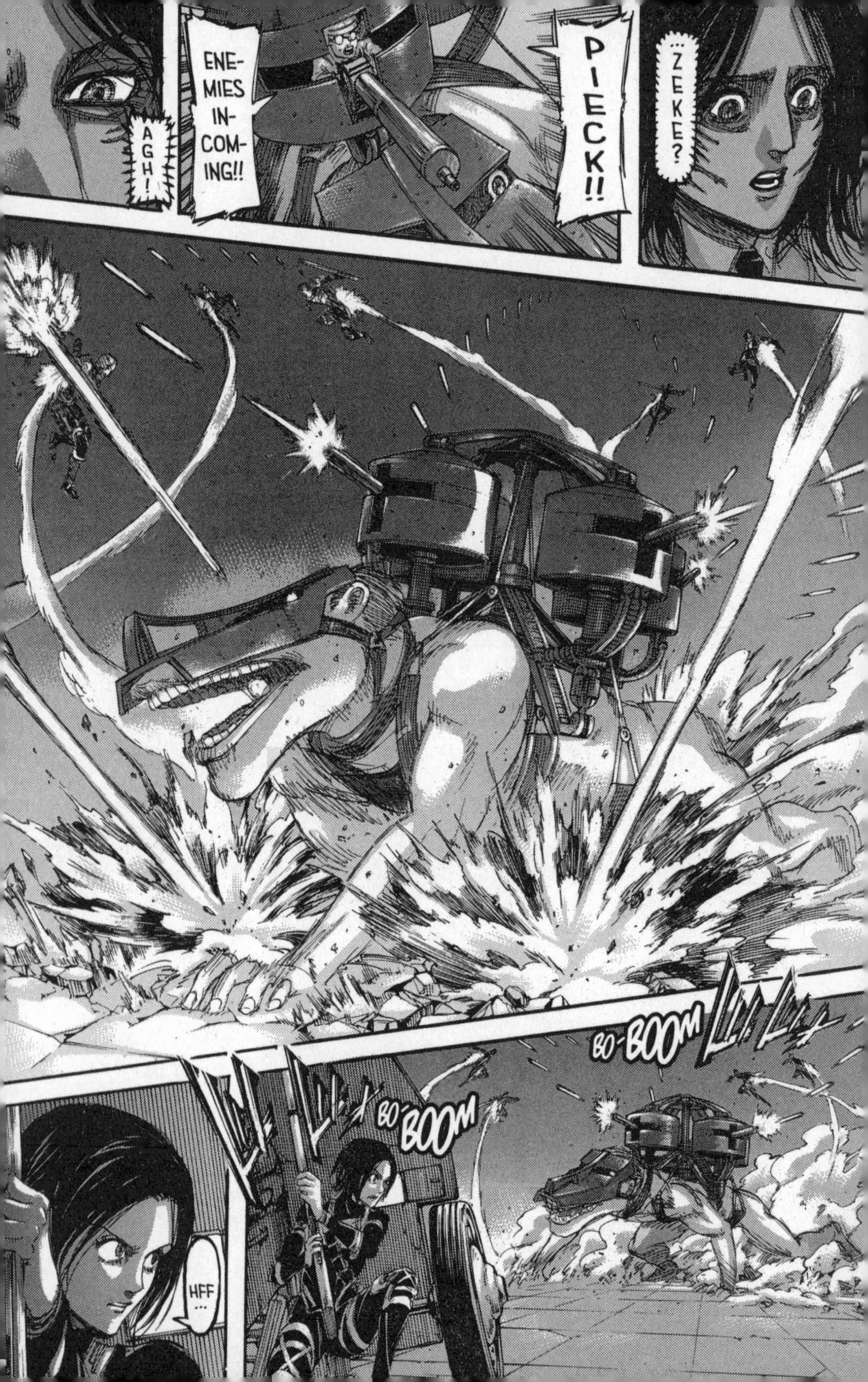
...ZEKE?
PIECK!!
ENEMIES INCOMING!!
AGH!
BO-BOOM
BO-BOOM
HFF...

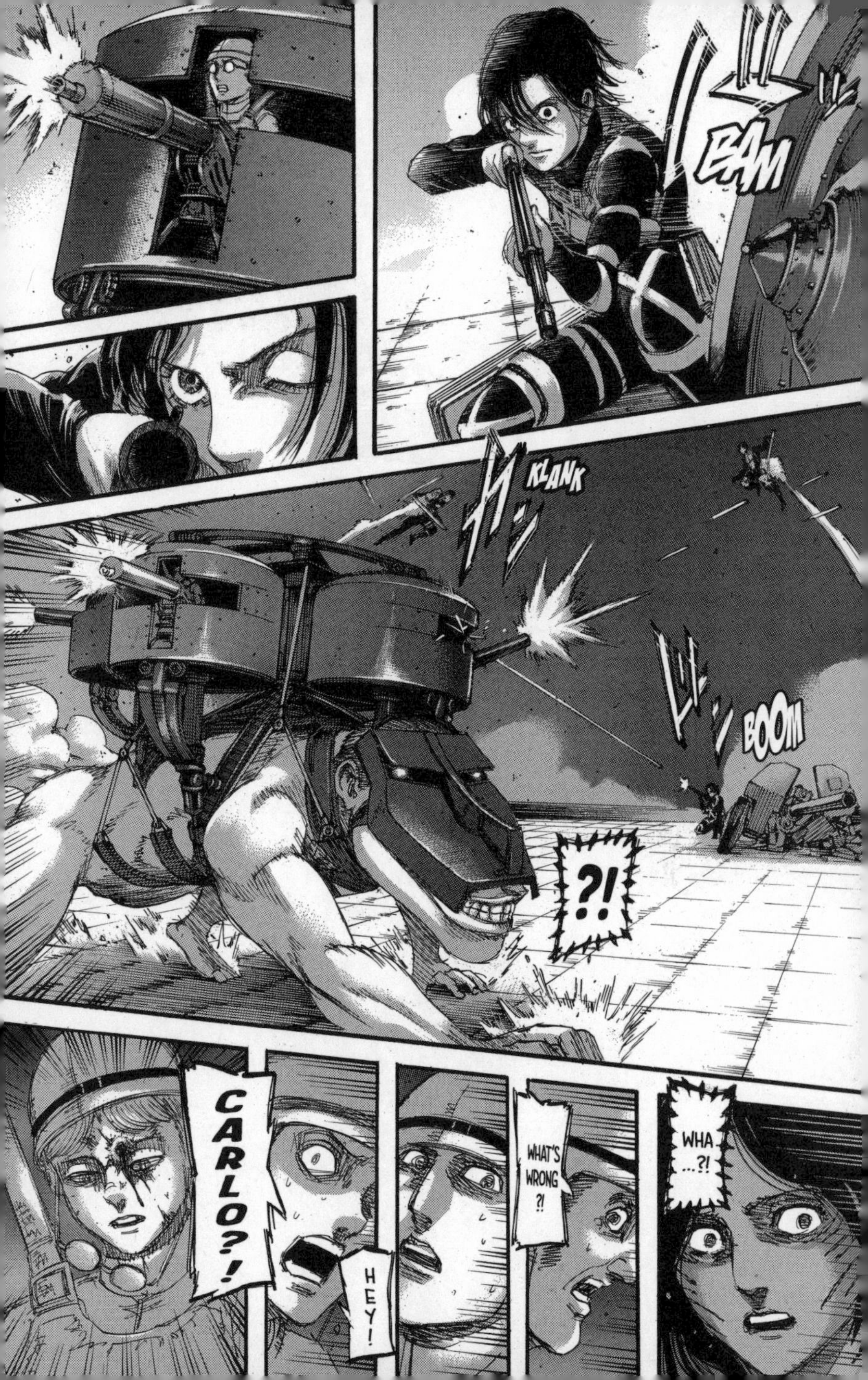
BAM
KLANK
BOOM
?!
WHA ...?!
WHAT'S WRONG ?!
CARLO?!
HEY!

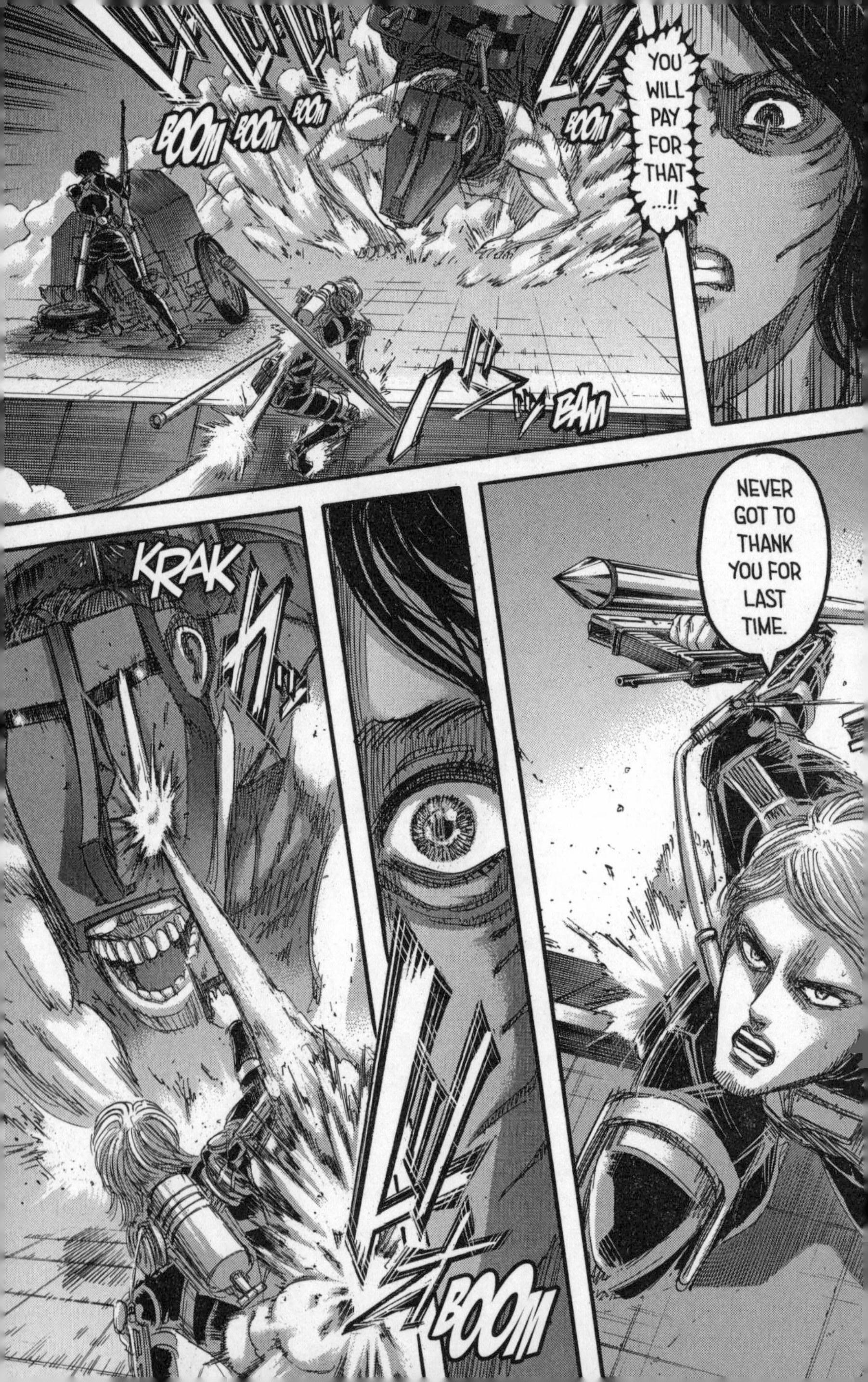
YOU WILL PAY FOR THAT...!!
BOOM
BOOM
BOOM
BOOM
BAM
NEVER GOT TO THANK YOU FOR LAST TIME.
KRAK
BOOM

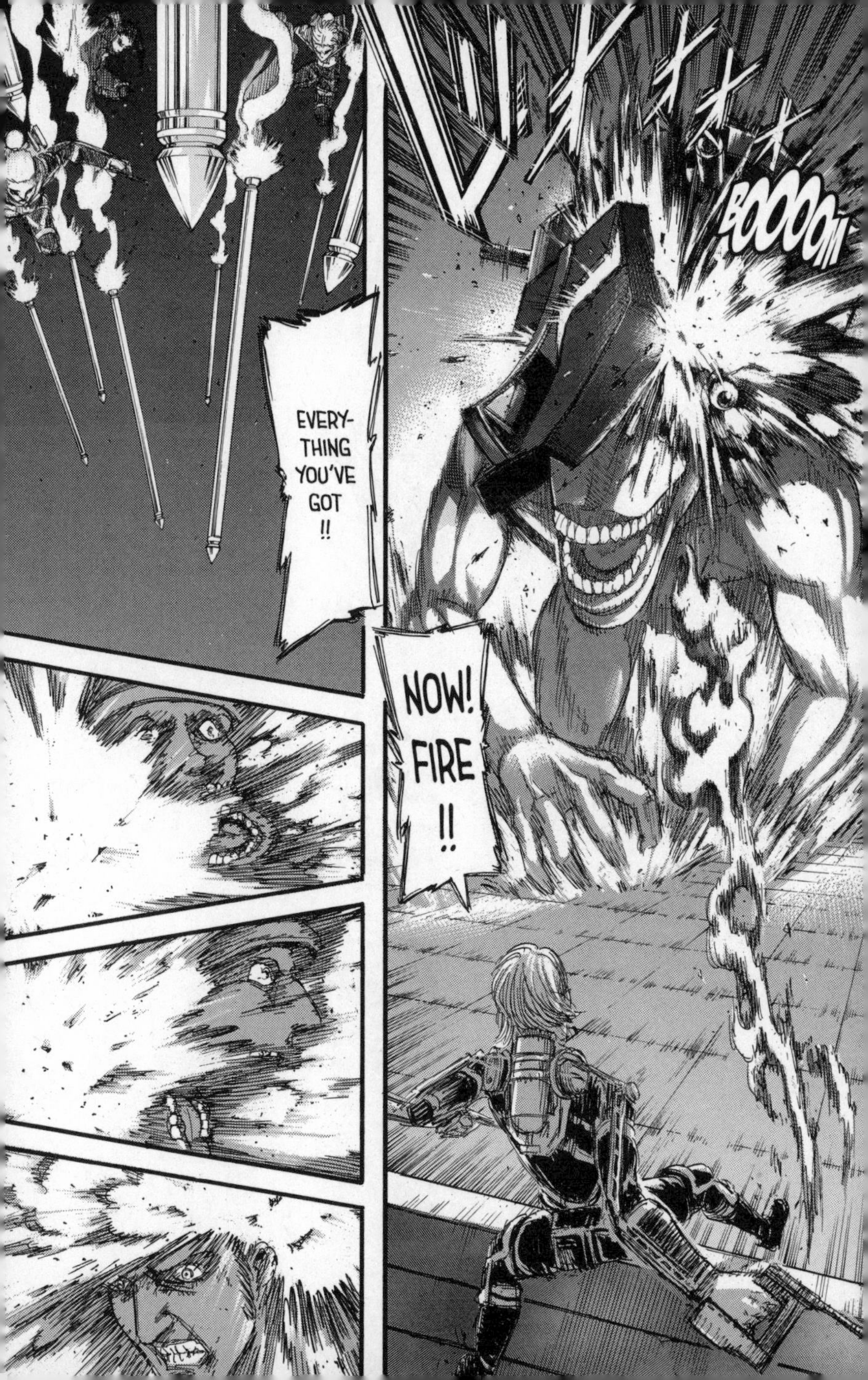
BOOOOM
NOW! FIRE !!
EVERY-THING YOU'VE GOT !!

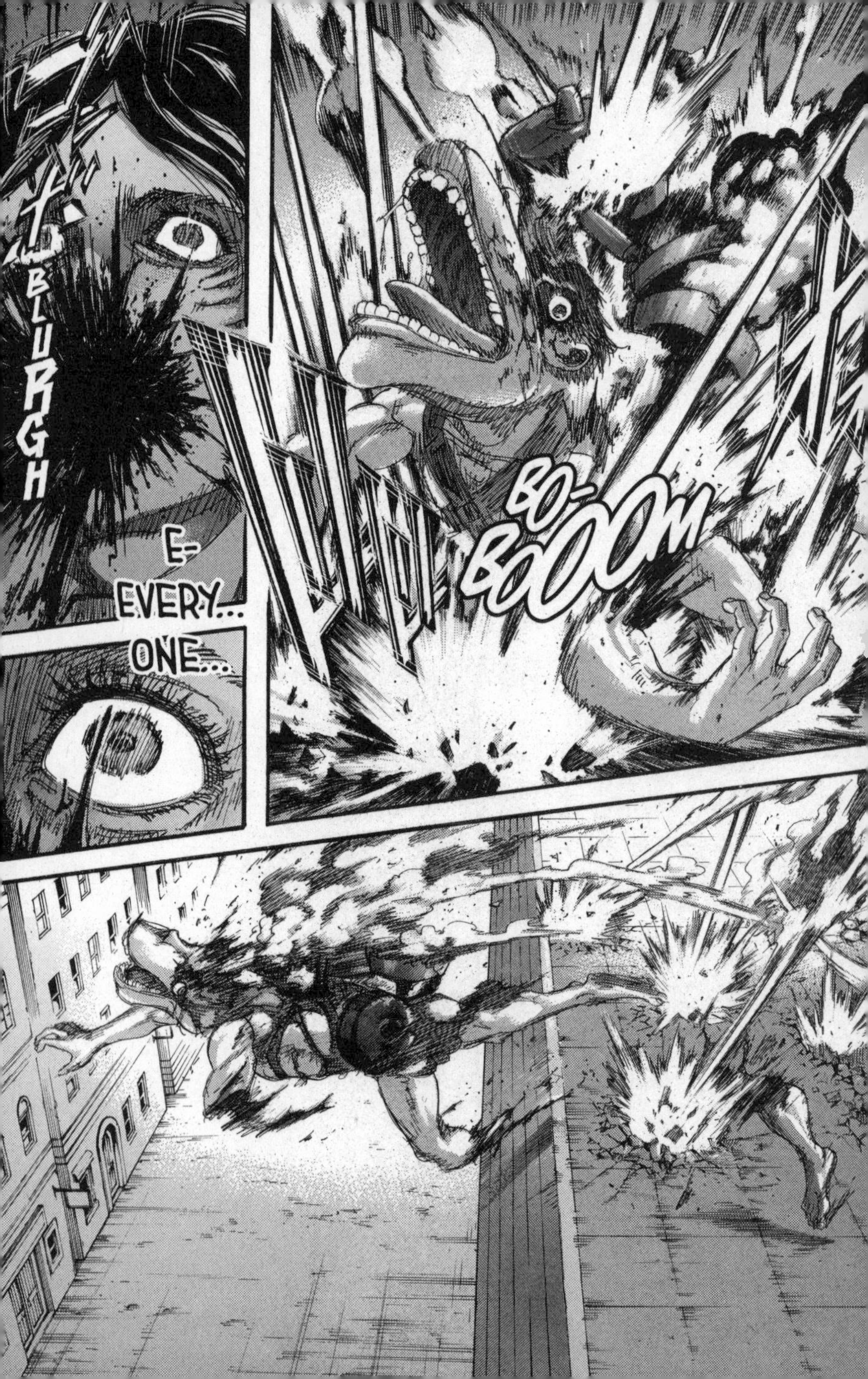
BO-
BOOOOM
BLURGH
E-
EVERY...
ONE...

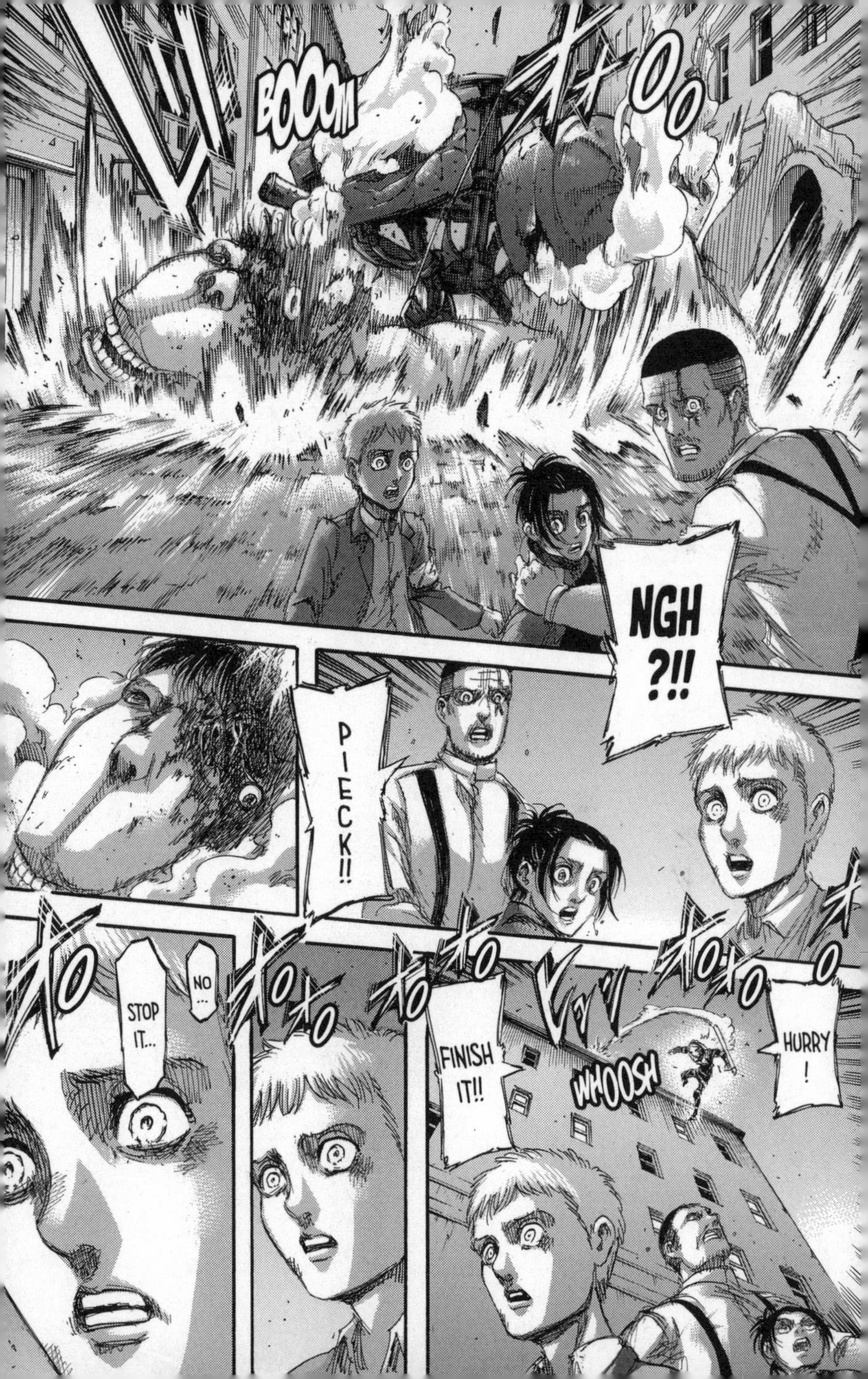
BOOOM
NGH ?!!
PIECK!!
HURRY !
FINISH IT!!
WHOOSH
NO ...
STOP IT...

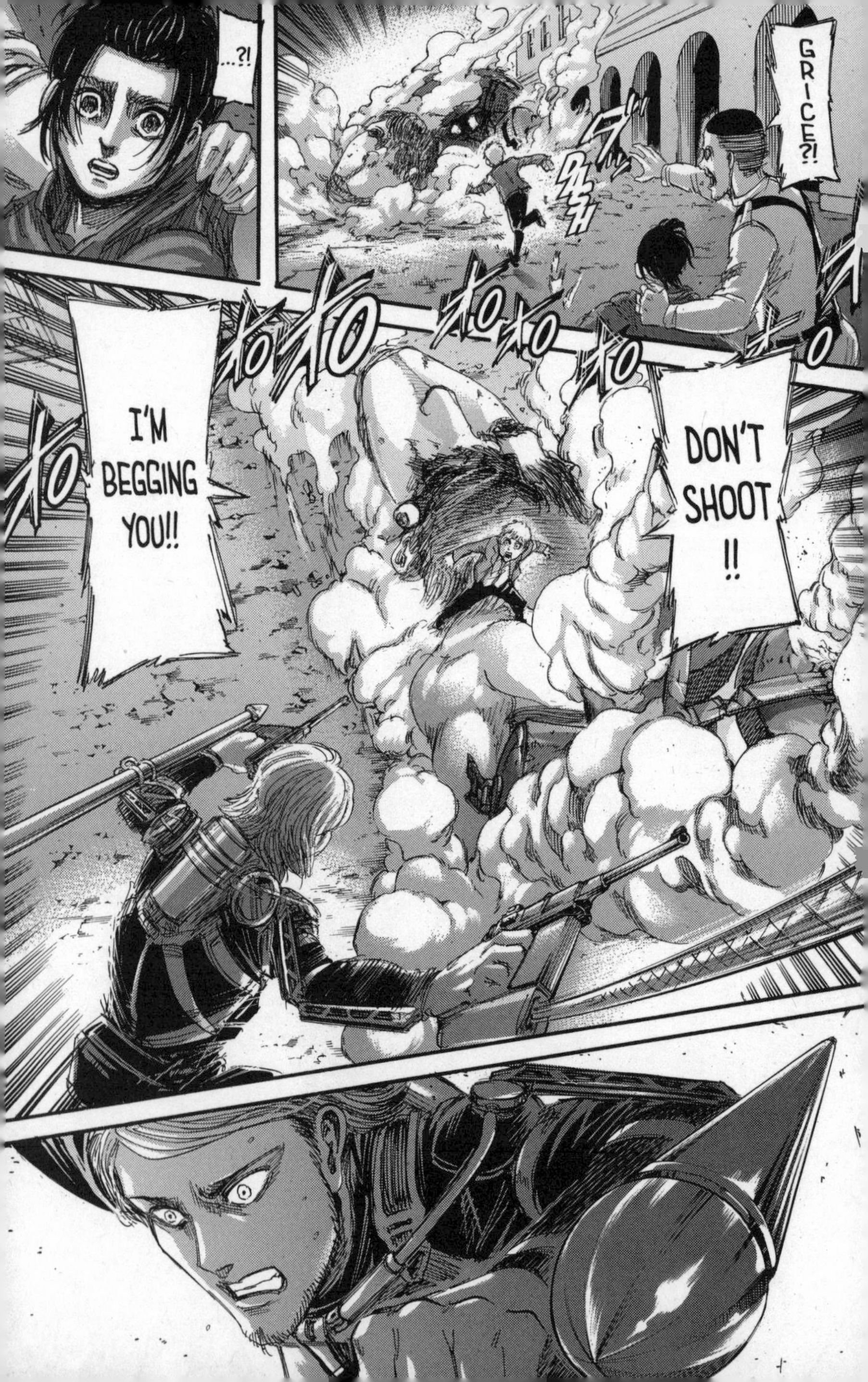
GRICE?!
DASH
...?!
DON'T SHOOT !!
I'M BEGGING YOU!!

ATTACK on TITAN

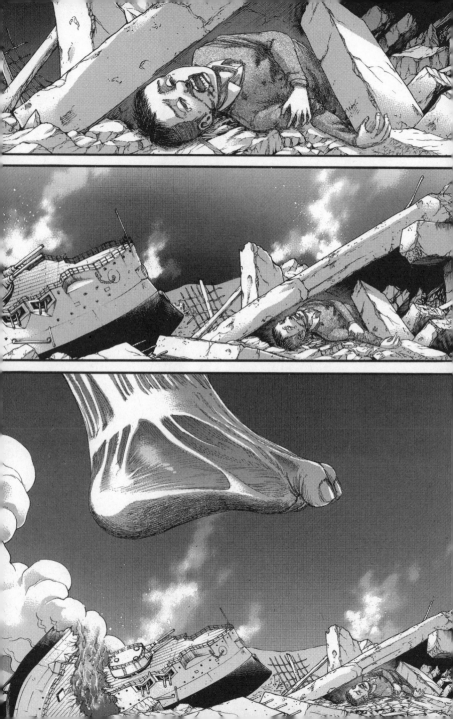

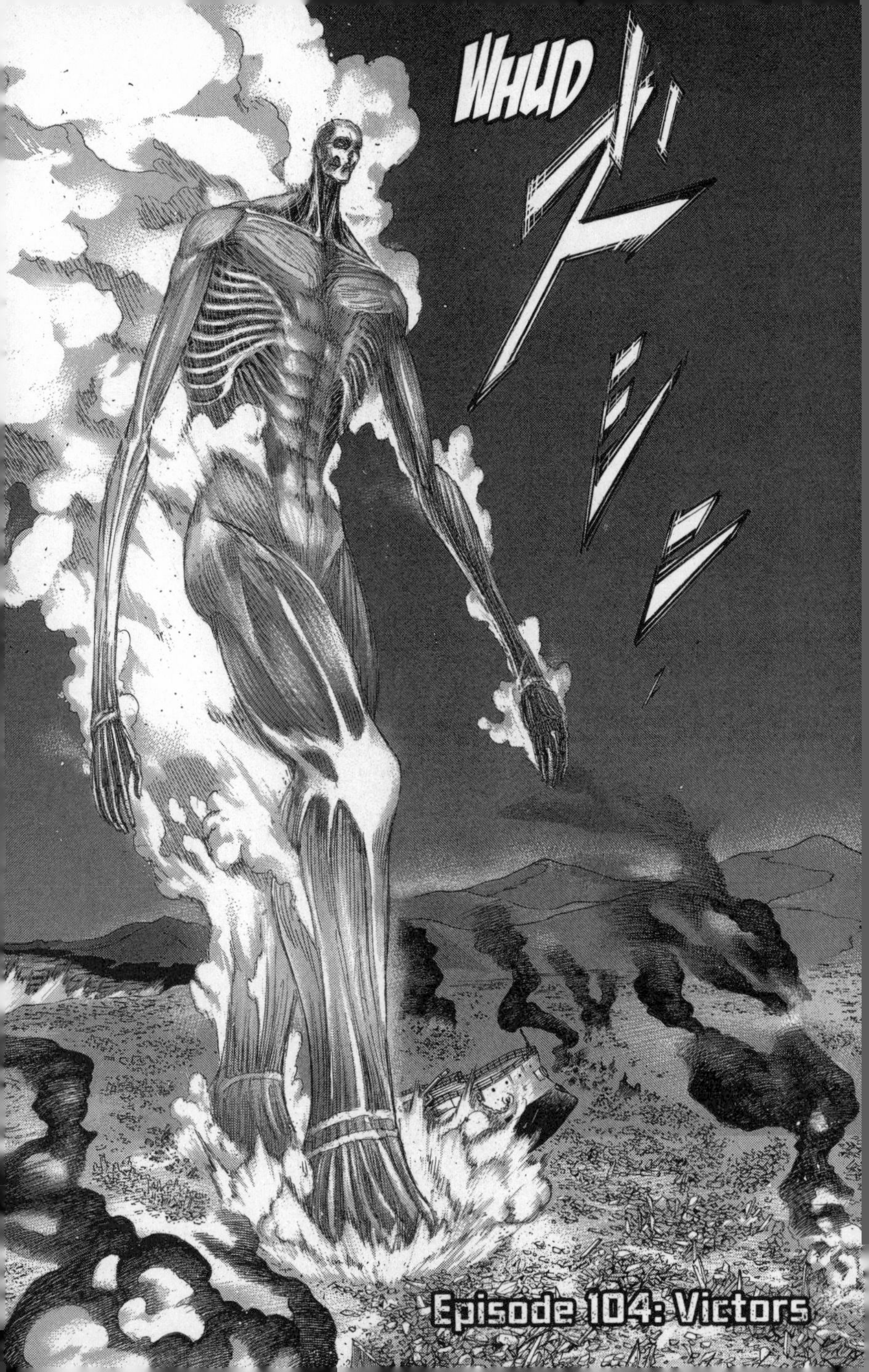
WHUD
Episode 104: Victors

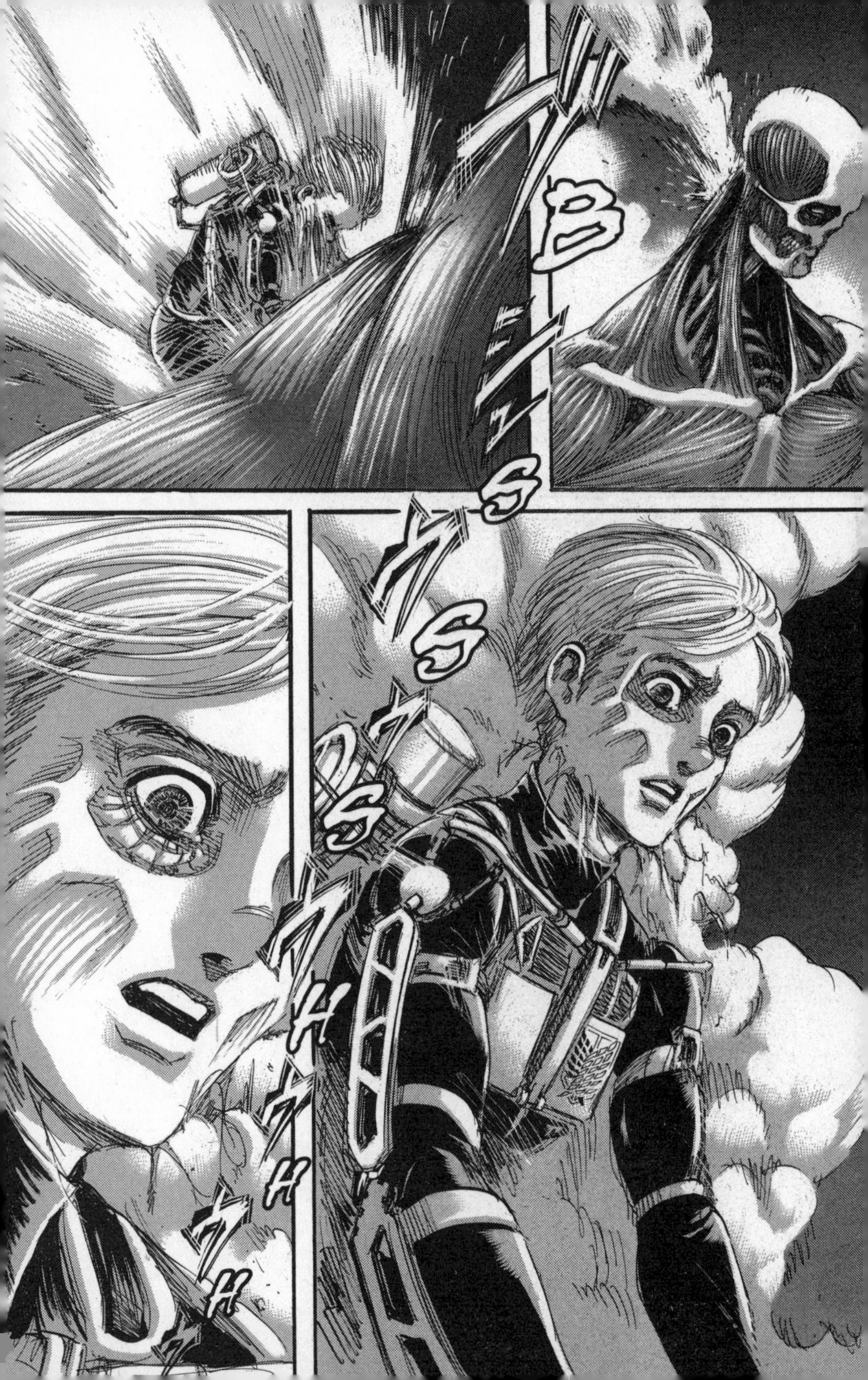
BSSSHHH

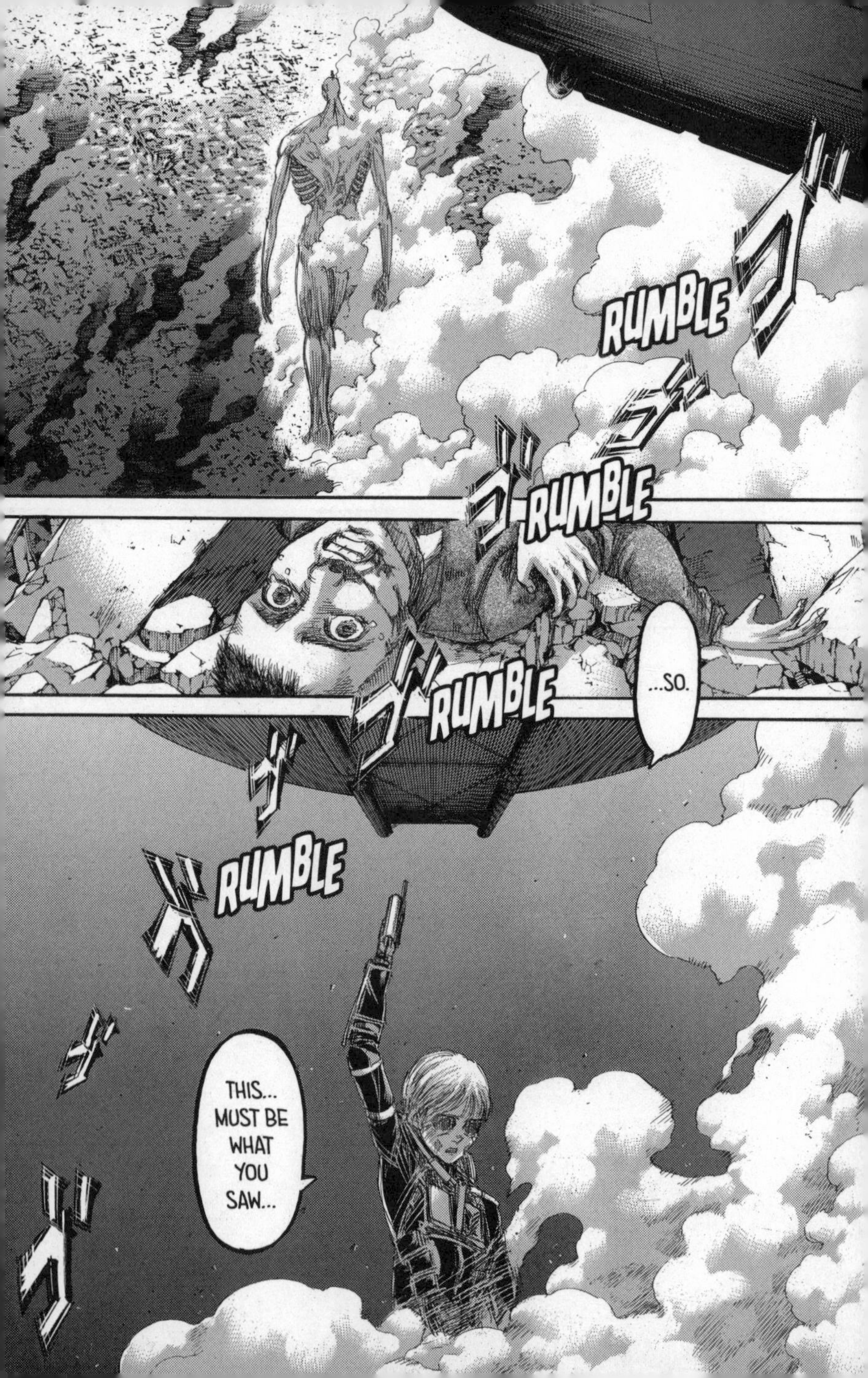
RUMBLE
RUMBLE
...SO.
RUMBLE
RUMBLE
THIS... MUST BE WHAT YOU SAW...

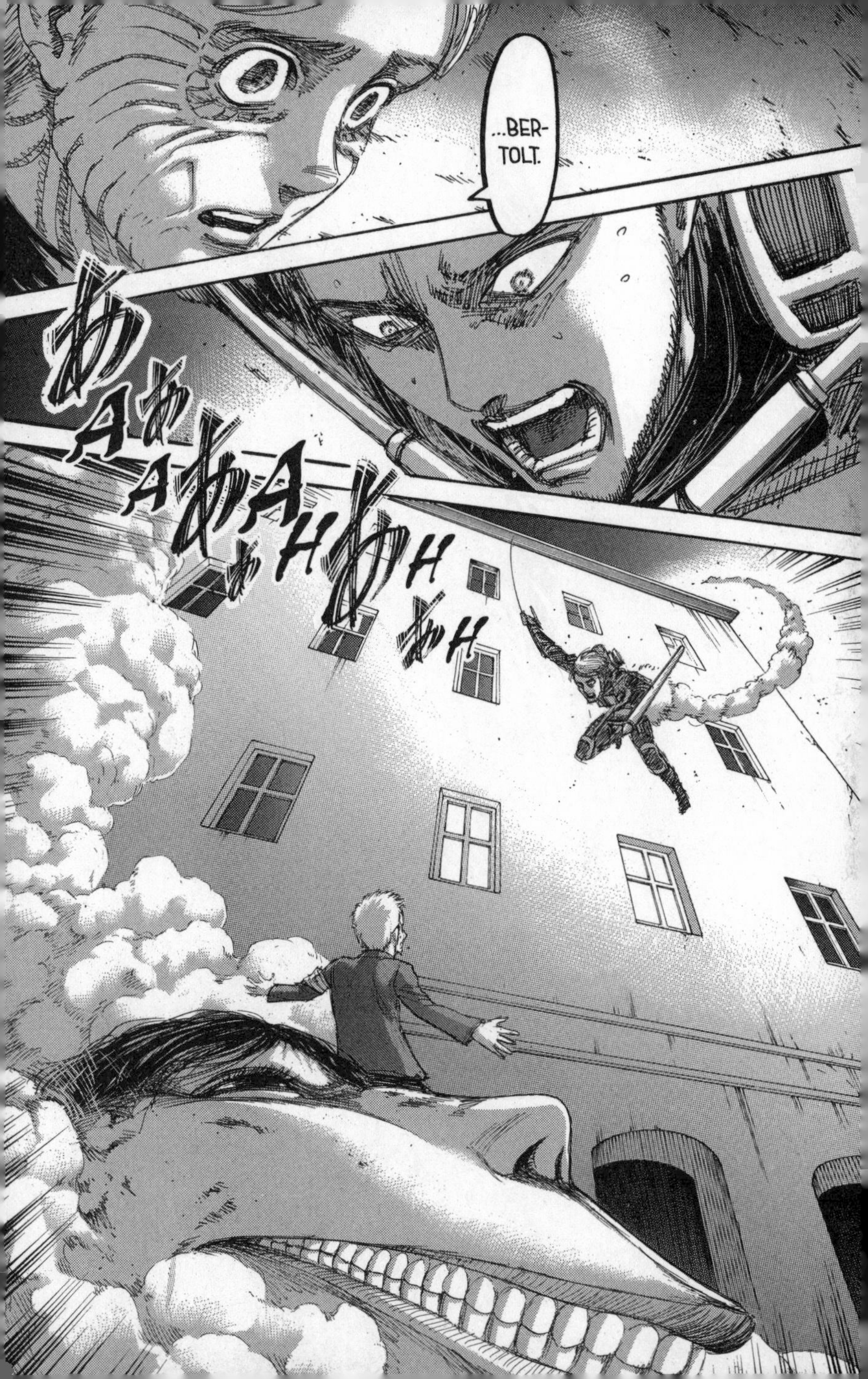
...BER-
TOLT.
AAAHHH

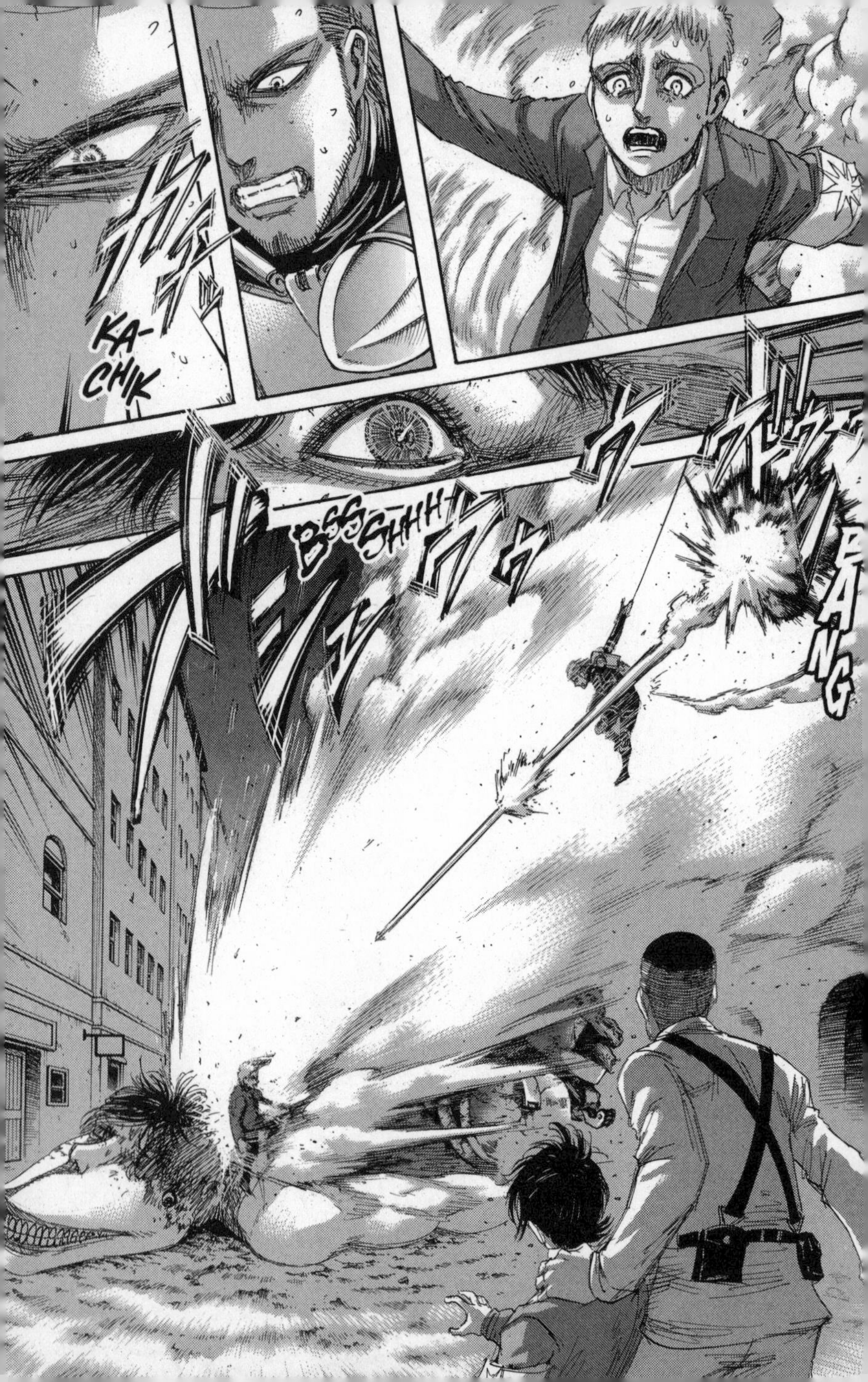
KA-CHIK
BANG
BSSSHHH

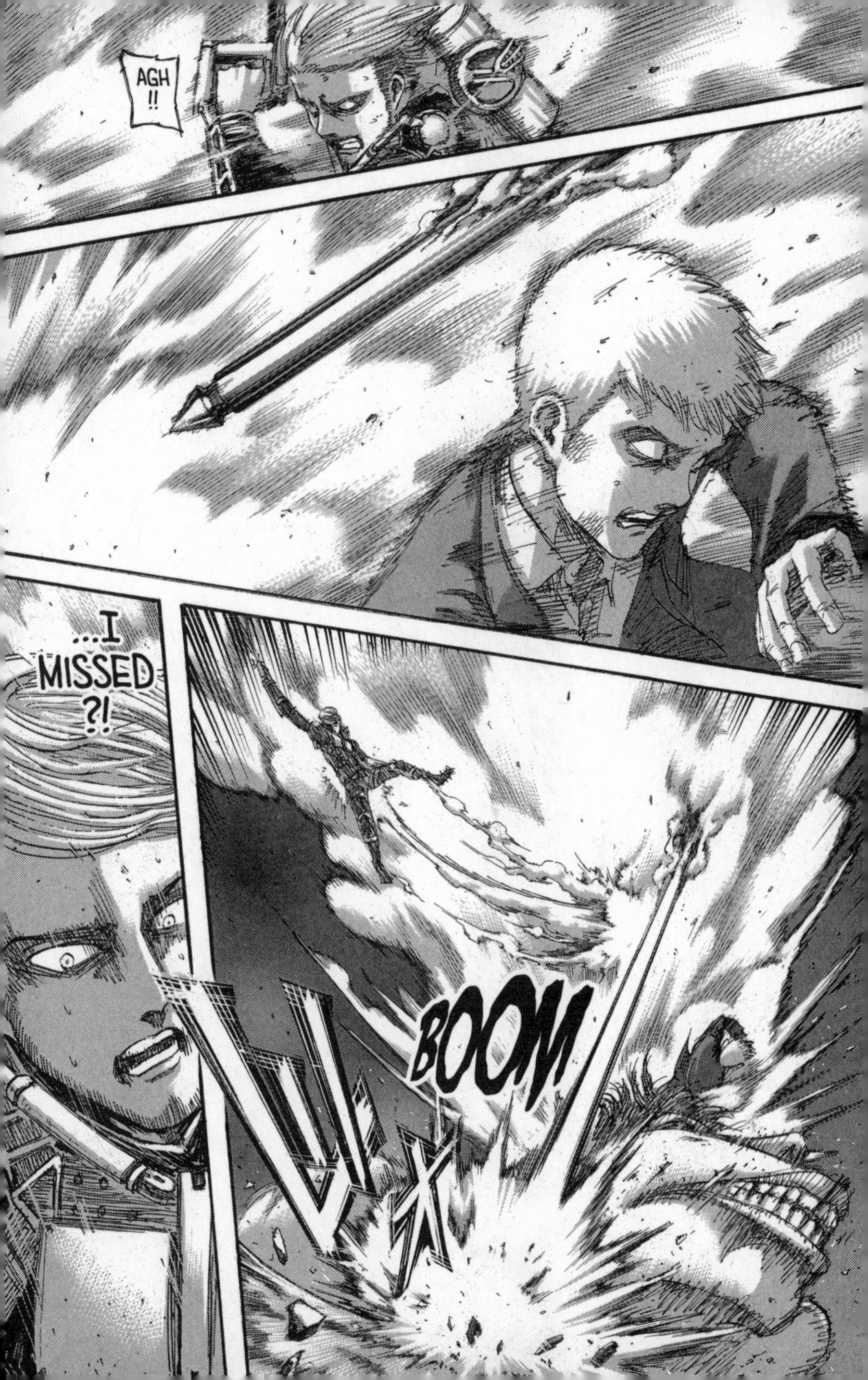
AGH!!
BOOM
...I MISSED?!

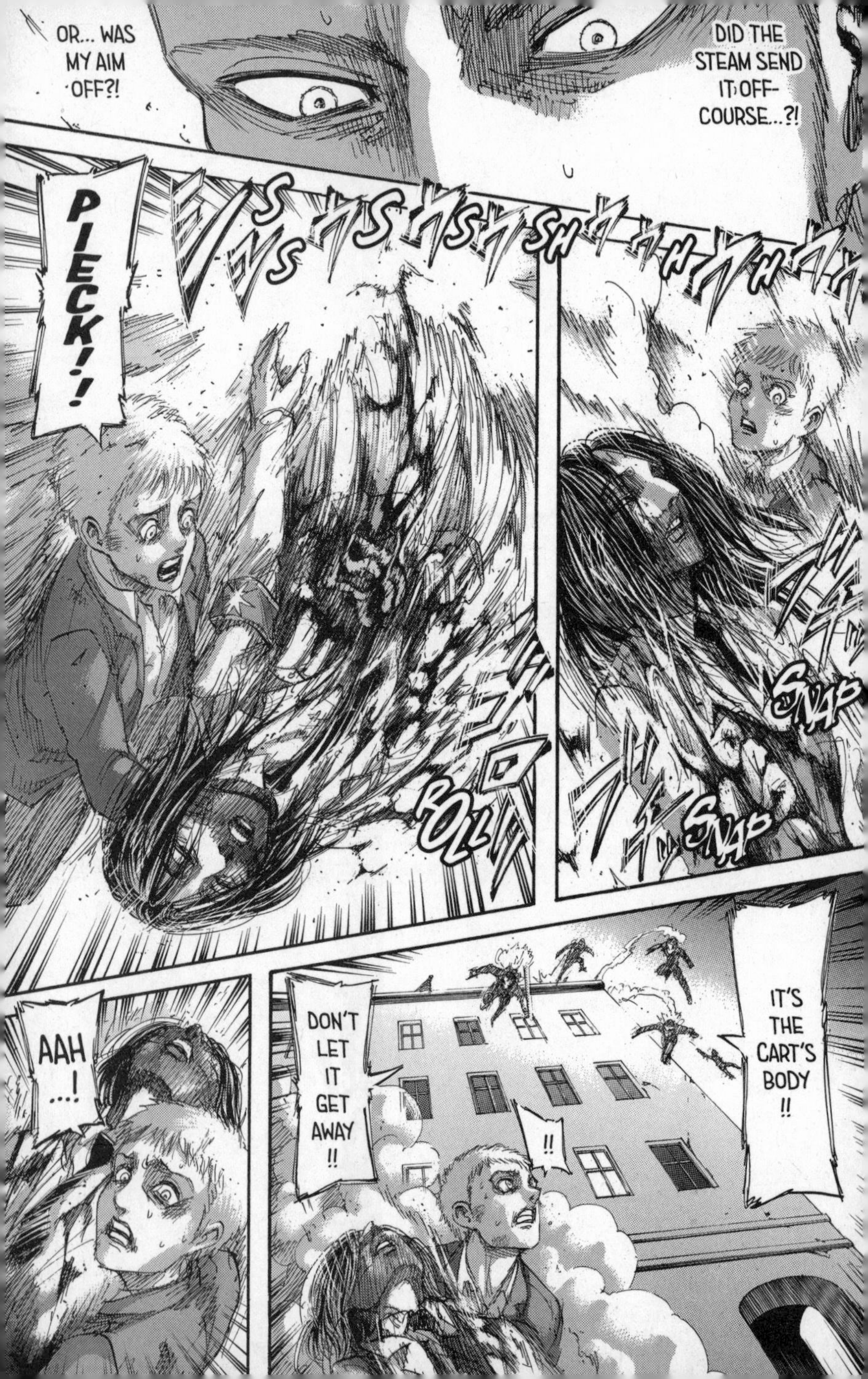
DID THE STEAM SEND IT OFF-COURSE...?!
OR... WAS MY AIM OFF?!
SNAP
SNAP
PIECK!!
ROLL
IT'S THE CART'S BODY !!
DON'T LET IT GET AWAY !!
!!
AAH ...!

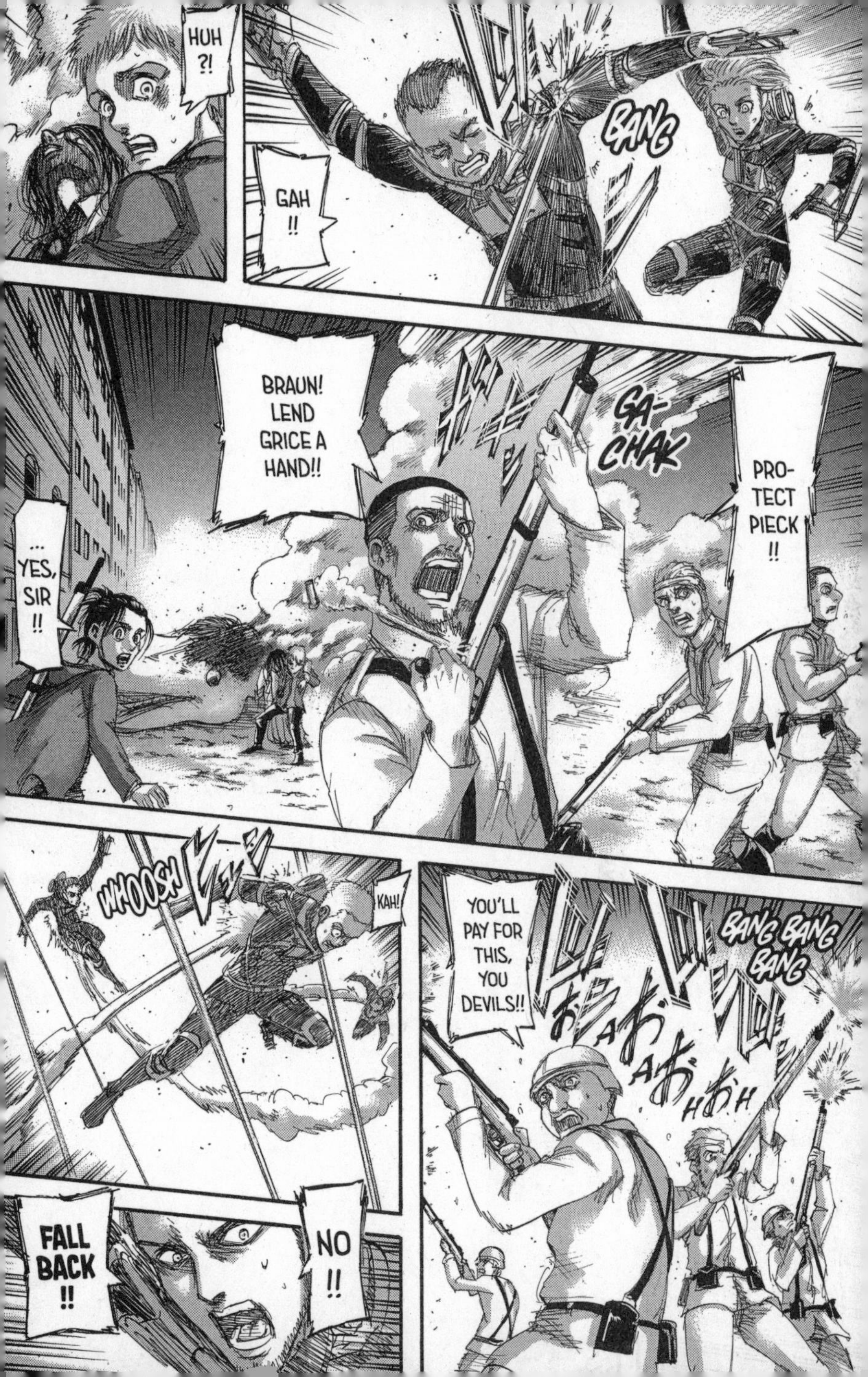
BANG
GAH !!
HUH ?!
PROTECT PIECK !!
GA-CHAK
BRAUN! LEND GRICE A HAND!!
... YES, SIR !!
BANG BANG BANG
YOU'LL PAY FOR THIS, YOU DEVILS!!
KAH!
WHOOSH
NO !!
FALL BACK !!

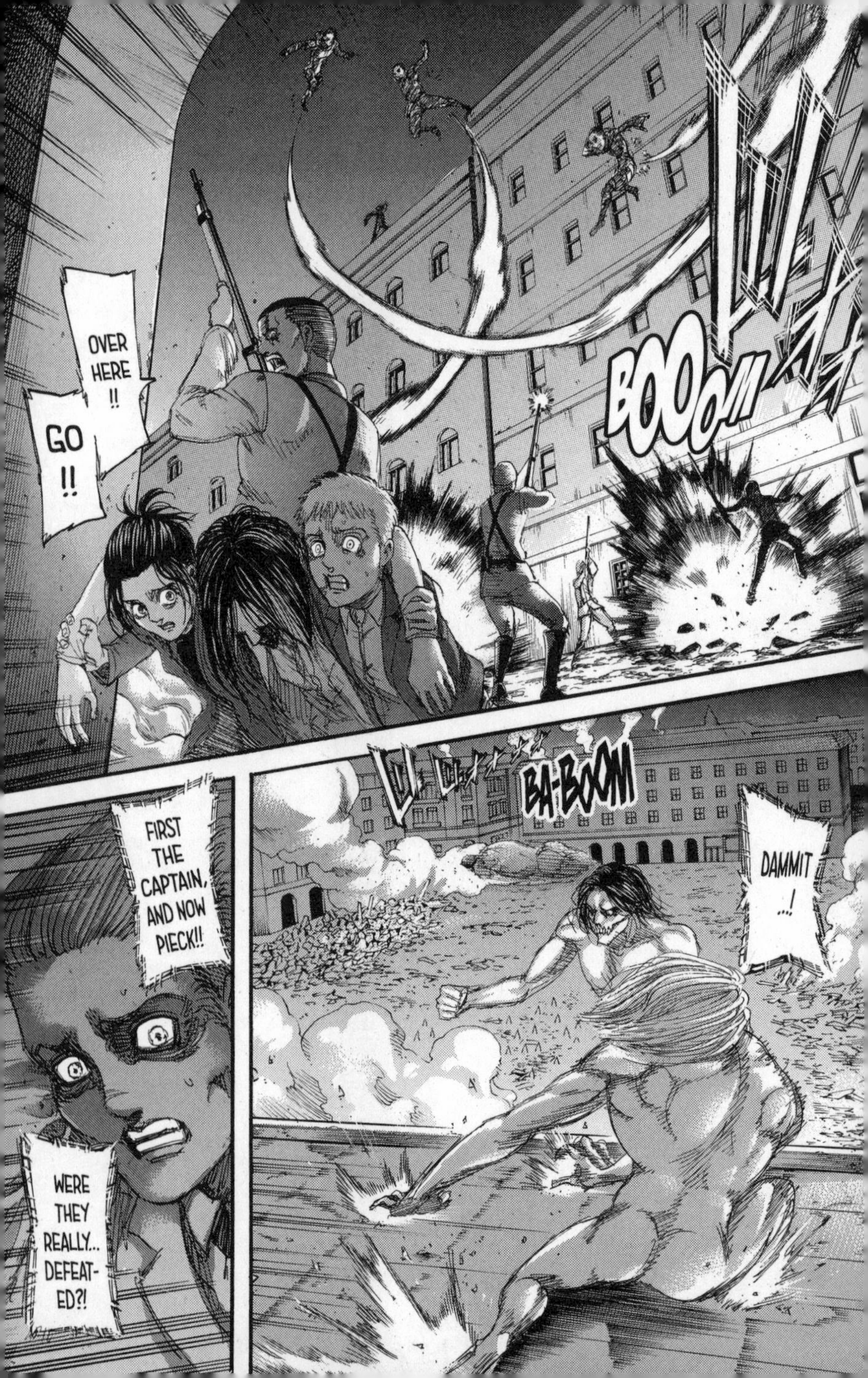
BOOOM
OVER HERE!!
GO!!
BA-BOOM
DAMMIT...!
FIRST THE CAPTAIN, AND NOW PIECK!!
WERE THEY REALLY... DEFEAT-ED?!

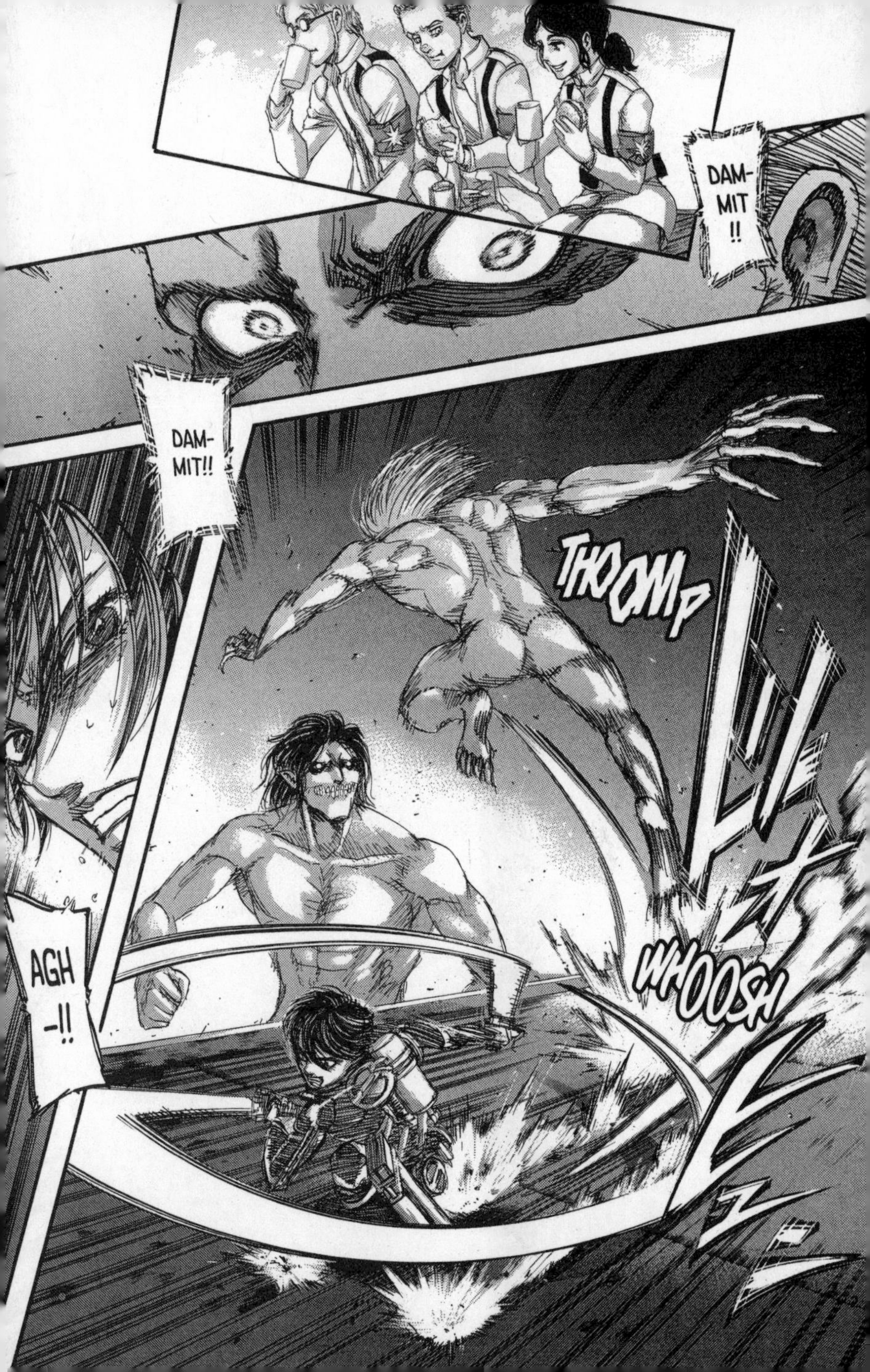
DAM-MIT!!
THOOMP
WHOOSH
DAM-MIT!!
AGH-!!

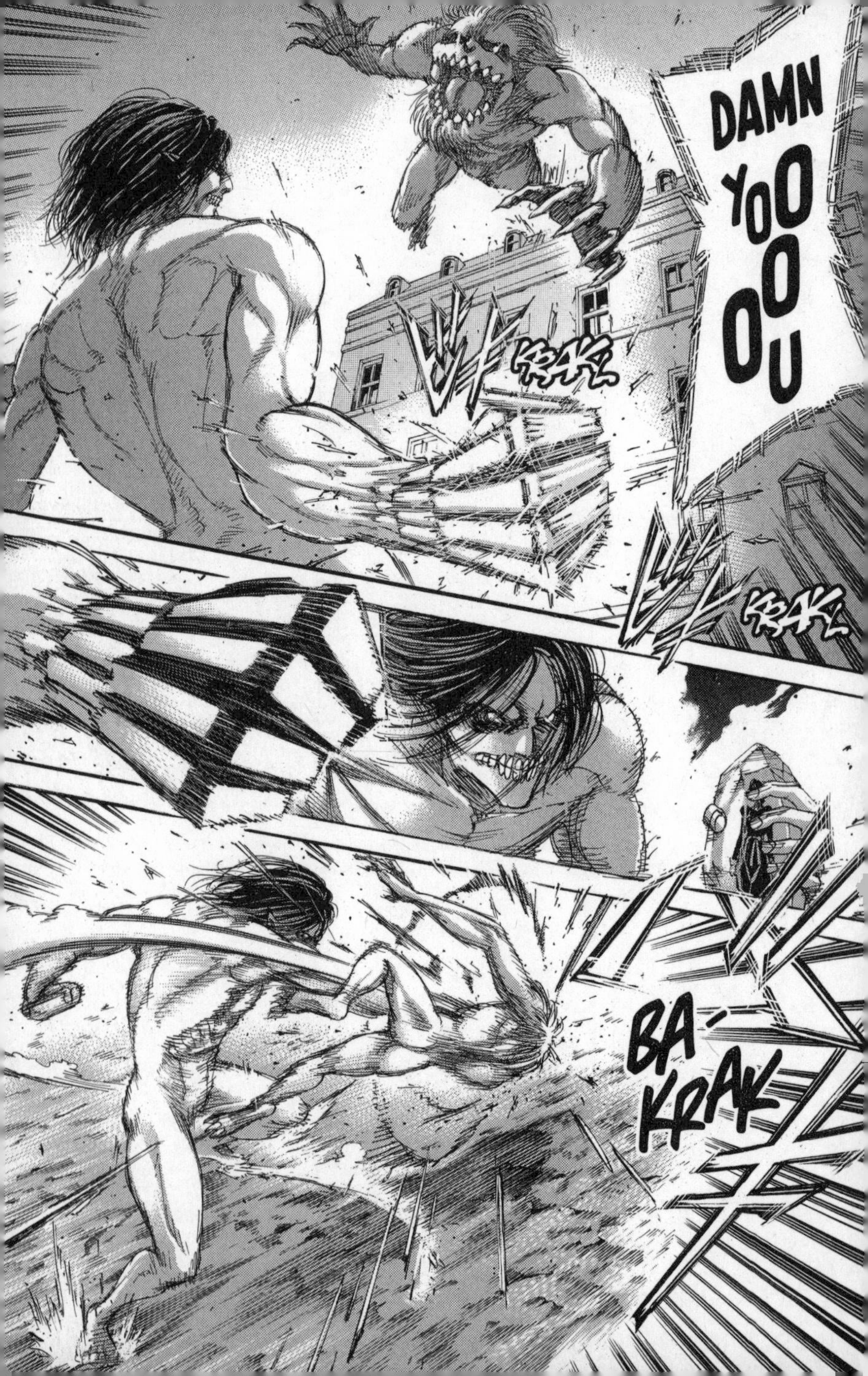
DAMN YOOOOOU
KRAK
KRAK
BA-KRAK

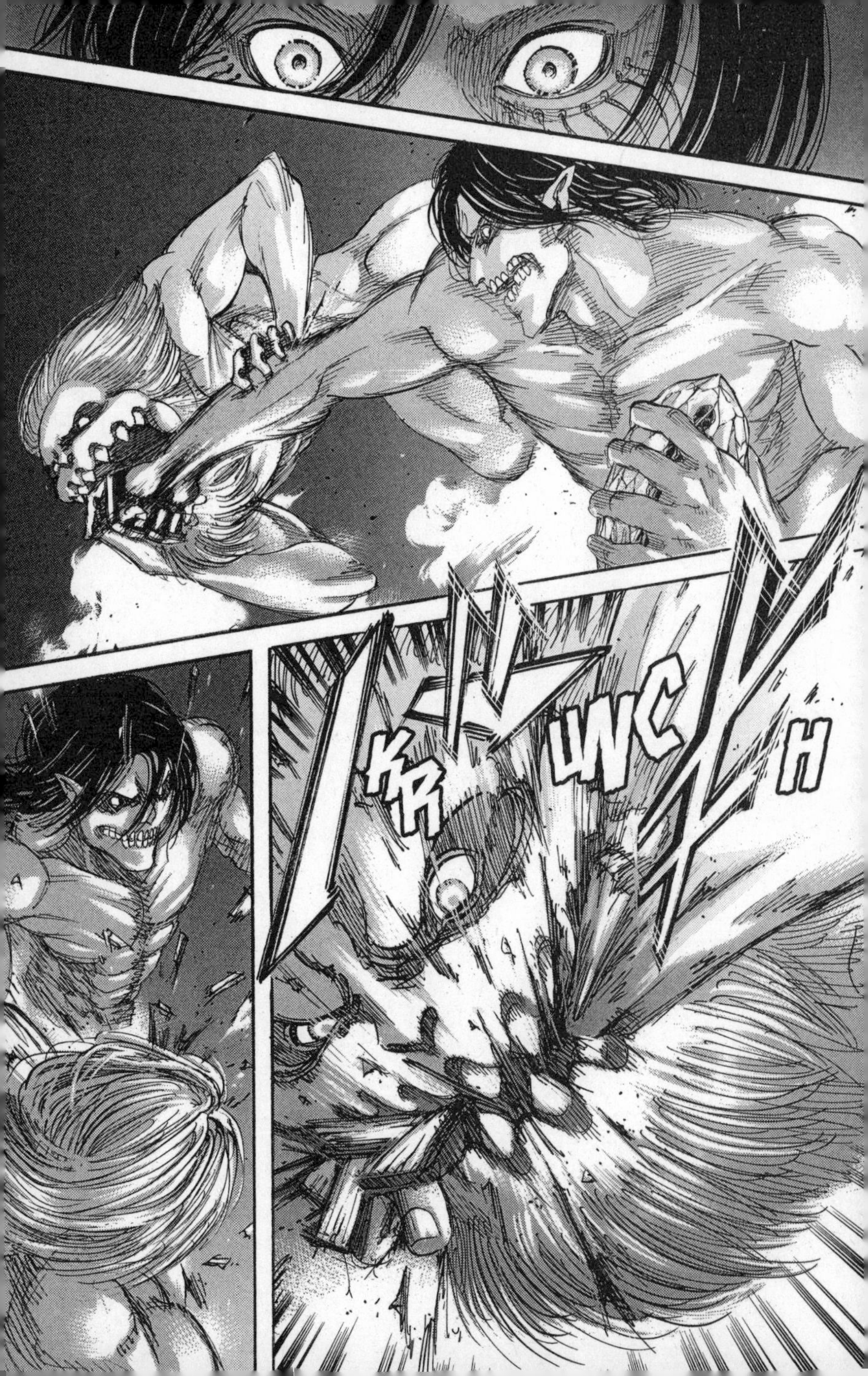
KRUNCH

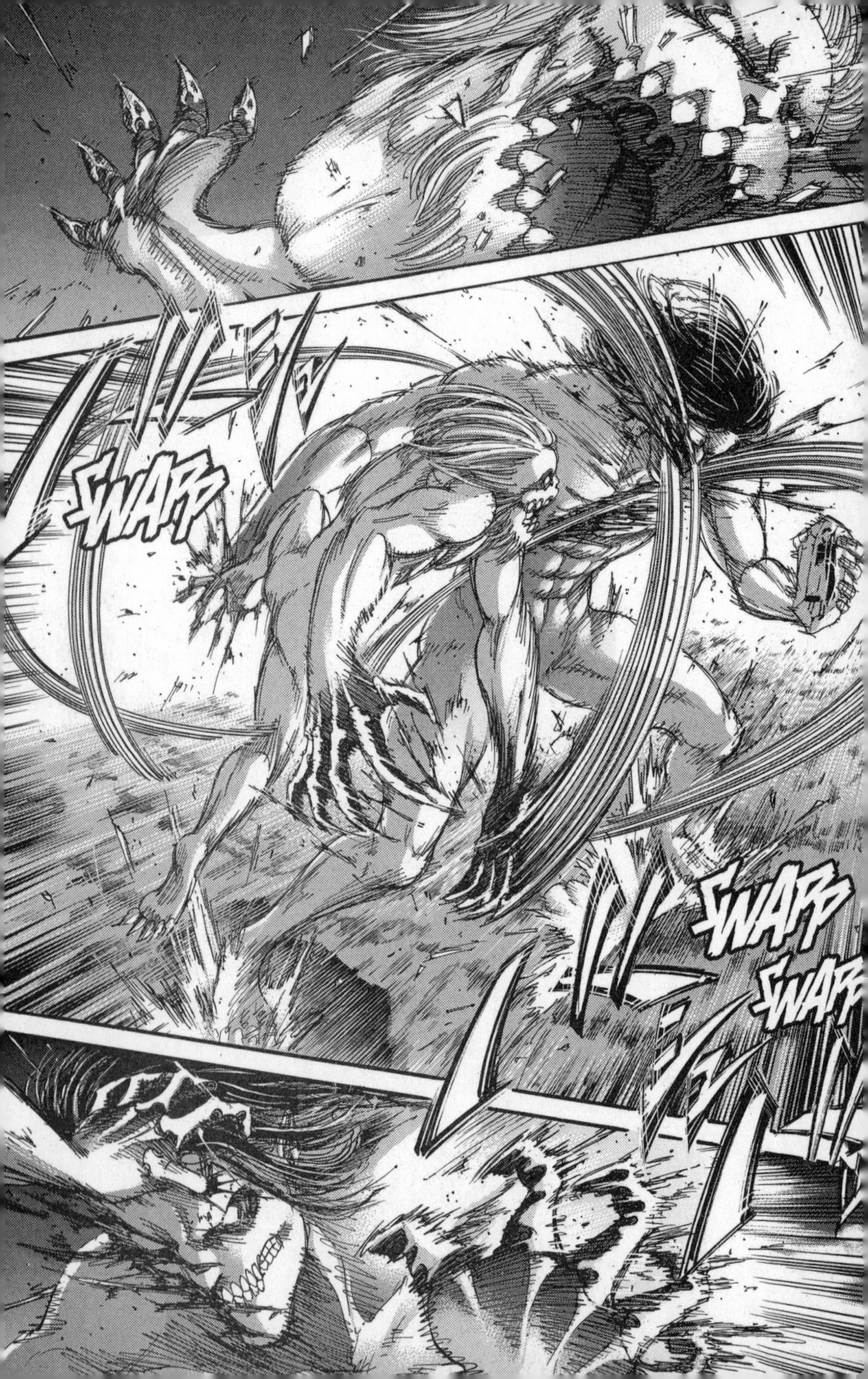
SWAP
SWAP
SWAP

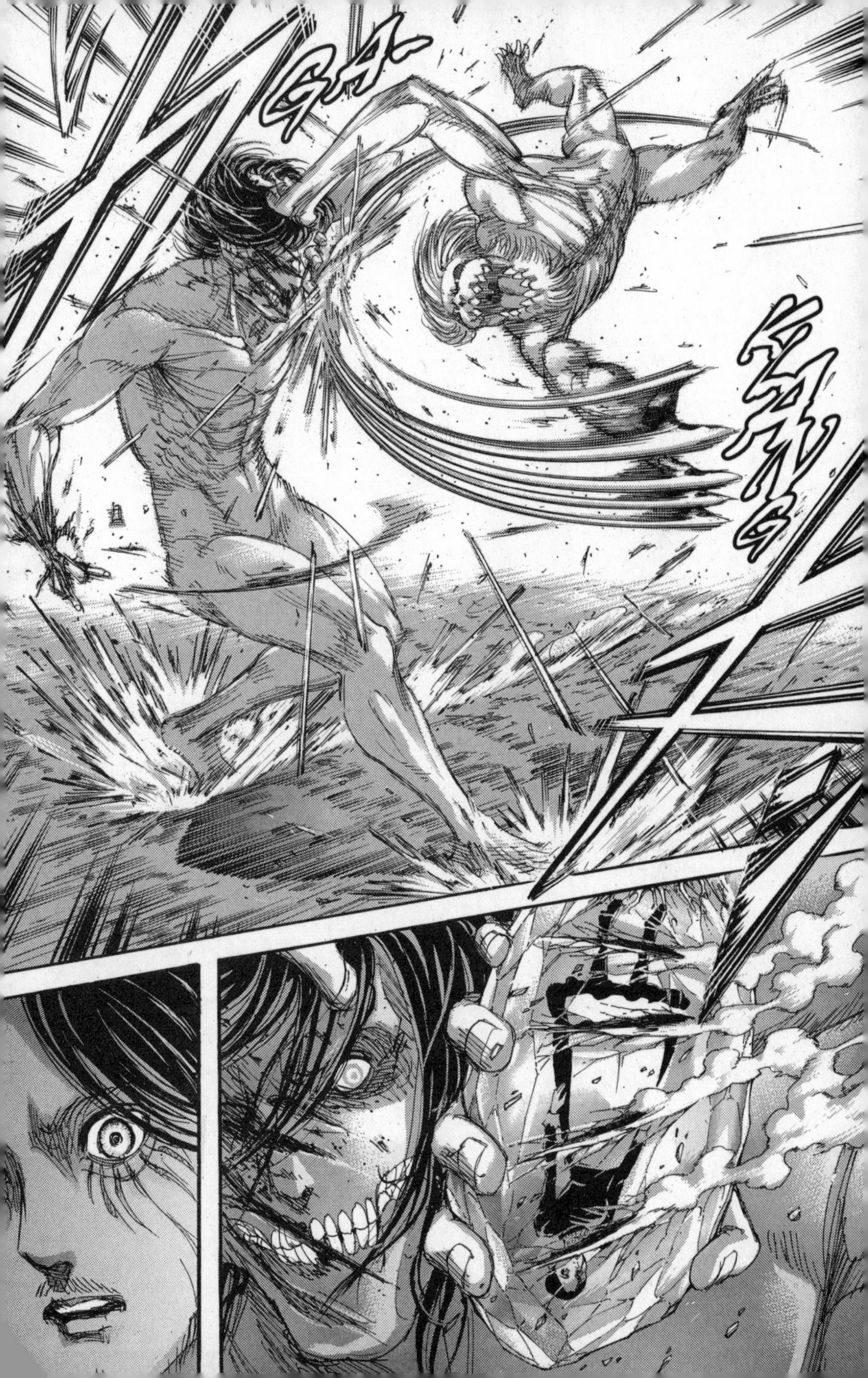
GRA
KLANG

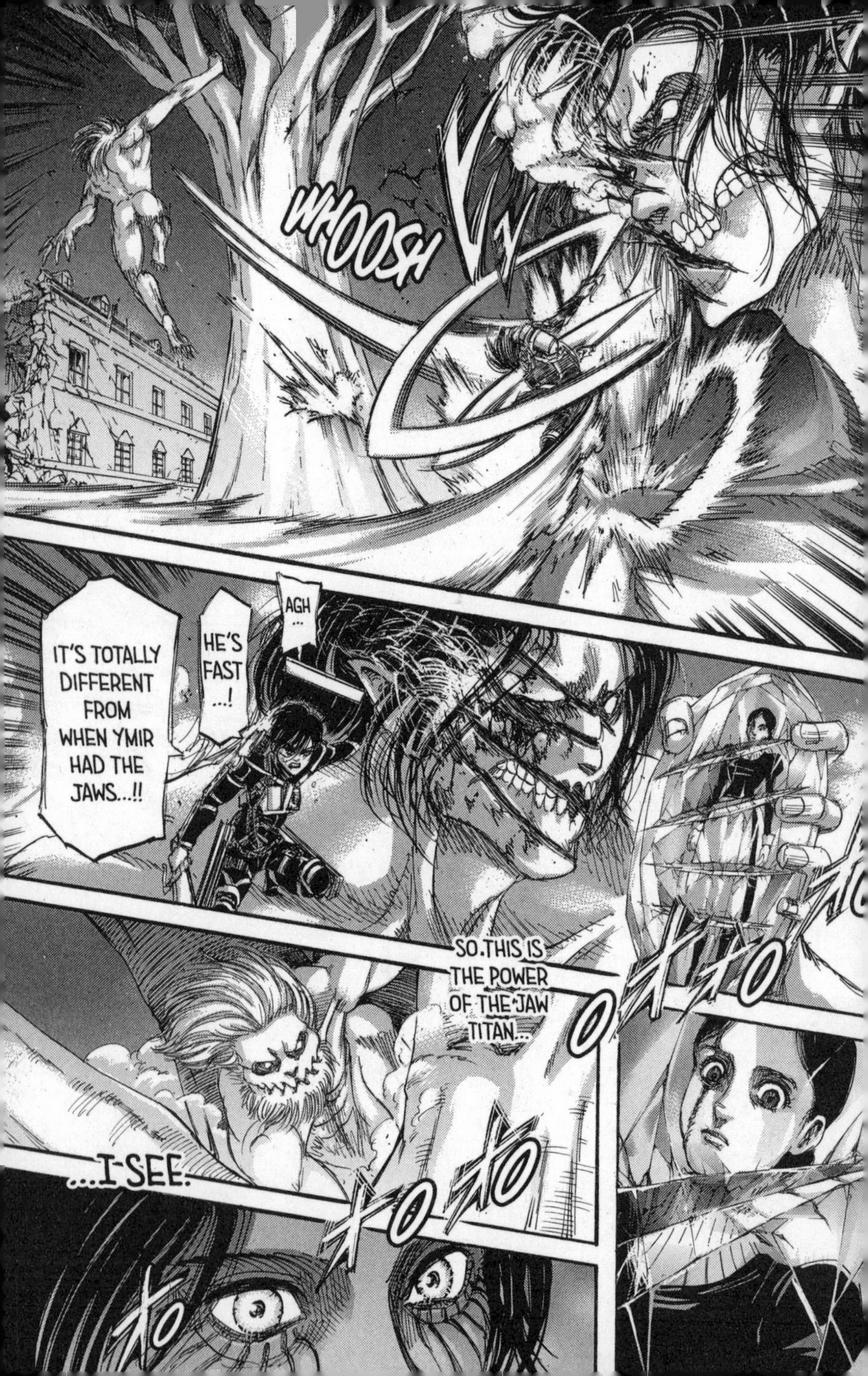
WHOOSH
AGH...
HE'S FAST...!
IT'S TOTALLY DIFFERENT FROM WHEN YMIR HAD THE JAWS...!!
SO, THIS IS THE POWER OF THE JAW TITAN...
...I SEE.

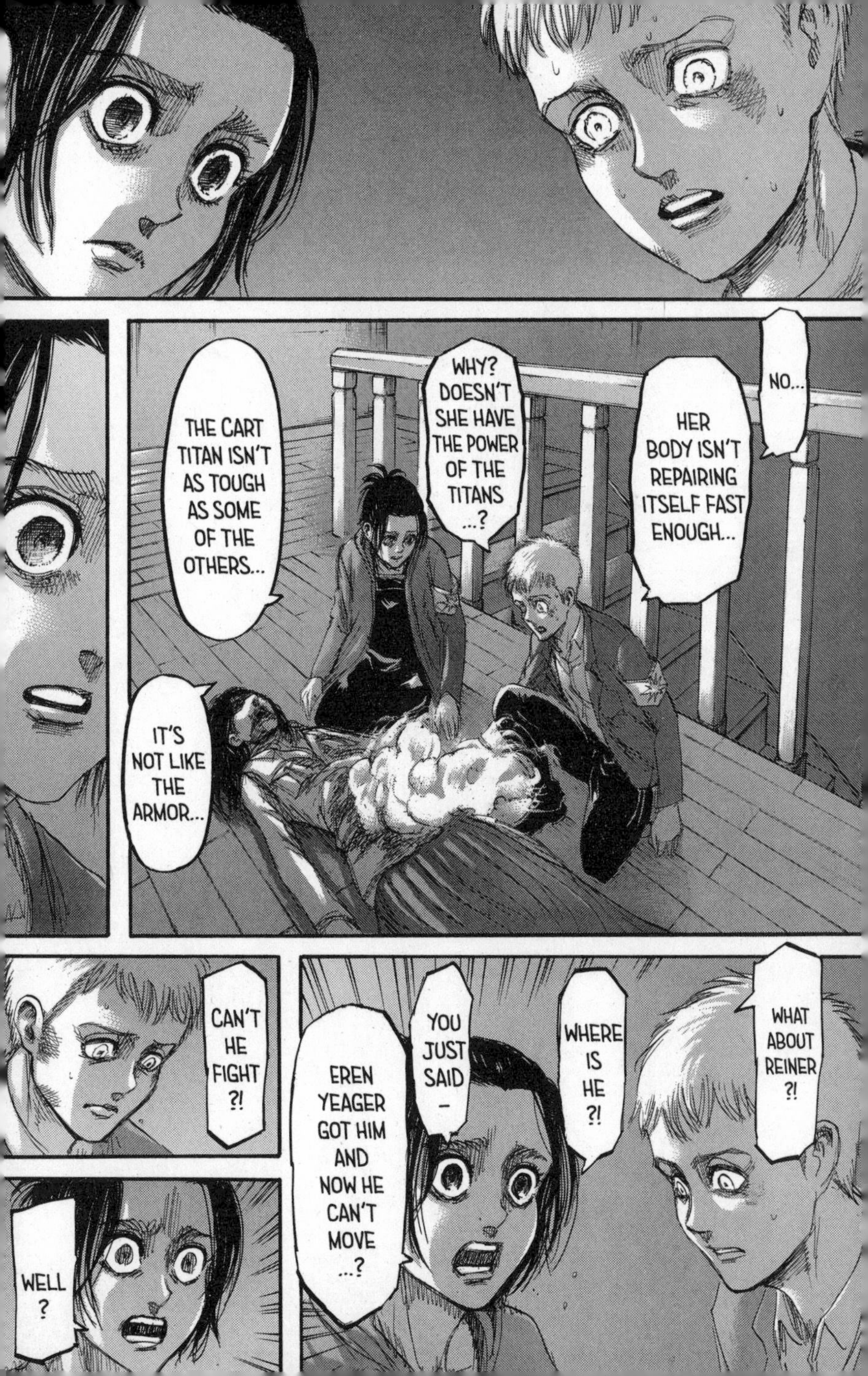
NO...
HER BODY ISN'T REPAIRING ITSELF FAST ENOUGH...
WHY? DOESN'T SHE HAVE THE POWER OF THE TITANS ...?
THE CART TITAN ISN'T AS TOUGH AS SOME OF THE OTHERS...
IT'S NOT LIKE THE ARMOR...
WHAT ABOUT REINER?!
WHERE IS HE?!
YOU JUST SAID –
EREN YEAGER GOT HIM AND NOW HE CAN'T MOVE ...?
CAN'T HE FIGHT?!
WELL?

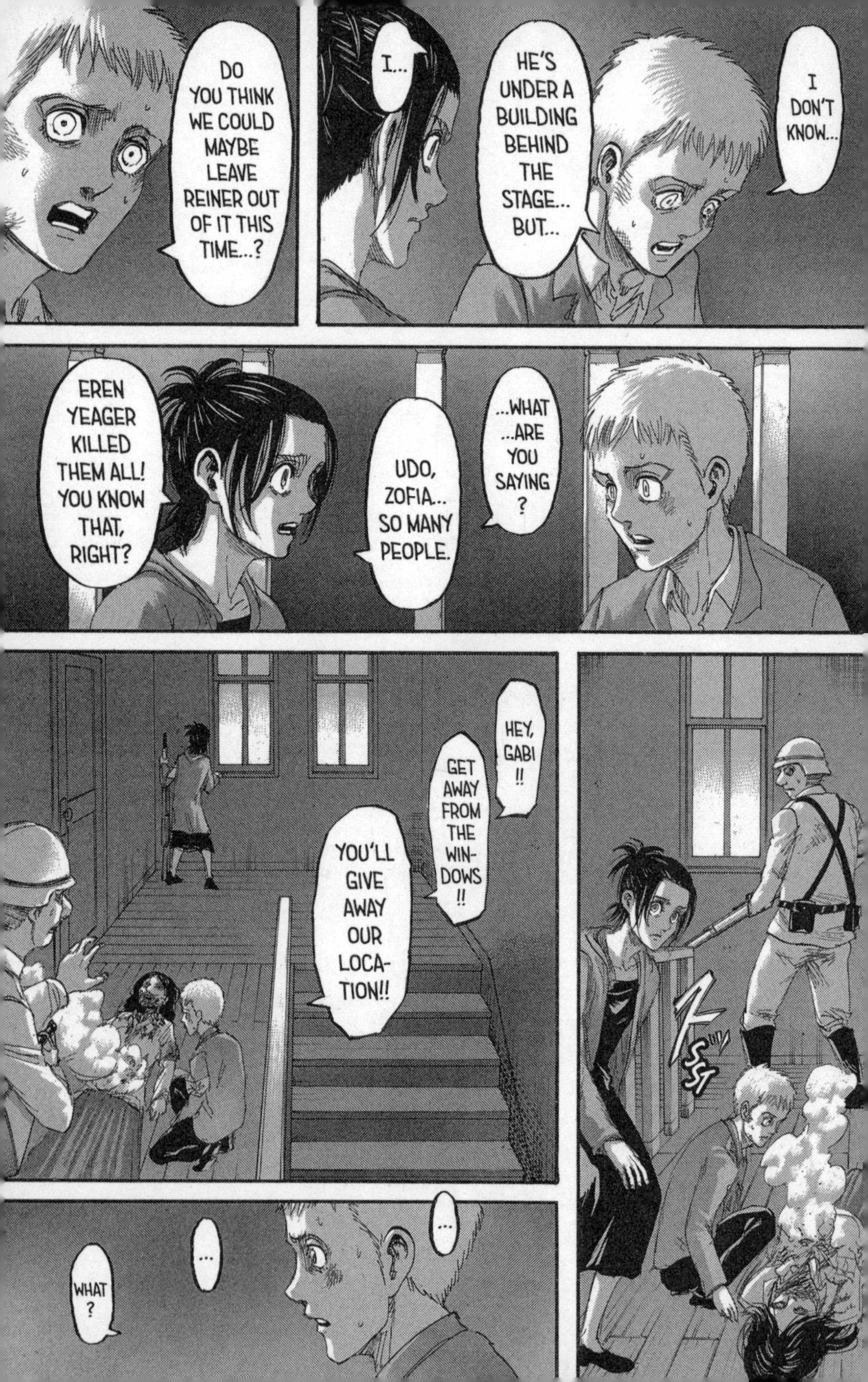
I DON'T KNOW...
HE'S UNDER A BUILDING BEHIND THE STAGE... BUT...
I...
DO YOU THINK WE COULD MAYBE LEAVE REINER OUT OF IT THIS TIME...?
...WHAT ...ARE YOU SAYING ?
UDO, ZOFIA... SO MANY PEOPLE.
EREN YEAGER KILLED THEM ALL! YOU KNOW THAT, RIGHT?
SSH
HEY, GABI !!
GET AWAY FROM THE WIN-DOWS !!
YOU'LL GIVE AWAY OUR LOCA-TION!!
...
...
WHAT ?

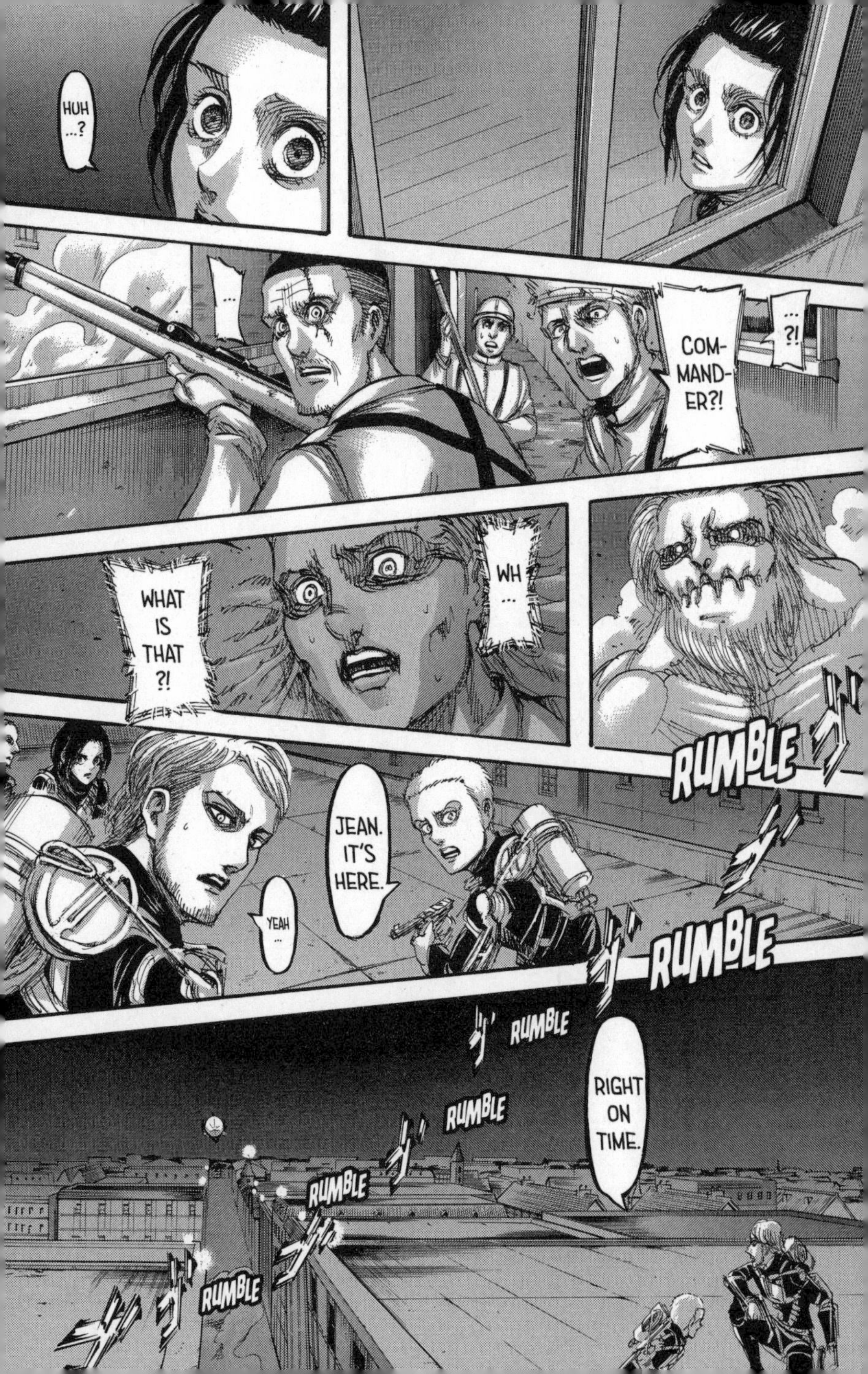
HUH ...?
...?!
COM-MAND-ER?!
...
WH ...
WHAT IS THAT ?!
RUMBLE
RUMBLE
JEAN. IT'S HERE.
YEAH ...
RUMBLE
RIGHT ON TIME.
RUMBLE
RUMBLE
RUMBLE

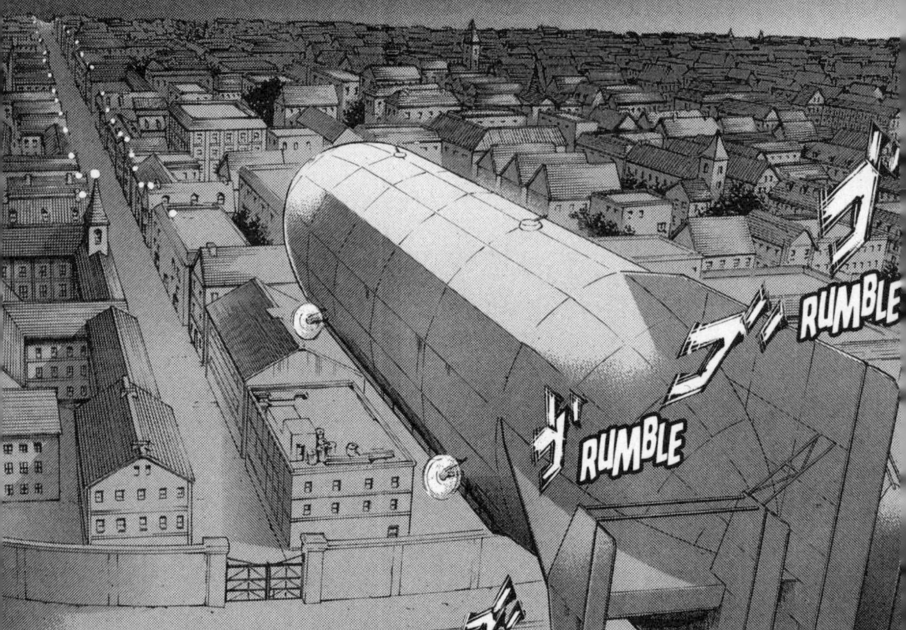
RUMBLE
RUMBLE
RUMBLE
RUMBLE
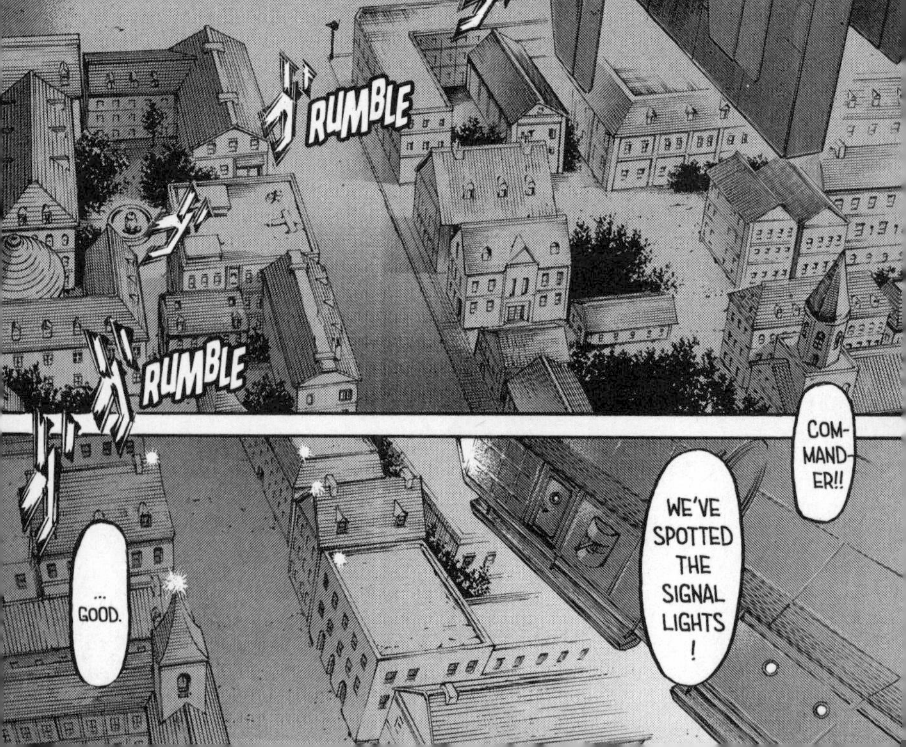
COMMANDER!!
WE'VE SPOTTED THE SIGNAL LIGHTS!
...GOOD.

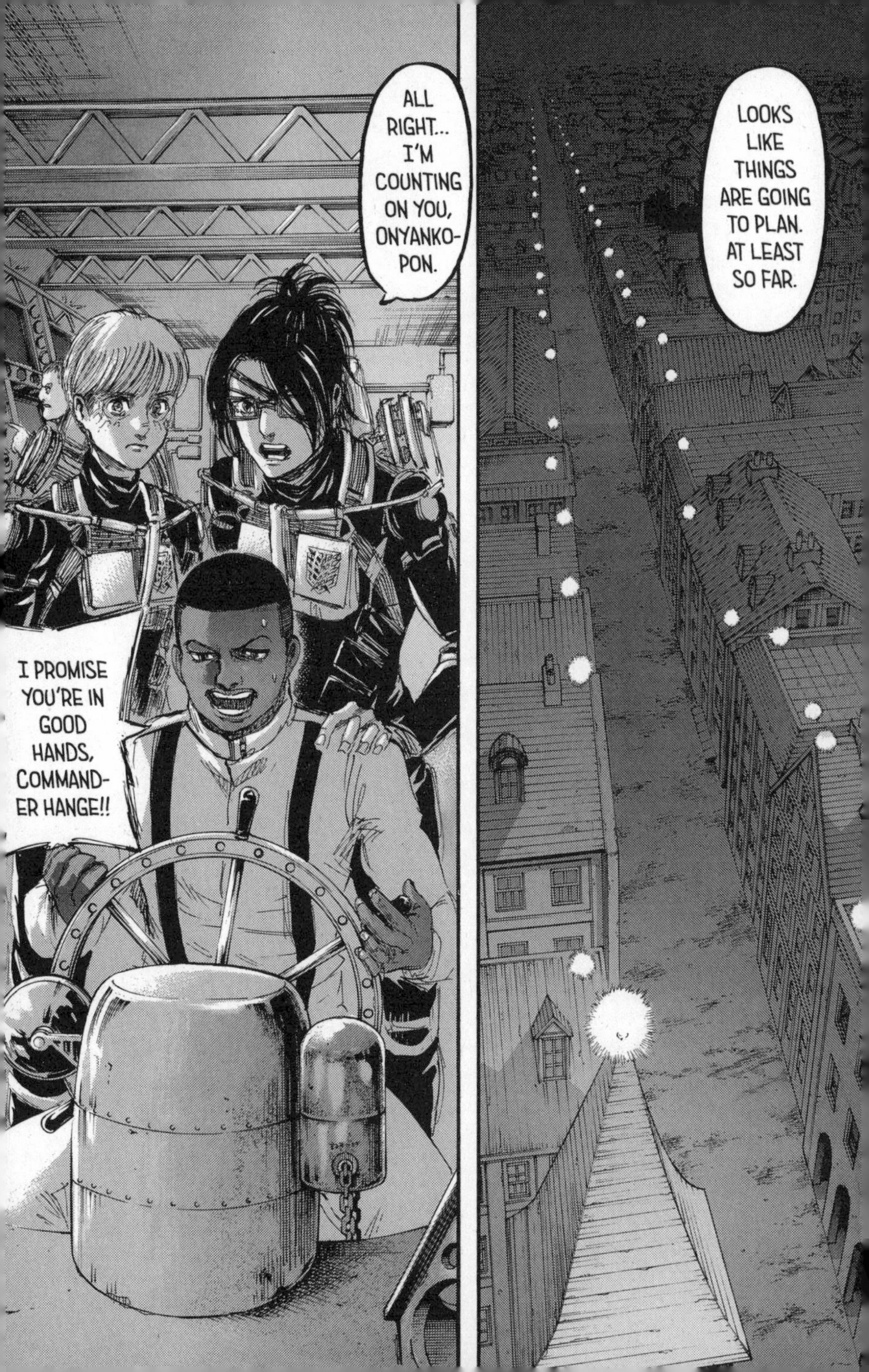
LOOKS LIKE THINGS ARE GOING TO PLAN. AT LEAST SO FAR.
ALL RIGHT... I'M COUNTING ON YOU, ONYANKO-PON.
I PROMISE YOU'RE IN GOOD HANDS, COMMANDER HANGE!!

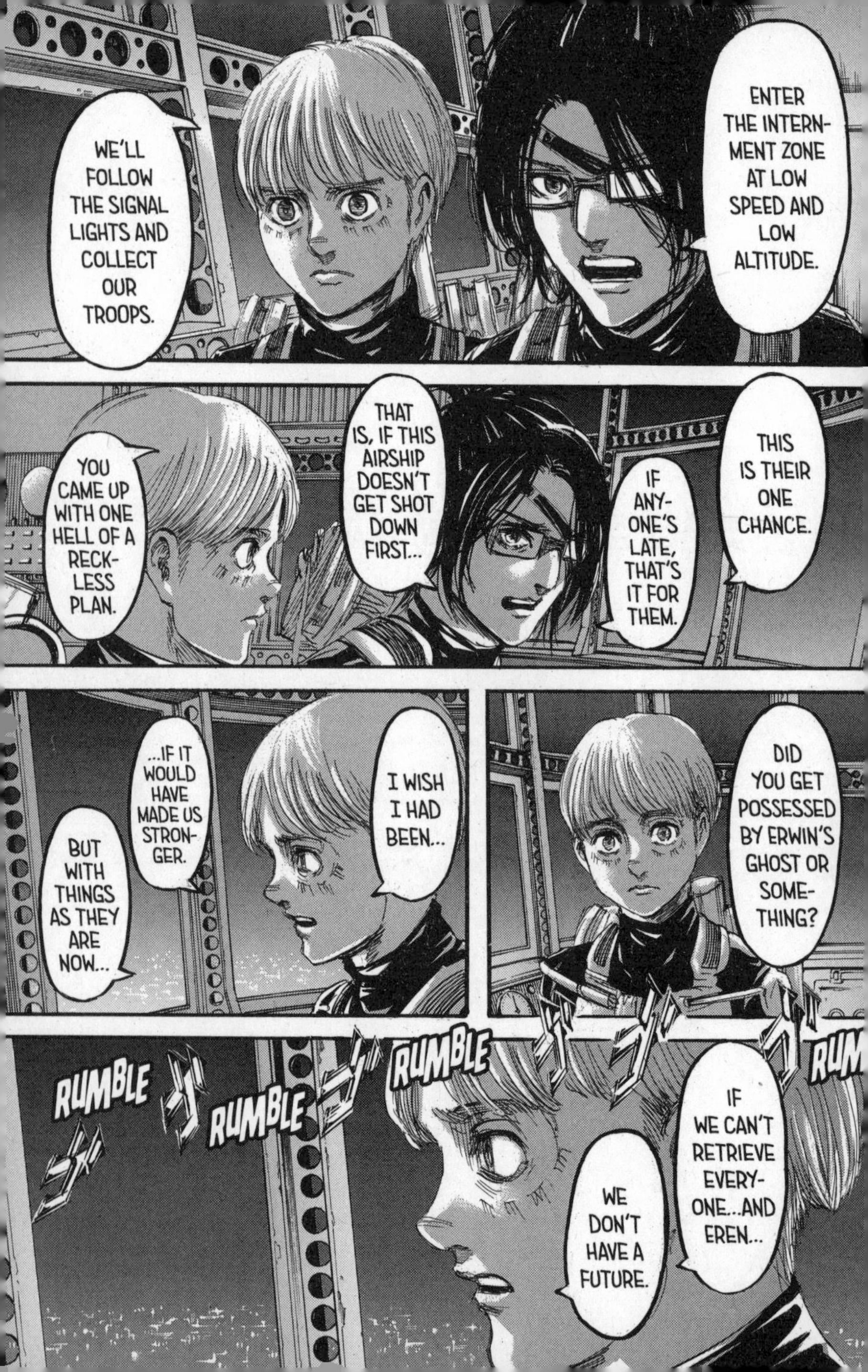
ENTER THE INTERNMENT ZONE AT LOW SPEED AND LOW ALTITUDE.
WE'LL FOLLOW THE SIGNAL LIGHTS AND COLLECT OUR TROOPS.
THIS IS THEIR ONE CHANCE.
IF ANYONE'S LATE, THAT'S IT FOR THEM.
THAT IS, IF THIS AIRSHIP DOESN'T GET SHOT DOWN FIRST...
YOU CAME UP WITH ONE HELL OF A RECKLESS PLAN.
DID YOU GET POSSESSED BY ERWIN'S GHOST OR SOMETHING?
I WISH I HAD BEEN...
...IF IT WOULD HAVE MADE US STRONGER.
BUT WITH THINGS AS THEY ARE NOW...
RUM
IF WE CAN'T RETRIEVE EVERYONE...AND EREN...
WE DON'T HAVE A FUTURE.
RUMBLE
RUMBLE
RUMBLE

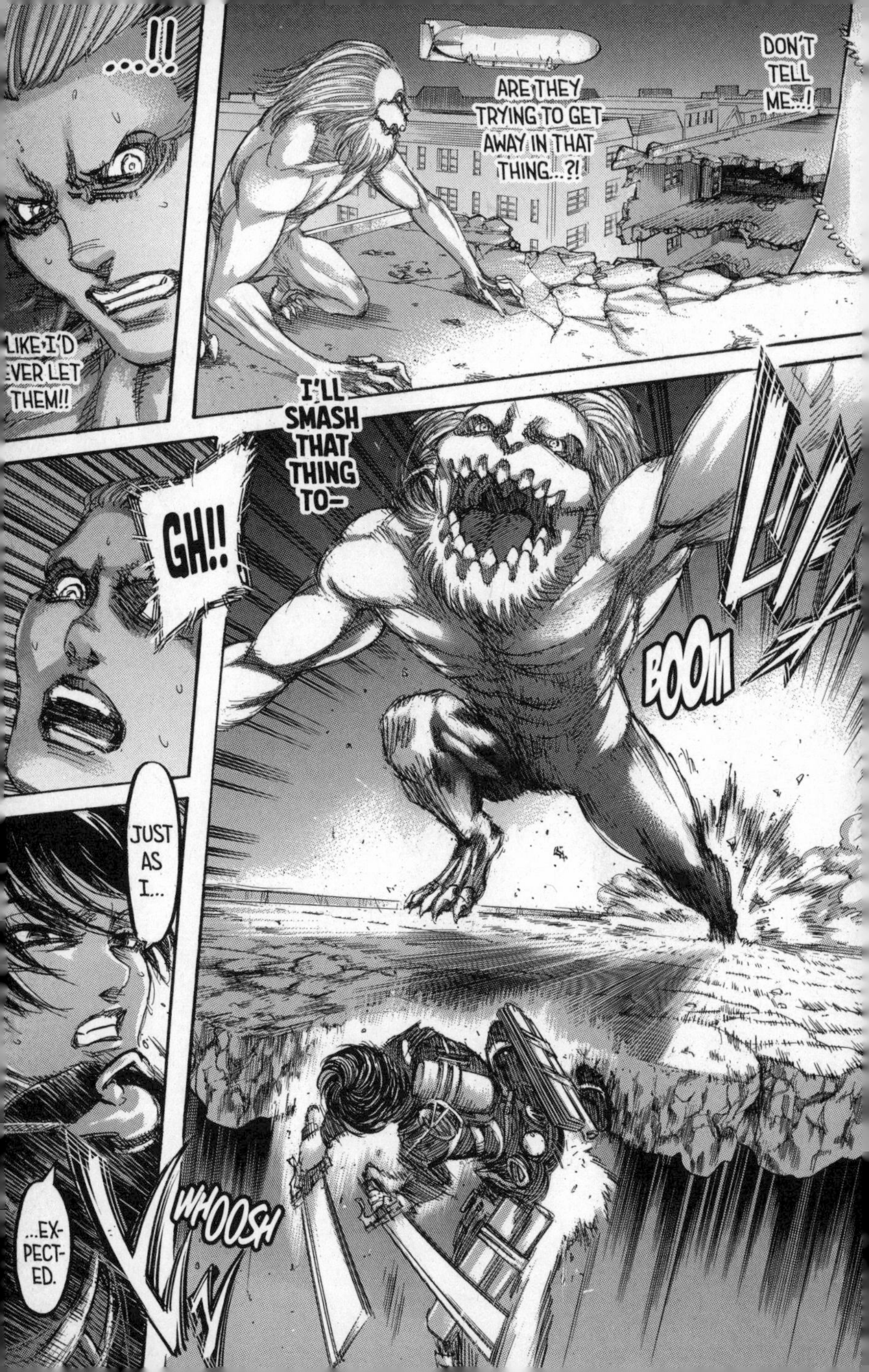
DON'T TELL ME...!
ARE THEY TRYING TO GET AWAY IN THAT THING...?!
...!!
LIKE I'D EVER LET THEM!!
I'LL SMASH THAT THING TO-
BOOM
GH!!
JUST AS I...
...EX-PECT-ED.
WHOOSH

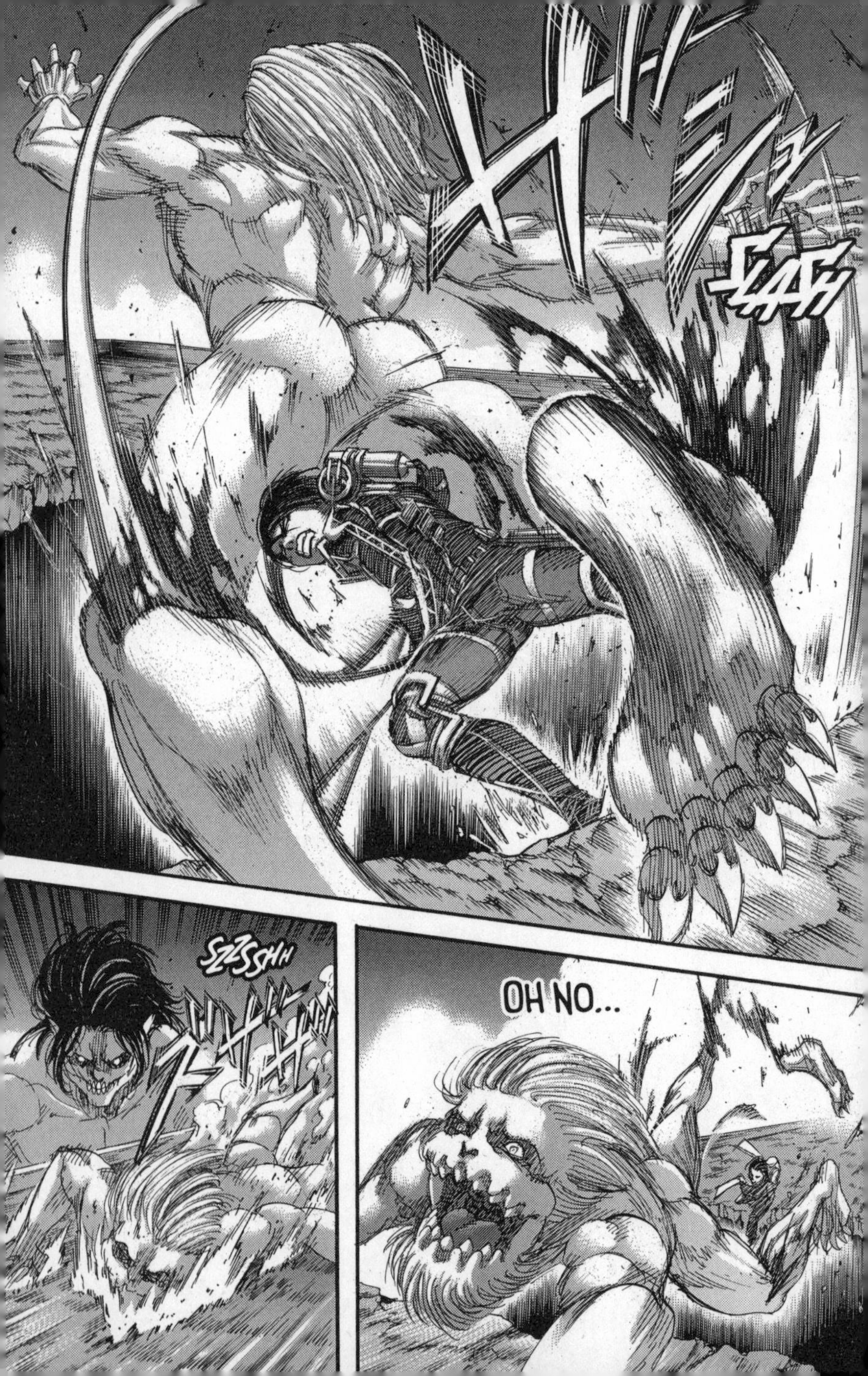
SLASH
OH NO...
SZZSSHH

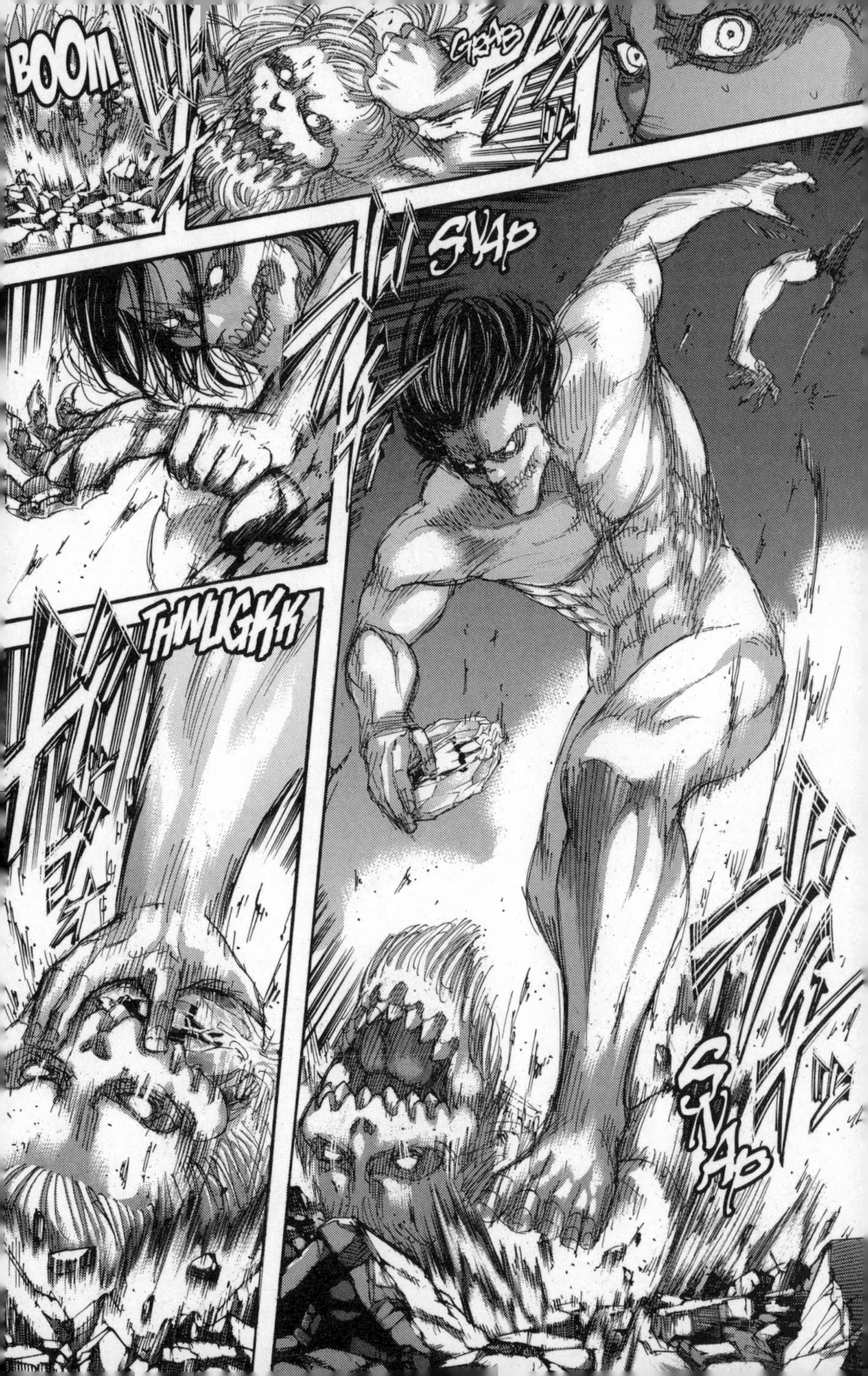
GRAB
BOOM
SNAP
SNAP
THWUGKK

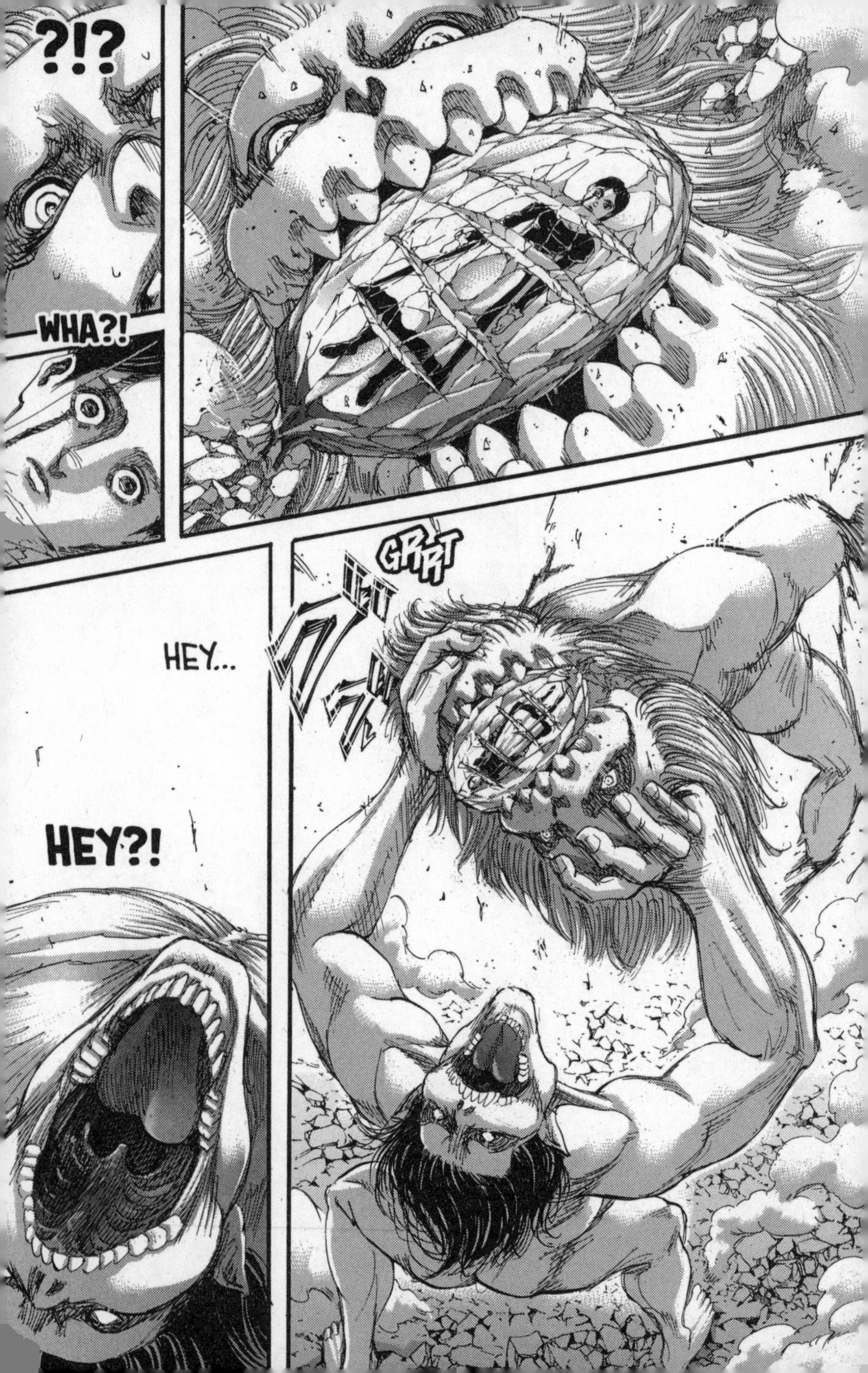
?!?
WHA?!
GRRT
HEY...
HEY?!

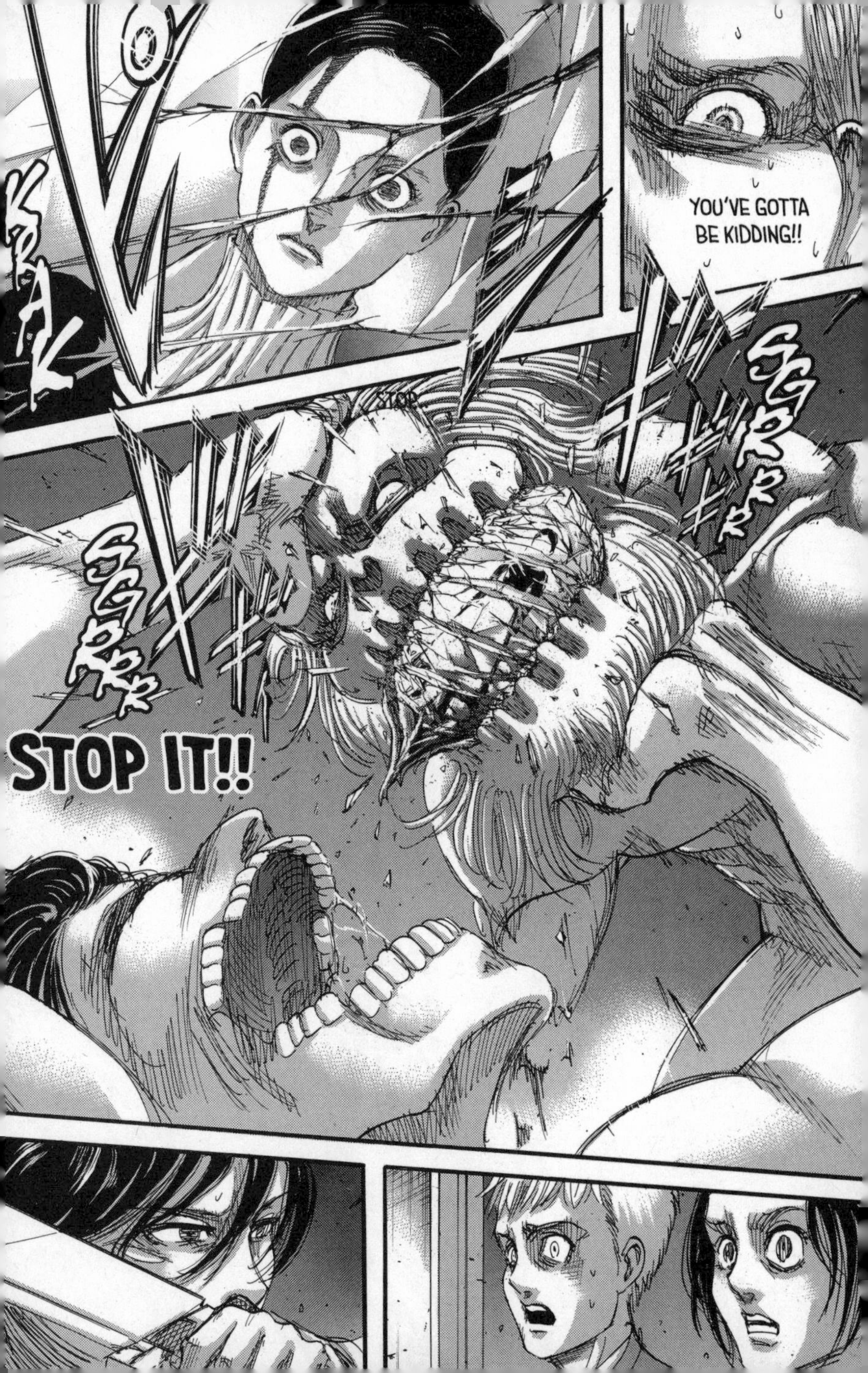
YOU'VE GOTTA BE KIDDING!!
STOP
STOP IT!!

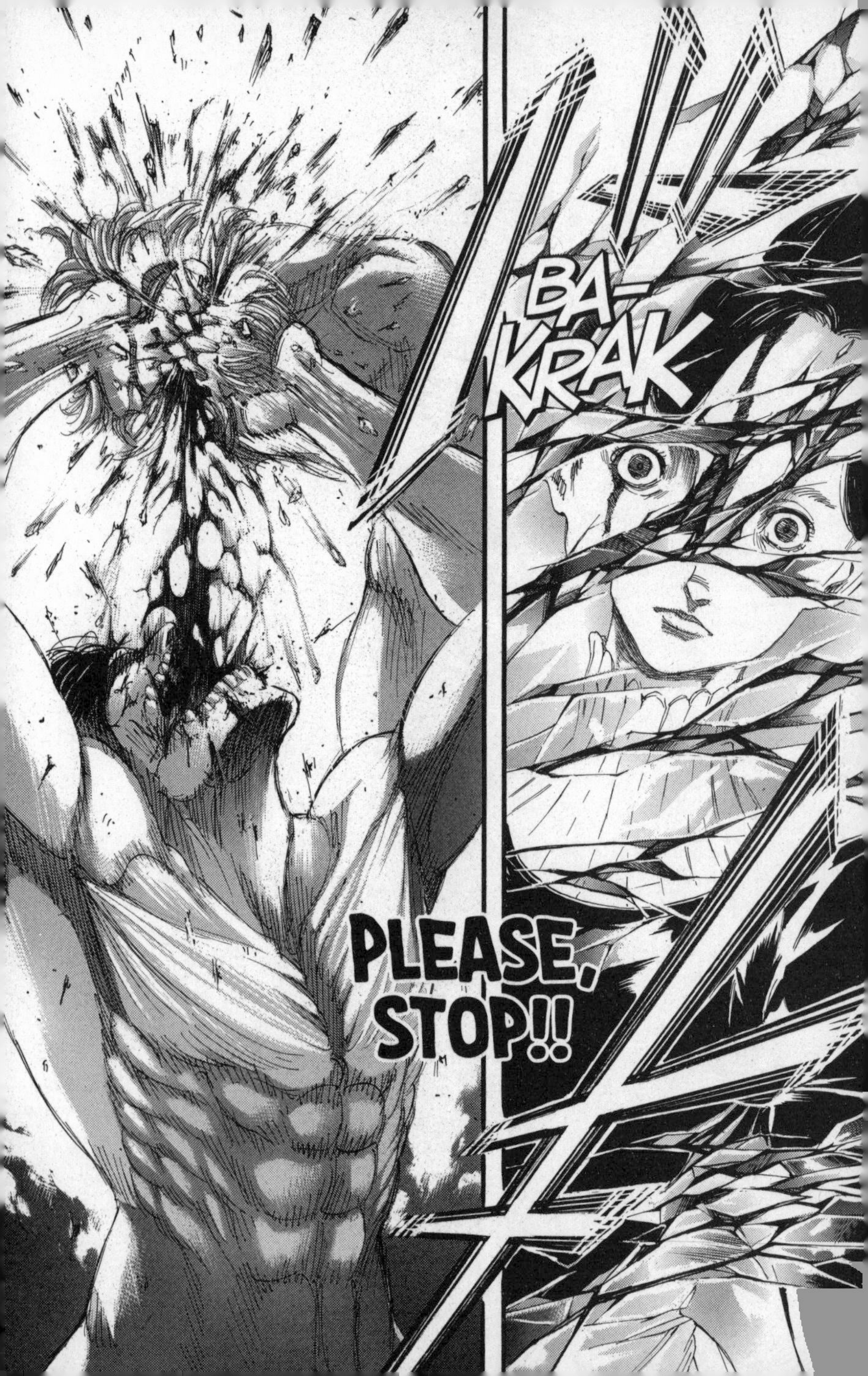
BA-KRAK
PLEASE, STOP!!

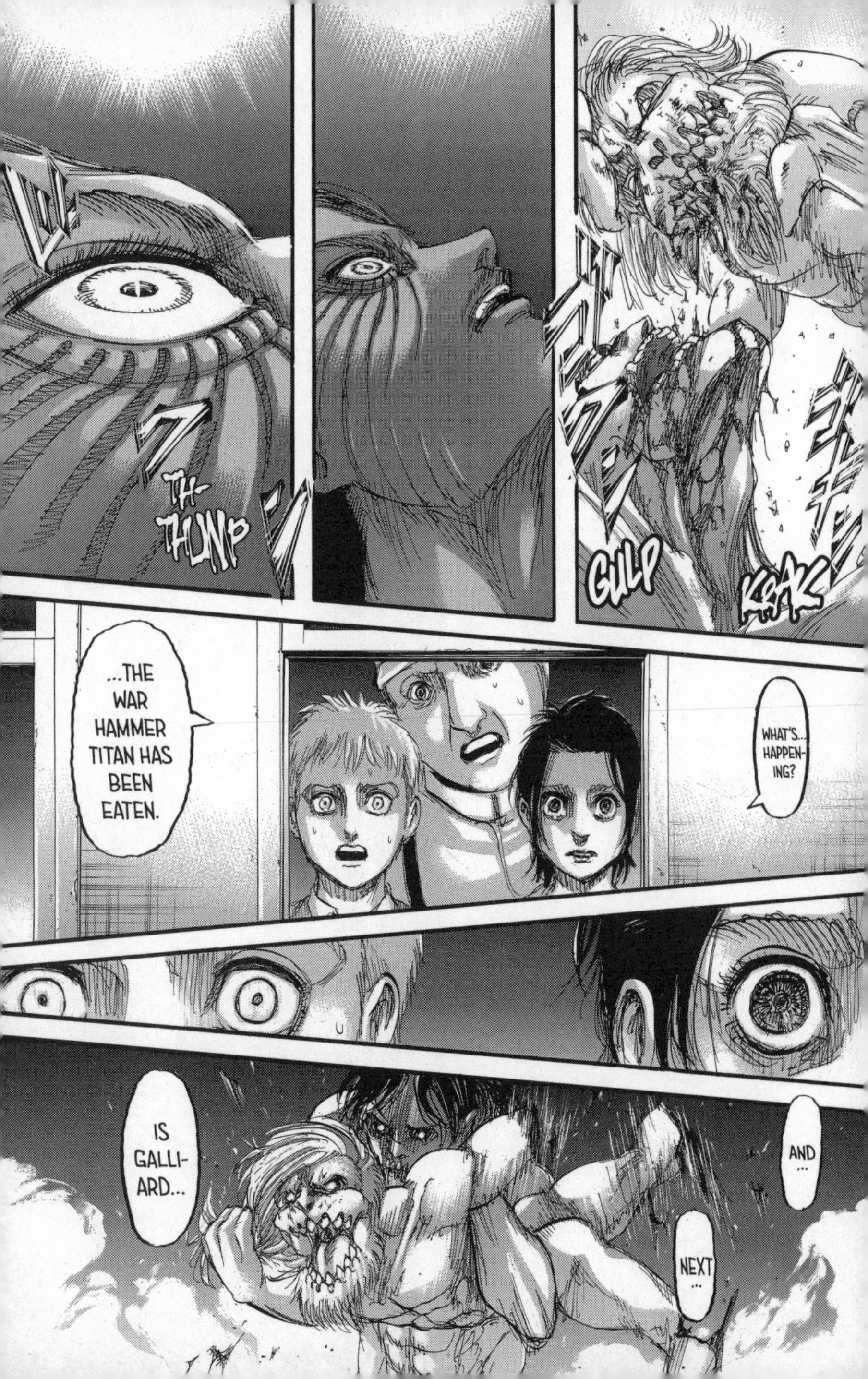
GULP
KRAK
TH-THUMP
WHAT'S... HAPPEN-ING?
...THE WAR HAMMER TITAN HAS BEEN EATEN.
AND...
NEXT...
IS GALLI-ARD...

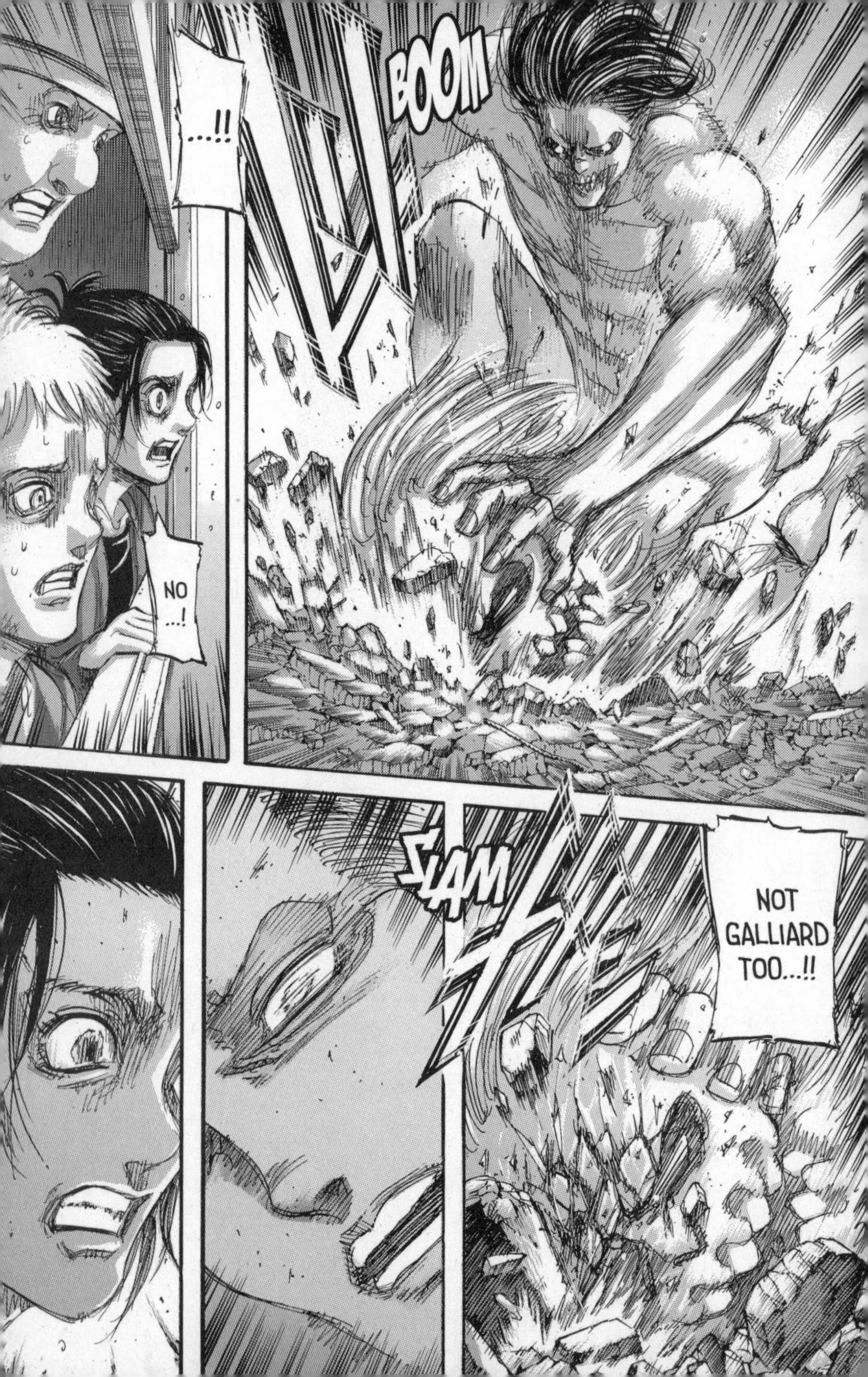
BOOM
...!!
NO ...!
SLAM
NOT GALLIARD TOO...!!

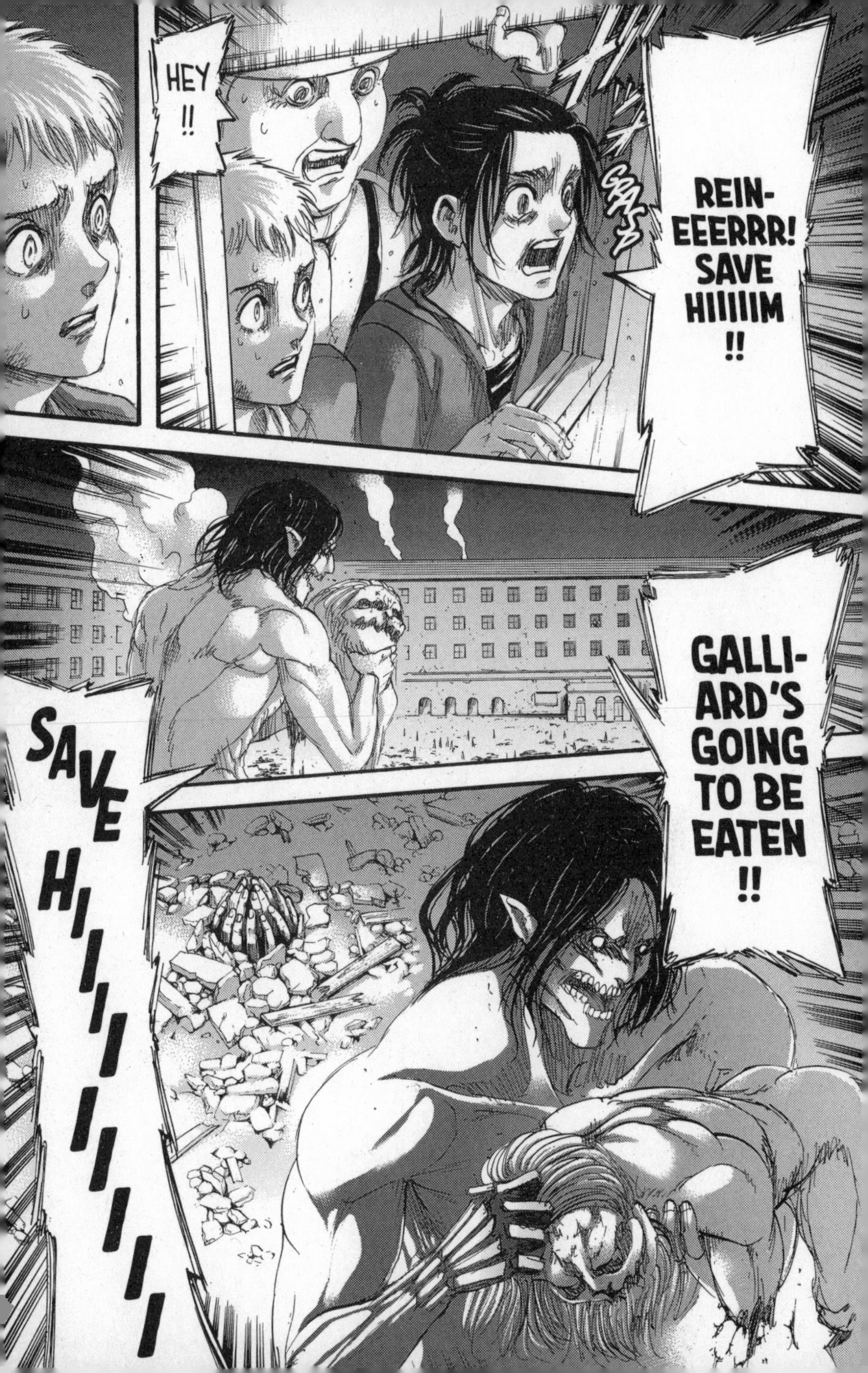
REIN-EEERRR! SAVE HIIIIIIM!!
GRASP
HEY!!
GALLIARD'S GOING TO BE EATEN!!
SAVE HIIIIIIIII

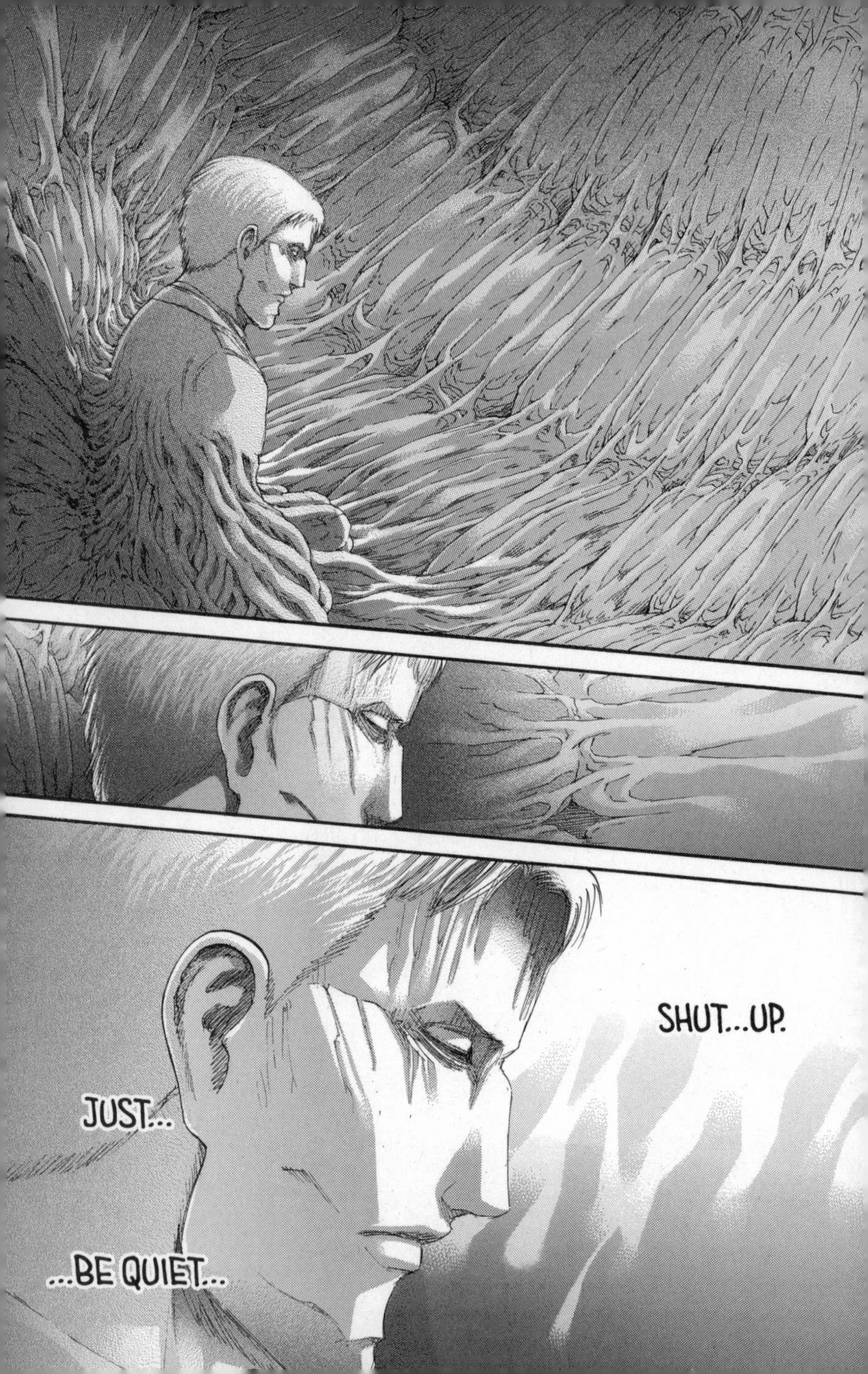
SHUT...UP.
JUST...
...BE QUIET...

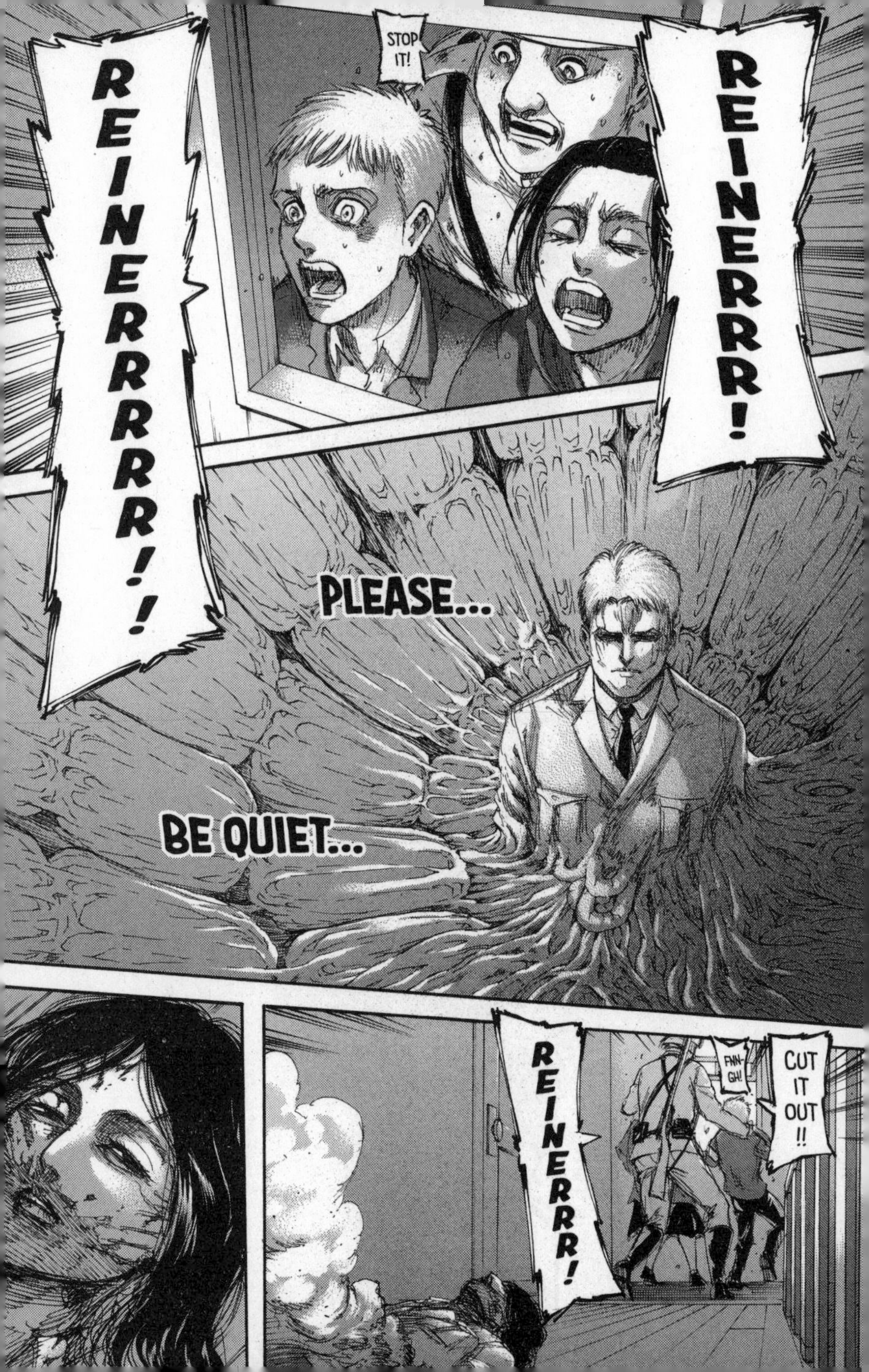
REINERRR!
STOP IT!
REINERRRRR!!
PLEASE...
BE QUIET...
CUT IT OUT!!
FNN-GH!
REINERRR!

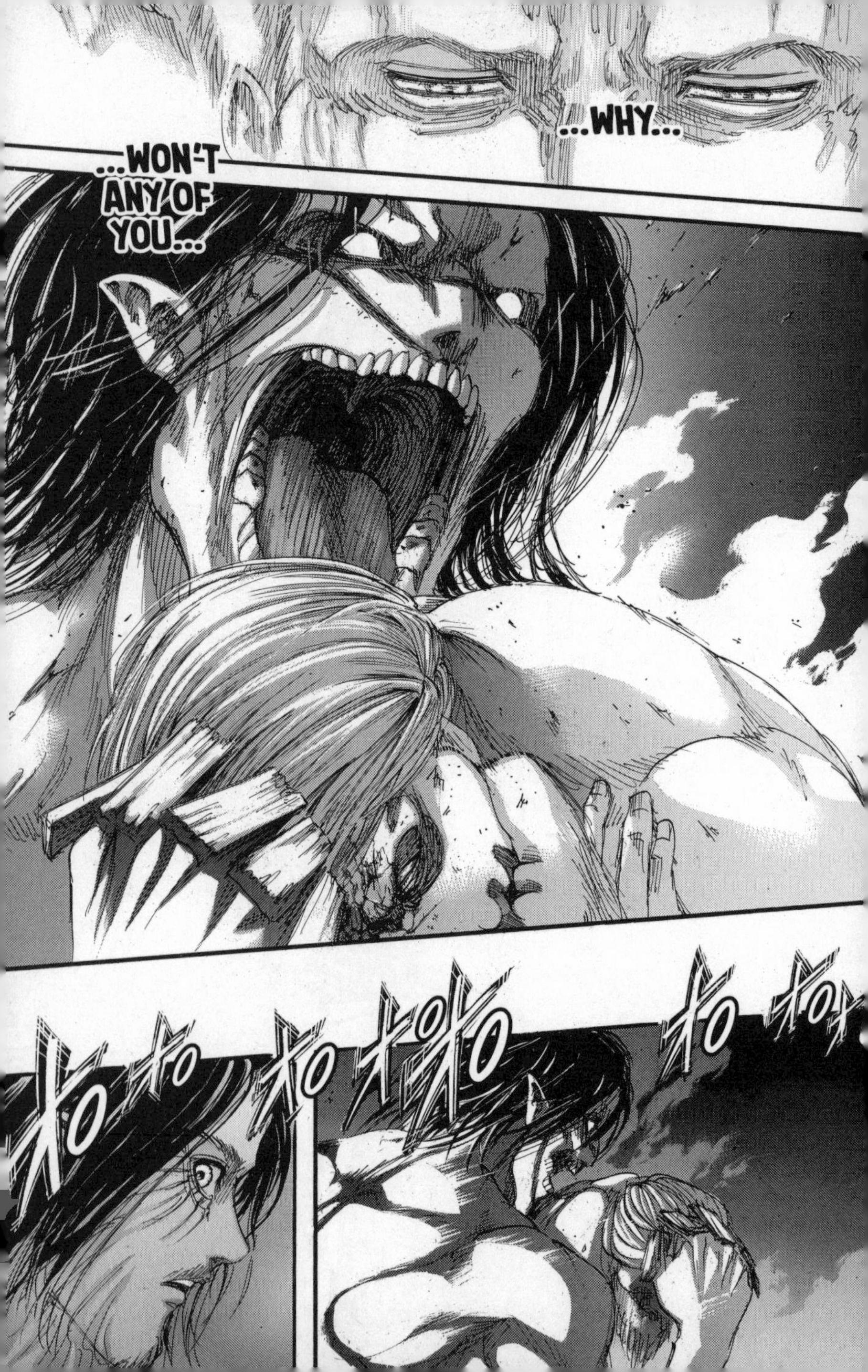
...WHY...
...WON'T ANY OF YOU...

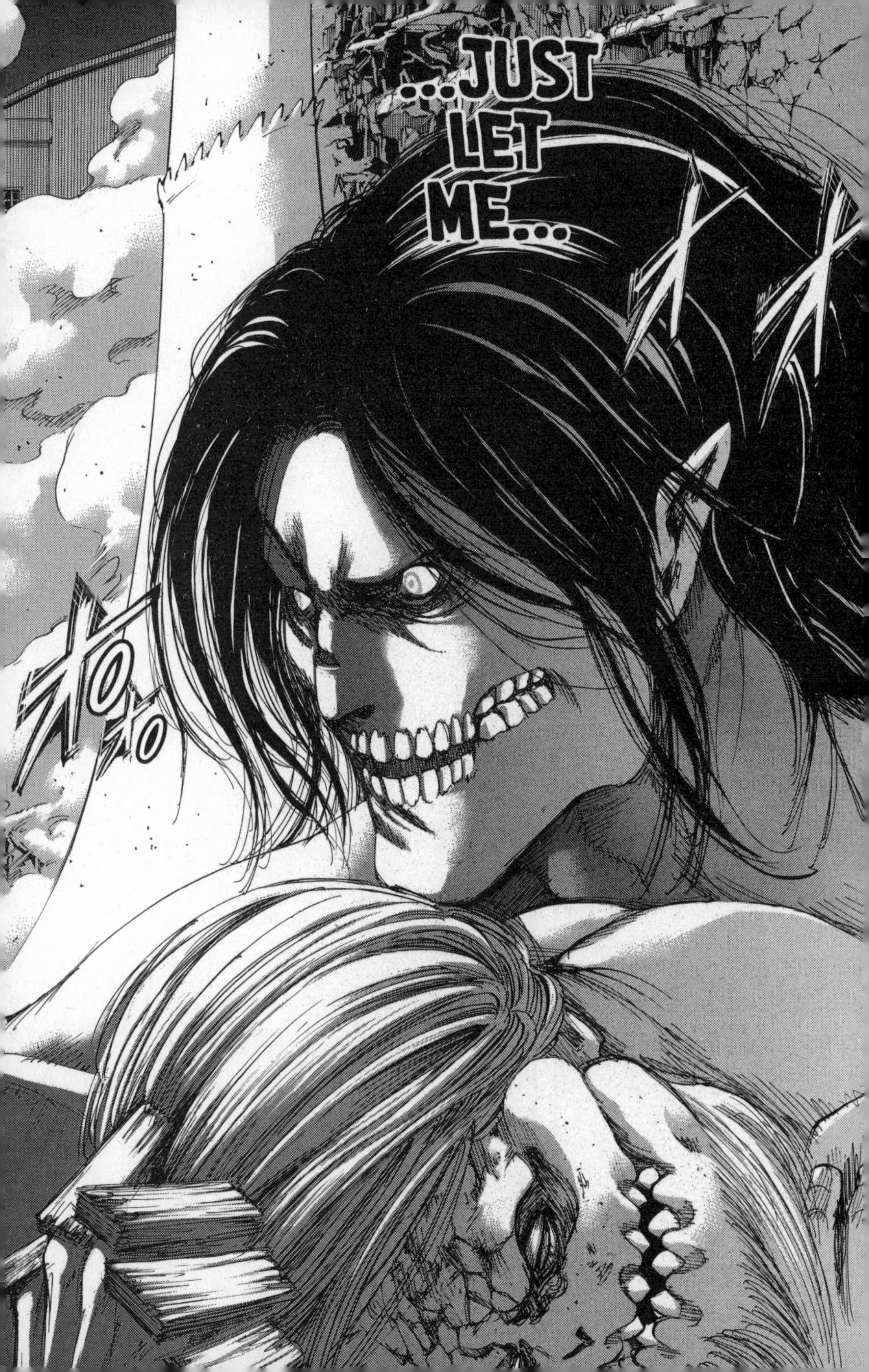
...JUST LET ME...

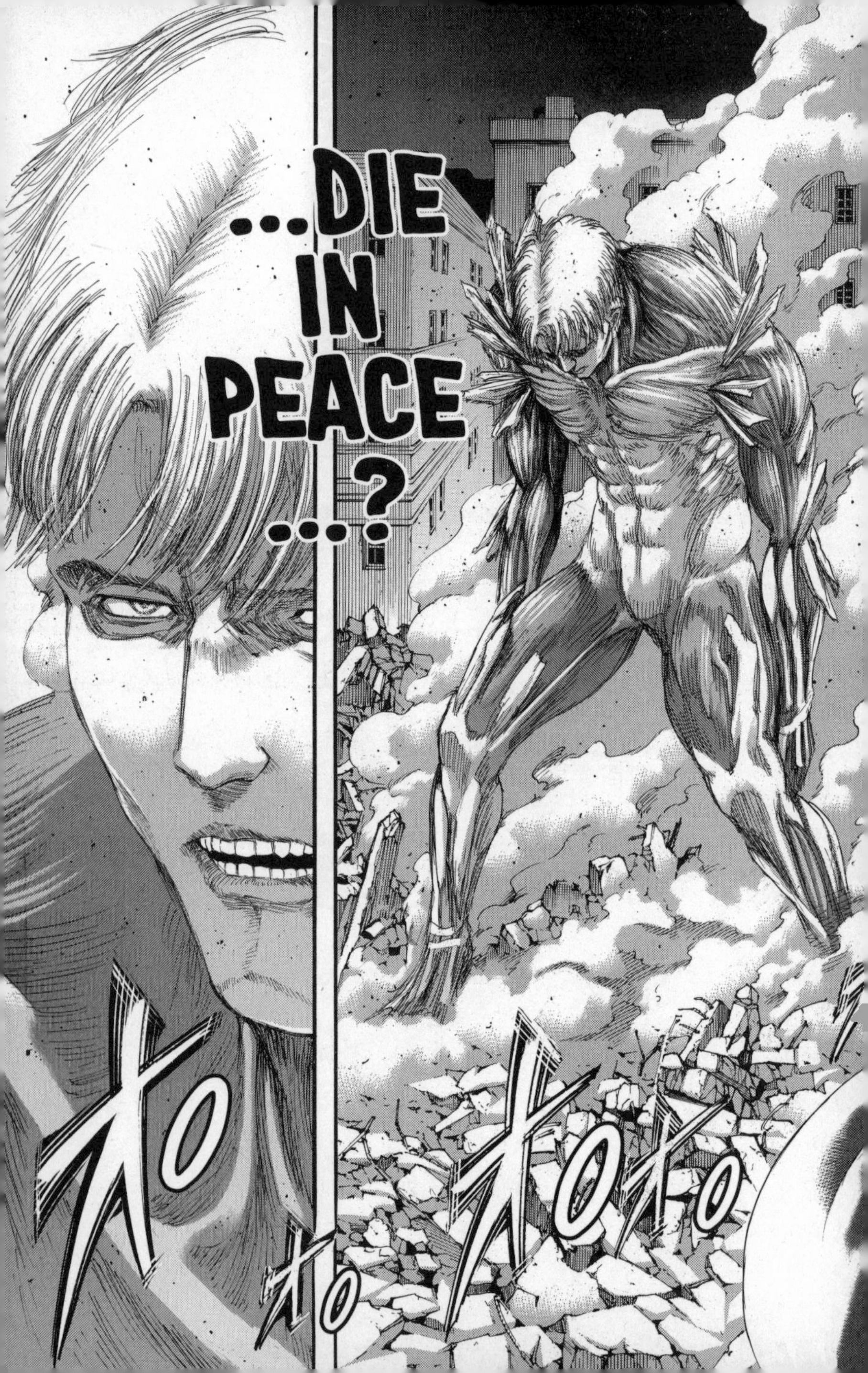
...DIE IN PEACE
...?

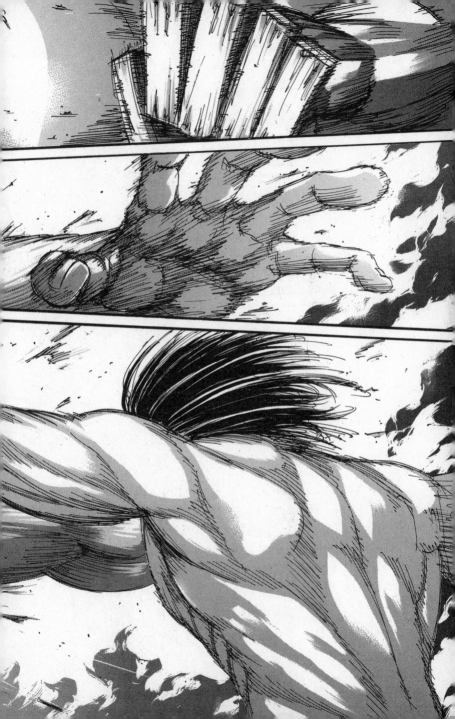

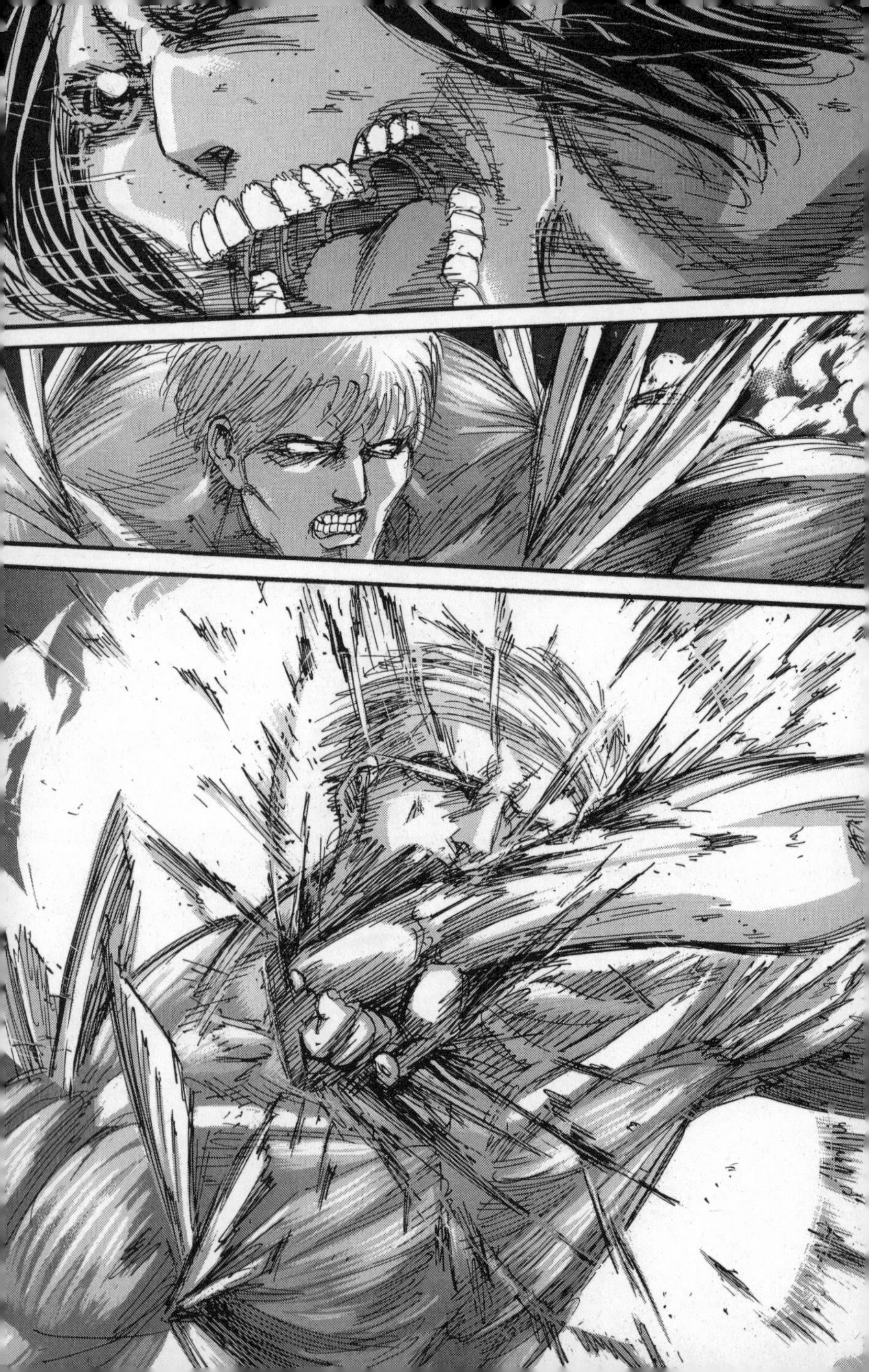

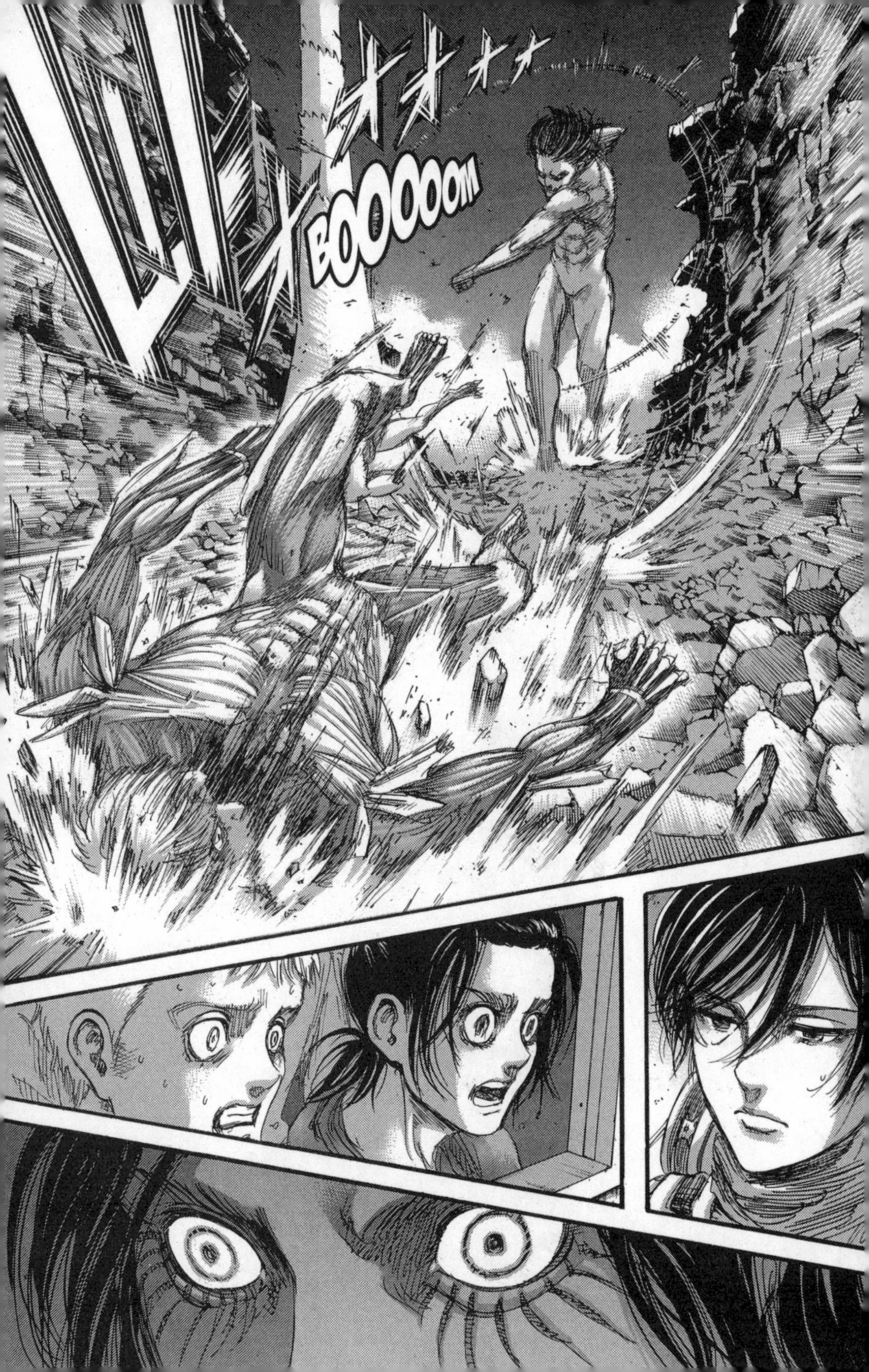
オオオオオ
BOOOOOM

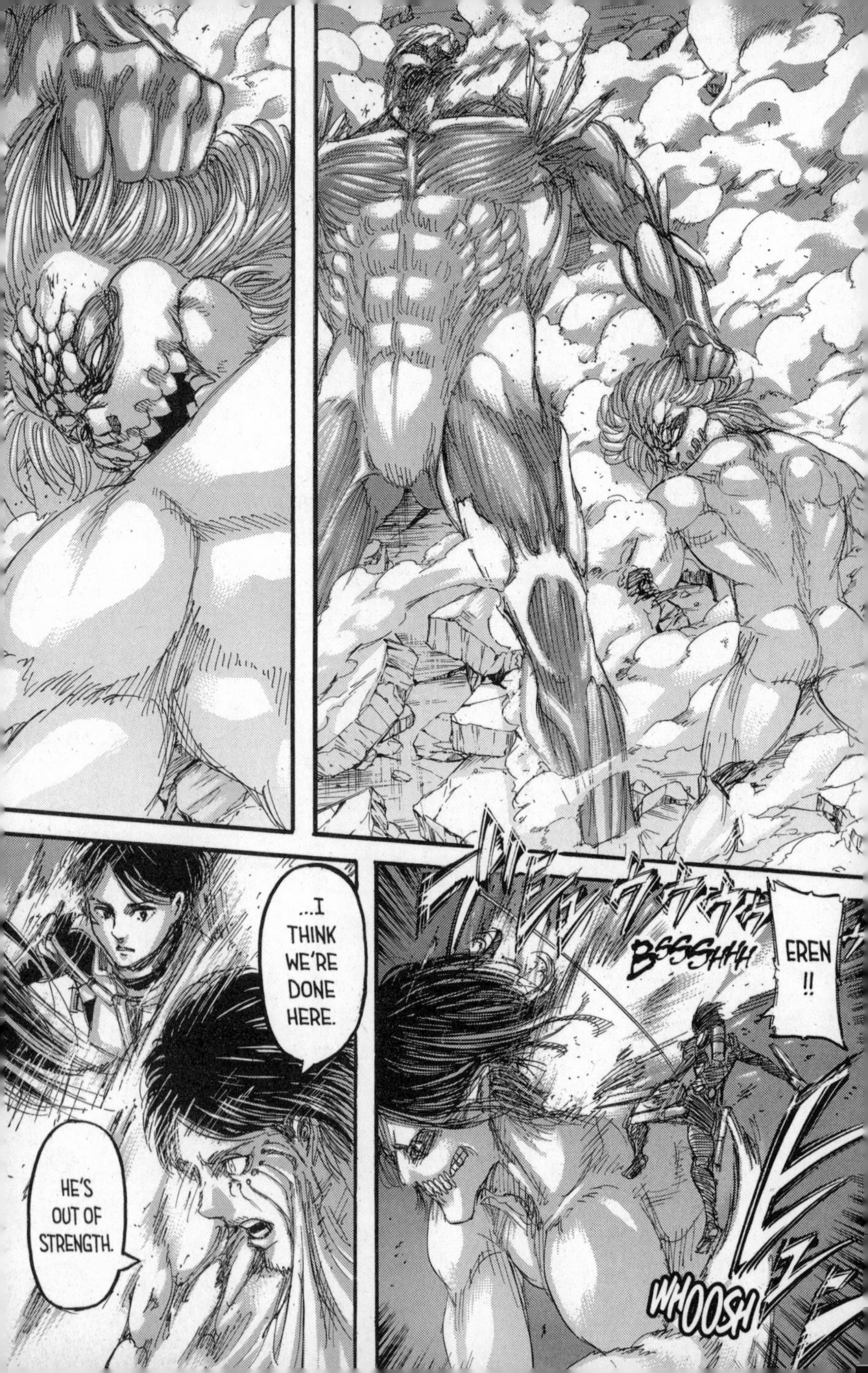
BSSSHHH
EREN!!
WHOOSH
...I THINK WE'RE DONE HERE.
HE'S OUT OF STRENGTH.

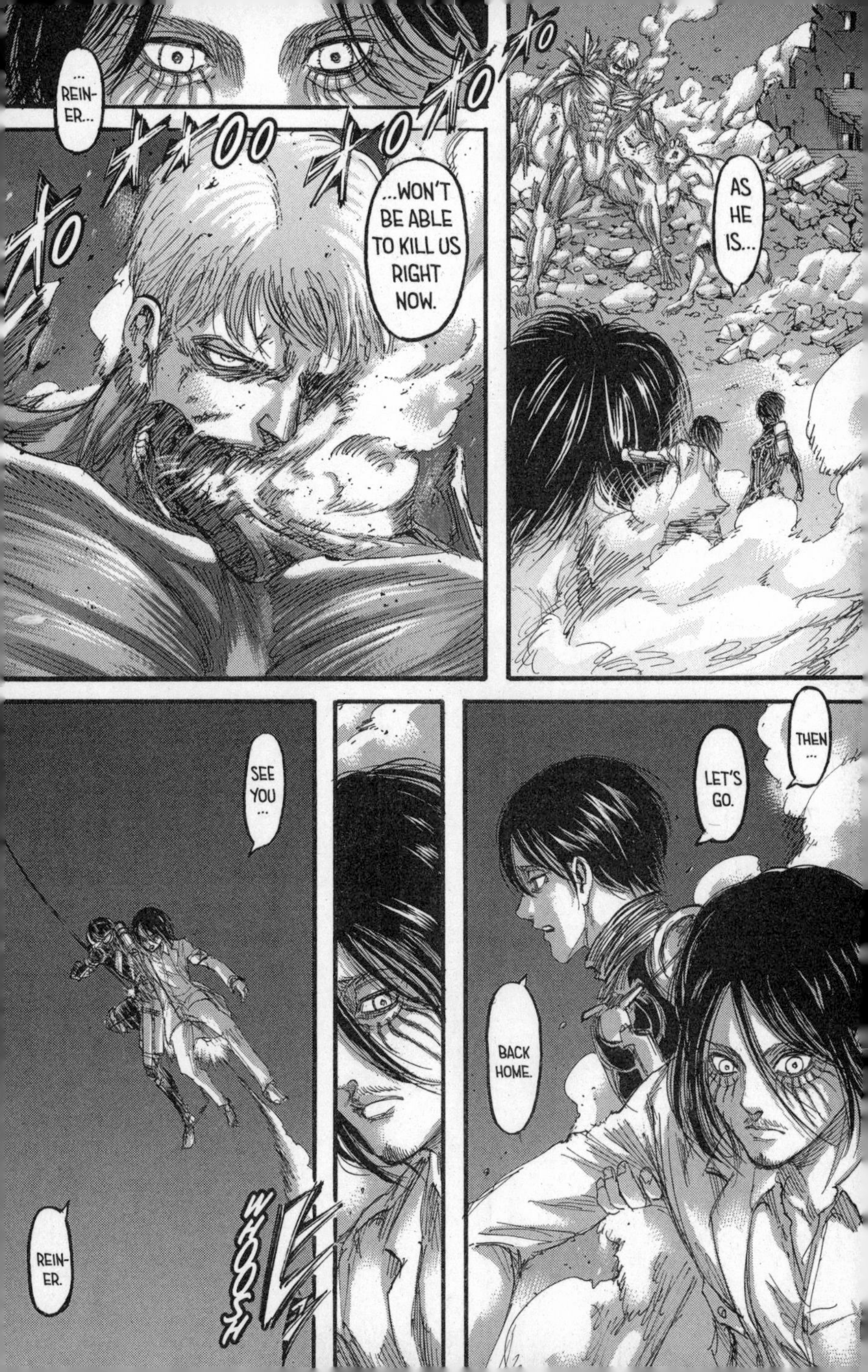
AS HE IS...
...REIN-ER...
...WON'T BE ABLE TO KILL US RIGHT NOW.
THEN...
LET'S GO.
BACK HOME.
SEE YOU...
REIN-ER.
WHOOSH

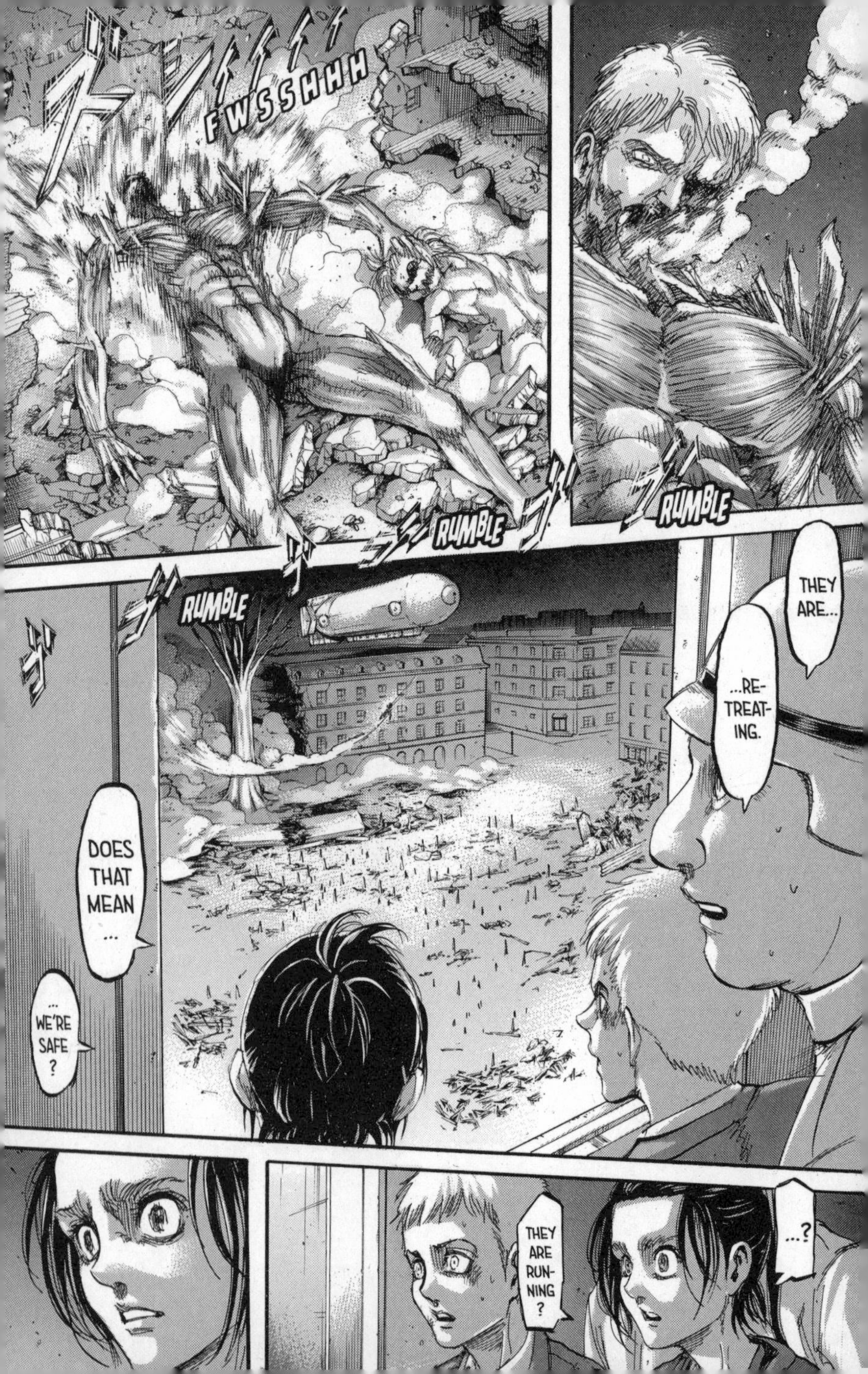
RUMBLE
FWSSHHH
RUMBLE
RUMBLE
THEY ARE...
...RETREATING.
DOES THAT MEAN ...
... WE'RE SAFE ?
...?
THEY ARE RUNNING ?

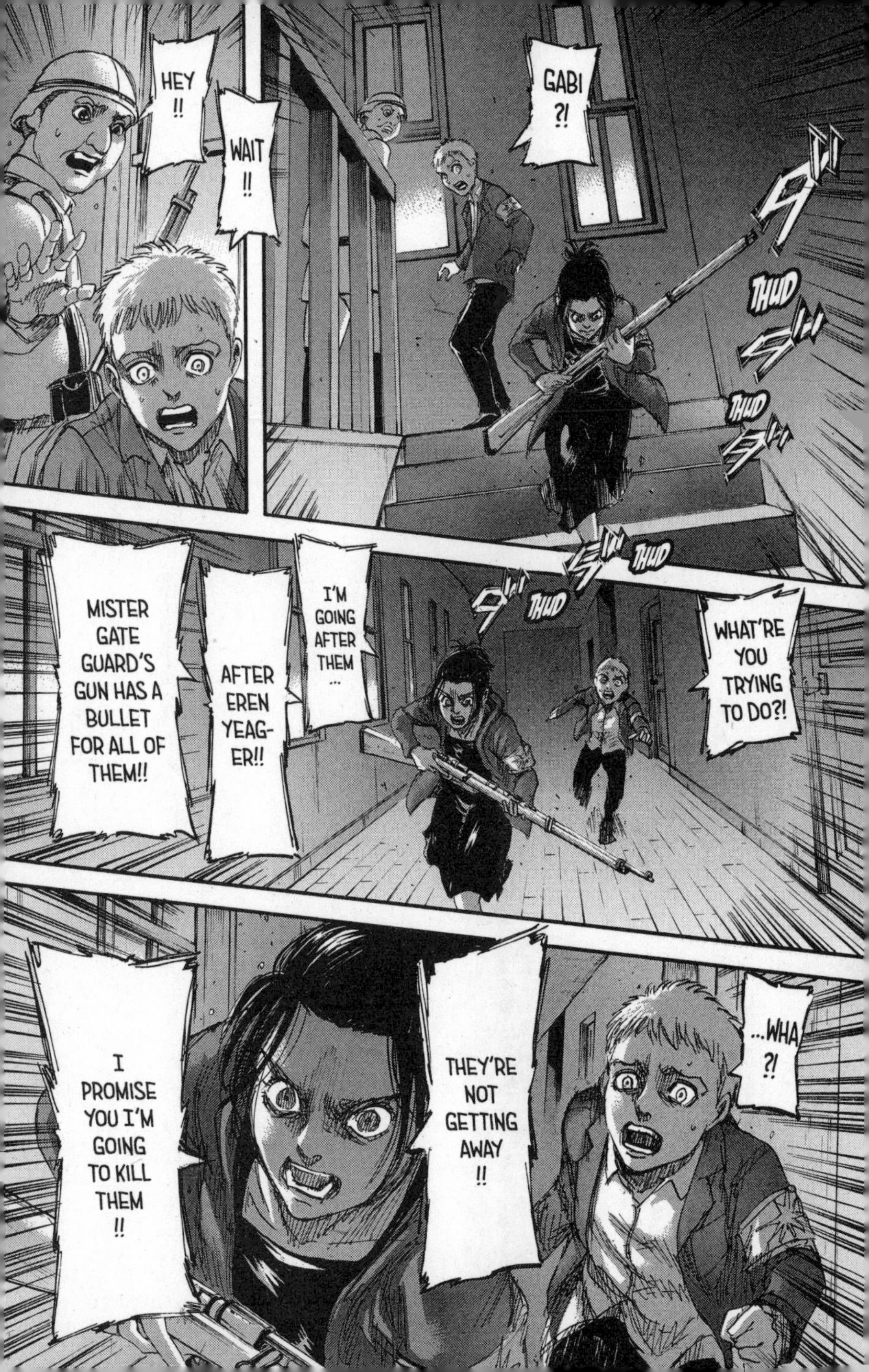
GABI ?!
THUD
THUD
HEY !!
WAIT !!
THUD
THUD
WHAT'RE YOU TRYING TO DO?!
I'M GOING AFTER THEM ...
AFTER EREN YEAGER!!
MISTER GATE GUARD'S GUN HAS A BULLET FOR ALL OF THEM!!
...WHA ?!
THEY'RE NOT GETTING AWAY !!
I PROMISE YOU I'M GOING TO KILL THEM !!

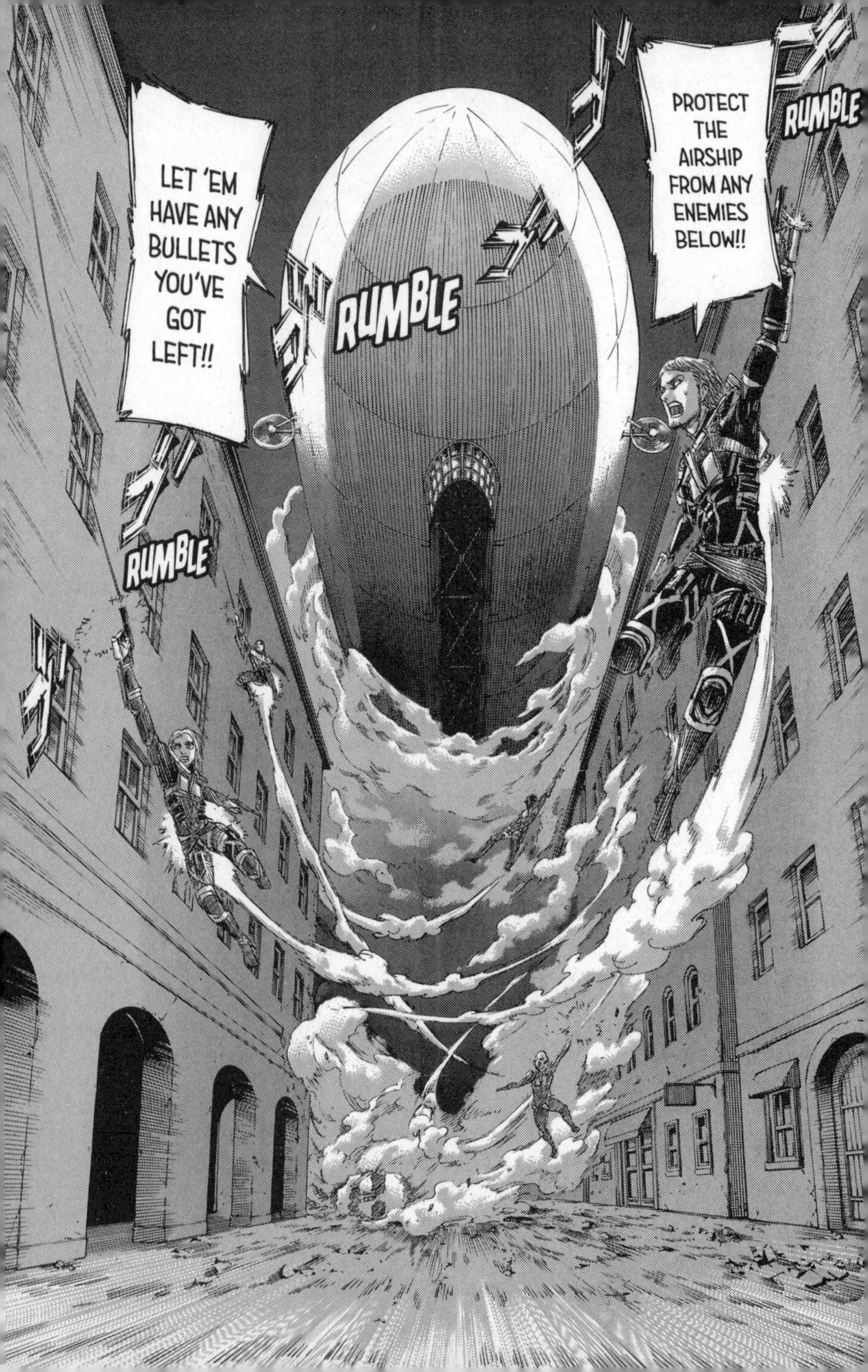
PROTECT THE AIRSHIP FROM ANY ENEMIES BELOW!!
RUMBLE
RUMBLE
LET 'EM HAVE ANY BULLETS YOU'VE GOT LEFT!!
RUMBLE

ATTACK on TITAN

Episode 105: Assassin's Bullet

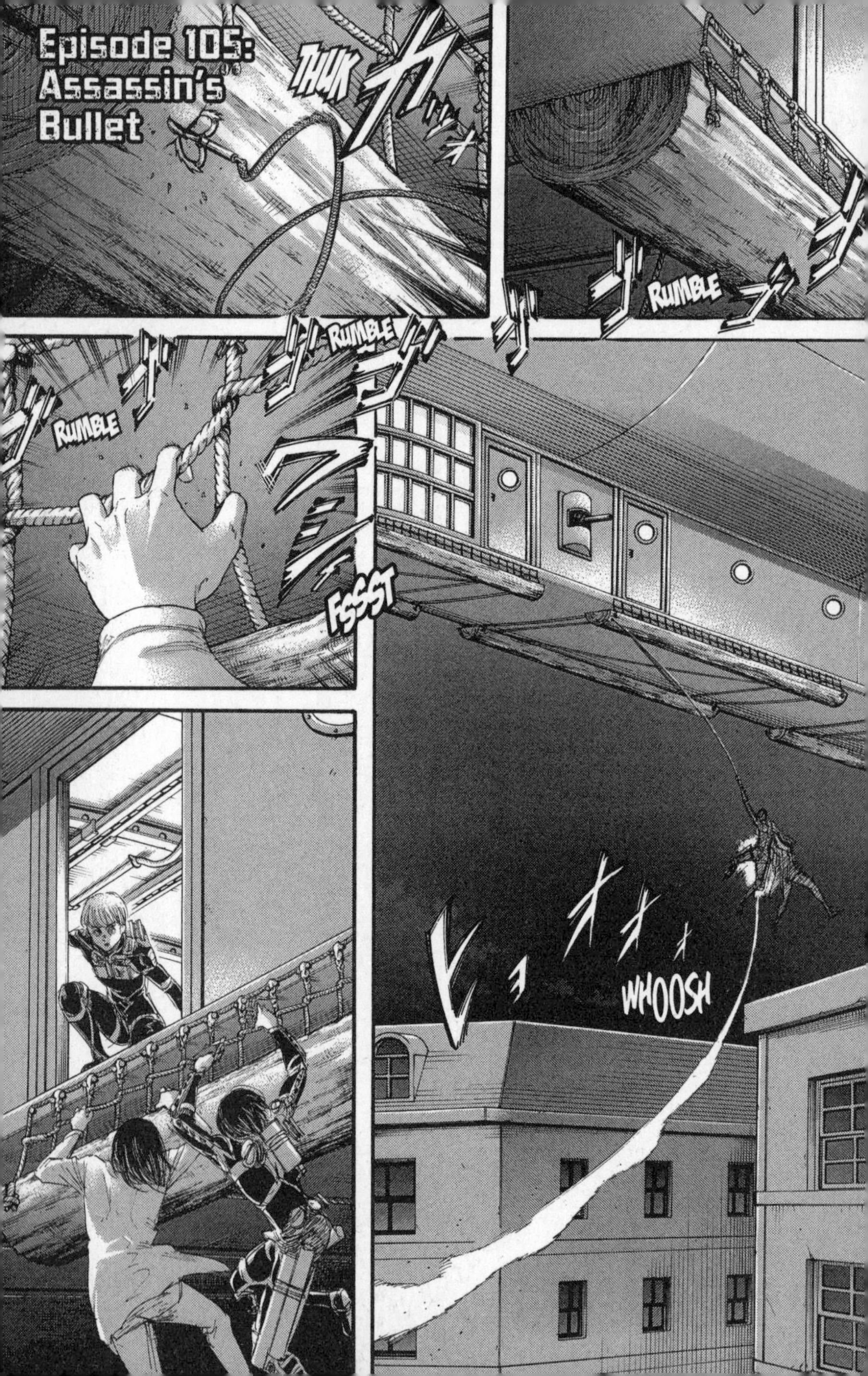
THUK
RUMBLE
WHOOSH
RUMBLE
RUMBLE
FSSST

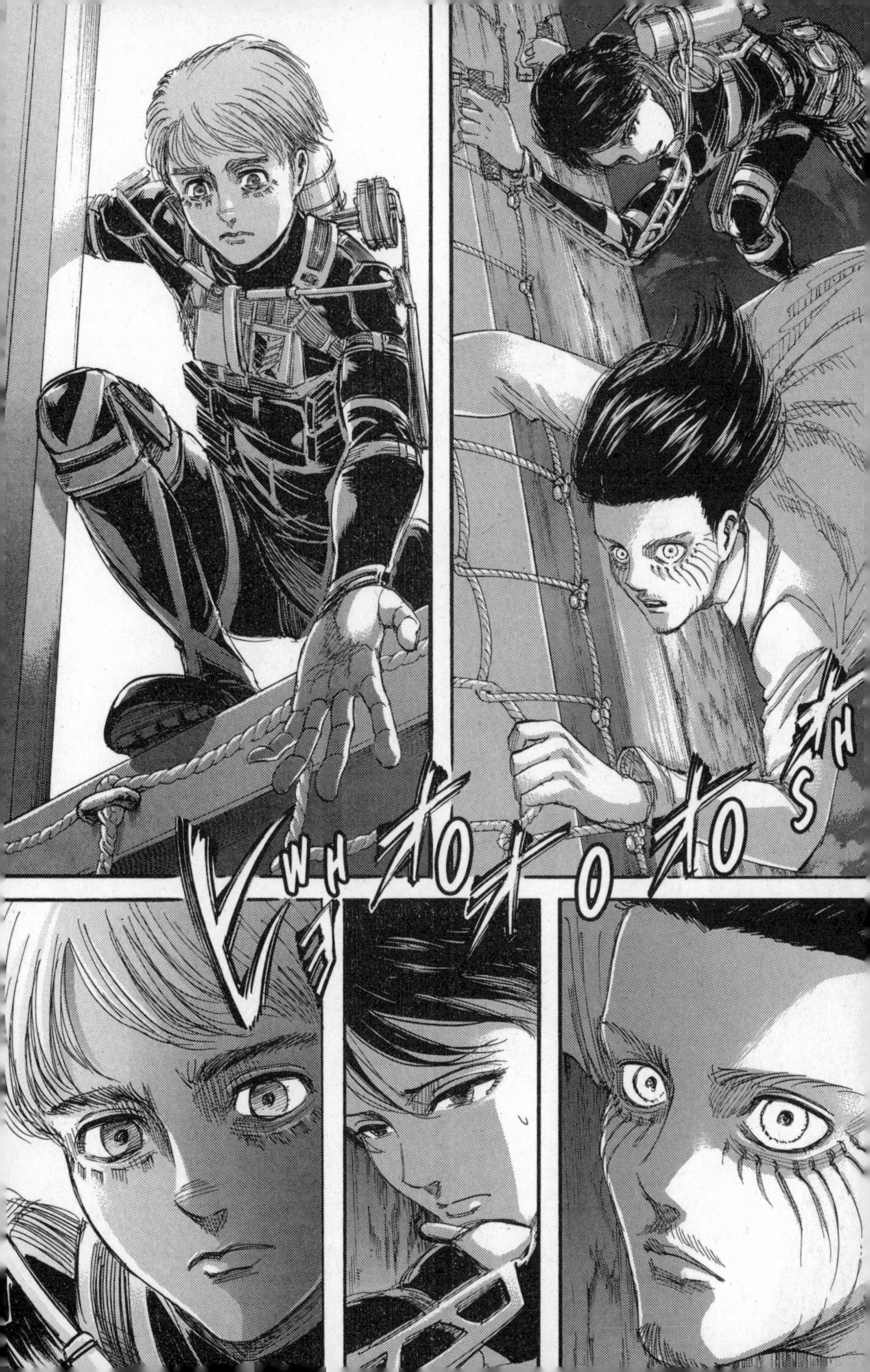
WHOOOOSH

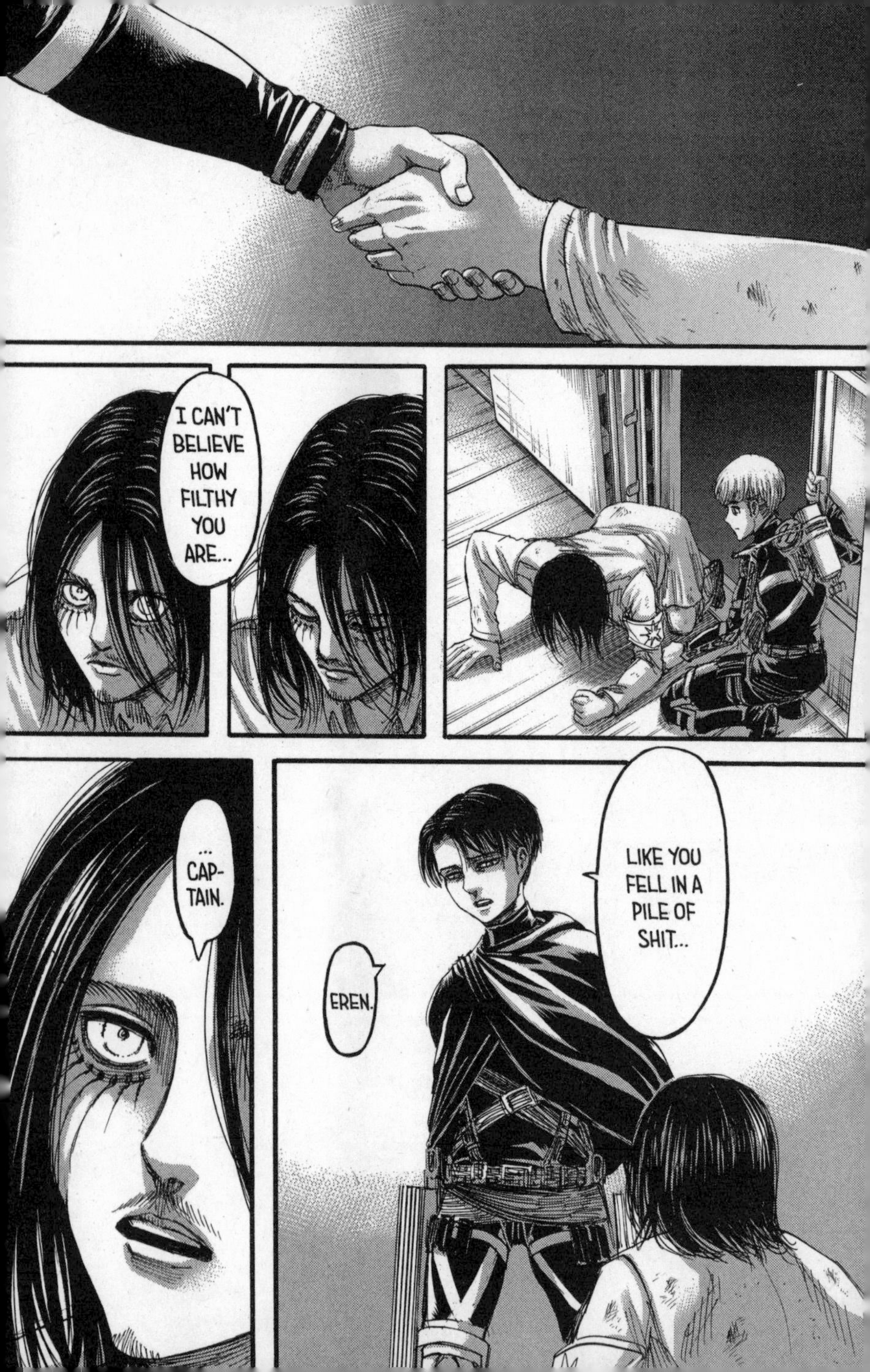
I CAN'T BELIEVE HOW FILTHY YOU ARE...
LIKE YOU FELL IN A PILE OF SHIT...
EREN.
... CAP-TAIN.

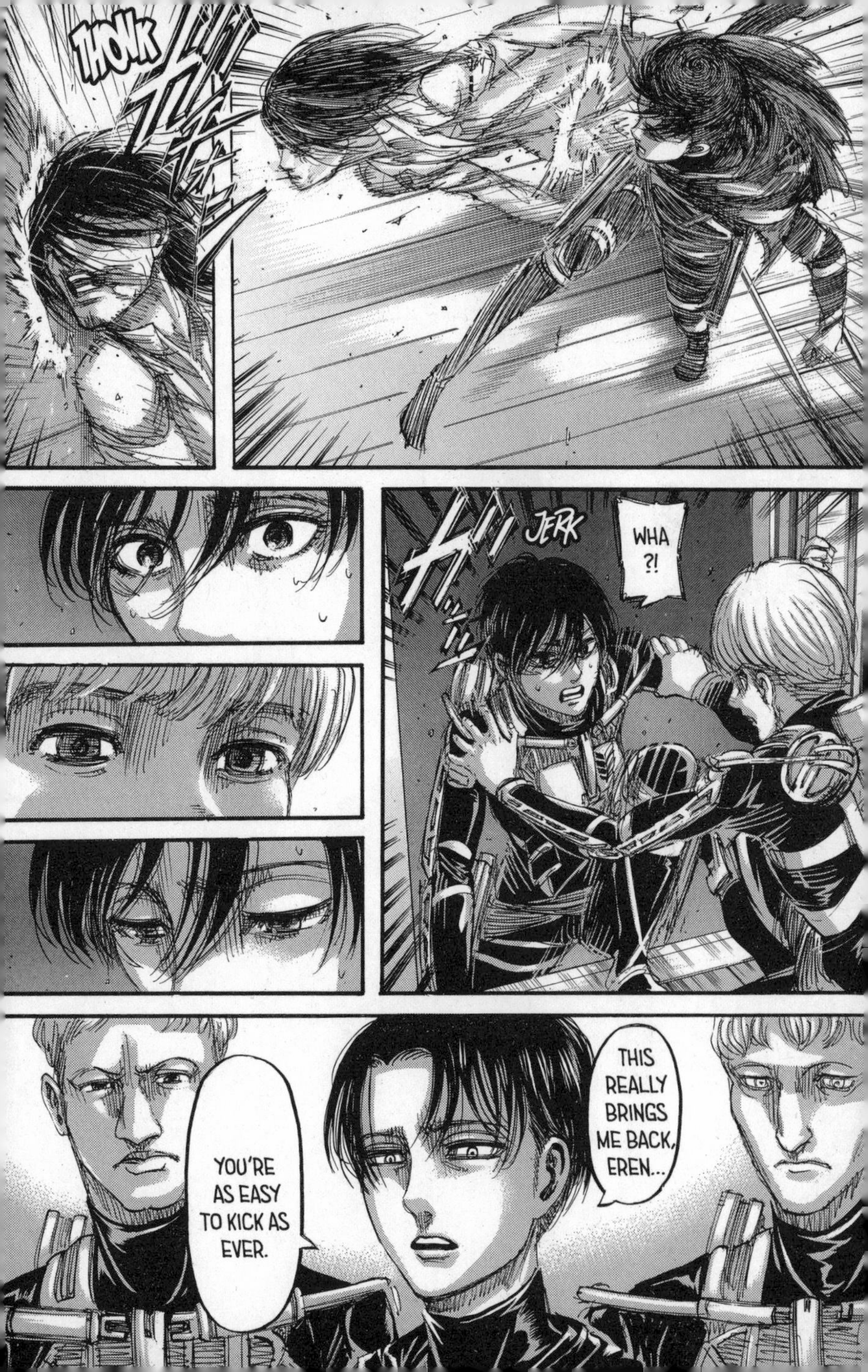
THONK
JERK
WHA ?!
THIS REALLY BRINGS ME BACK, EREN...
YOU'RE AS EASY TO KICK AS EVER.

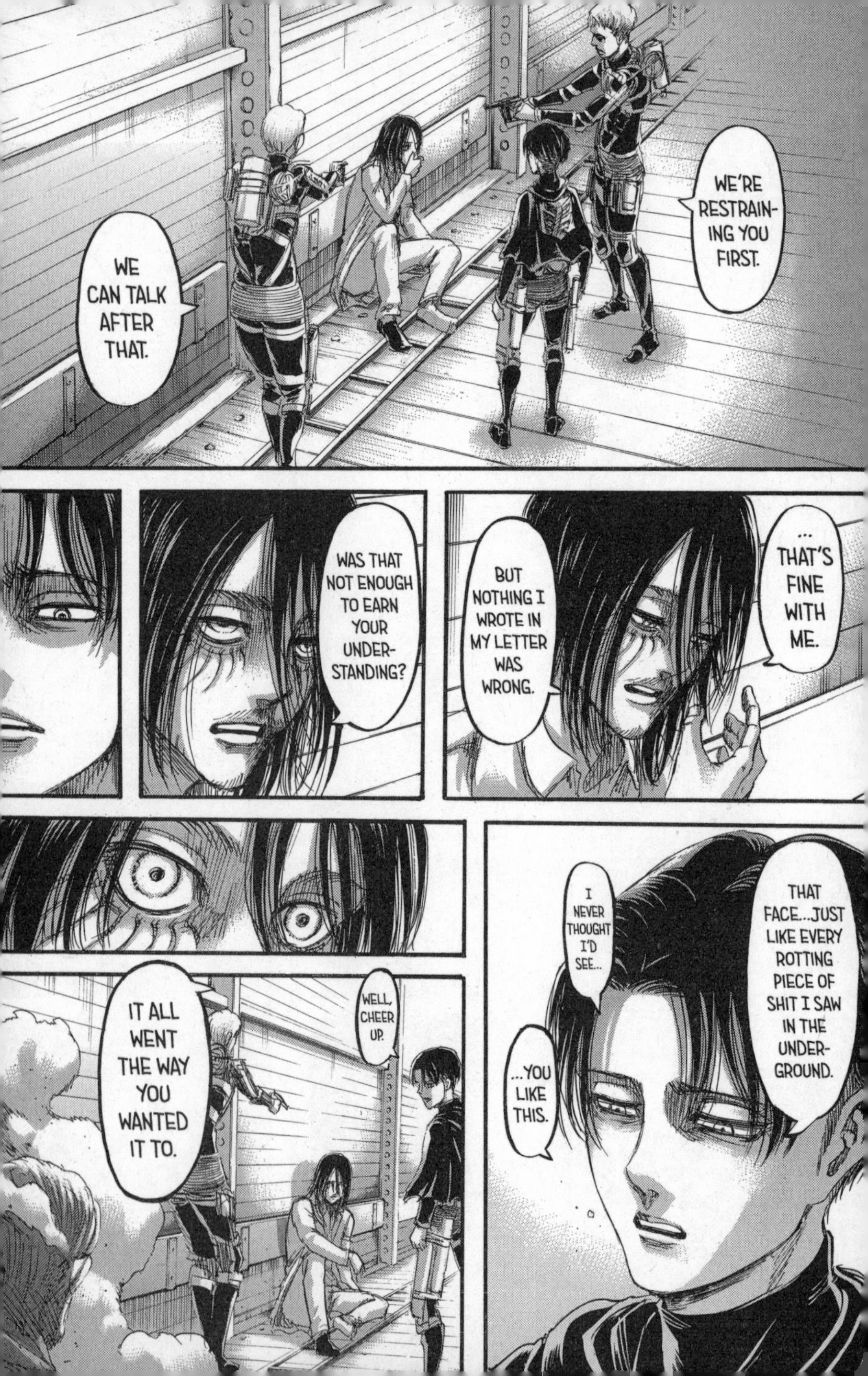
WE'RE RESTRAINING YOU FIRST.
WE CAN TALK AFTER THAT.
... THAT'S FINE WITH ME.
BUT NOTHING I WROTE IN MY LETTER WAS WRONG.
WAS THAT NOT ENOUGH TO EARN YOUR UNDERSTANDING?
THAT FACE...JUST LIKE EVERY ROTTING PIECE OF SHIT I SAW IN THE UNDERGROUND.
I NEVER THOUGHT I'D SEE...
...YOU LIKE THIS.
WELL, CHEER UP.
IT ALL WENT THE WAY YOU WANTED IT TO.

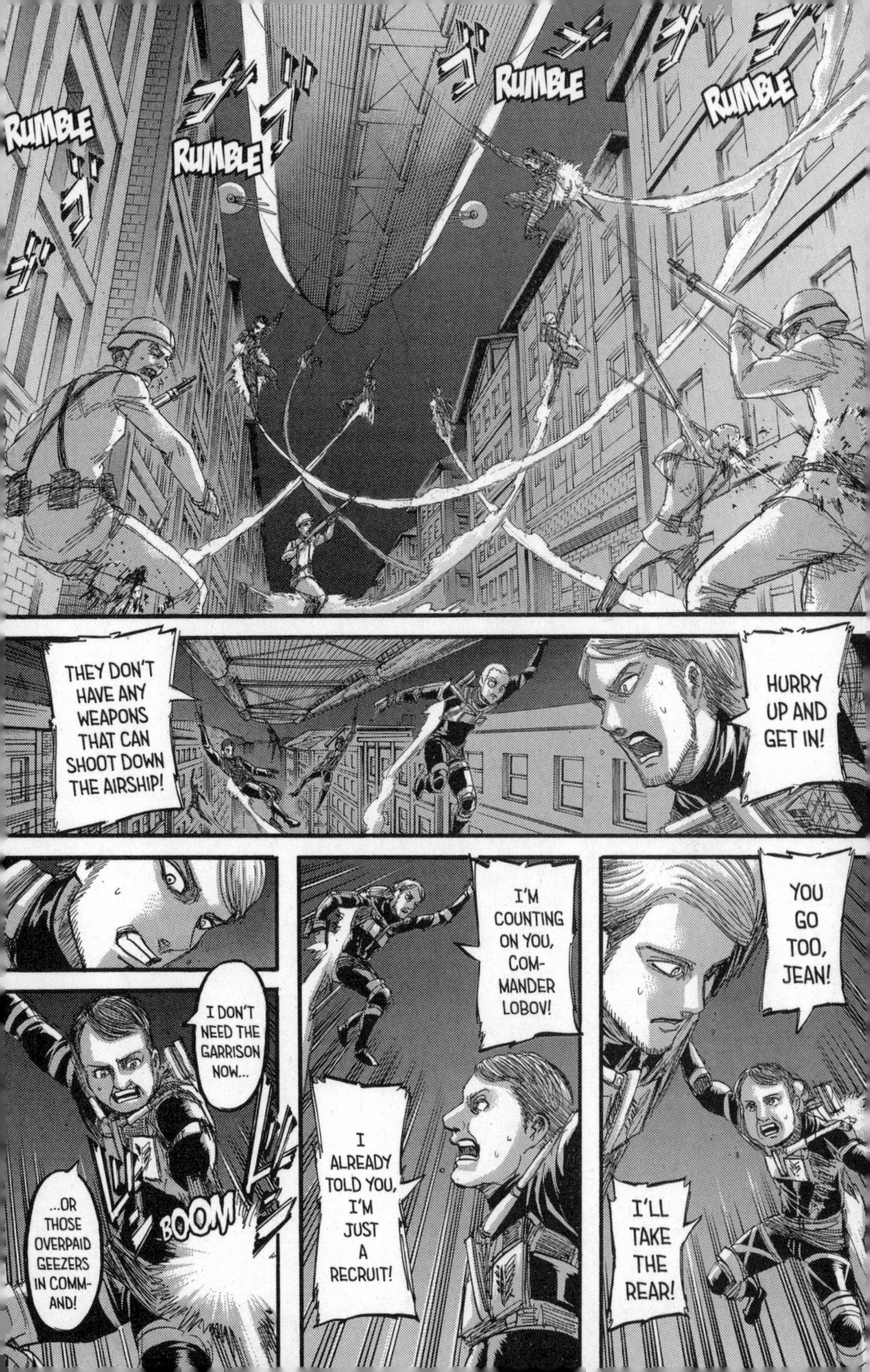
RUMBLE
RUMBLE
RUMBLE
RUMBLE
HURRY UP AND GET IN!
THEY DON'T HAVE ANY WEAPONS THAT CAN SHOOT DOWN THE AIRSHIP!
YOU GO TOO, JEAN!
I'LL TAKE THE REAR!
I'M COUNTING ON YOU, COMMANDER LOBOV!
I ALREADY TOLD YOU, I'M JUST A RECRUIT!
I DON'T NEED THE GARRISON NOW...
BOOM
...OR THOSE OVERPAID GEEZERS IN COMMAND!

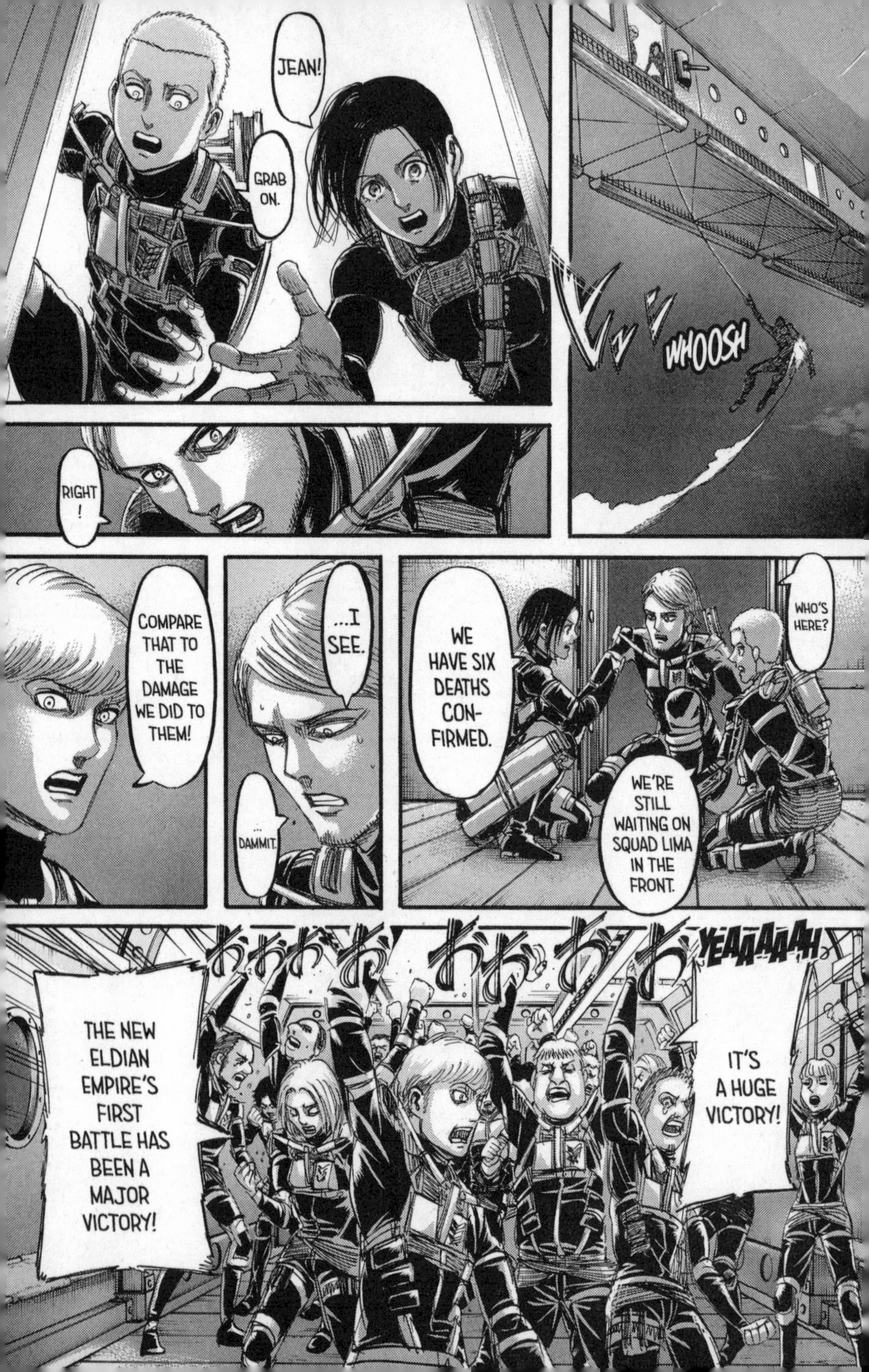
WHOOSH
JEAN!
GRAB ON.
RIGHT!
WHO'S HERE?
WE HAVE SIX DEATHS CON-FIRMED.
WE'RE STILL WAITING ON SQUAD LIMA IN THE FRONT.
...I SEE.
...DAMMIT.
COMPARE THAT TO THE DAMAGE WE DID TO THEM!
YEAAAAAH
IT'S A HUGE VICTORY!
THE NEW ELDIAN EMPIRE'S FIRST BATTLE HAS BEEN A MAJOR VICTORY!

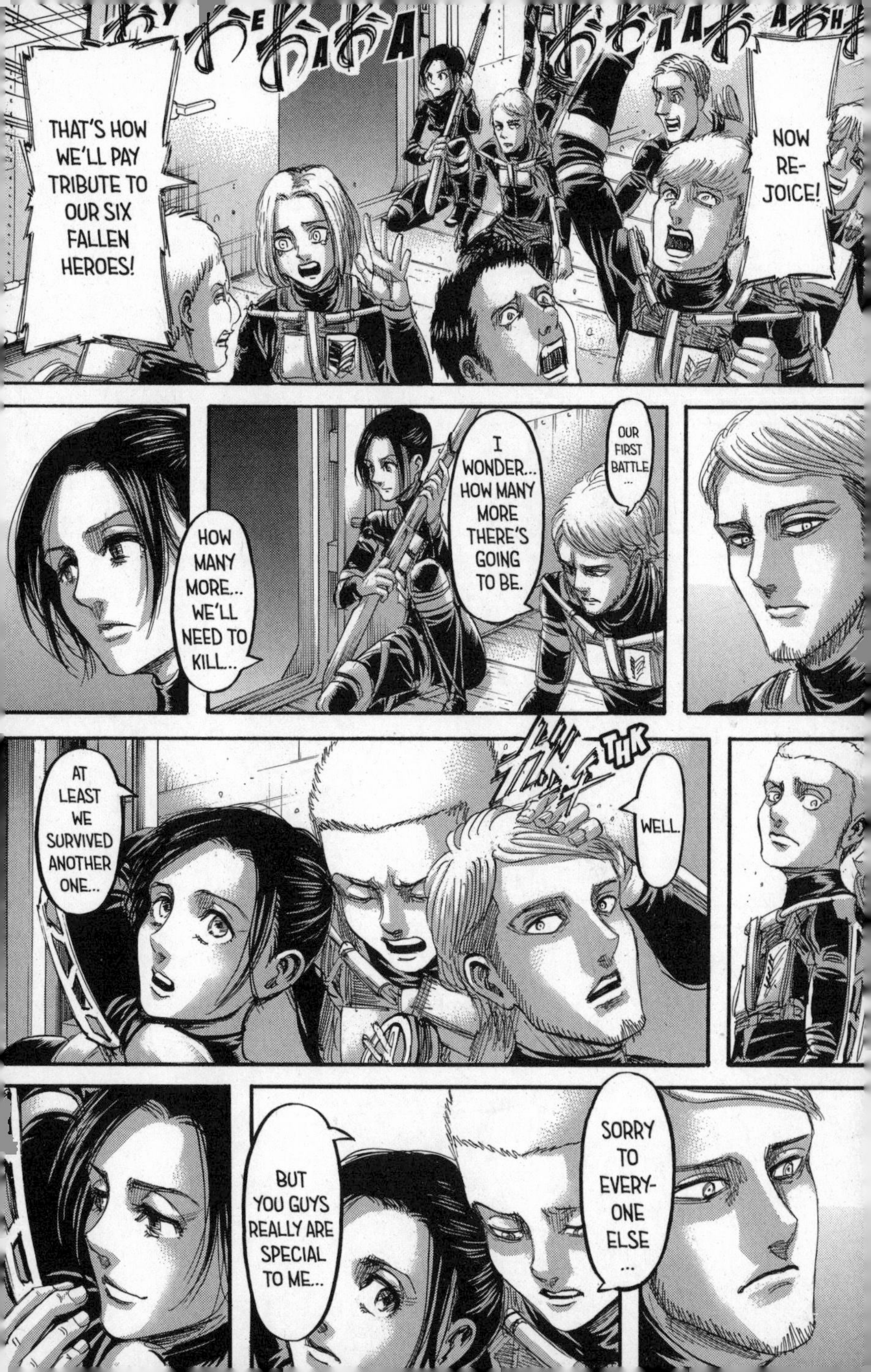
NOW RE-JOICE!
THAT'S HOW WE'LL PAY TRIBUTE TO OUR SIX FALLEN HEROES!
OUR FIRST BATTLE...
I WONDER... HOW MANY MORE THERE'S GOING TO BE.
HOW MANY MORE... WE'LL NEED TO KILL...
THK
WELL.
AT LEAST WE SURVIVED ANOTHER ONE...
SORRY TO EVERY-ONE ELSE...
BUT YOU GUYS REALLY ARE SPECIAL TO ME...

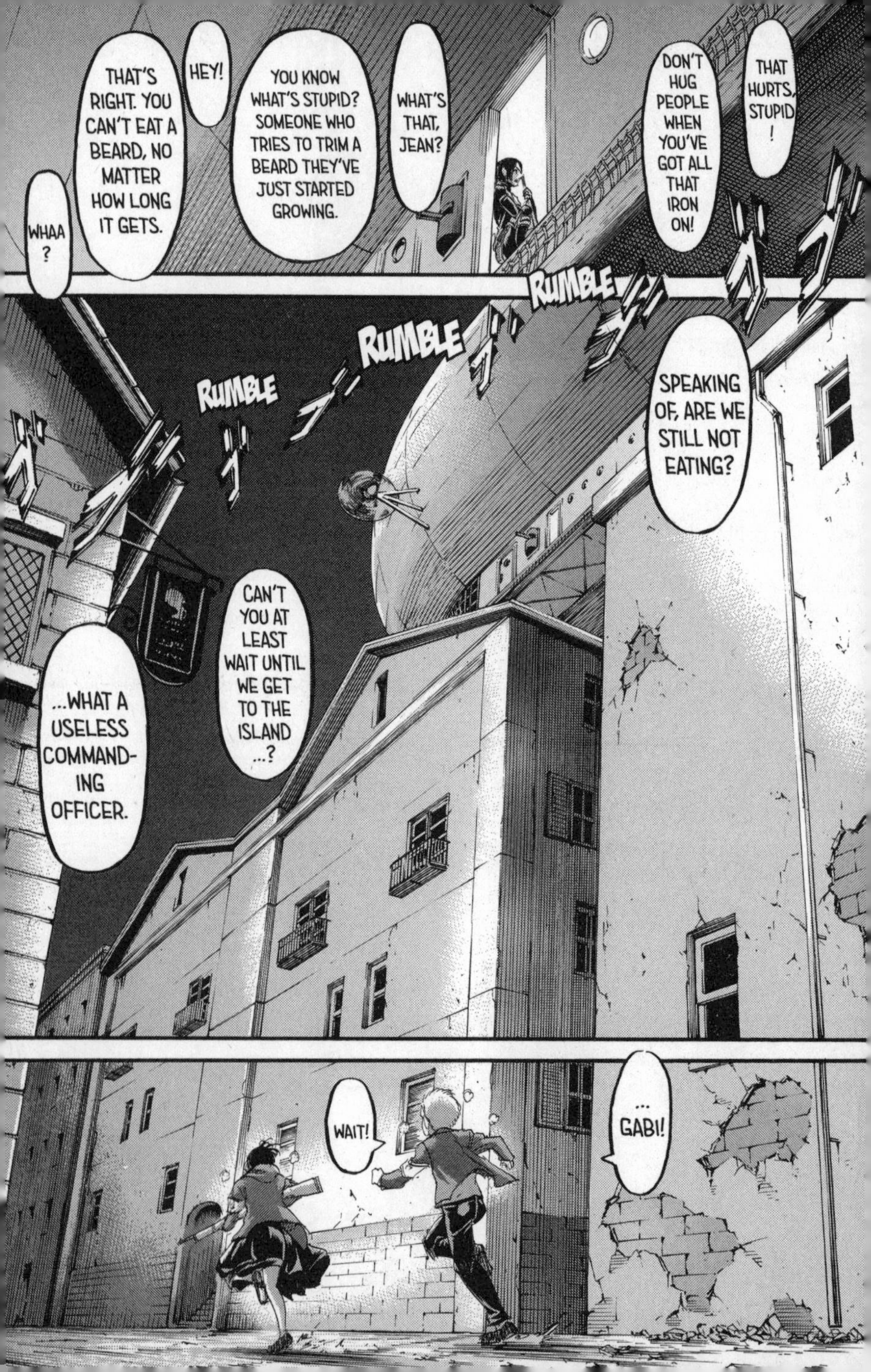
THAT HURTS, STUPID!
DON'T HUG PEOPLE WHEN YOU'VE GOT ALL THAT IRON ON!
WHAT'S THAT, JEAN?
YOU KNOW WHAT'S STUPID? SOMEONE WHO TRIES TO TRIM A BEARD THEY'VE JUST STARTED GROWING.
HEY!
THAT'S RIGHT. YOU CAN'T EAT A BEARD, NO MATTER HOW LONG IT GETS.
WHAA?
RUMBLE
SPEAKING OF, ARE WE STILL NOT EATING?
RUMBLE
RUMBLE
CAN'T YOU AT LEAST WAIT UNTIL WE GET TO THE ISLAND...?
...WHAT A USELESS COMMAND-ING OFFICER.
... GABI!
WAIT!

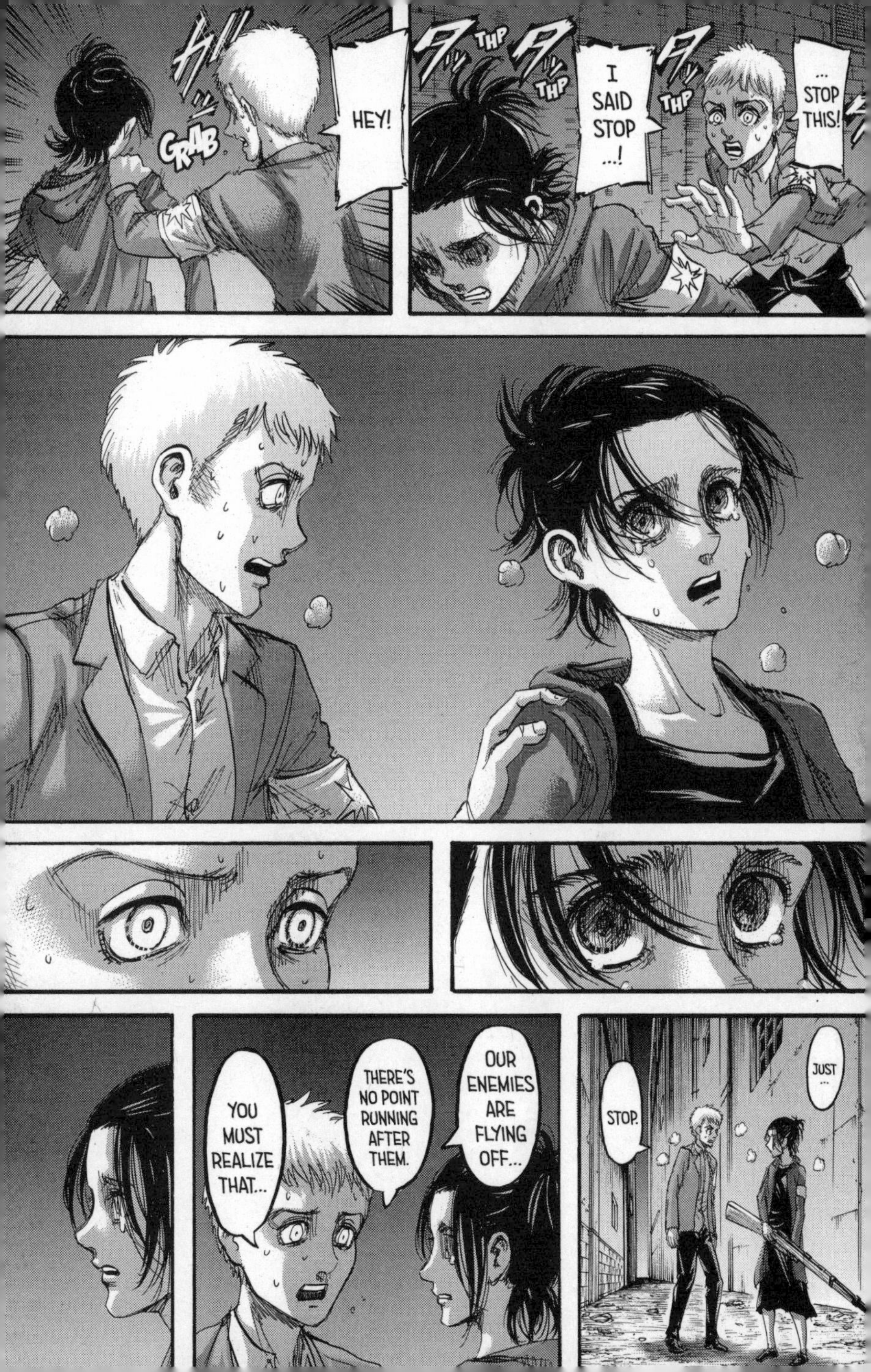
THP
... STOP THIS!
THP
I SAID STOP ...!
THP
HEY!
GRAB
JUST ...
STOP.
OUR ENEMIES ARE FLYING OFF...
THERE'S NO POINT RUNNING AFTER THEM.
YOU MUST REALIZE THAT...

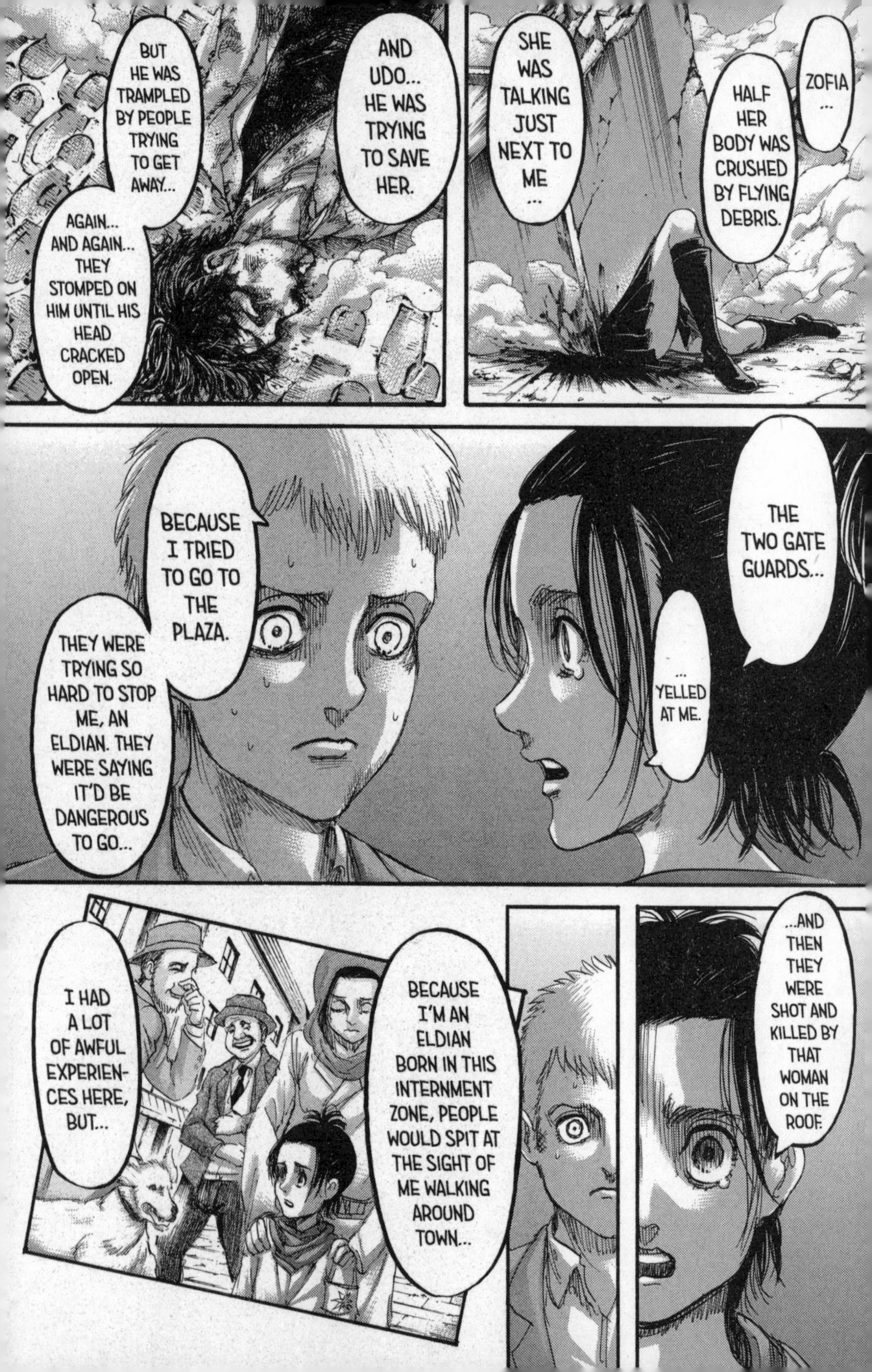
ZOFIA...
HALF HER BODY WAS CRUSHED BY FLYING DEBRIS.
SHE WAS TALKING JUST NEXT TO ME...
AND UDO... HE WAS TRYING TO SAVE HER.
BUT HE WAS TRAMPLED BY PEOPLE TRYING TO GET AWAY...
AGAIN... AND AGAIN... THEY STOMPED ON HIM UNTIL HIS HEAD CRACKED OPEN.
THE TWO GATE GUARDS...
...YELLED AT ME.
BECAUSE I TRIED TO GO TO THE PLAZA.
THEY WERE TRYING SO HARD TO STOP ME, AN ELDIAN. THEY WERE SAYING IT'D BE DANGEROUS TO GO...
...AND THEN THEY WERE SHOT AND KILLED BY THAT WOMAN ON THE ROOF.
BECAUSE I'M AN ELDIAN BORN IN THIS INTERNMENT ZONE, PEOPLE WOULD SPIT AT THE SIGHT OF ME WALKING AROUND TOWN...
I HAD A LOT OF AWFUL EXPERIEN-CES HERE, BUT...

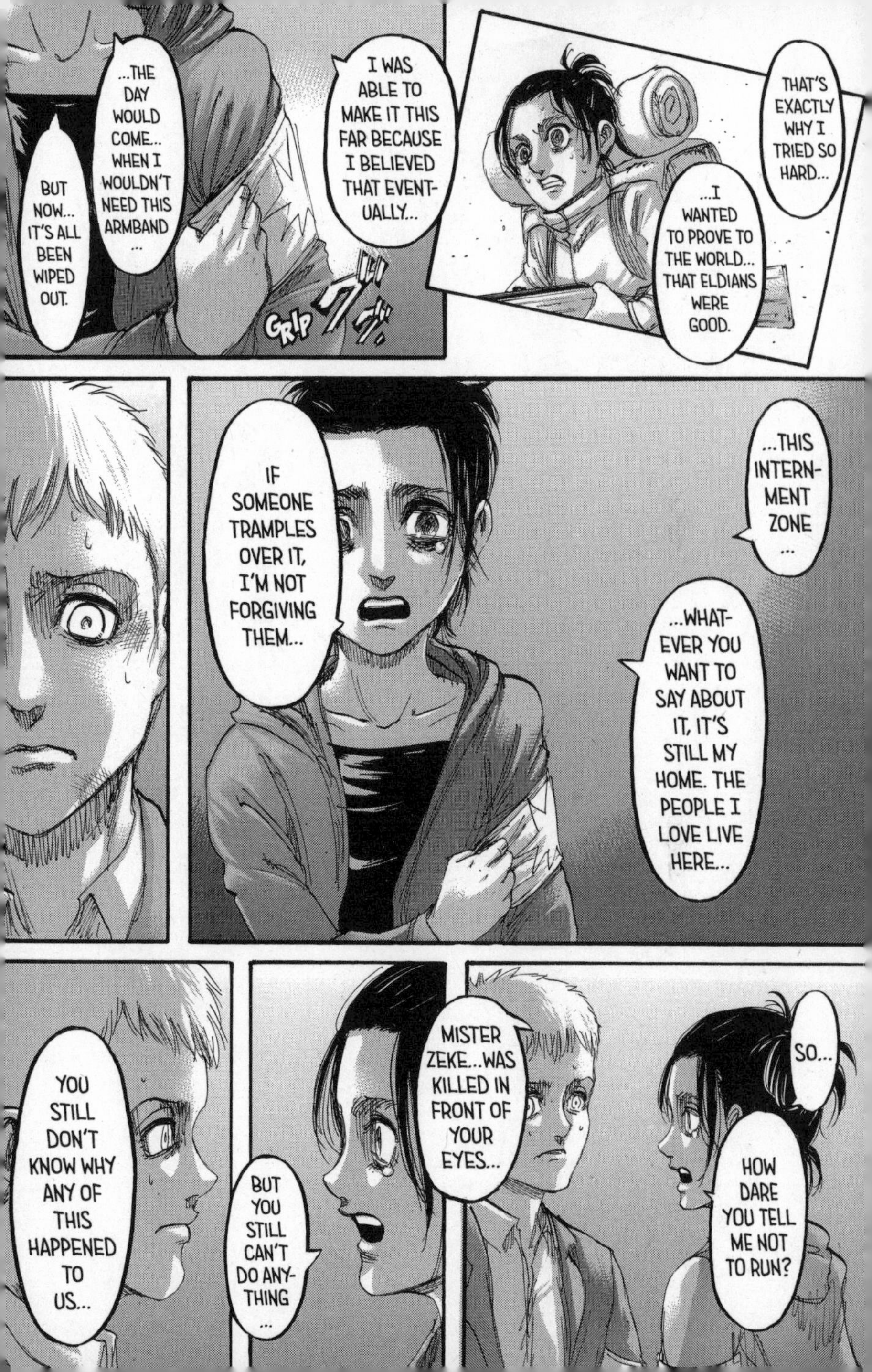
THAT'S EXACTLY WHY I TRIED SO HARD...
...I WANTED TO PROVE TO THE WORLD... THAT ELDIANS WERE GOOD.
I WAS ABLE TO MAKE IT THIS FAR BECAUSE I BELIEVED THAT EVENTUALLY...
...THE DAY WOULD COME... WHEN I WOULDN'T NEED THIS ARMBAND...
BUT NOW... IT'S ALL BEEN WIPED OUT.
GRIP
...THIS INTERNMENT ZONE...
...WHATEVER YOU WANT TO SAY ABOUT IT, IT'S STILL MY HOME. THE PEOPLE I LOVE LIVE HERE...
IF SOMEONE TRAMPLES OVER IT, I'M NOT FORGIVING THEM...
SO...
HOW DARE YOU TELL ME NOT TO RUN?
MISTER ZEKE...WAS KILLED IN FRONT OF YOUR EYES...
BUT YOU STILL CAN'T DO ANYTHING...
YOU STILL DON'T KNOW WHY ANY OF THIS HAPPENED TO US...

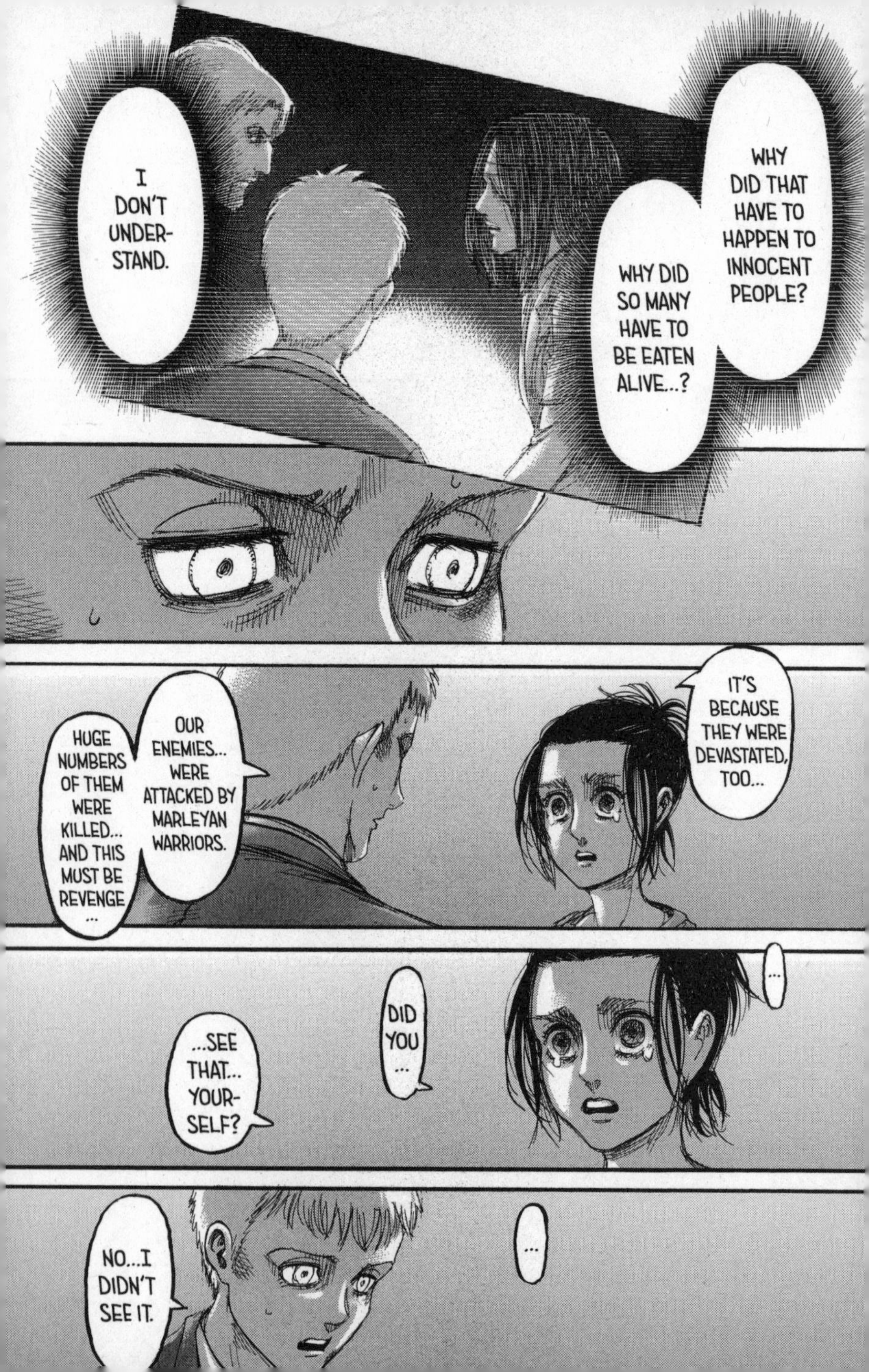
WHY DID THAT HAVE TO HAPPEN TO INNOCENT PEOPLE?
WHY DID SO MANY HAVE TO BE EATEN ALIVE...?
I DON'T UNDER-STAND.
IT'S BECAUSE THEY WERE DEVASTATED, TOO...
OUR ENEMIES... WERE ATTACKED BY MARLEYAN WARRIORS.
HUGE NUMBERS OF THEM WERE KILLED... AND THIS MUST BE REVENGE...
...
DID YOU...
...SEE THAT... YOURSELF?
...
NO...I DIDN'T SEE IT.

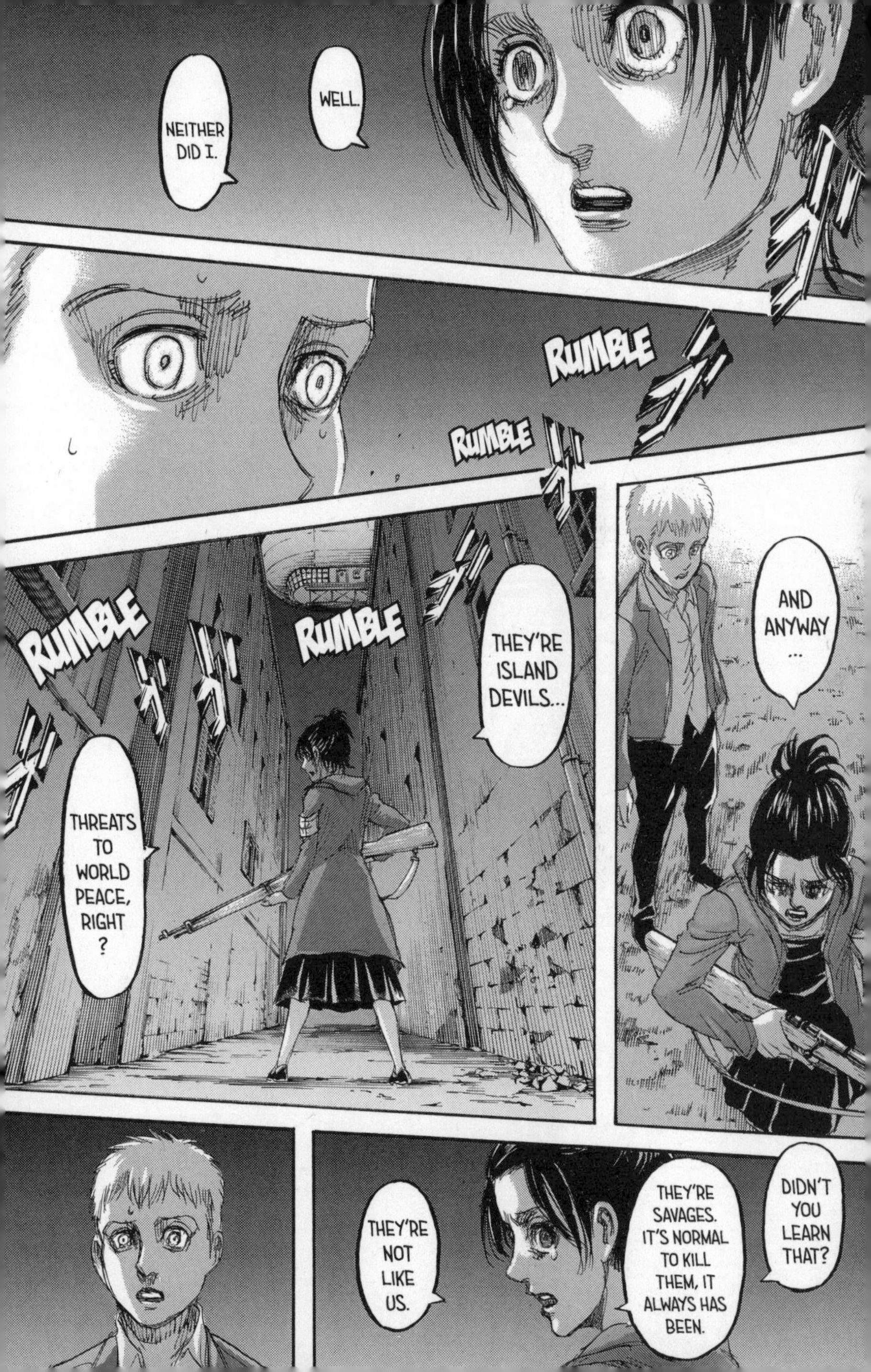
WELL.
NEITHER DID I.
RUMBLE
RUMBLE
AND ANYWAY ...
THEY'RE ISLAND DEVILS...
RUMBLE
RUMBLE
THREATS TO WORLD PEACE, RIGHT ?
DIDN'T YOU LEARN THAT?
THEY'RE SAVAGES. IT'S NORMAL TO KILL THEM, IT ALWAYS HAS BEEN.
THEY'RE NOT LIKE US.

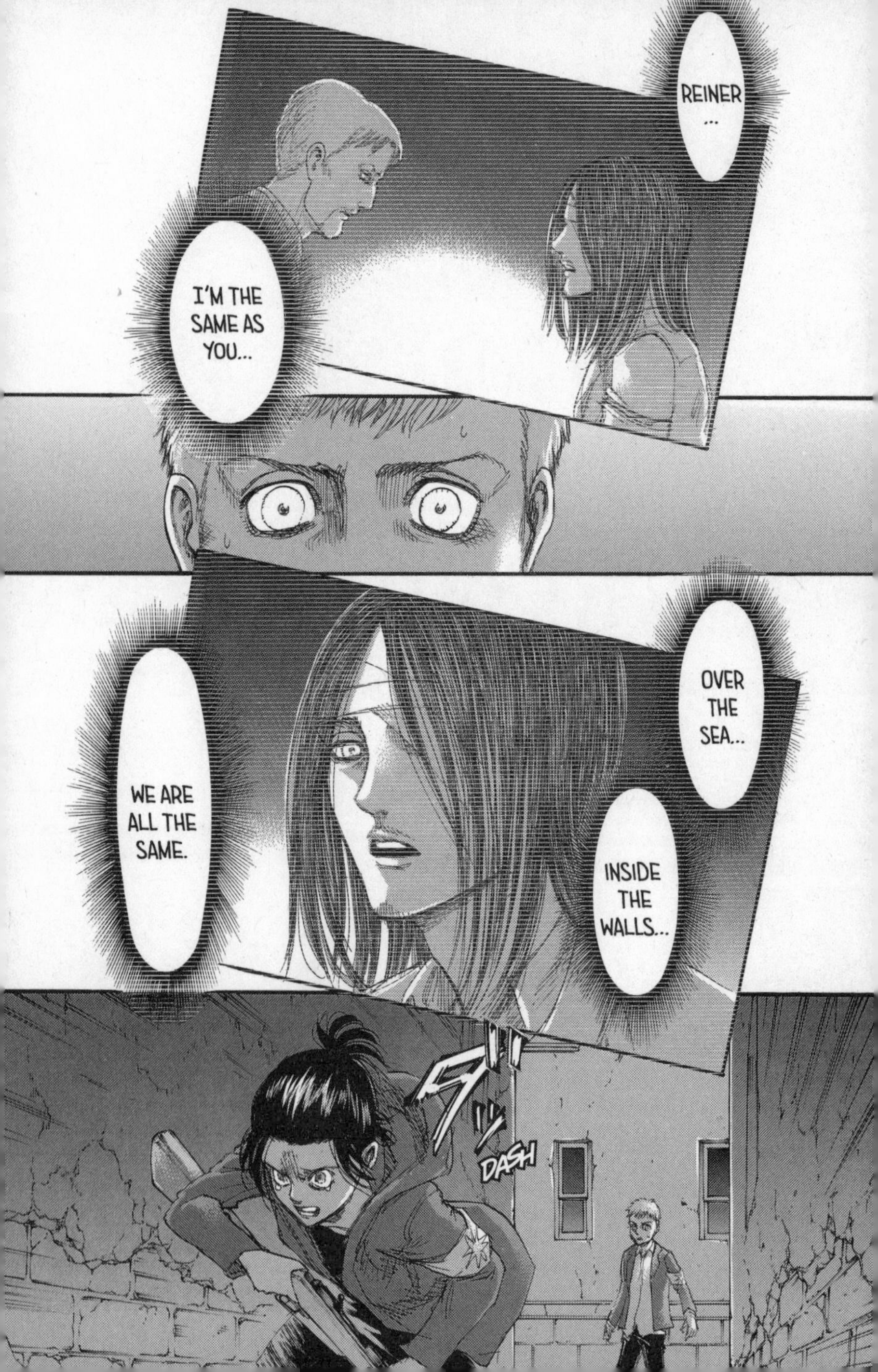
REINER...
I'M THE SAME AS YOU...
OVER THE SEA...
INSIDE THE WALLS...
WE ARE ALL THE SAME.
DASH

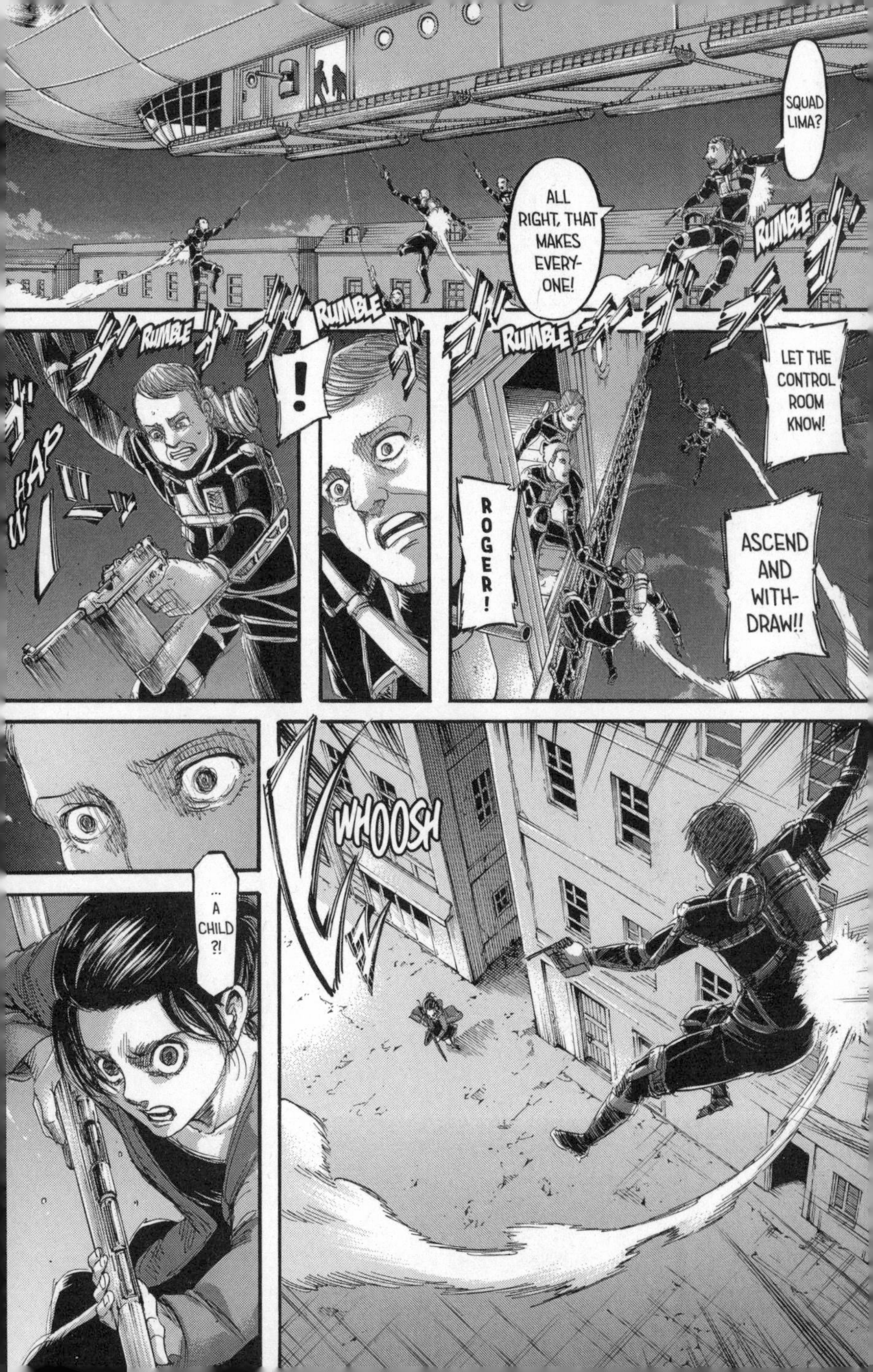
SQUAD LIMA?
ALL RIGHT, THAT MAKES EVERY-ONE!
RUMBLE
RUMBLE
LET THE CONTROL ROOM KNOW!
ASCEND AND WITH-DRAW!!
ROGER!
RUMBLE
!
RUMBLE
RUMBLE
WHAP
WHOOSH
... A CHILD ?!

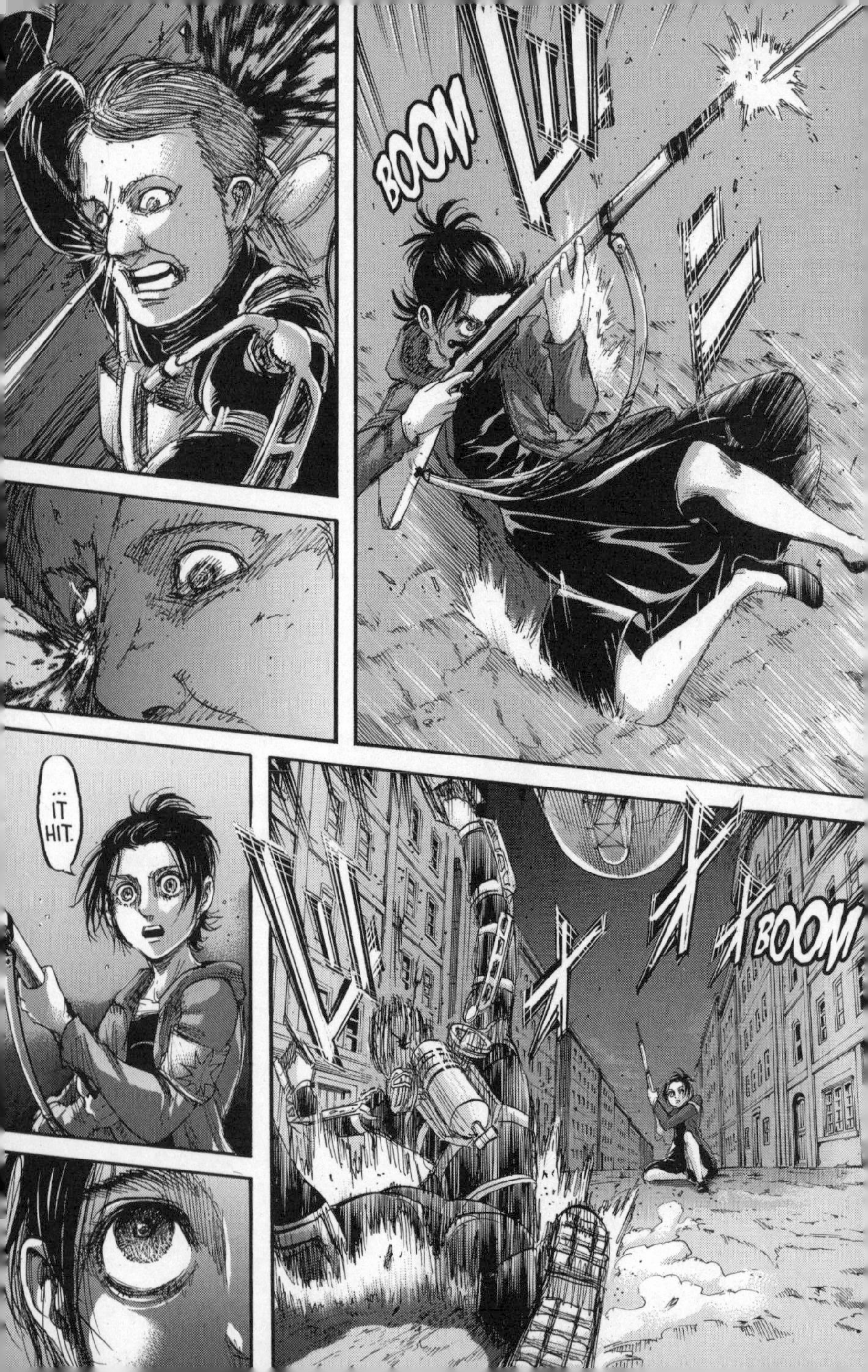
BOOM
BOOM
...IT HIT.

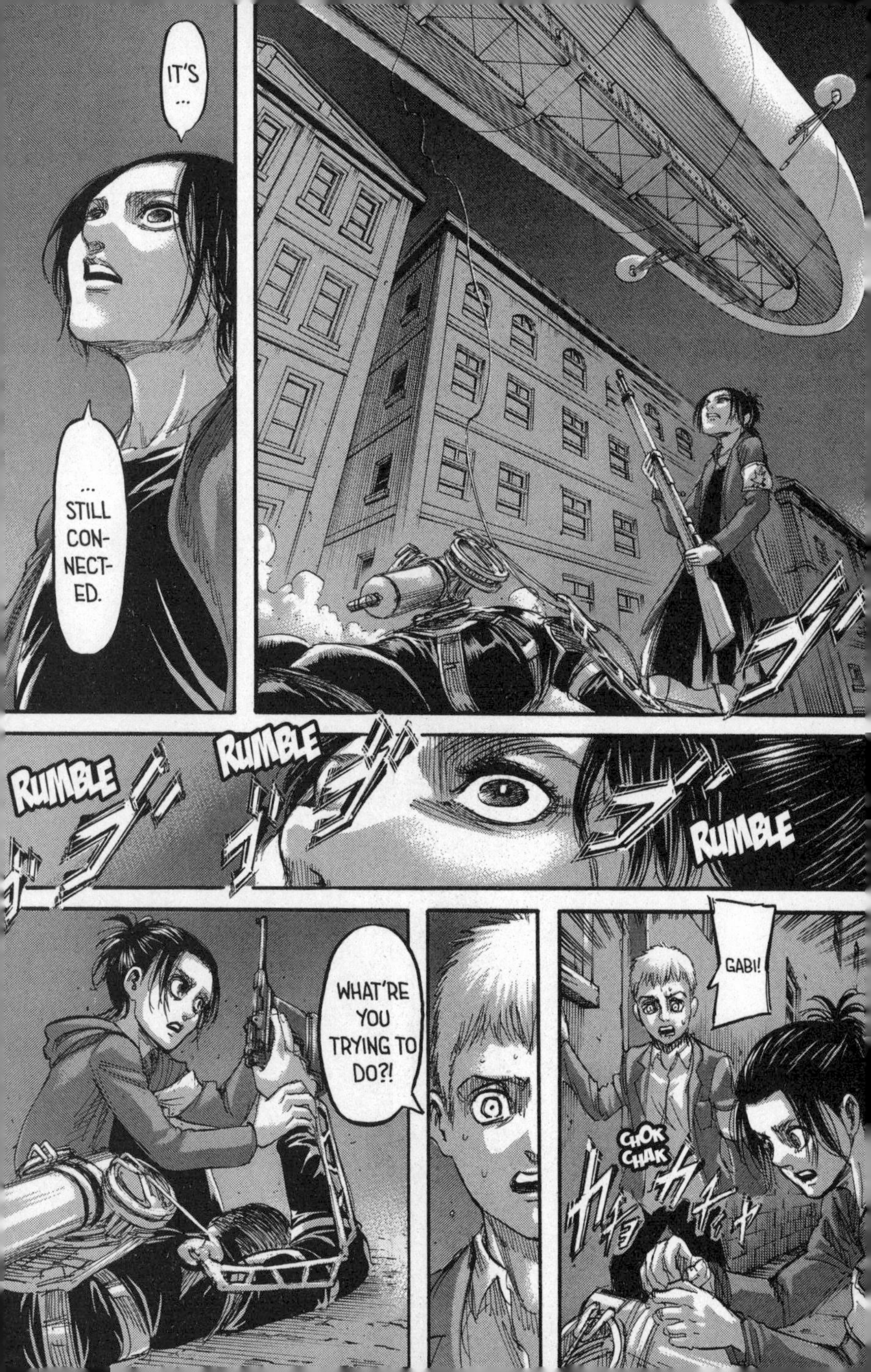
IT'S ...
... STILL CON- NECT- ED.
RUMBLE
RUMBLE
RUMBLE
GABI!
CHOK CHAK
WHAT'RE YOU TRYING TO DO?!

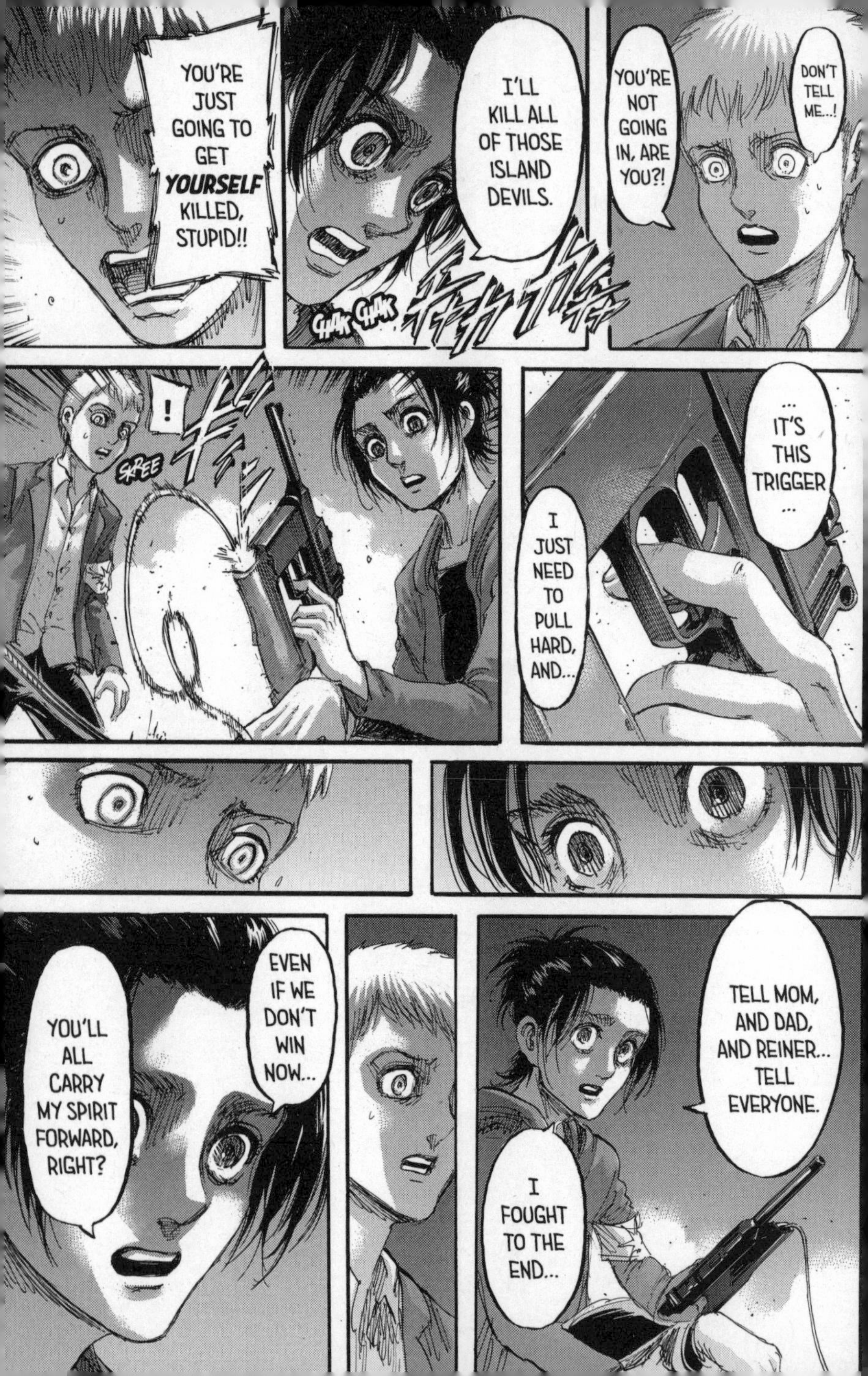
DON'T TELL ME...!
YOU'RE NOT GOING IN, ARE YOU?!
I'LL KILL ALL OF THOSE ISLAND DEVILS.
CHAK CHAK
YOU'RE JUST GOING TO GET YOURSELF KILLED, STUPID!!
... IT'S THIS TRIGGER ...
I JUST NEED TO PULL HARD, AND...
!
SKREE
TELL MOM, AND DAD, AND REINER... TELL EVERYONE.
I FOUGHT TO THE END...
EVEN IF WE DON'T WIN NOW...
YOU'LL ALL CARRY MY SPIRIT FORWARD, RIGHT?

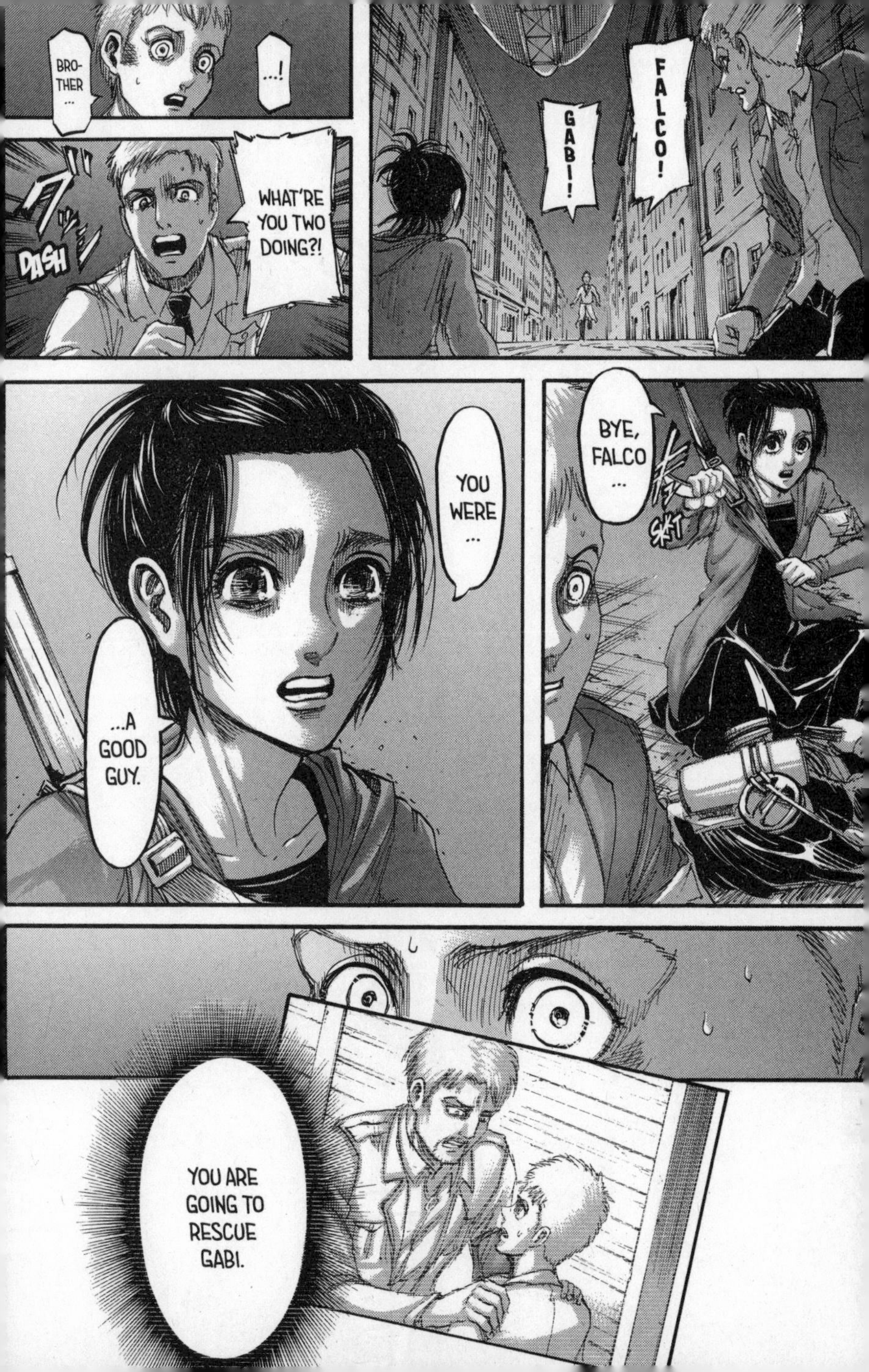
FALCO!
GABI!!
...!
BRO-THER ...
WHAT'RE YOU TWO DOING?!
DASH
BYE, FALCO ...
SKT
YOU WERE ...
...A GOOD GUY.
YOU ARE GOING TO RESCUE GABI.

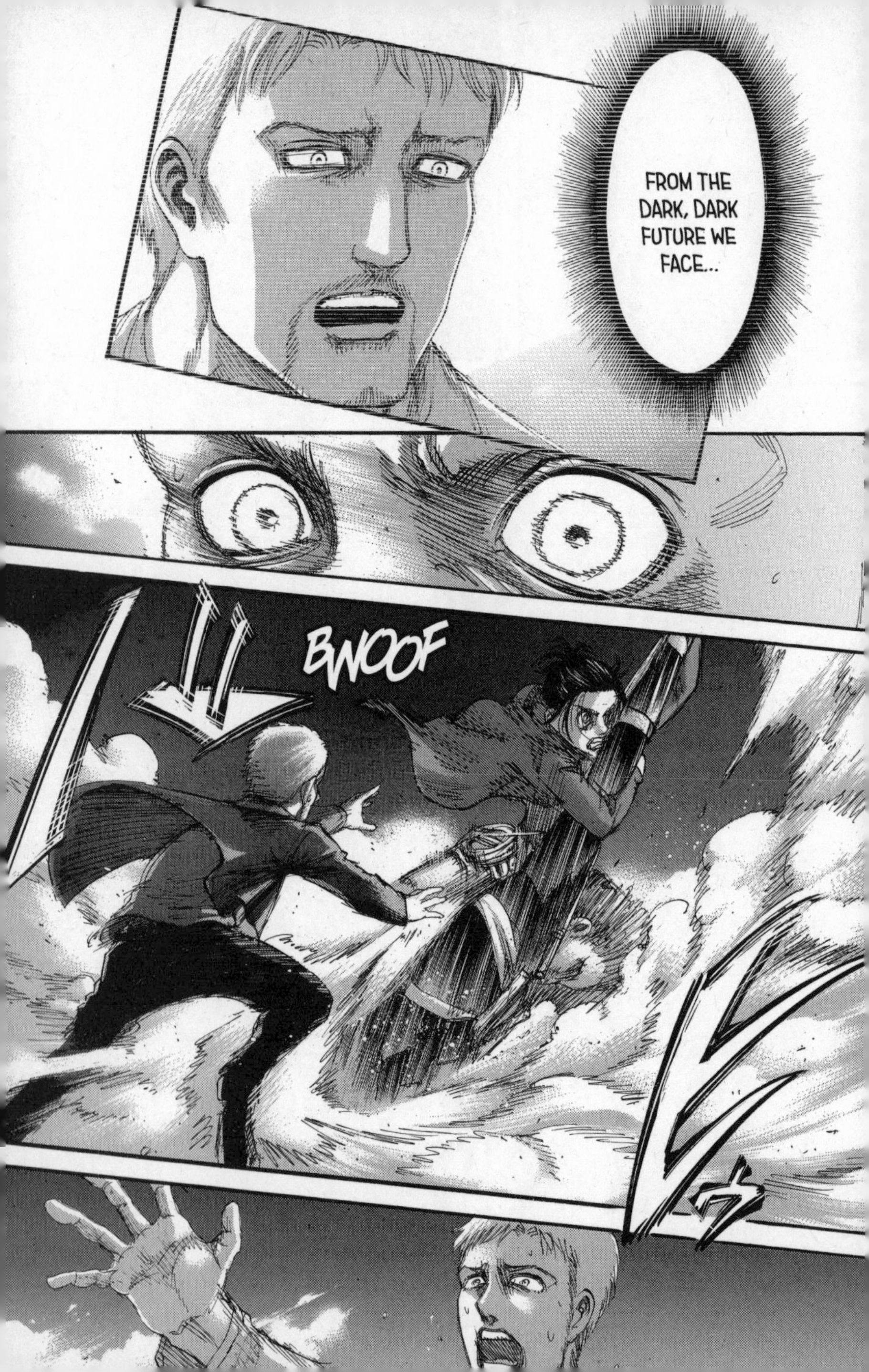
FROM THE DARK, DARK FUTURE WE FACE...
BWOOF

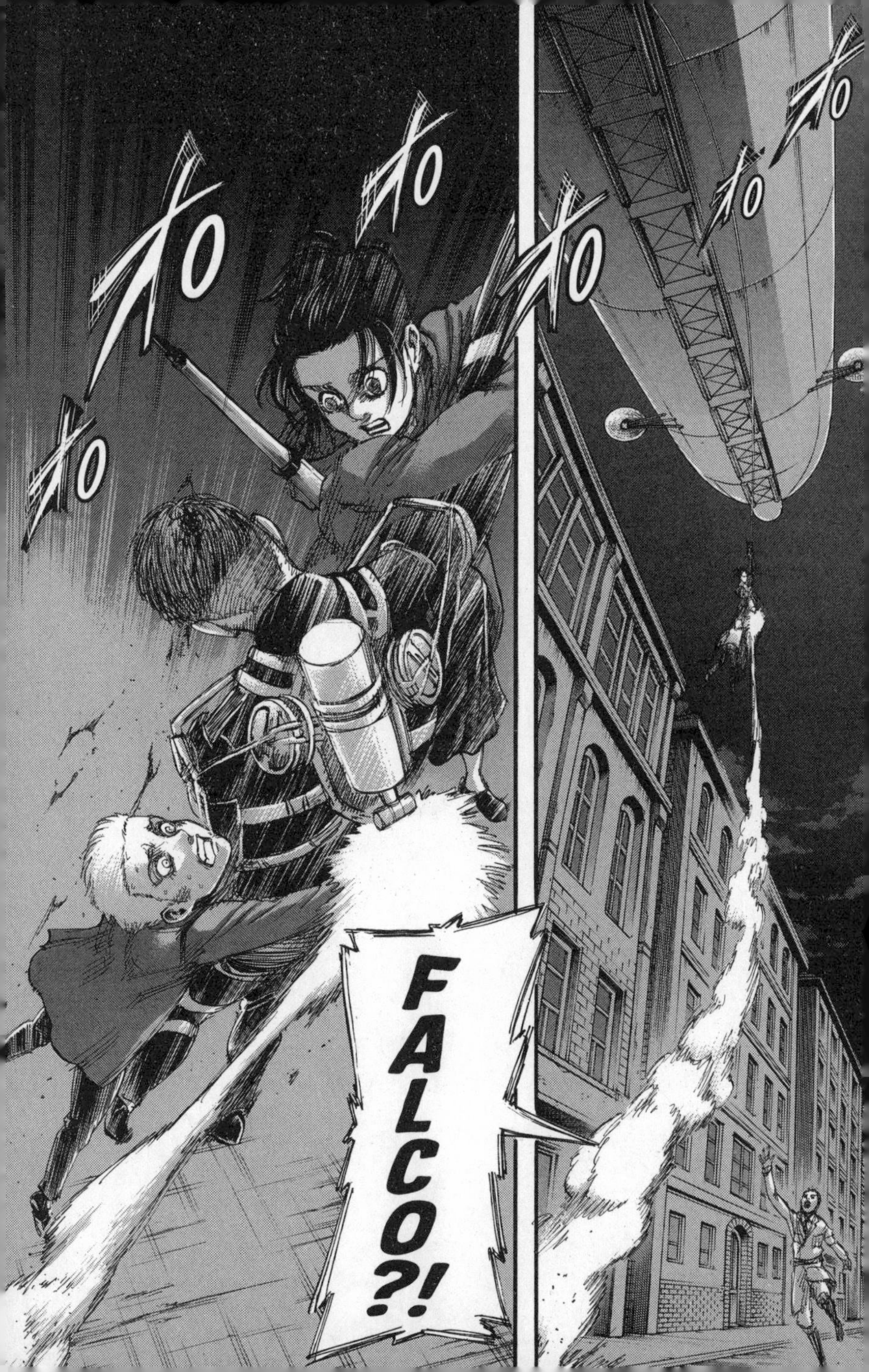
オォ
オォ
オォ
オォ
オォ
オォ
FALCO?!

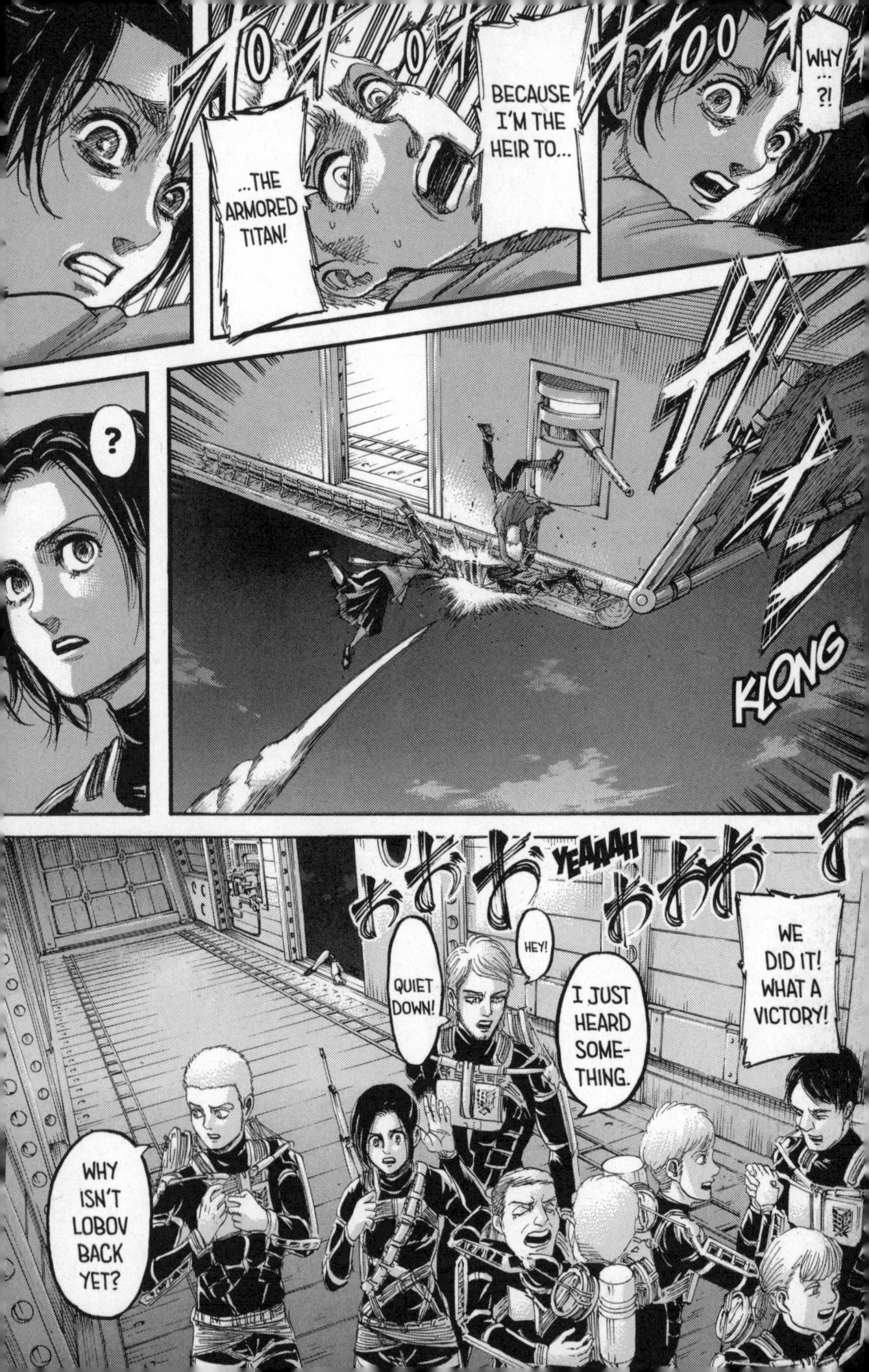
WHY...?!
BECAUSE I'M THE HEIR TO...
...THE ARMORED TITAN!
KLONG
?
YEAAAH
WE DID IT! WHAT A VICTORY!
HEY!
I JUST HEARD SOMETHING.
QUIET DOWN!
WHY ISN'T LOBOV BACK YET?

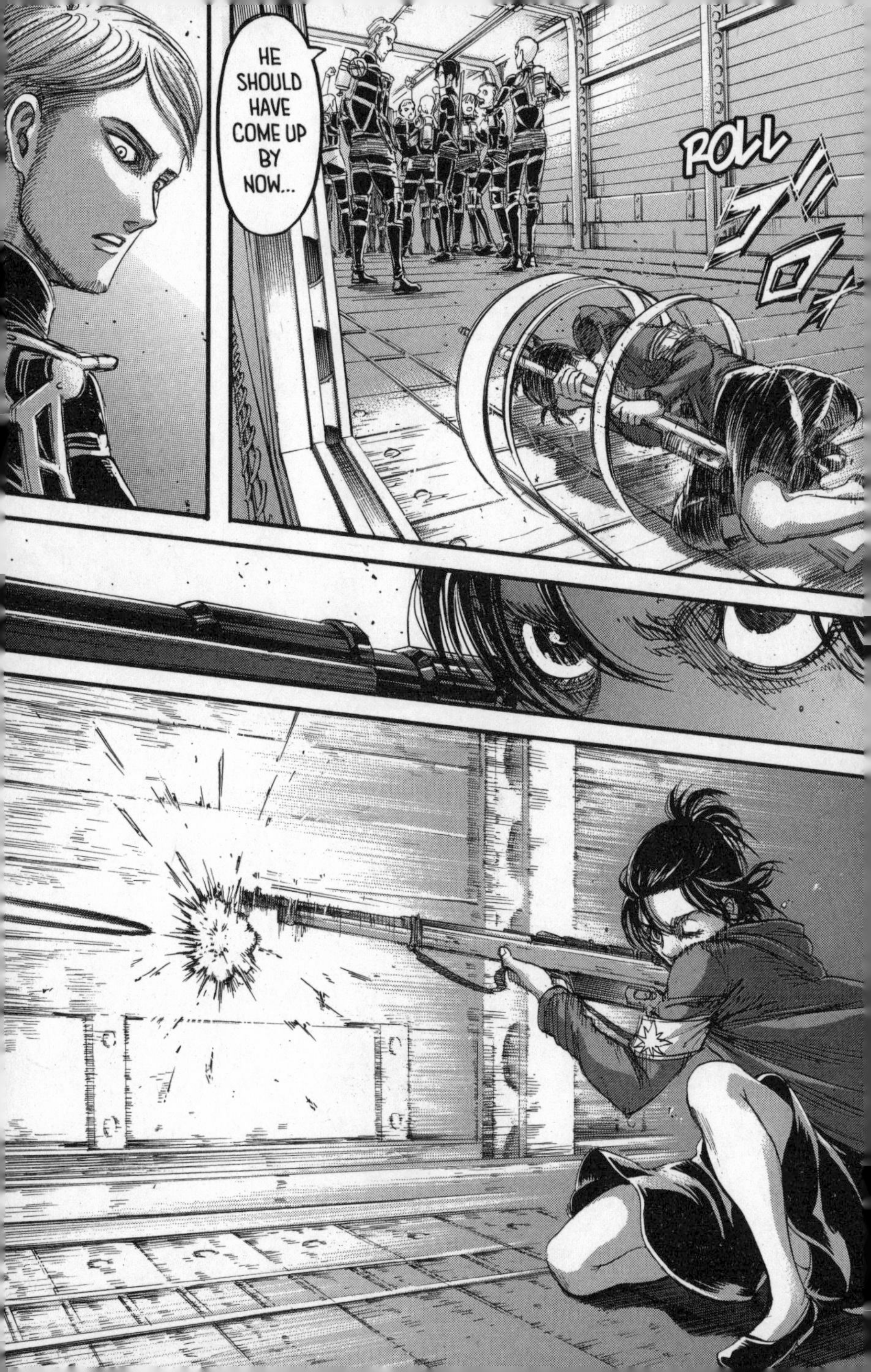
ROLL
ゴロッ
HE SHOULD HAVE COME UP BY NOW...

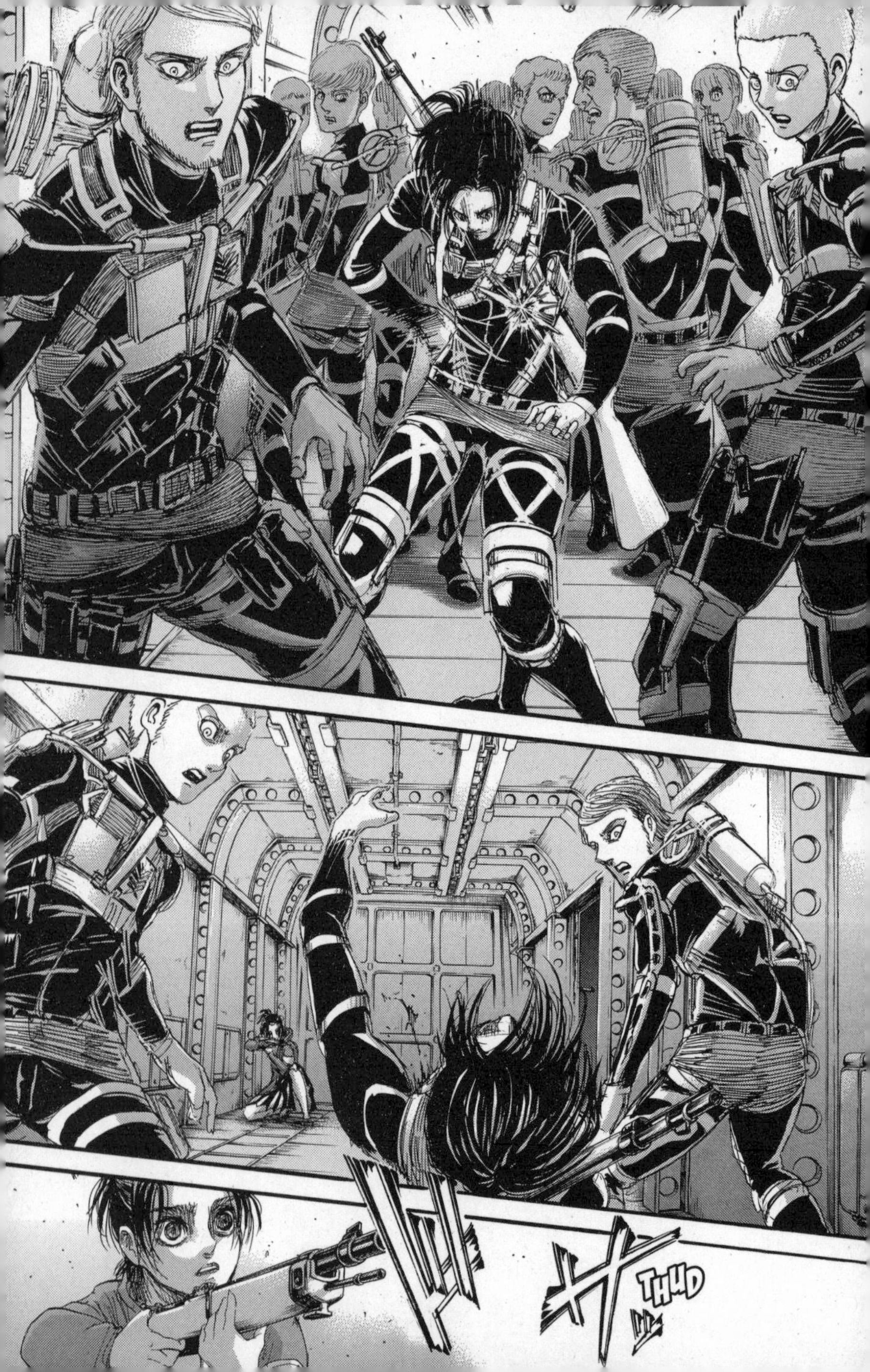
THUD

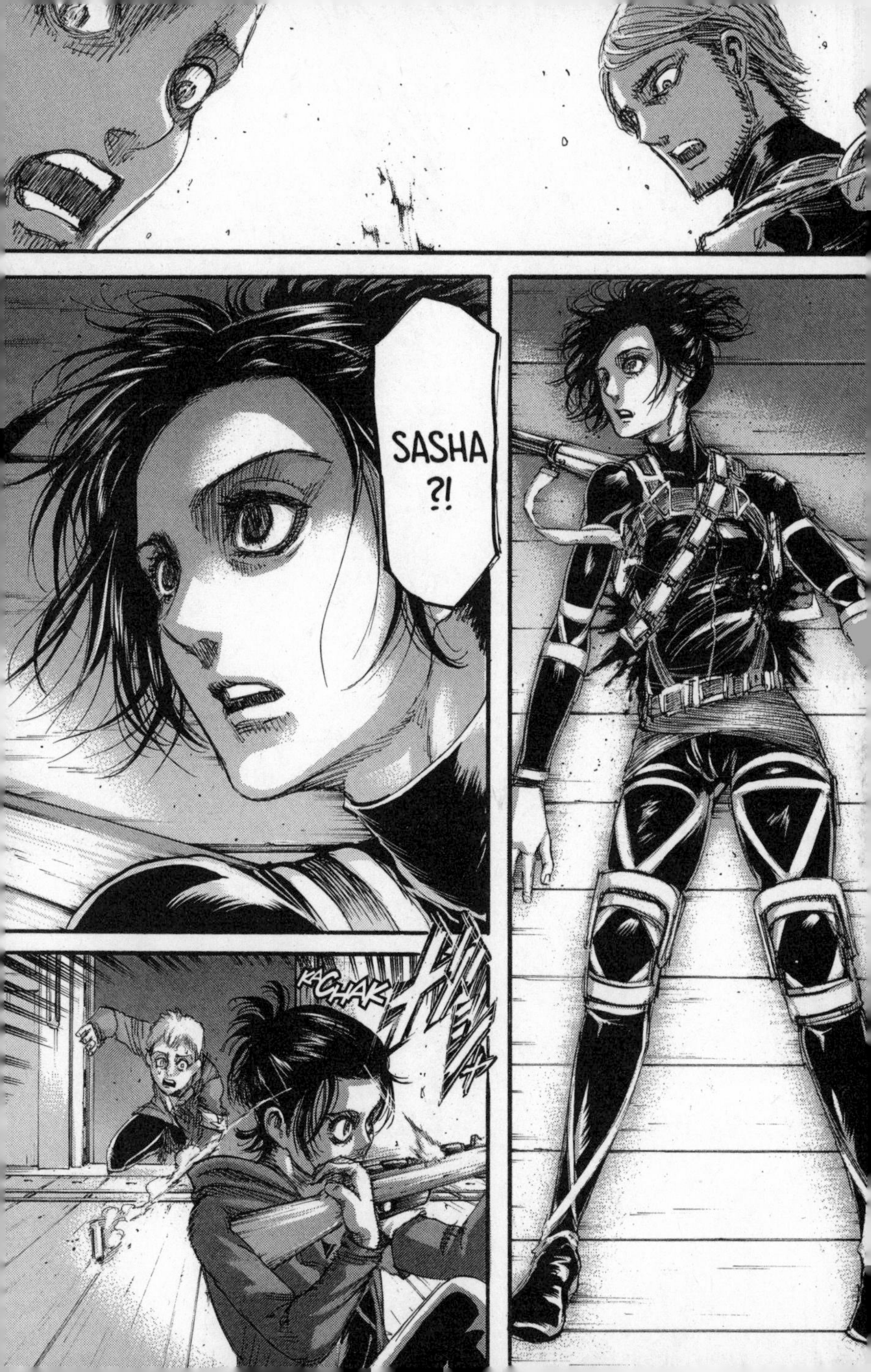
SASHA
?!
KACHAK

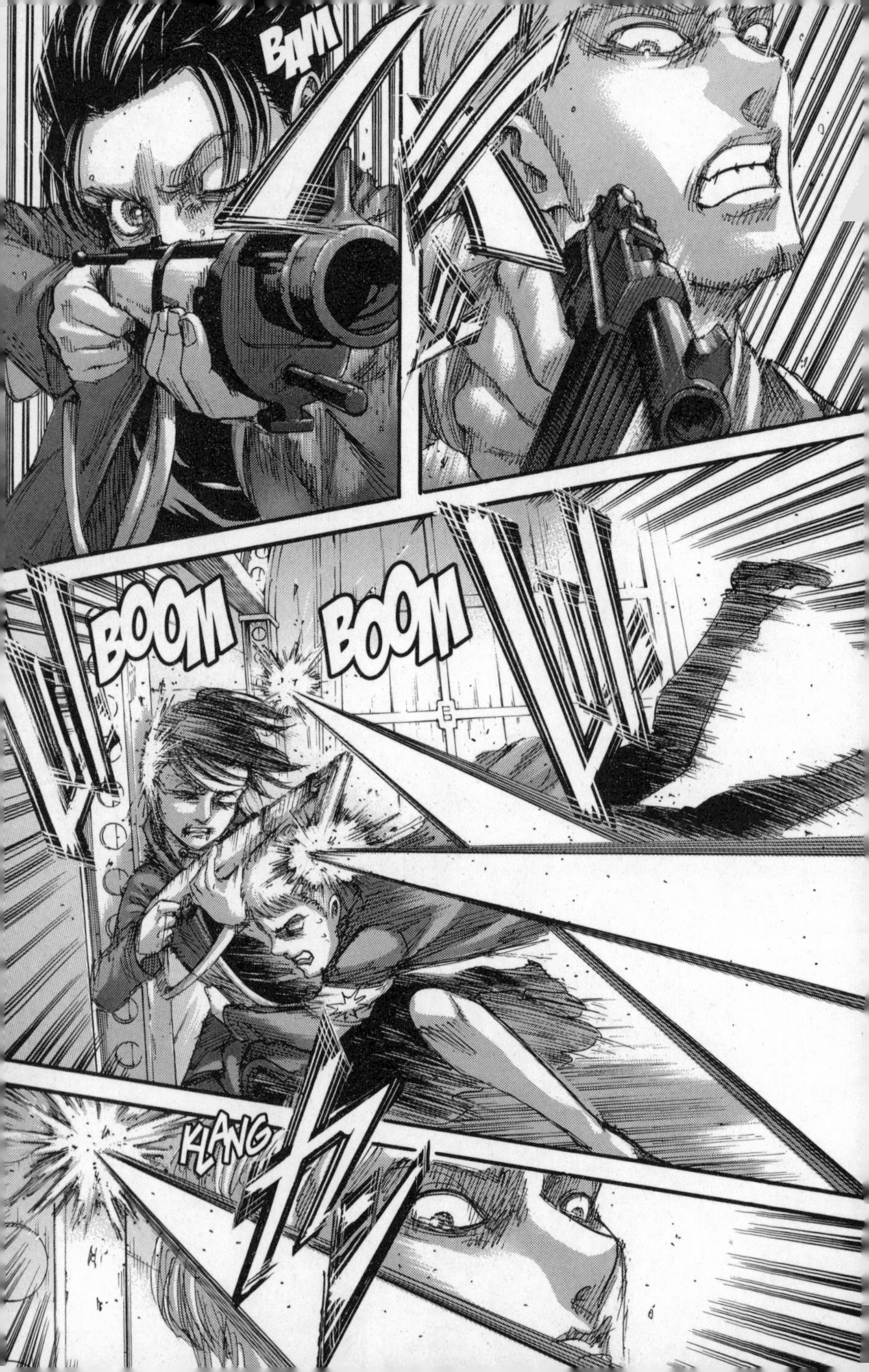
BAM
BOOM
BOOM
KLANG

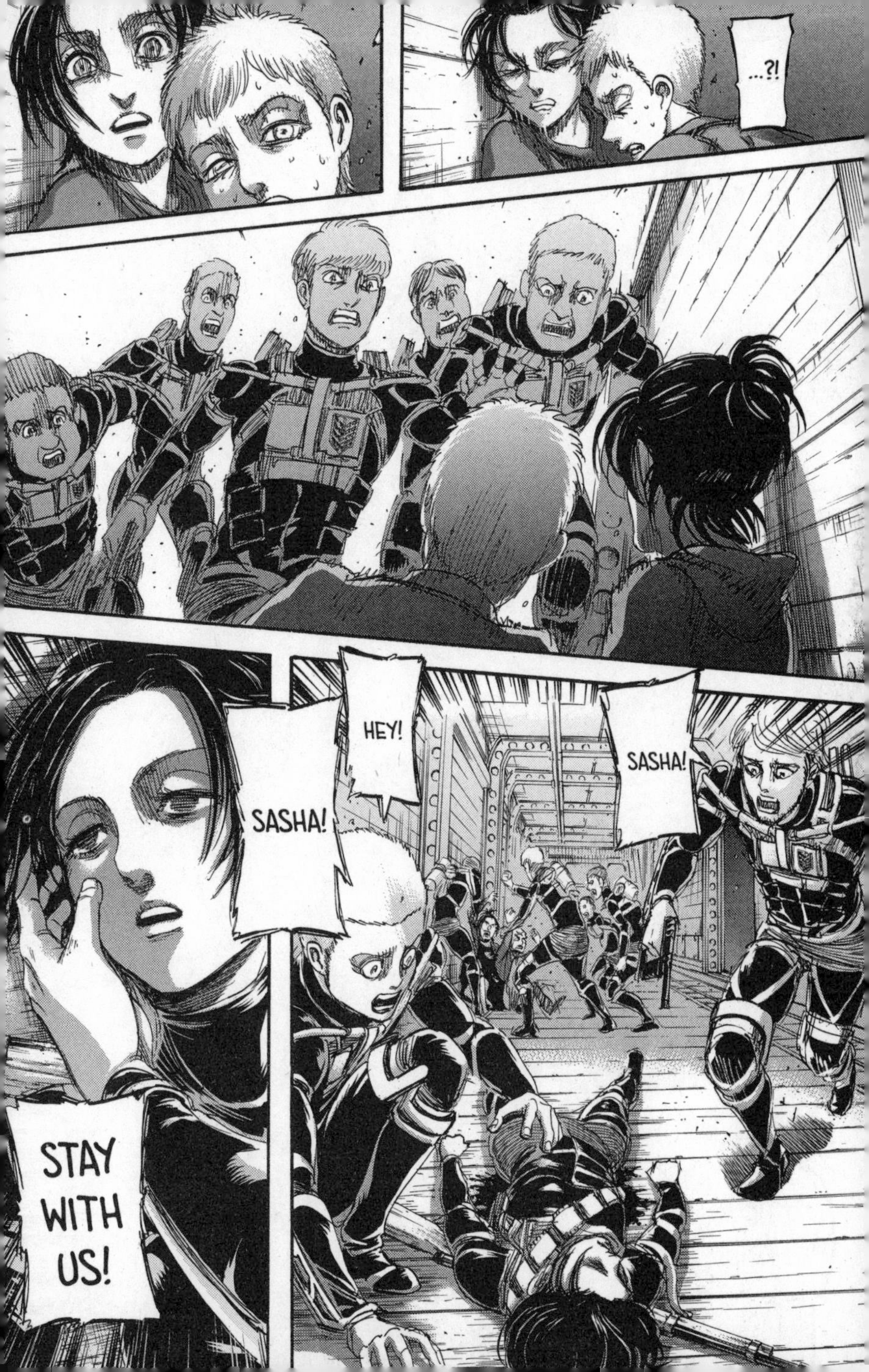
...?!
SASHA!
HEY!
SASHA!
STAY WITH US!

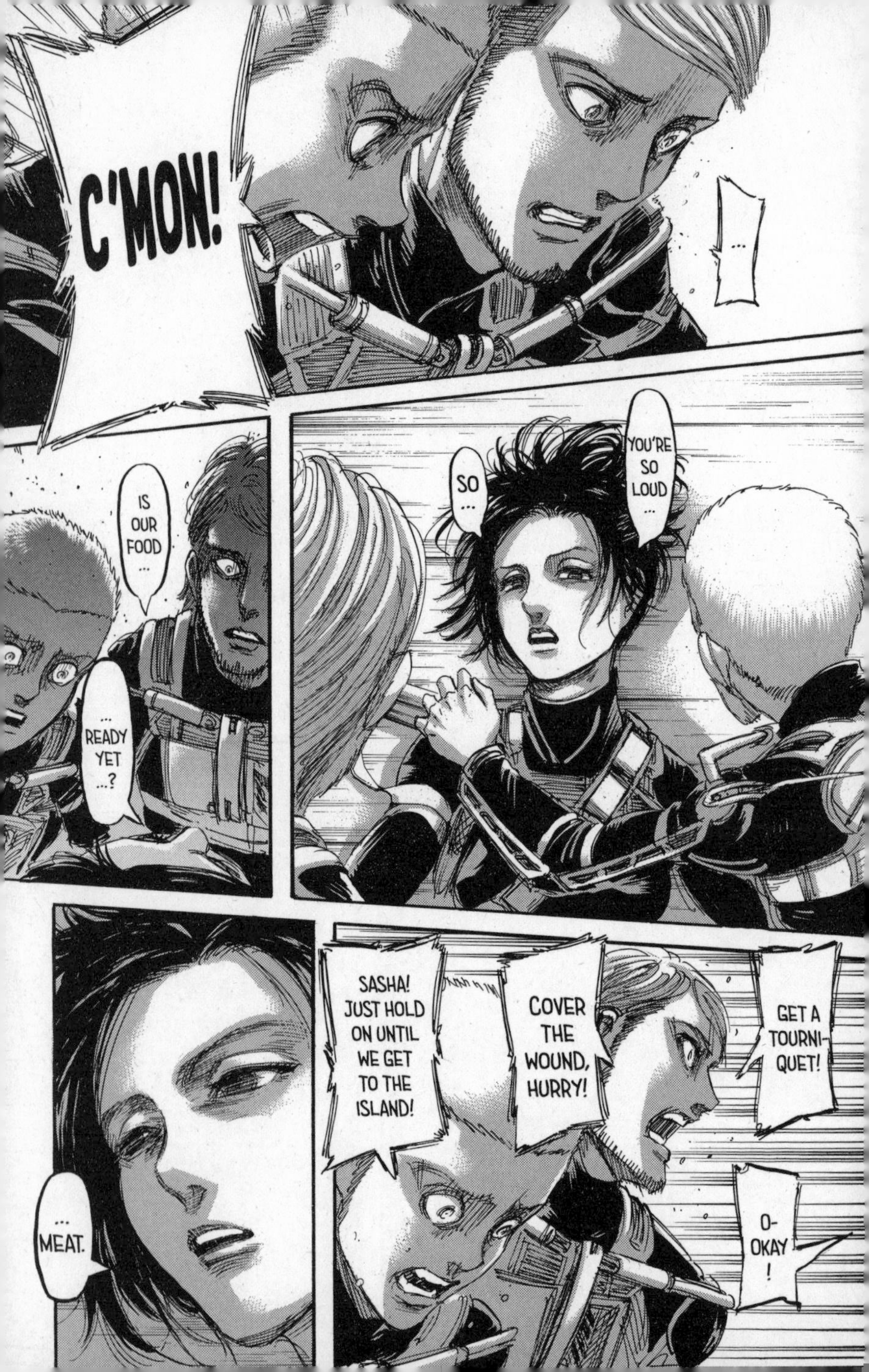
...
C'MON!
YOU'RE SO LOUD ...
SO ...
IS OUR FOOD ...
... READY YET ...?
GET A TOURNI-QUET!
COVER THE WOUND, HURRY!
SASHA! JUST HOLD ON UNTIL WE GET TO THE ISLAND!
O-OKAY!
... MEAT.

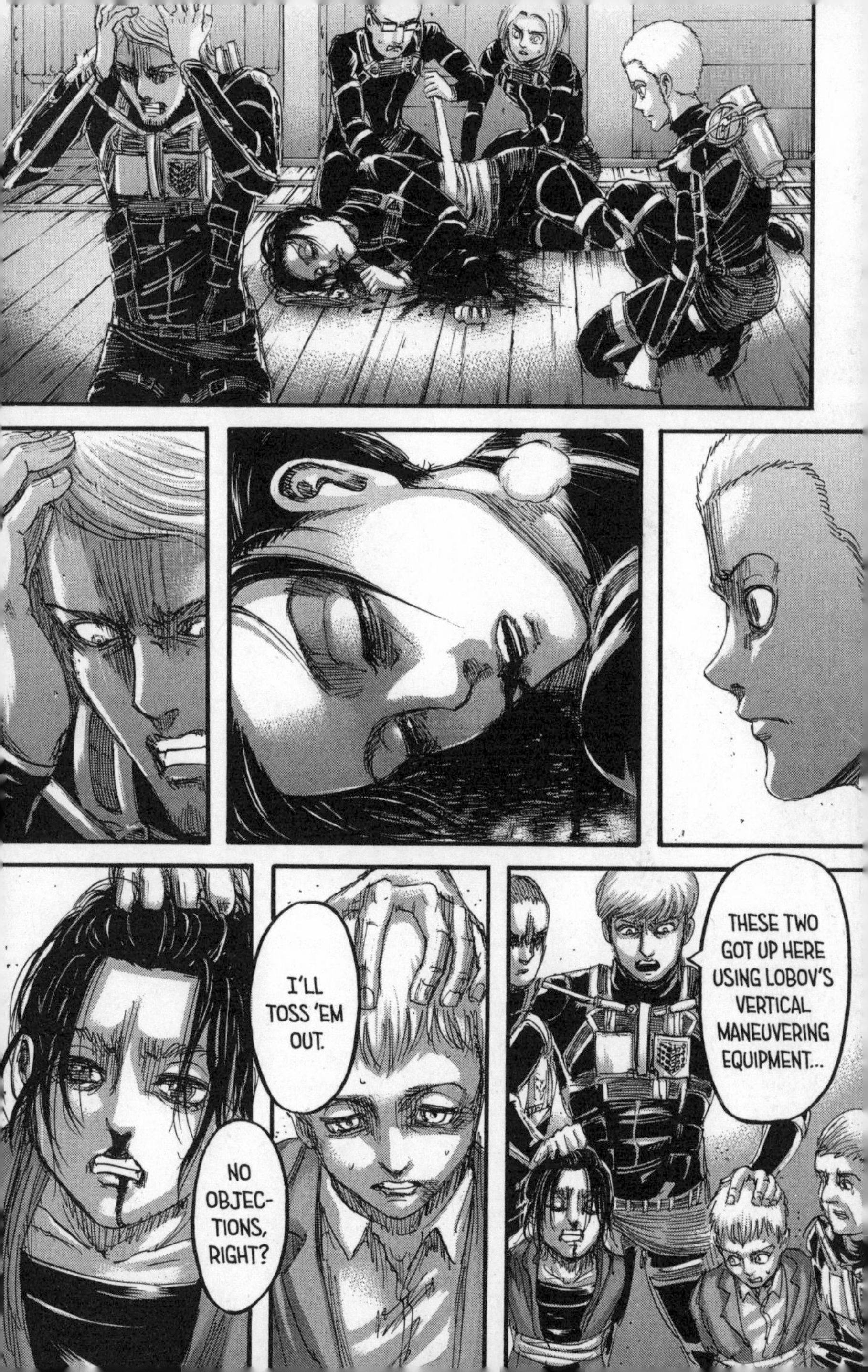
THESE TWO GOT UP HERE USING LOBOV'S VERTICAL MANEUVERING EQUIPMENT...
I'LL TOSS 'EM OUT.
NO OBJECTIONS, RIGHT?

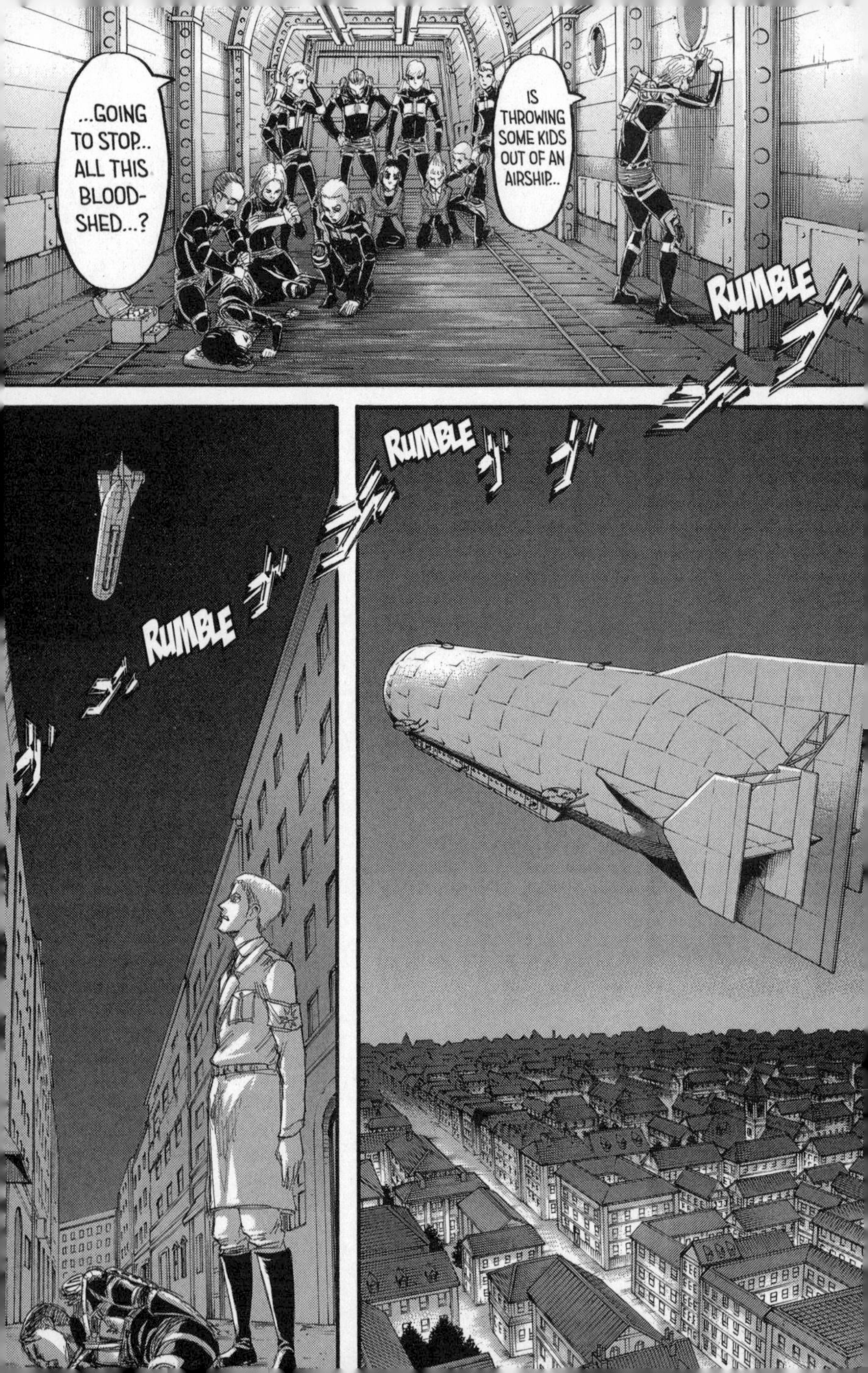
IS THROWING SOME KIDS OUT OF AN AIRSHIP...
...GOING TO STOP... ALL THIS BLOOD-SHED...?
RUMBLE
RUMBLE
RUMBLE

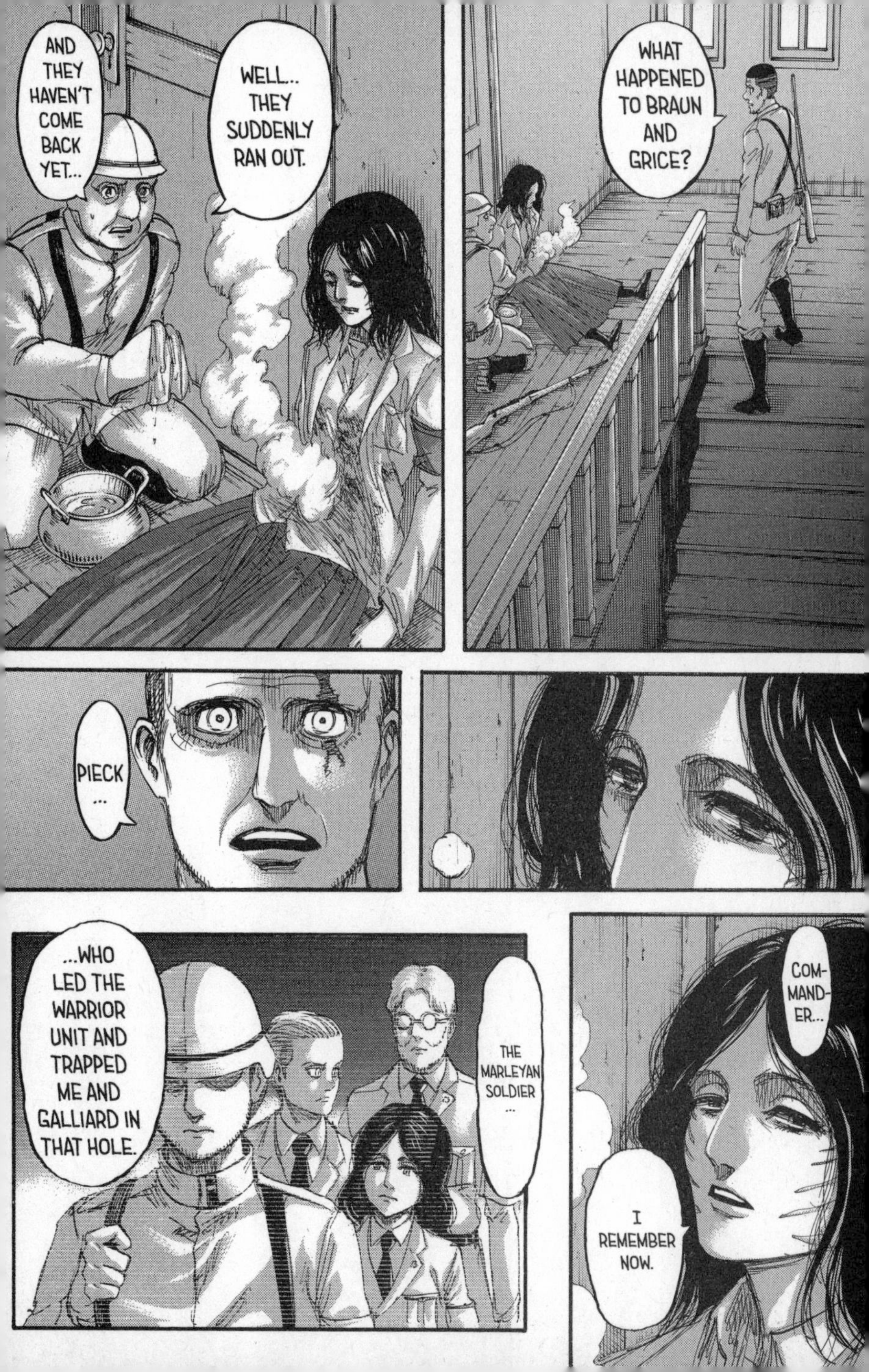
WHAT HAPPENED TO BRAUN AND GRICE?
WELL... THEY SUDDENLY RAN OUT.
AND THEY HAVEN'T COME BACK YET...
PIECK ...
COMMANDER...
I REMEMBER NOW.
THE MARLEYAN SOLDIER ...
...WHO LED THE WARRIOR UNIT AND TRAPPED ME AND GALLIARD IN THAT HOLE.

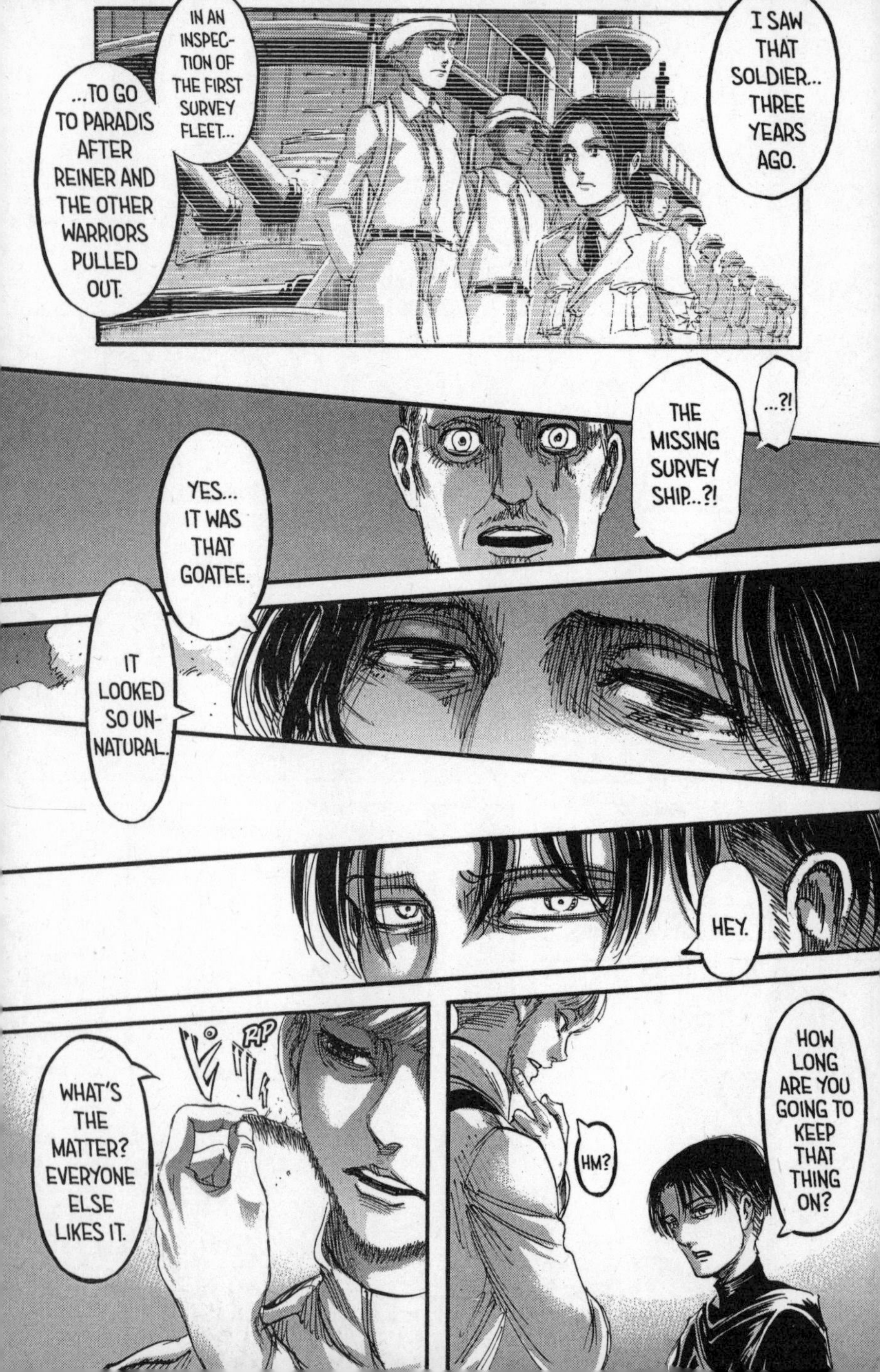
I SAW THAT SOLDIER... THREE YEARS AGO.
IN AN INSPECTION OF THE FIRST SURVEY FLEET...
...TO GO TO PARADIS AFTER REINER AND THE OTHER WARRIORS PULLED OUT.
...?!
THE MISSING SURVEY SHIP...?!
YES... IT WAS THAT GOATEE.
IT LOOKED SO UN-NATURAL.
HEY.
HOW LONG ARE YOU GOING TO KEEP THAT THING ON?
HM?
RIP
WHAT'S THE MATTER? EVERYONE ELSE LIKES IT.

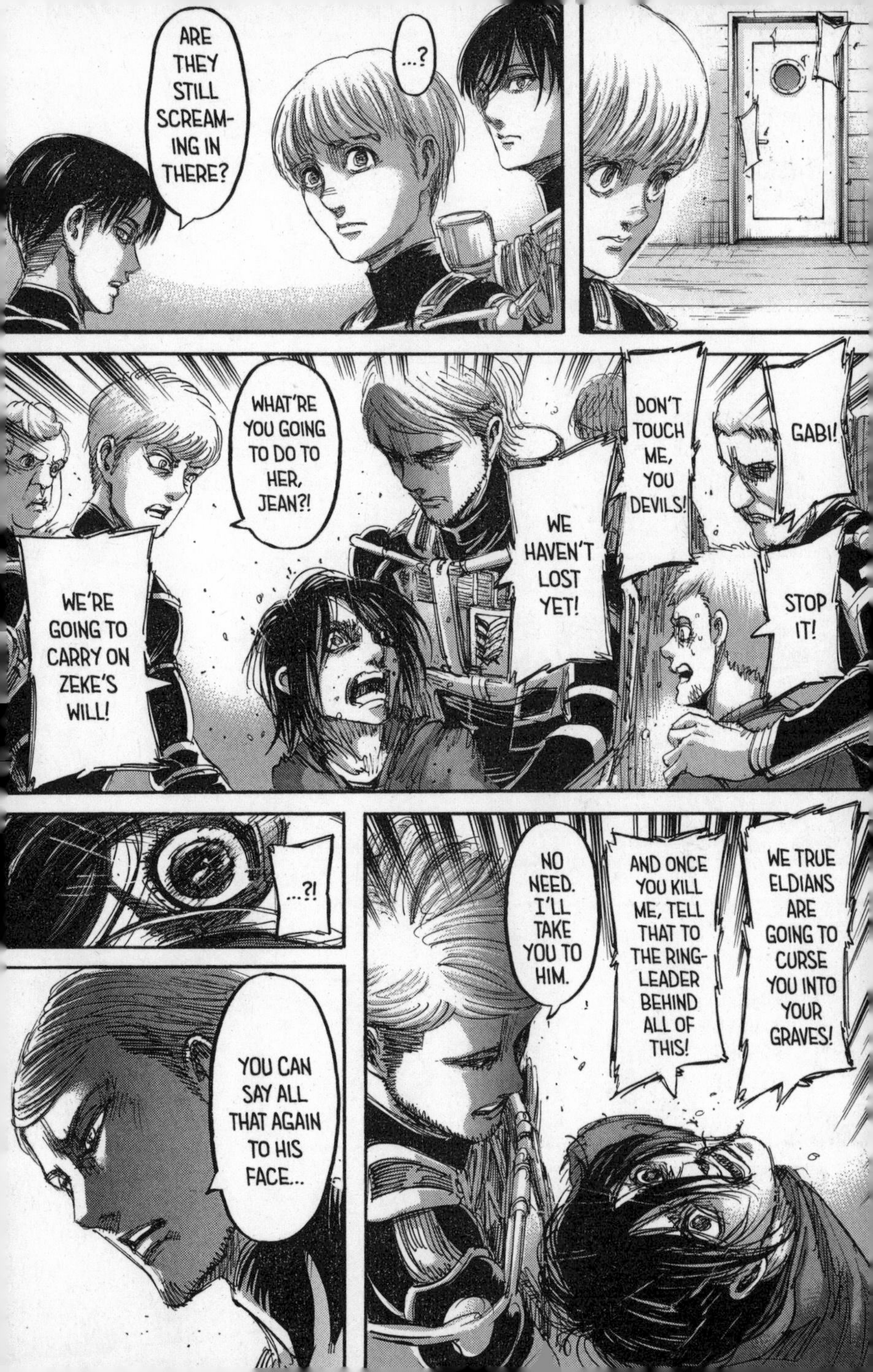
...?
ARE THEY STILL SCREAMING IN THERE?
GABI!
DON'T TOUCH ME, YOU DEVILS!
STOP IT!
WE HAVEN'T LOST YET!
WHAT'RE YOU GOING TO DO TO HER, JEAN?!
WE'RE GOING TO CARRY ON ZEKE'S WILL!
WE TRUE ELDIANS ARE GOING TO CURSE YOU INTO YOUR GRAVES!
AND ONCE YOU KILL ME, TELL THAT TO THE RING-LEADER BEHIND ALL OF THIS!
NO NEED. I'LL TAKE YOU TO HIM.
...?!
YOU CAN SAY ALL THAT AGAIN TO HIS FACE...

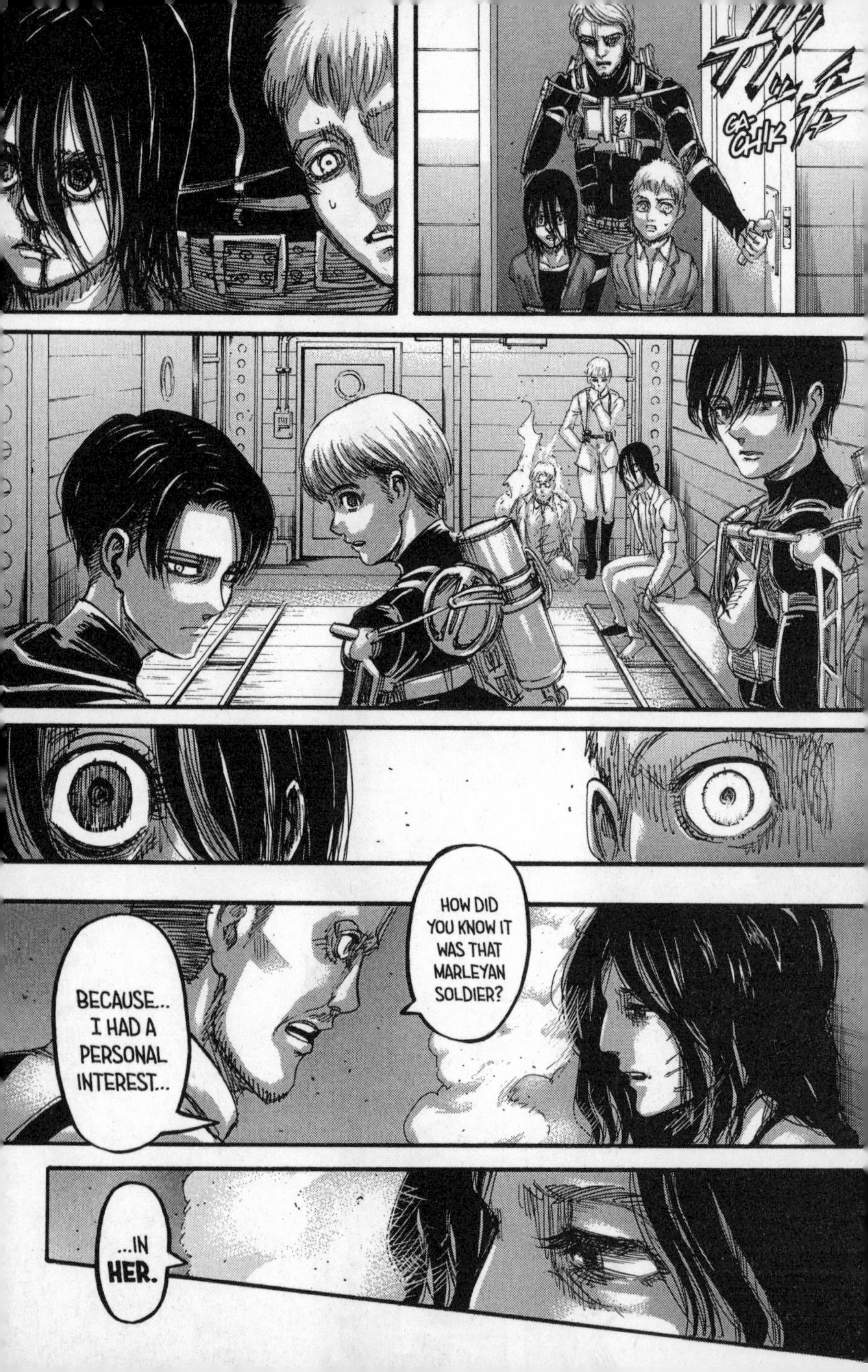
CA-CHIK
HOW DID YOU KNOW IT WAS THAT MARLEYAN SOLDIER?
BECAUSE... I HAD A PERSONAL INTEREST...
...IN HER.

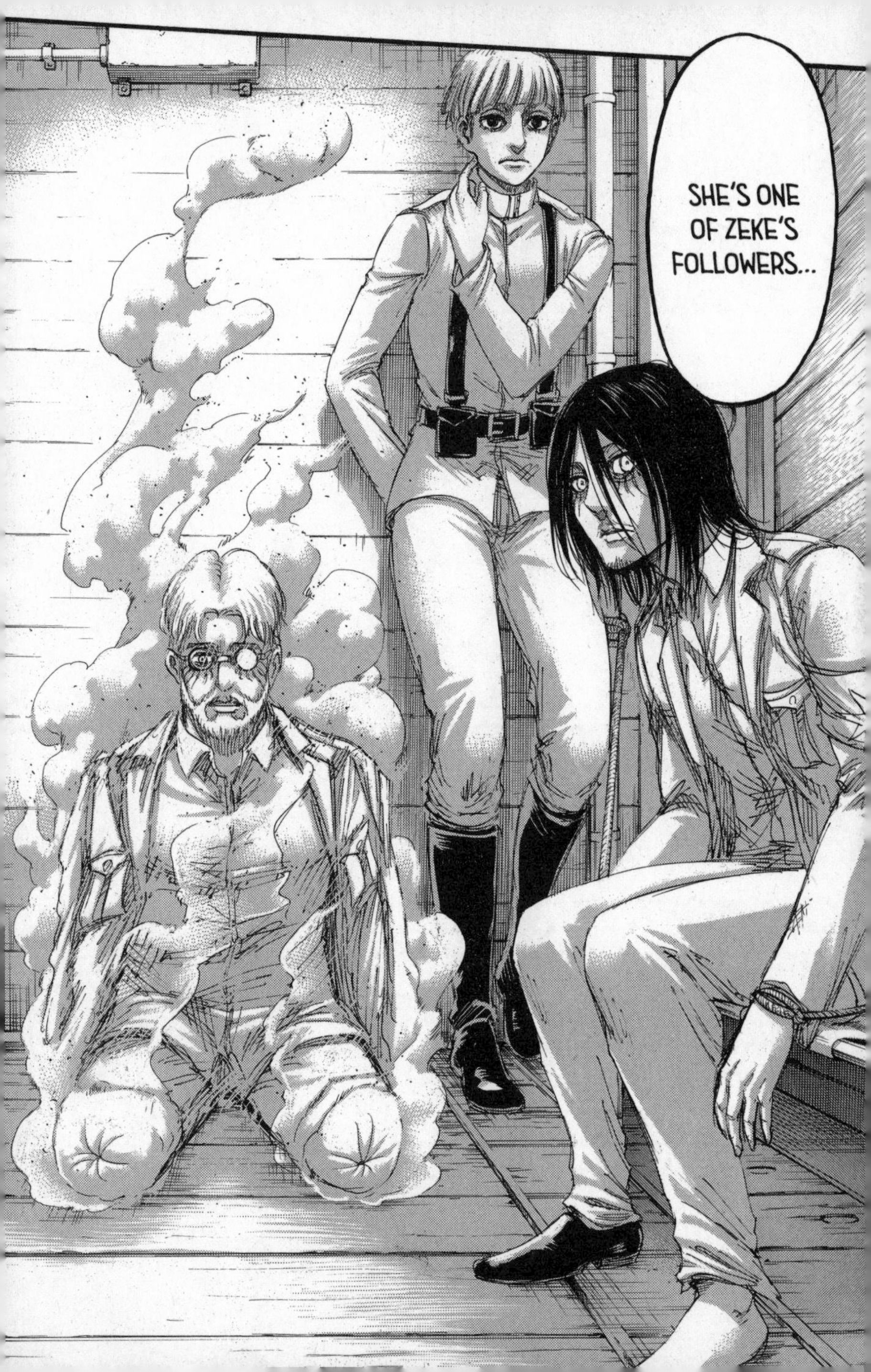
SHE'S ONE OF ZEKE'S FOLLOWERS...

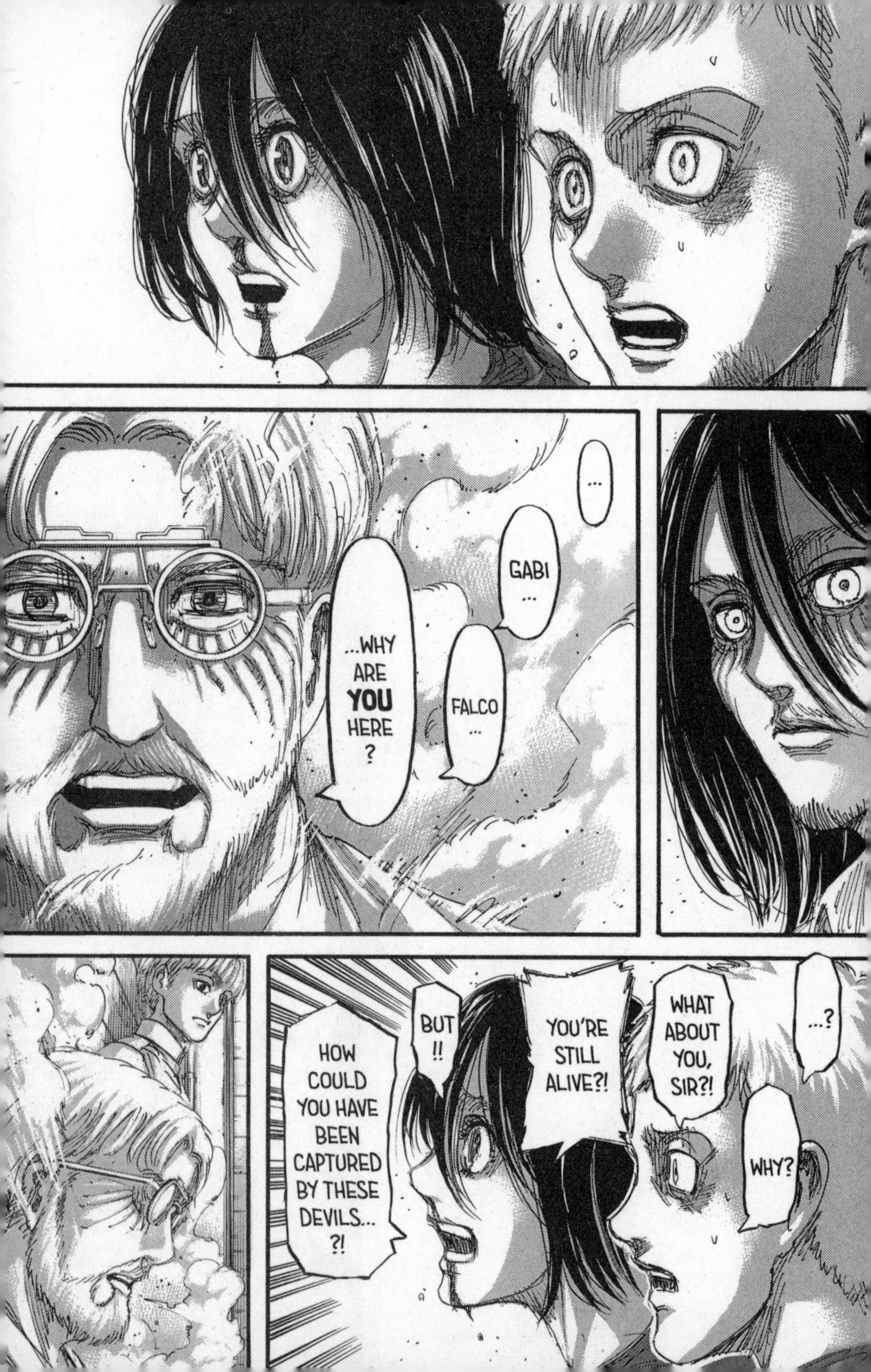
...
GABI ...
FALCO ...
...WHY ARE **YOU** HERE ?
...?
WHAT ABOUT YOU, SIR?!
WHY?
YOU'RE STILL ALIVE?!
BUT !!
HOW COULD YOU HAVE BEEN CAPTURED BY THESE DEVILS... ?!

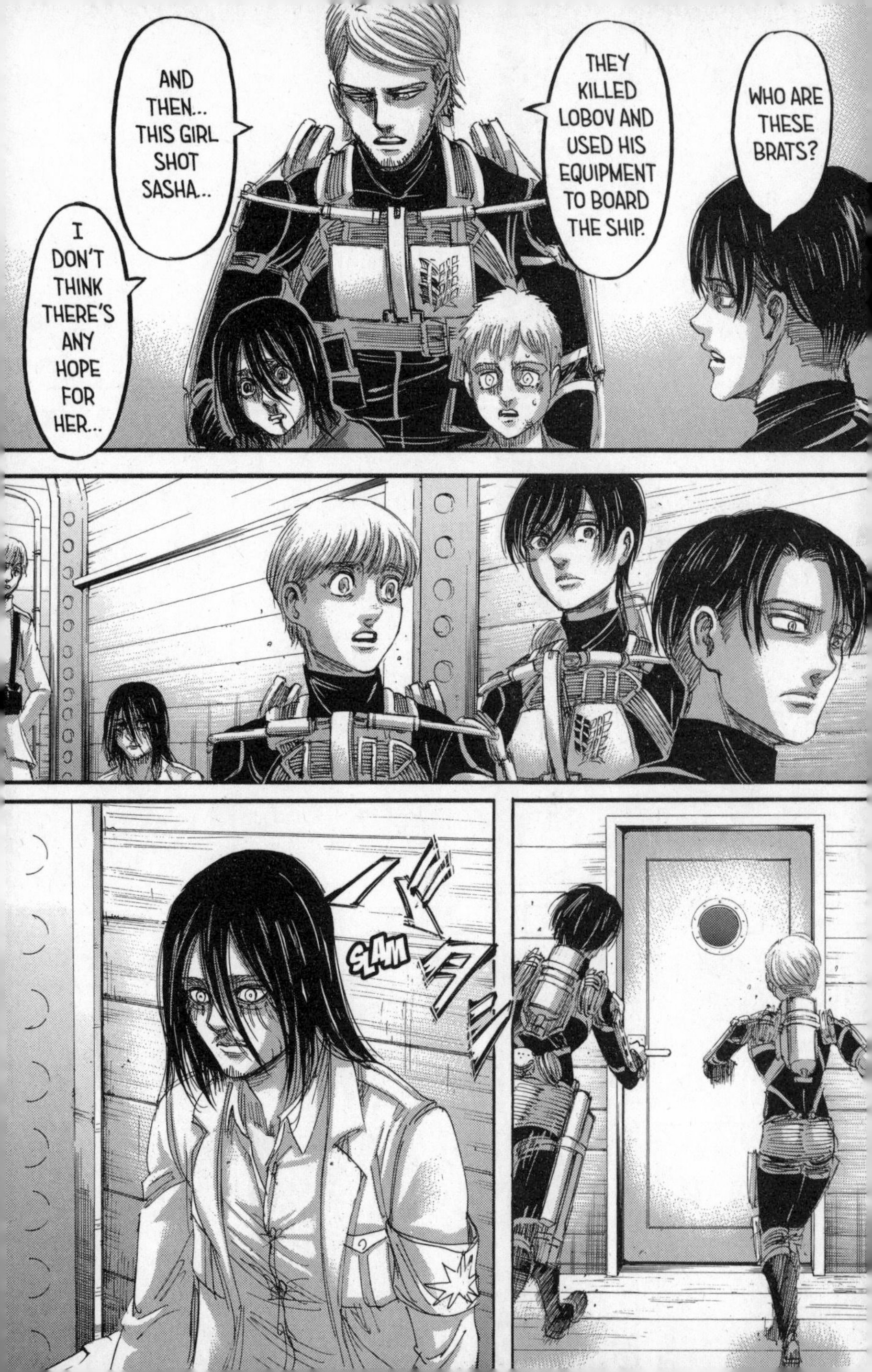
WHO ARE THESE BRATS?
THEY KILLED LOBOV AND USED HIS EQUIPMENT TO BOARD THE SHIP.
AND THEN... THIS GIRL SHOT SASHA...
I DON'T THINK THERE'S ANY HOPE FOR HER...
SLAM

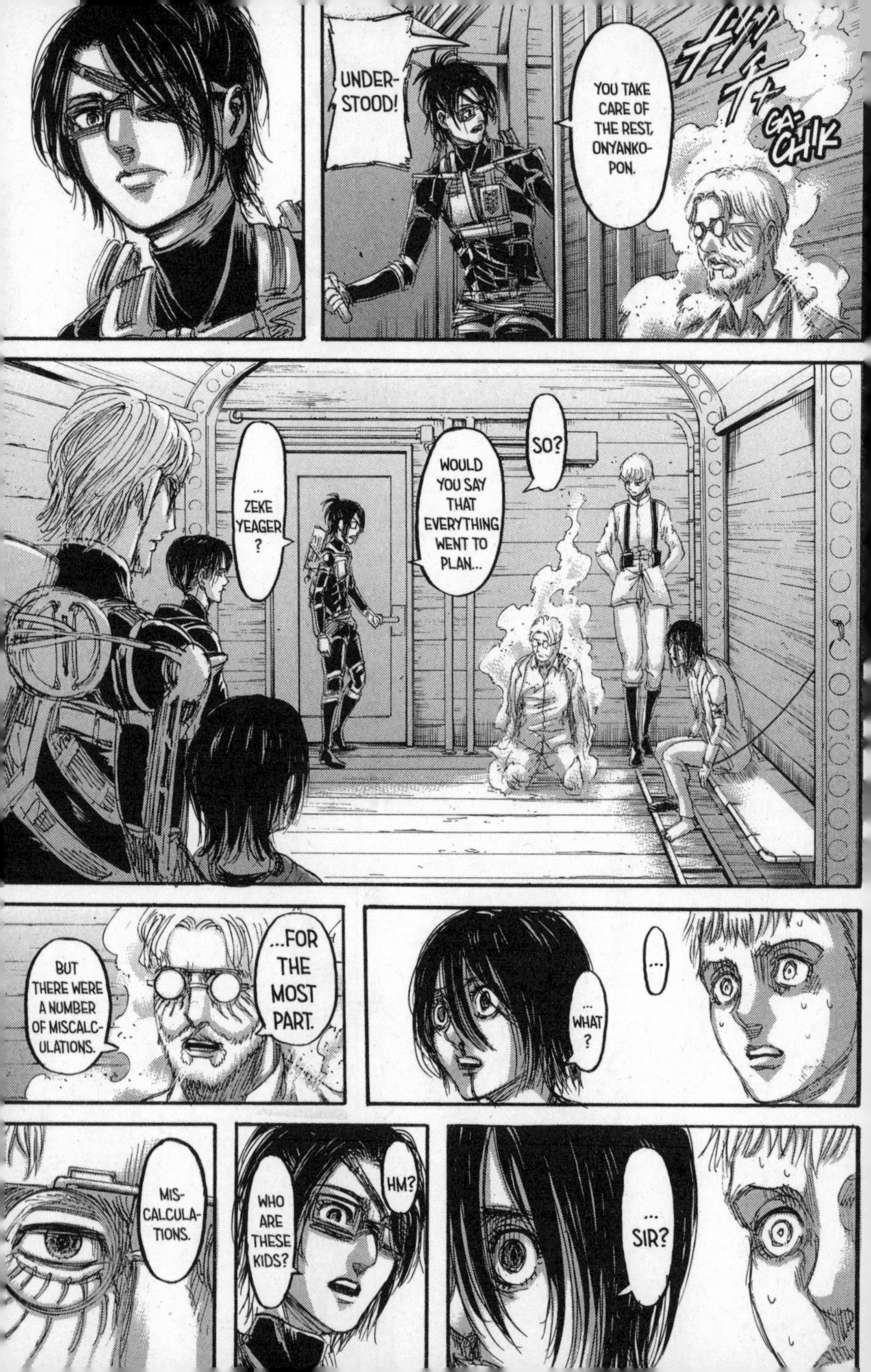
GA-CHIK
YOU TAKE CARE OF THE REST, ONYANKOPON.
UNDER-STOOD!
SO?
WOULD YOU SAY THAT EVERYTHING WENT TO PLAN...
...ZEKE YEAGER?
...
...WHAT?
...FOR THE MOST PART.
BUT THERE WERE A NUMBER OF MISCALC-ULATIONS.
...SIR?
HM?
WHO ARE THESE KIDS?
MIS-CALCULA-TIONS.

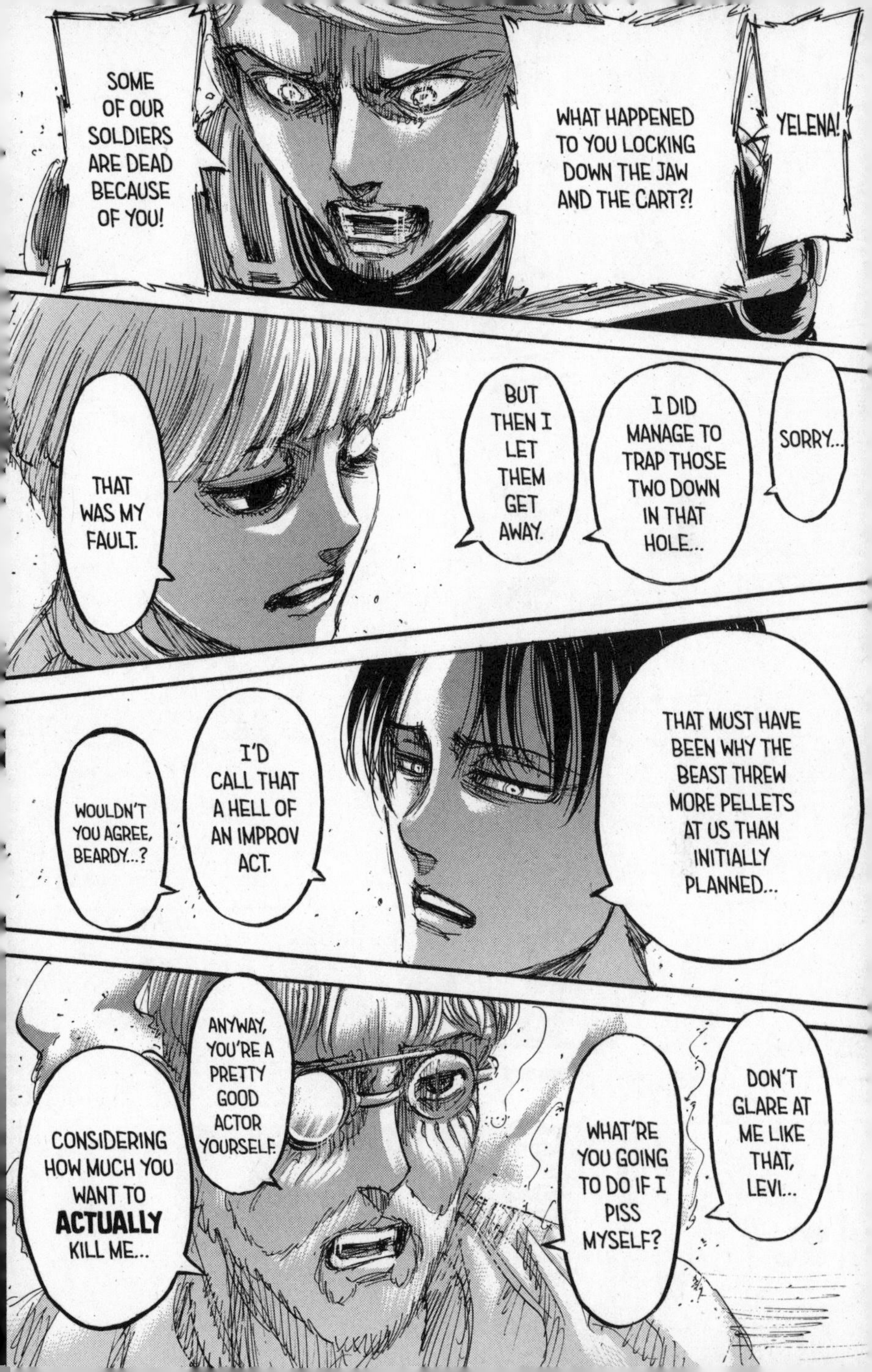
YELENA!
WHAT HAPPENED TO YOU LOCKING DOWN THE JAW AND THE CART?!
SOME OF OUR SOLDIERS ARE DEAD BECAUSE OF YOU!
SORRY...
I DID MANAGE TO TRAP THOSE TWO DOWN IN THAT HOLE...
BUT THEN I LET THEM GET AWAY.
THAT WAS MY FAULT.
THAT MUST HAVE BEEN WHY THE BEAST THREW MORE PELLETS AT US THAN INITIALLY PLANNED...
I'D CALL THAT A HELL OF AN IMPROV ACT.
WOULDN'T YOU AGREE, BEARDY...?
DON'T GLARE AT ME LIKE THAT, LEVI...
WHAT'RE YOU GOING TO DO IF I PISS MYSELF?
ANYWAY, YOU'RE A PRETTY GOOD ACTOR YOURSELF.
CONSIDERING HOW MUCH YOU WANT TO **ACTUALLY** KILL ME...

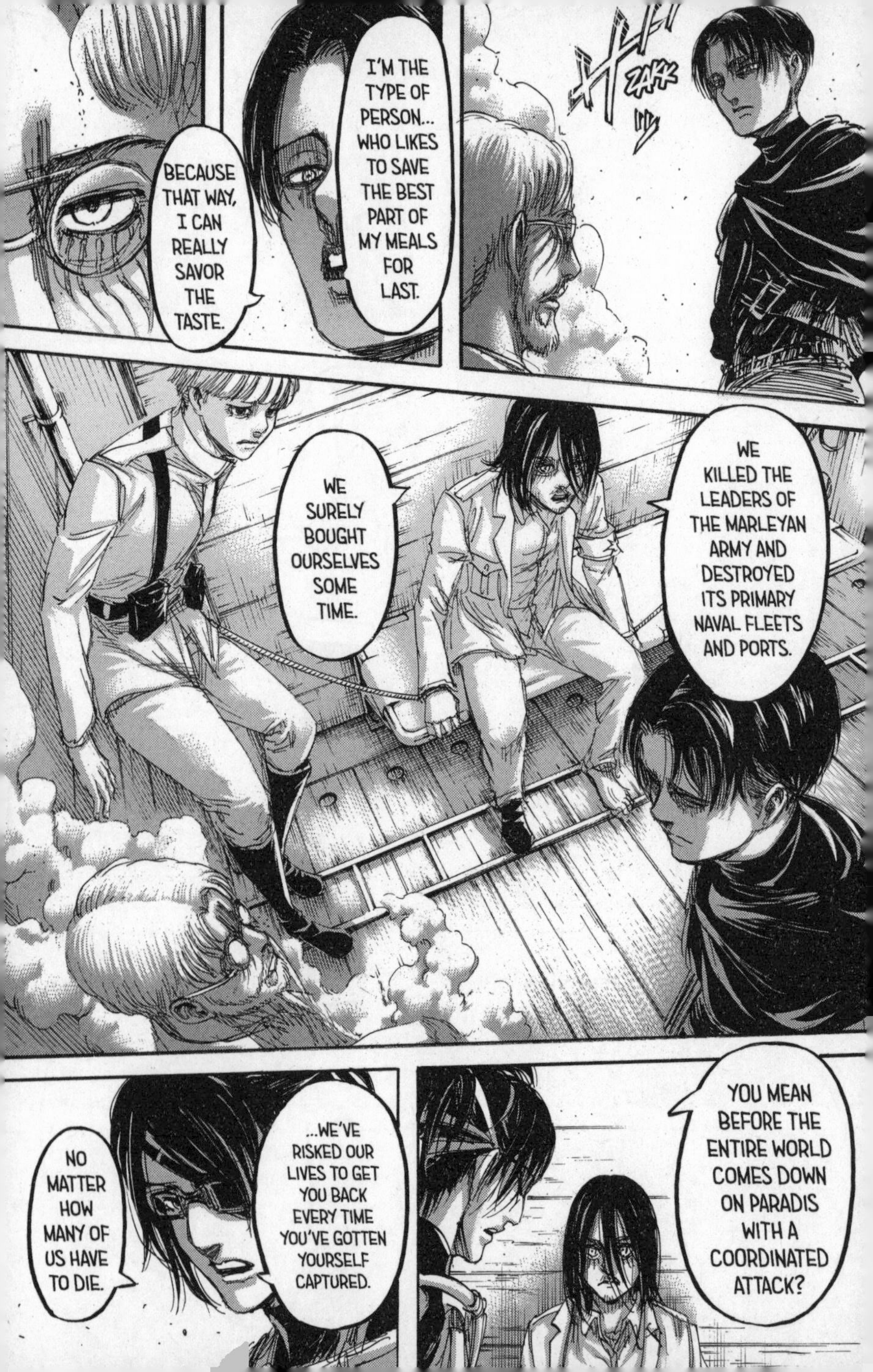
ZAKK
I'M THE TYPE OF PERSON... WHO LIKES TO SAVE THE BEST PART OF MY MEALS FOR LAST.
BECAUSE THAT WAY, I CAN REALLY SAVOR THE TASTE.
WE KILLED THE LEADERS OF THE MARLEYAN ARMY AND DESTROYED ITS PRIMARY NAVAL FLEETS AND PORTS.
WE SURELY BOUGHT OURSELVES SOME TIME.
YOU MEAN BEFORE THE ENTIRE WORLD COMES DOWN ON PARADIS WITH A COORDINATED ATTACK?
...WE'VE RISKED OUR LIVES TO GET YOU BACK EVERY TIME YOU'VE GOTTEN YOURSELF CAPTURED.
NO MATTER HOW MANY OF US HAVE TO DIE.

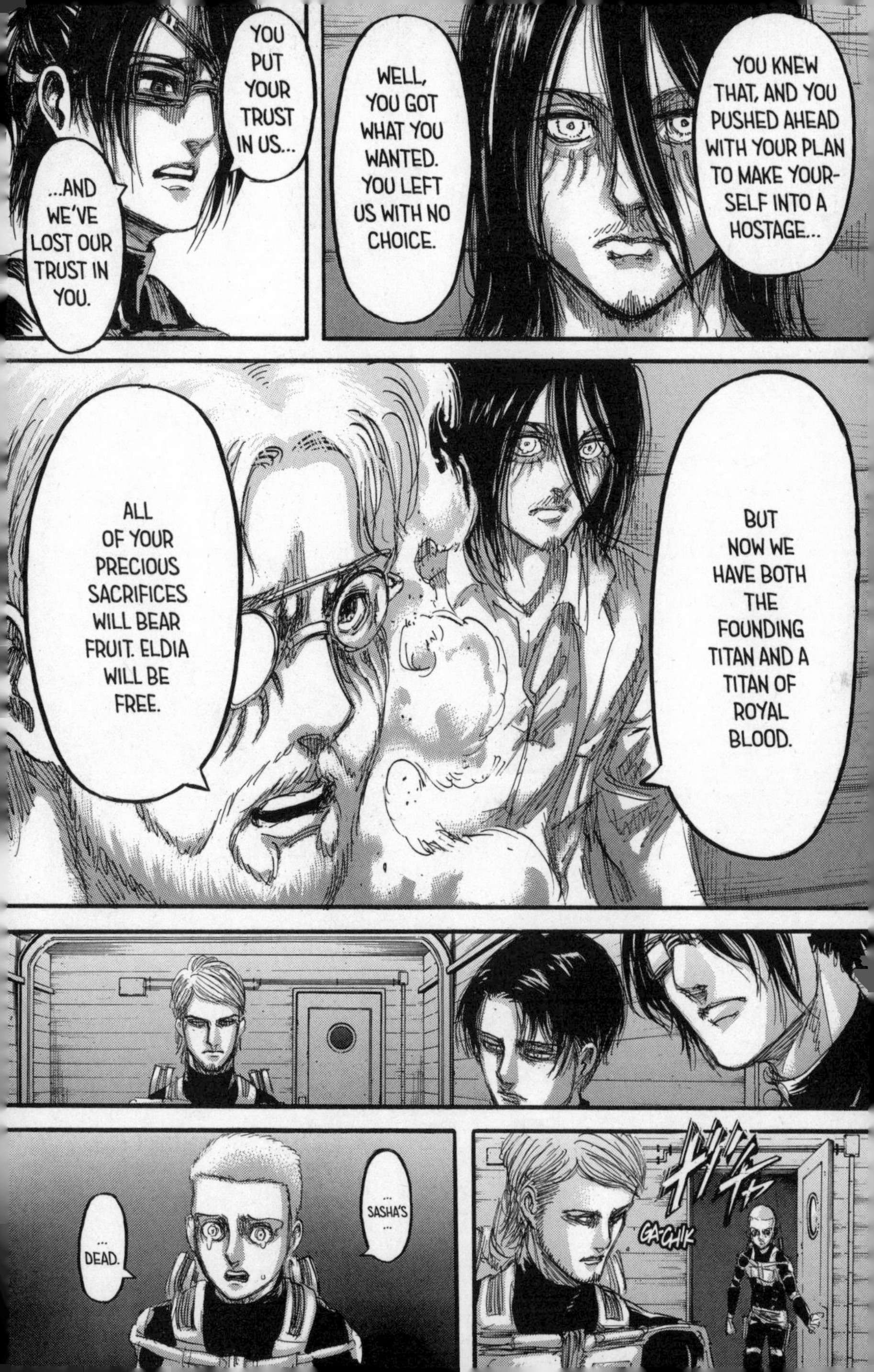
YOU KNEW THAT, AND YOU PUSHED AHEAD WITH YOUR PLAN TO MAKE YOUR-SELF INTO A HOSTAGE...
WELL, YOU GOT WHAT YOU WANTED. YOU LEFT US WITH NO CHOICE.
YOU PUT YOUR TRUST IN US...
...AND WE'VE LOST OUR TRUST IN YOU.
BUT NOW WE HAVE BOTH THE FOUNDING TITAN AND A TITAN OF ROYAL BLOOD.
ALL OF YOUR PRECIOUS SACRIFICES WILL BEAR FRUIT. ELDIA WILL BE FREE.
GA-CHIK
... SASHA'S ...
... DEAD.

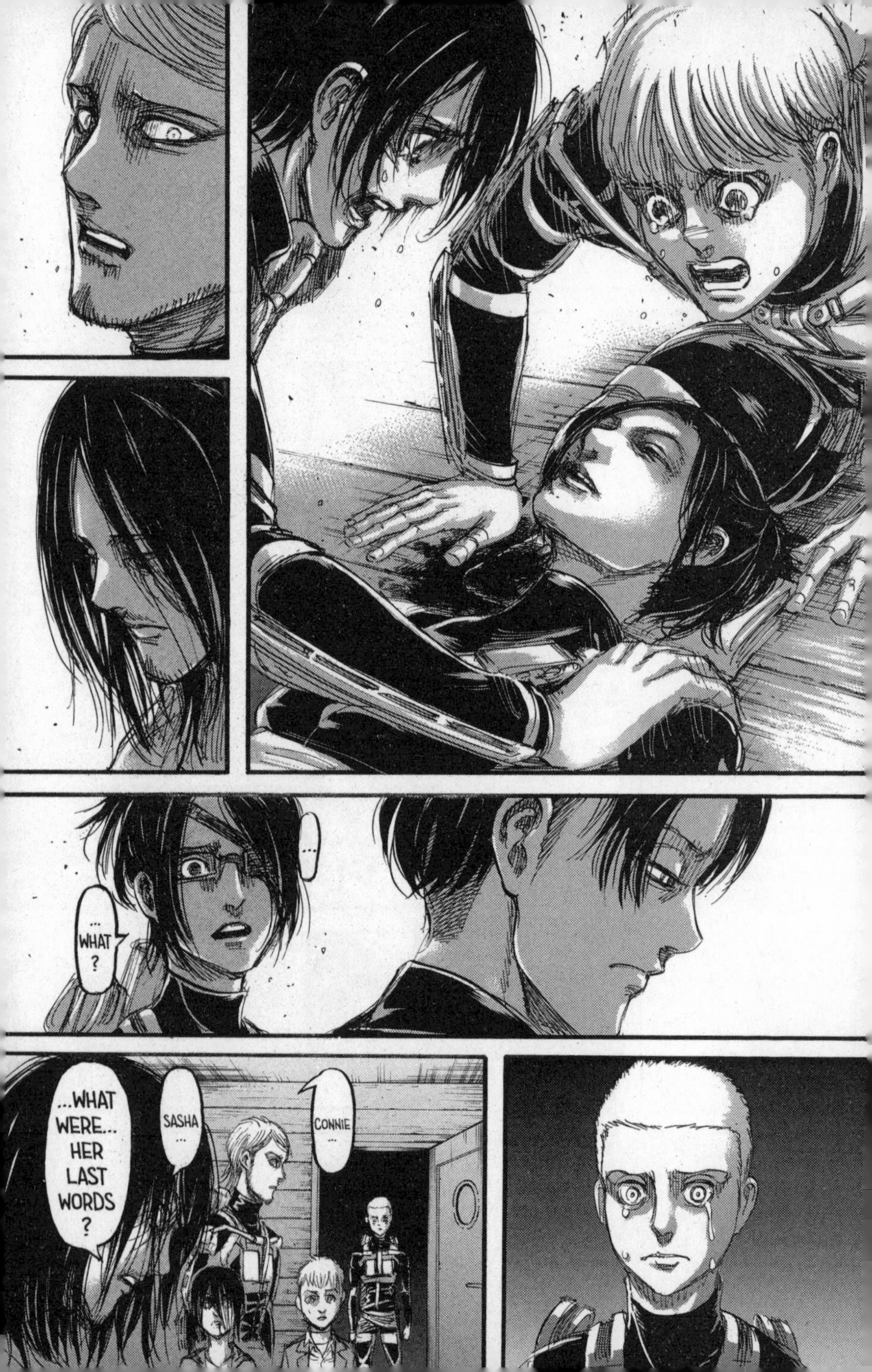
...
... WHAT ?
CONNIE ...
SASHA ...
...WHAT WERE... HER LAST WORDS ?

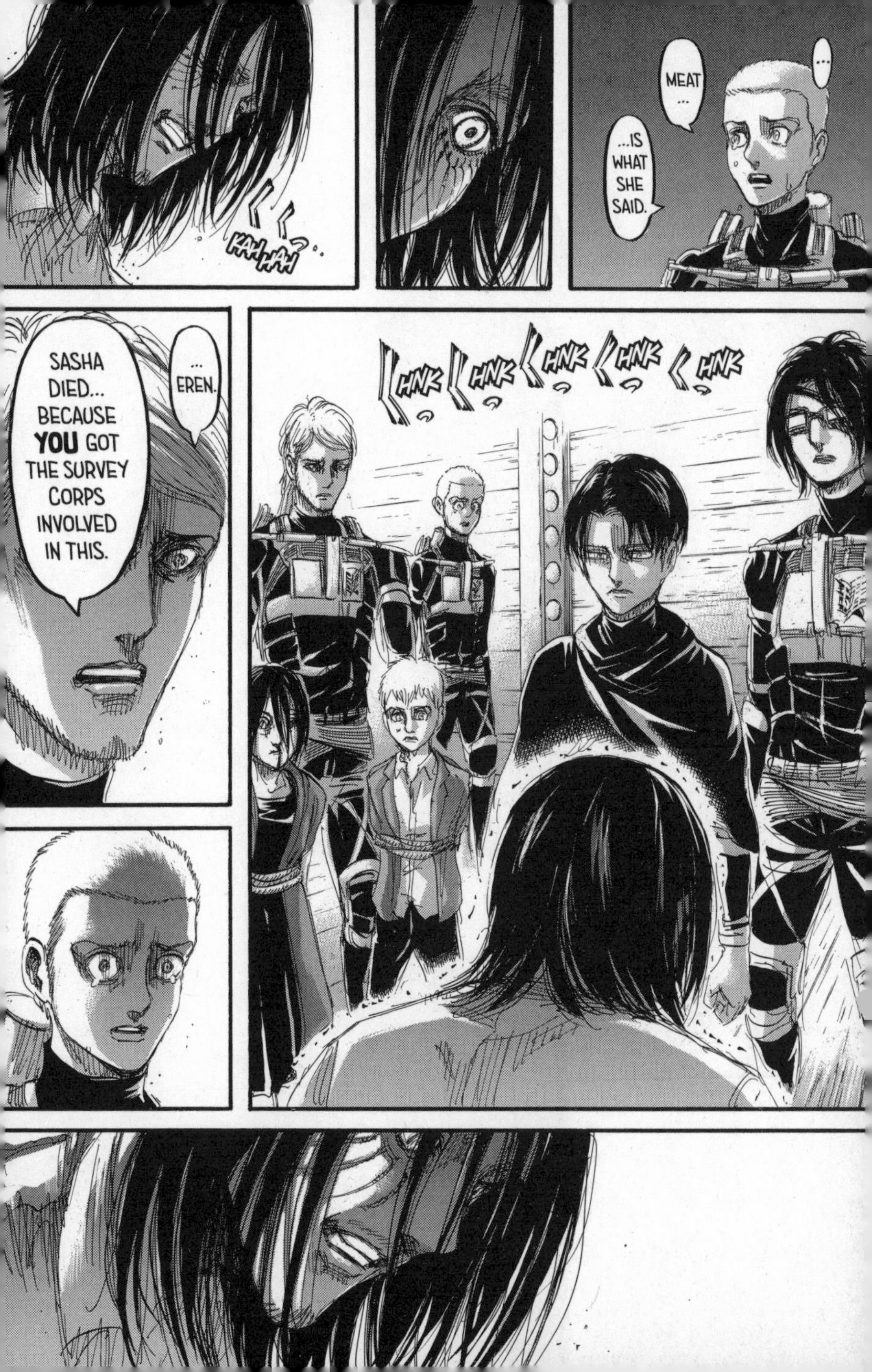
...
MEAT ...
...IS WHAT SHE SAID.
KAH HAH
HNK HNK HNK HNK HNK
... EREN.
SASHA DIED... BECAUSE YOU GOT THE SURVEY CORPS INVOLVED IN THIS.

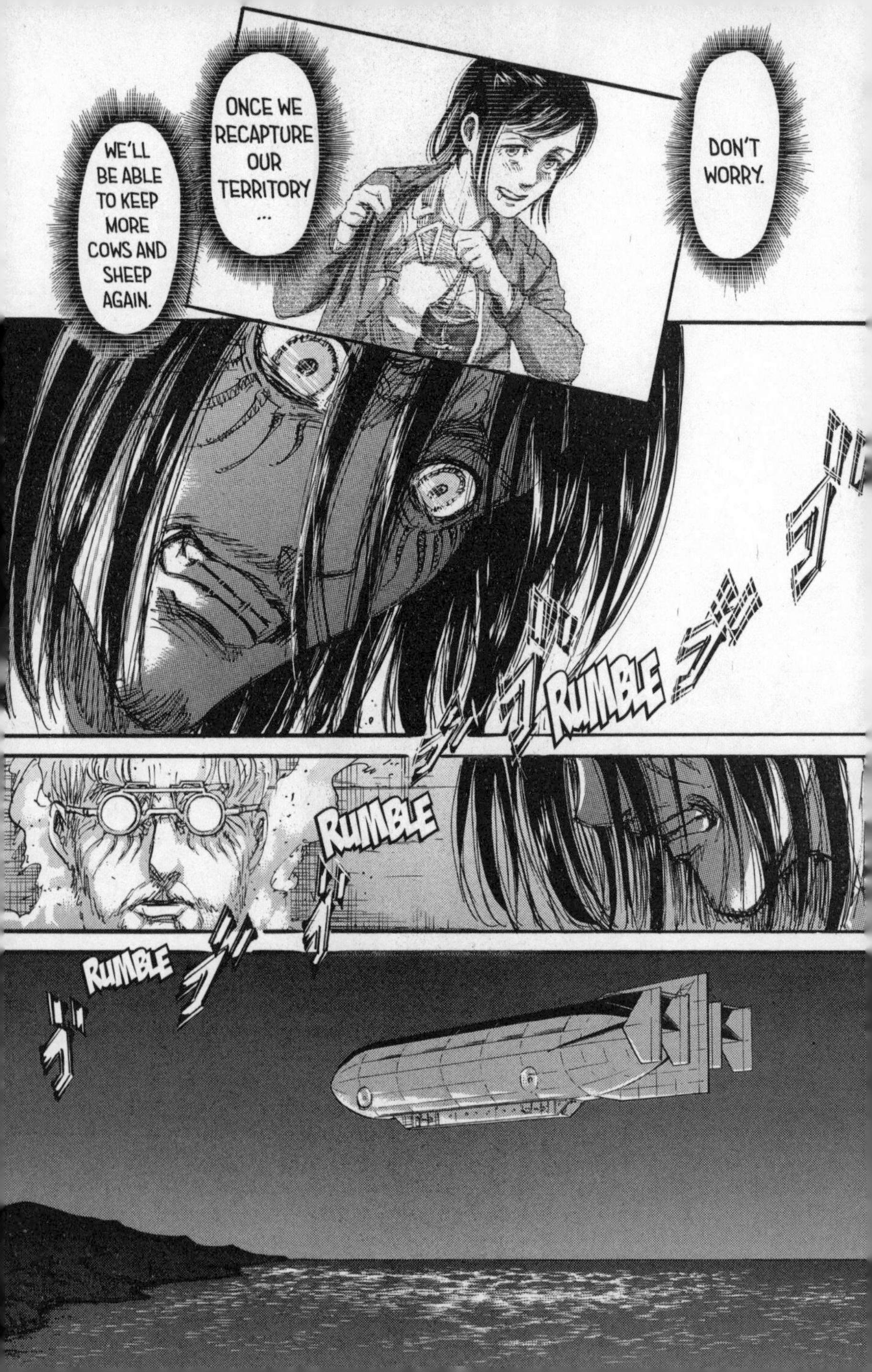
DON'T WORRY.
ONCE WE RECAPTURE OUR TERRITORY ...
WE'LL BE ABLE TO KEEP MORE COWS AND SHEEP AGAIN.
RUMBLE
RUMBLE
RUMBLE

ATTACK on TITAN

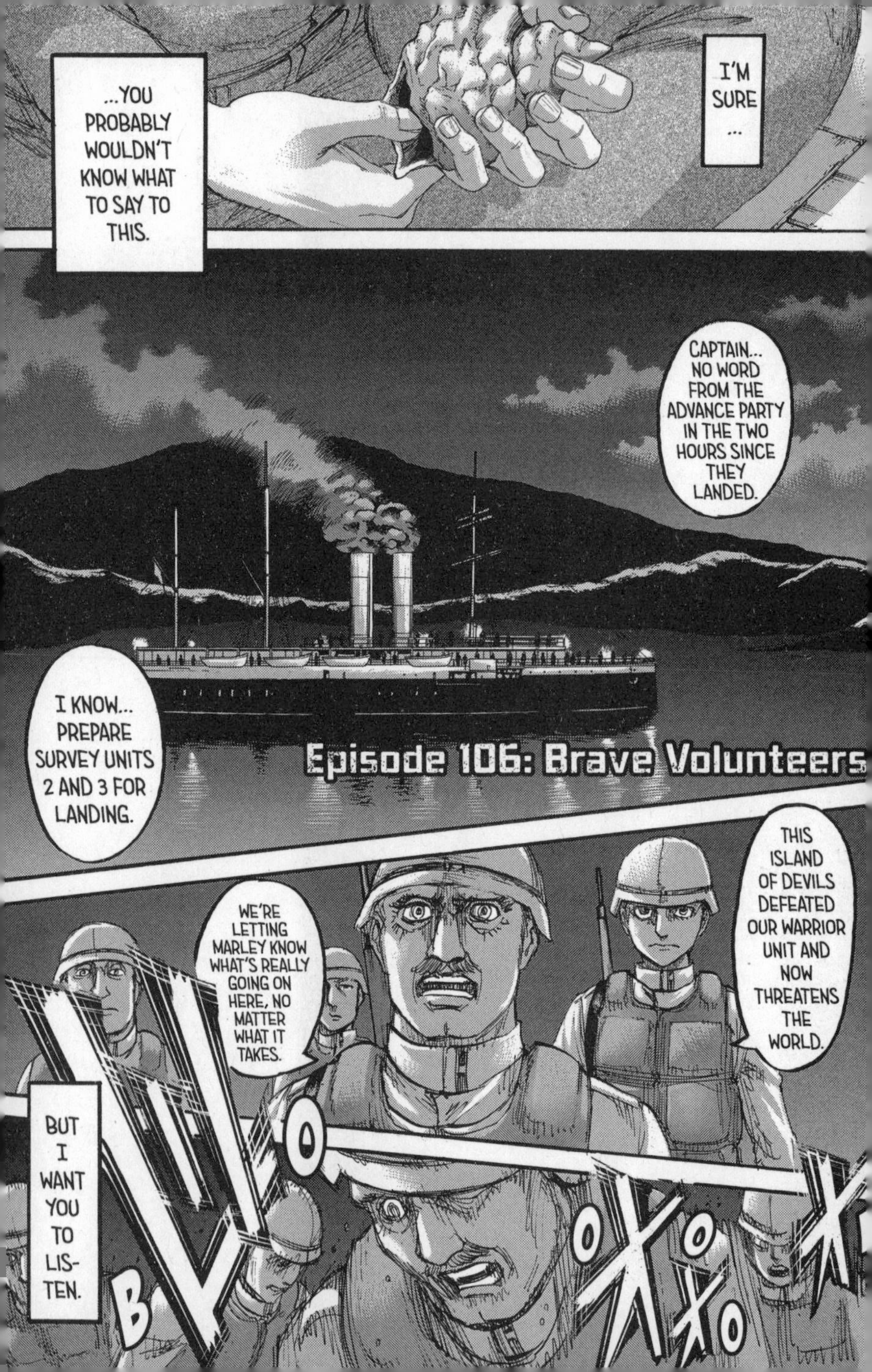
I'M SURE ...
...YOU PROBABLY WOULDN'T KNOW WHAT TO SAY TO THIS.
CAPTAIN... NO WORD FROM THE ADVANCE PARTY IN THE TWO HOURS SINCE THEY LANDED.
I KNOW... PREPARE SURVEY UNITS 2 AND 3 FOR LANDING.
Episode 106: Brave Volunteers
THIS ISLAND OF DEVILS DEFEATED OUR WARRIOR UNIT AND NOW THREATENS THE WORLD.
WE'RE LETTING MARLEY KNOW WHAT'S REALLY GOING ON HERE, NO MATTER WHAT IT TAKES.
BUT I WANT YOU TO LIS-TEN.

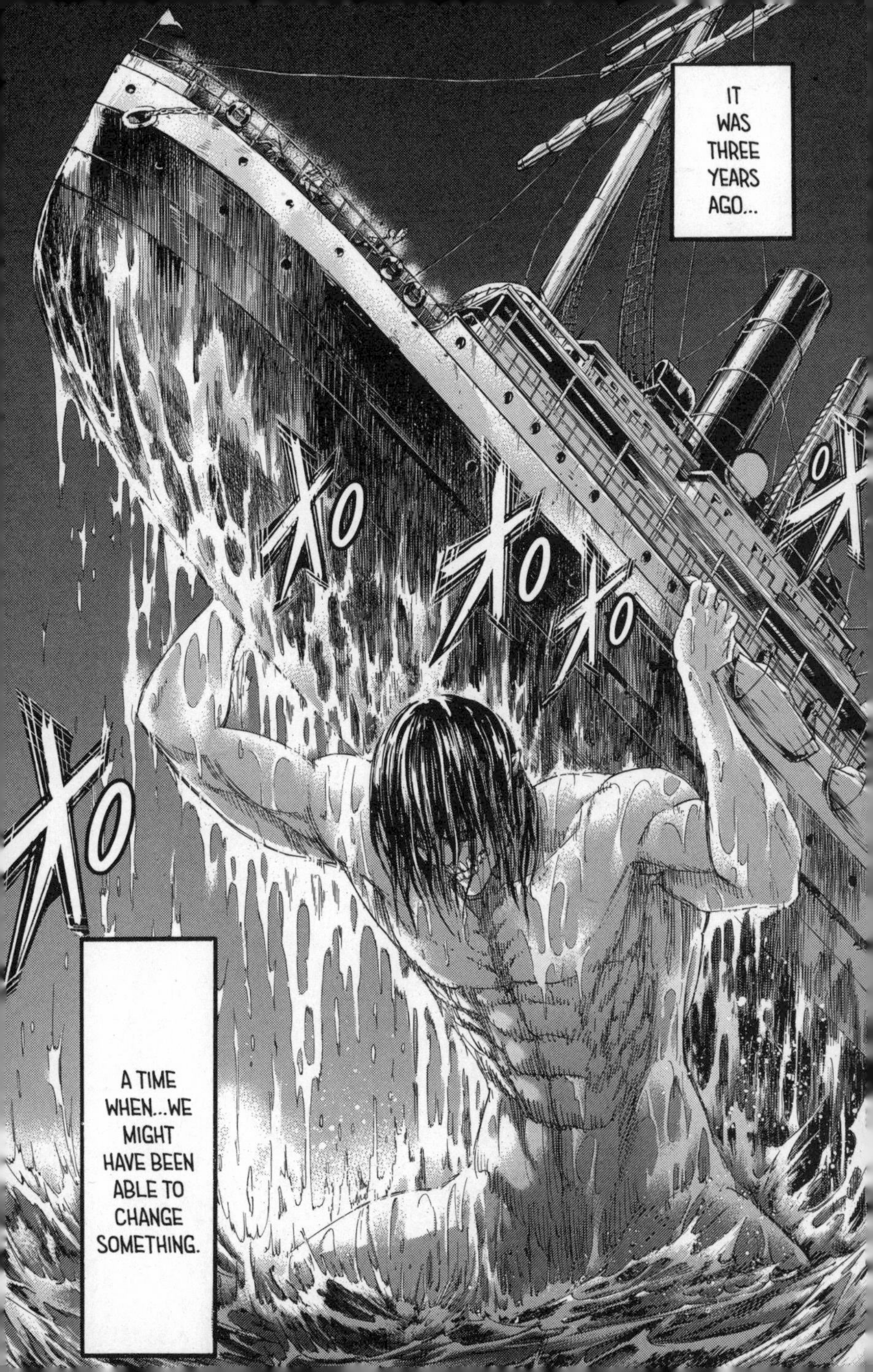
IT WAS THREE YEARS AGO...
A TIME WHEN...WE MIGHT HAVE BEEN ABLE TO CHANGE SOMETHING.

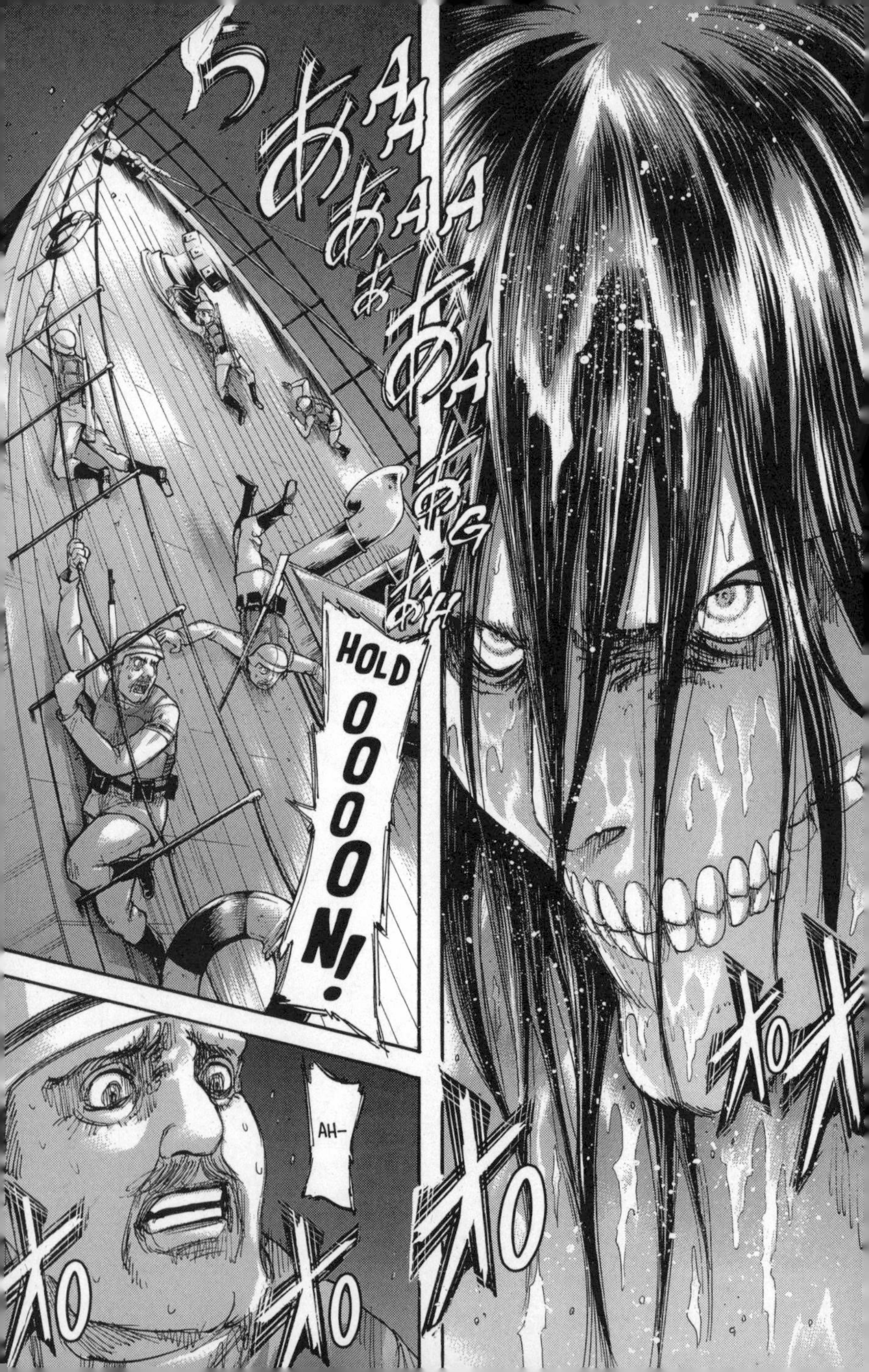
AAAAAAARGH
HOLD OOOOOON!
AH—

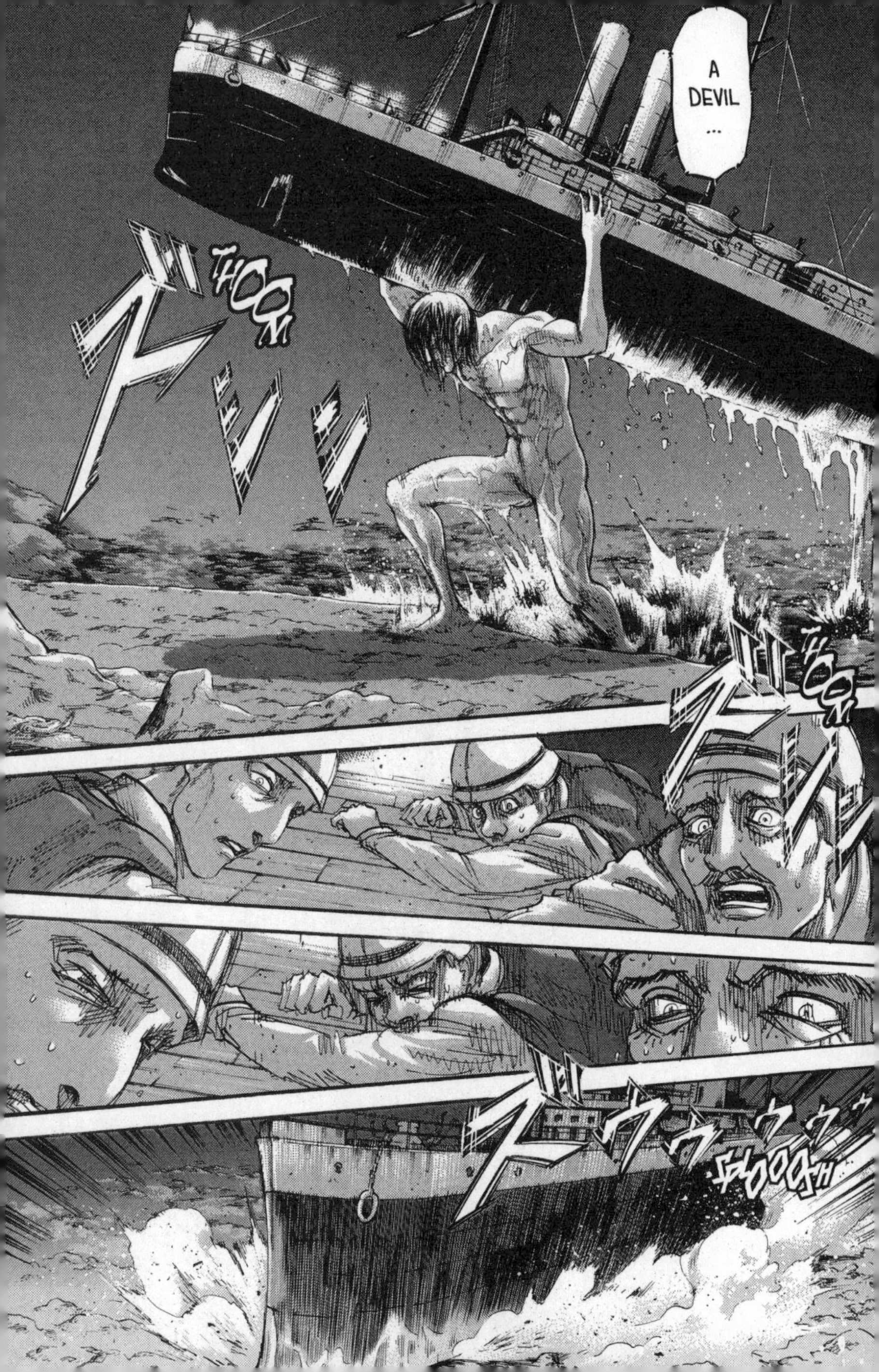
A DEVIL ...
THOOM
THOOM
SPLOOSH

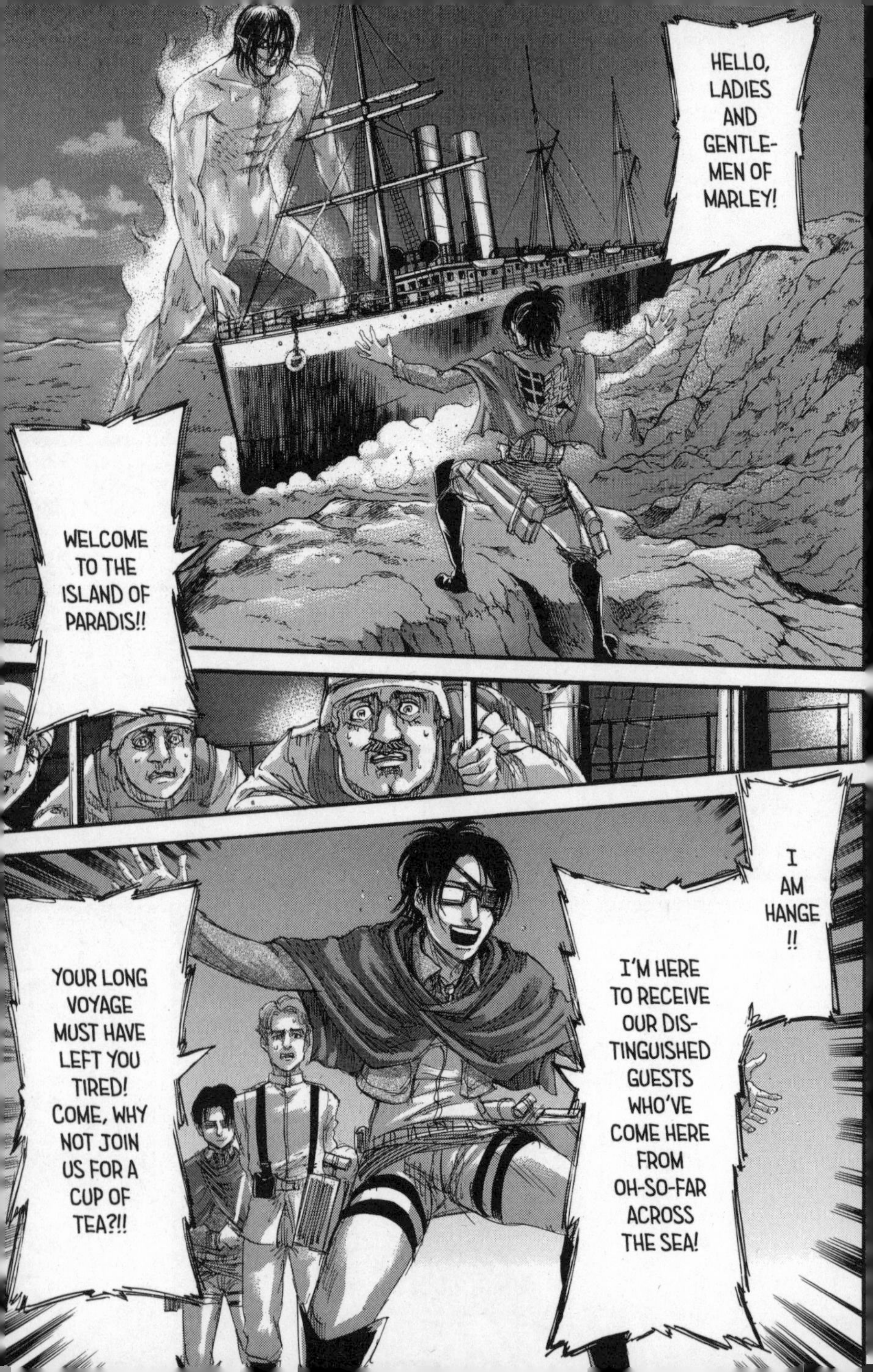
HELLO, LADIES AND GENTLE- MEN OF MARLEY!
WELCOME TO THE ISLAND OF PARADIS!!
I AM HANGE !!
I'M HERE TO RECEIVE OUR DIS- TINGUISHED GUESTS WHO'VE COME HERE FROM OH-SO-FAR ACROSS THE SEA!
YOUR LONG VOYAGE MUST HAVE LEFT YOU TIRED! COME, WHY NOT JOIN US FOR A CUP OF TEA?!!

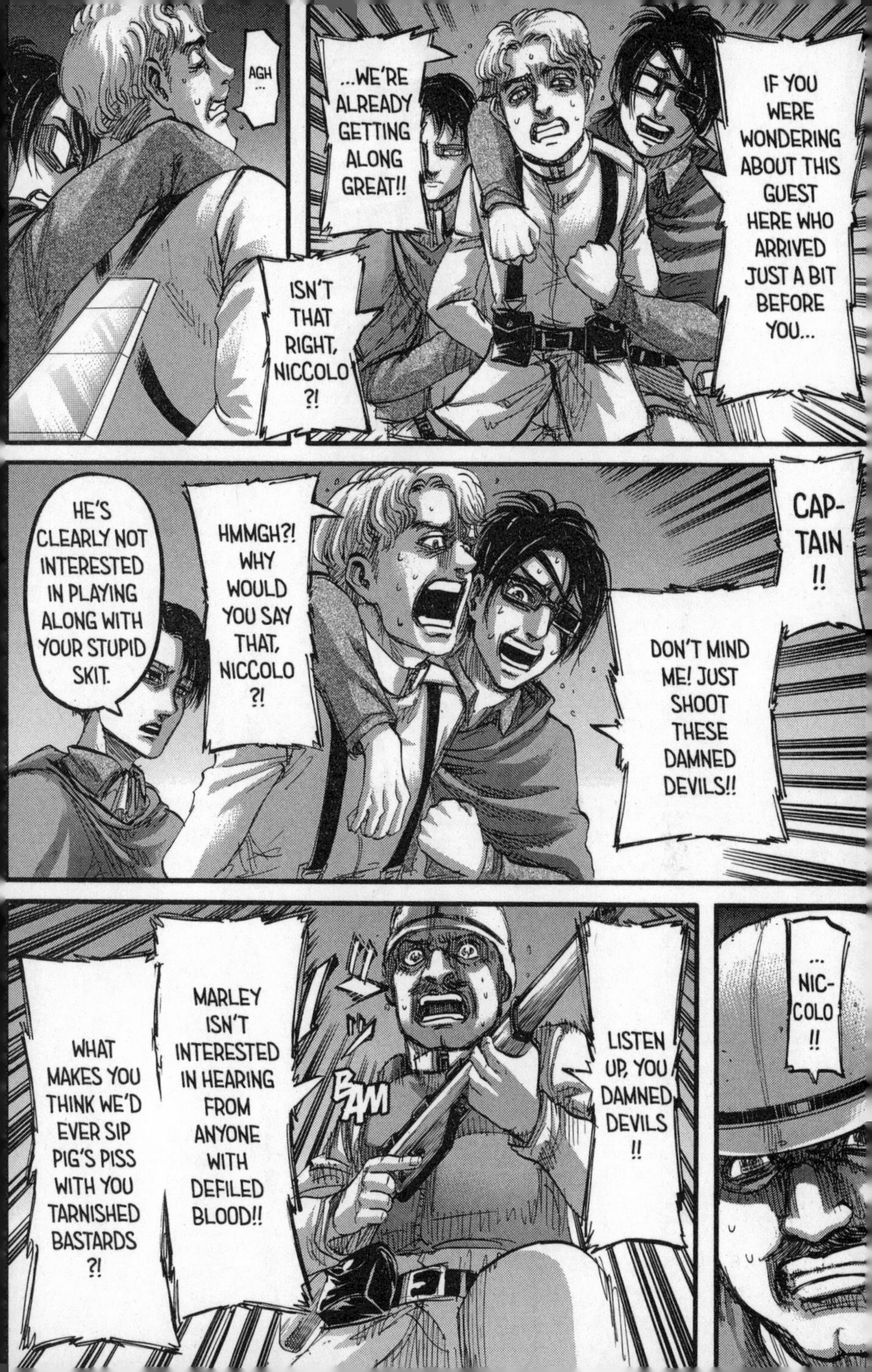
IF YOU WERE WONDERING ABOUT THIS GUEST HERE WHO ARRIVED JUST A BIT BEFORE YOU...
...WE'RE ALREADY GETTING ALONG GREAT!!
ISN'T THAT RIGHT, NICCOLO?!
AGH...
CAPTAIN!!
DON'T MIND ME! JUST SHOOT THESE DAMNED DEVILS!!
HMMGH?! WHY WOULD YOU SAY THAT, NICCOLO?!
HE'S CLEARLY NOT INTERESTED IN PLAYING ALONG WITH YOUR STUPID SKIT.
...NICCOLO!!
LISTEN UP, YOU DAMNED DEVILS!!
BAM
MARLEY ISN'T INTERESTED IN HEARING FROM ANYONE WITH DEFILED BLOOD!!
WHAT MAKES YOU THINK WE'D EVER SIP PIG'S PISS WITH YOU TARNISHED BASTARDS?!

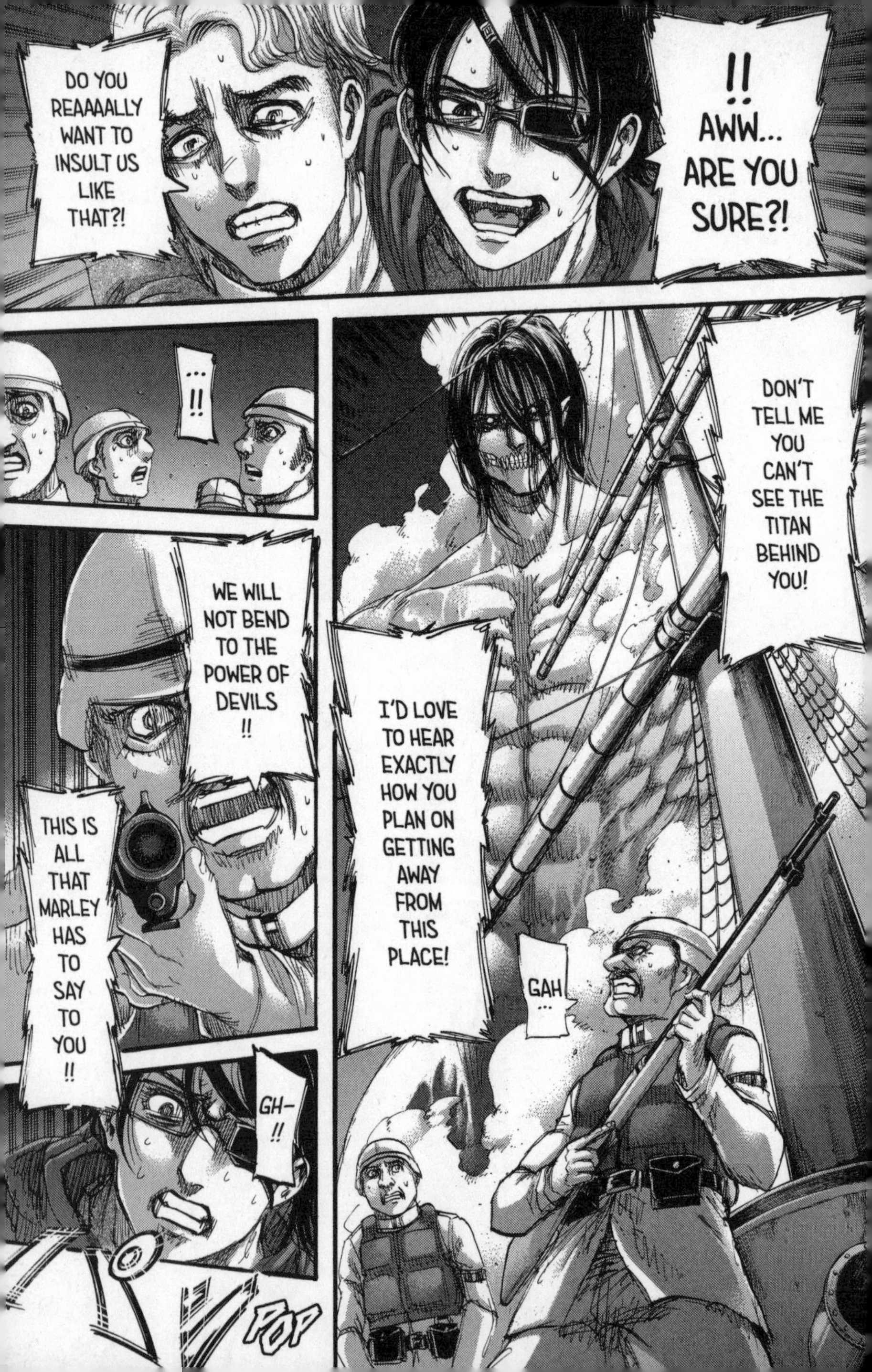
!! AWW... ARE YOU SURE?!
DO YOU REAAAALLY WANT TO INSULT US LIKE THAT?!
DON'T TELL ME YOU CAN'T SEE THE TITAN BEHIND YOU!
I'D LOVE TO HEAR EXACTLY HOW YOU PLAN ON GETTING AWAY FROM THIS PLACE!
GAH...
...!!
WE WILL NOT BEND TO THE POWER OF DEVILS!!
THIS IS ALL THAT MARLEY HAS TO SAY TO YOU!!
GH-!!
POP

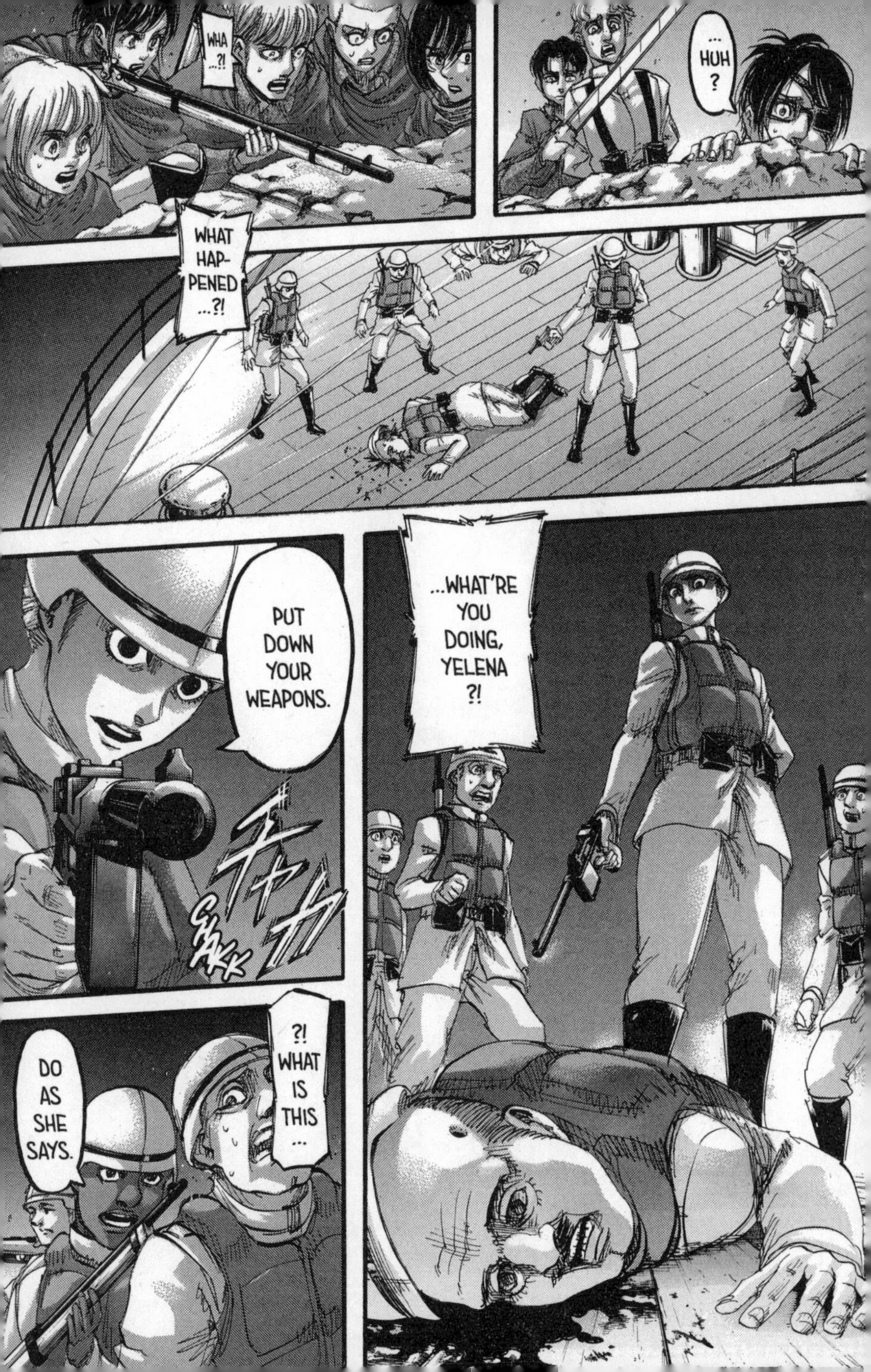
... HUH ?
WHA ...?!
WHAT HAP-PENED ...?!
...WHAT'RE YOU DOING, YELENA ?!
PUT DOWN YOUR WEAPONS.
CHAKK
?! WHAT IS THIS ...
DO AS SHE SAYS.

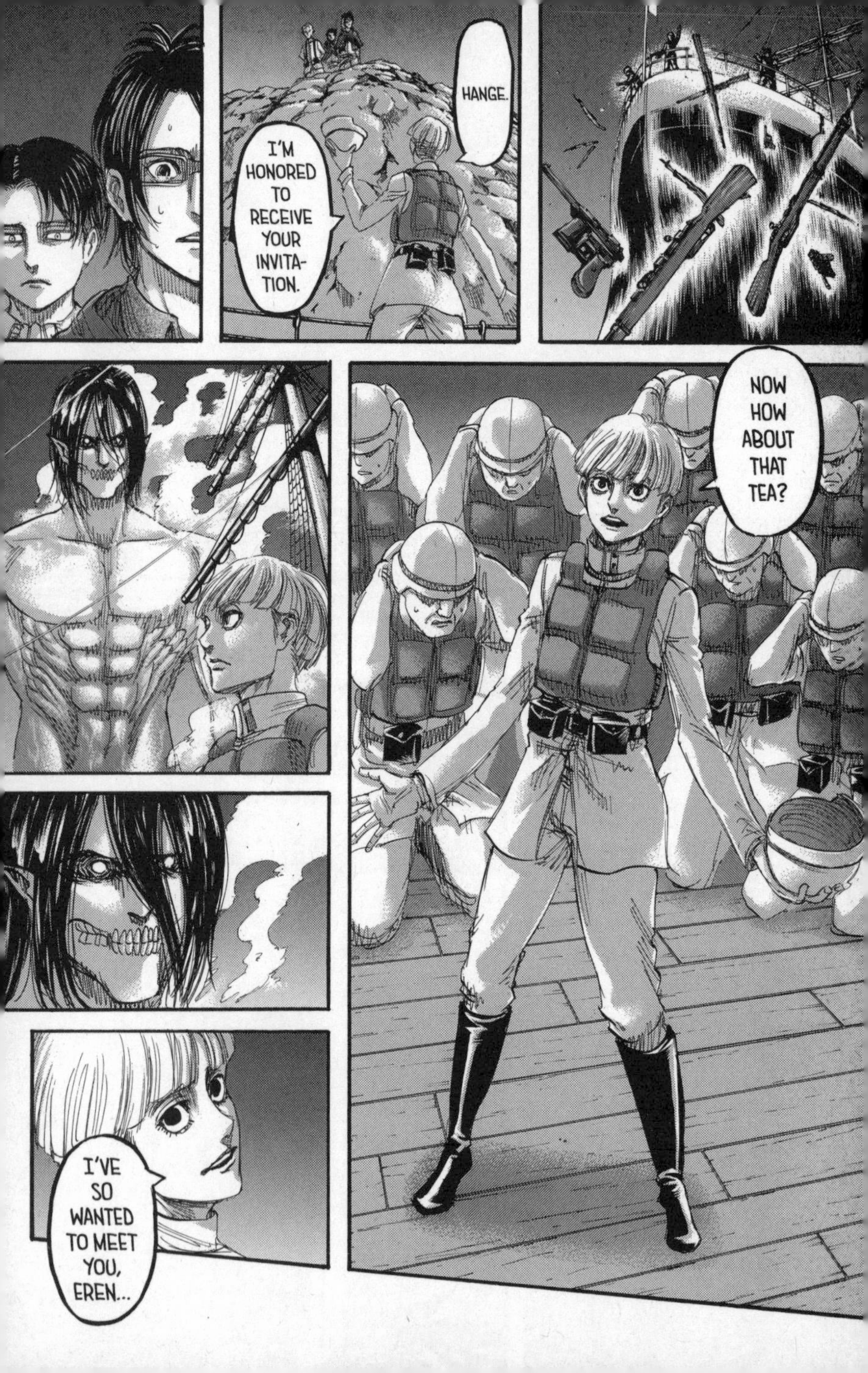
HANGE.
I'M HONORED TO RECEIVE YOUR INVITATION.
NOW HOW ABOUT THAT TEA?
I'VE SO WANTED TO MEET YOU, EREN...

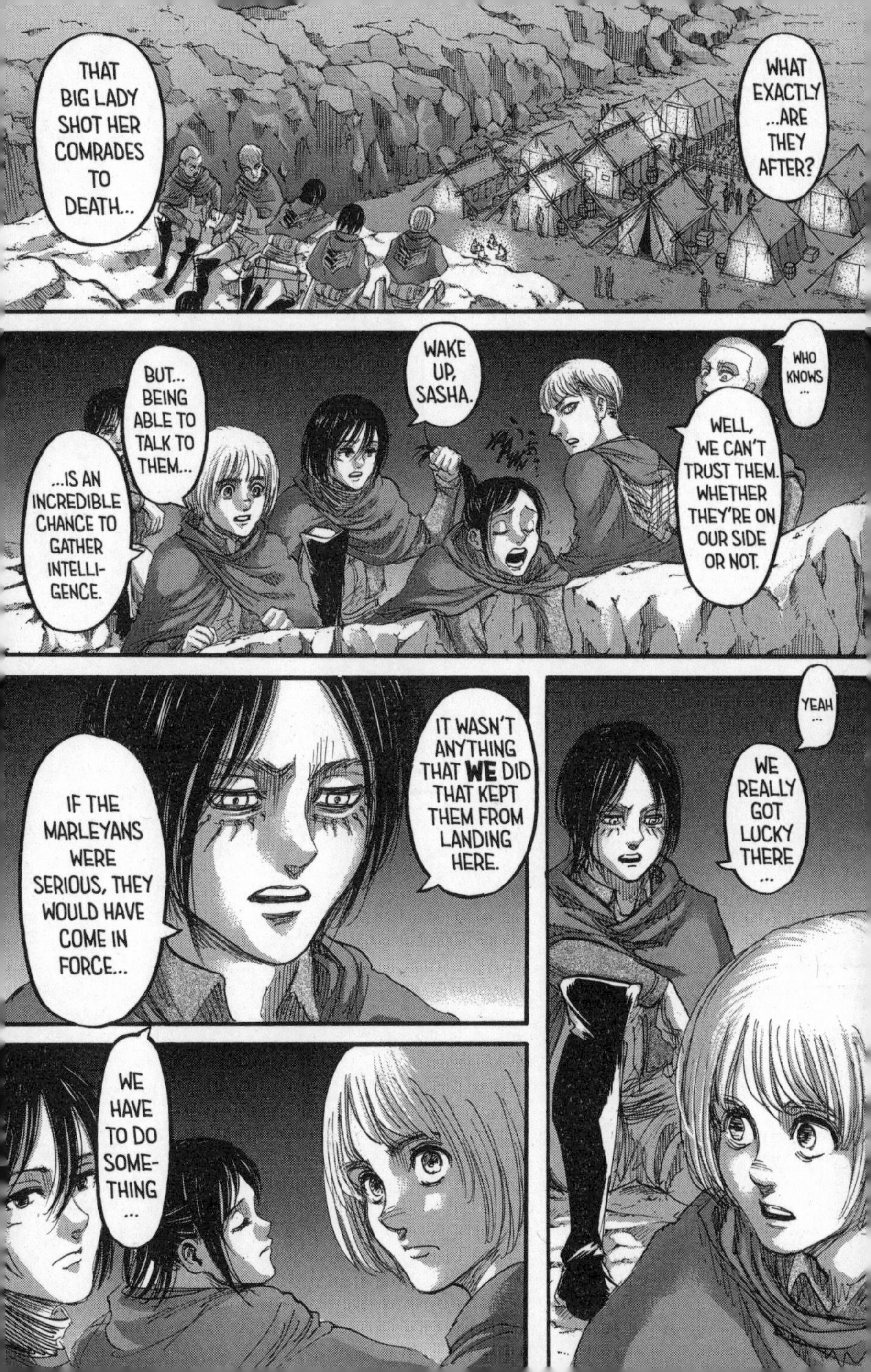
WHAT EXACTLY ...ARE THEY AFTER?
THAT BIG LADY SHOT HER COMRADES TO DEATH...
WHO KNOWS ...
WELL, WE CAN'T TRUST THEM. WHETHER THEY'RE ON OUR SIDE OR NOT.
WAKE UP, SASHA.
BUT... BEING ABLE TO TALK TO THEM...
...IS AN INCREDIBLE CHANCE TO GATHER INTELLIGENCE.
YEAH ...
WE REALLY GOT LUCKY THERE ...
IT WASN'T ANYTHING THAT **WE** DID THAT KEPT THEM FROM LANDING HERE.
IF THE MARLEYANS WERE SERIOUS, THEY WOULD HAVE COME IN FORCE...
WE HAVE TO DO SOMETHING ...

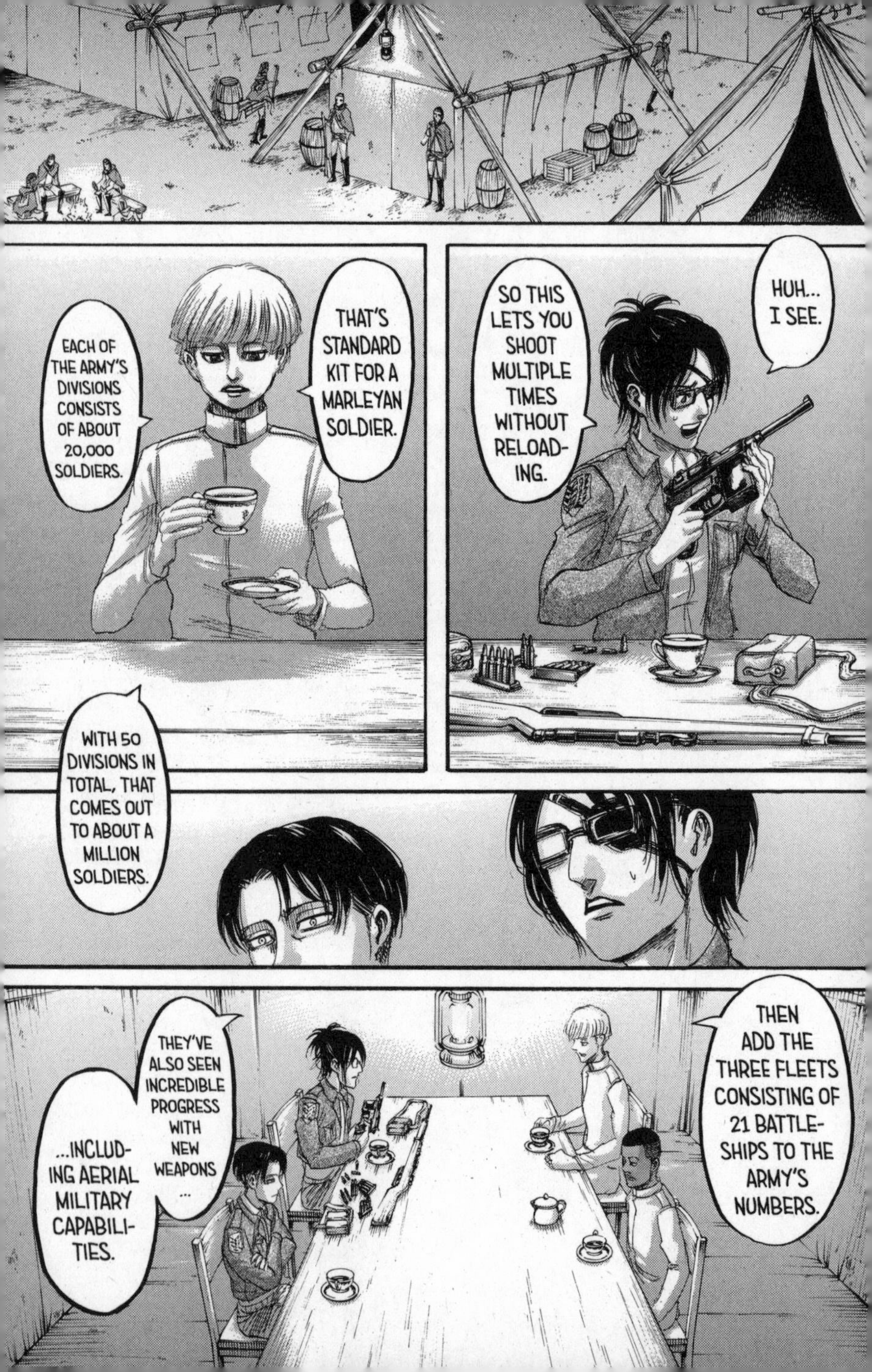
HUH... I SEE.
SO THIS LETS YOU SHOOT MULTIPLE TIMES WITHOUT RELOAD-ING.
THAT'S STANDARD KIT FOR A MARLEYAN SOLDIER.
EACH OF THE ARMY'S DIVISIONS CONSISTS OF ABOUT 20,000 SOLDIERS.
WITH 50 DIVISIONS IN TOTAL, THAT COMES OUT TO ABOUT A MILLION SOLDIERS.
THEN ADD THE THREE FLEETS CONSISTING OF 21 BATTLE-SHIPS TO THE ARMY'S NUMBERS.
THEY'VE ALSO SEEN INCREDIBLE PROGRESS WITH NEW WEAPONS ...
...INCLUD-ING AERIAL MILITARY CAPABILI-TIES.

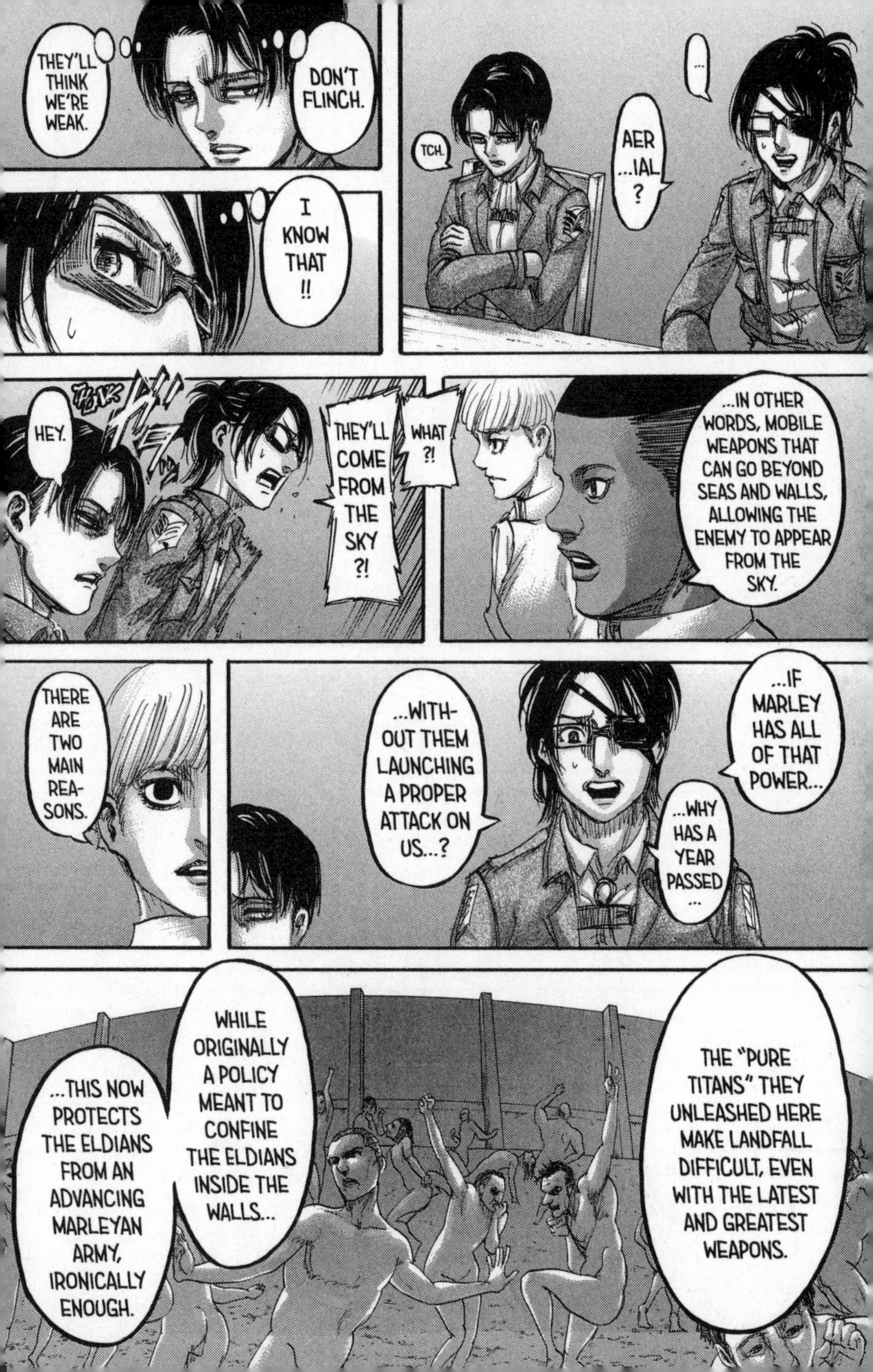
...
AER ...IAL ?
TCH.
DON'T FLINCH.
THEY'LL THINK WE'RE WEAK.
I KNOW THAT !!
...IN OTHER WORDS, MOBILE WEAPONS THAT CAN GO BEYOND SEAS AND WALLS, ALLOWING THE ENEMY TO APPEAR FROM THE SKY.
WHAT ?!
THEY'LL COME FROM THE SKY ?!
HEY.
...IF MARLEY HAS ALL OF THAT POWER...
...WHY HAS A YEAR PASSED ...
...WITH-OUT THEM LAUNCHING A PROPER ATTACK ON US...?
THERE ARE TWO MAIN REA-SONS.
THE "PURE TITANS" THEY UNLEASHED HERE MAKE LANDFALL DIFFICULT, EVEN WITH THE LATEST AND GREATEST WEAPONS.
WHILE ORIGINALLY A POLICY MEANT TO CONFINE THE ELDIANS INSIDE THE WALLS...
...THIS NOW PROTECTS THE ELDIANS FROM AN ADVANCING MARLEYAN ARMY, IRONICALLY ENOUGH.

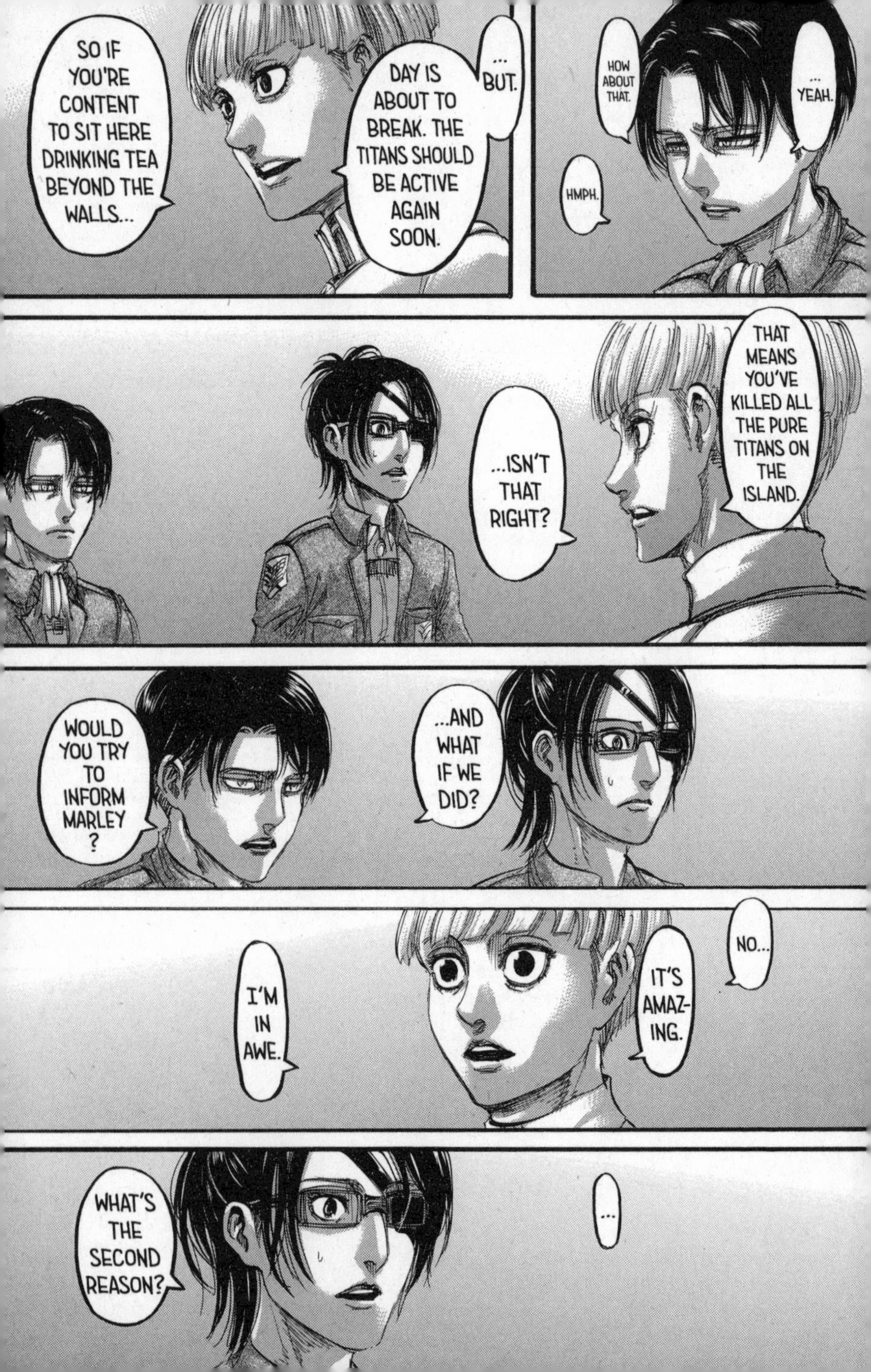

... YEAH.
HOW ABOUT THAT.
HMPH.
... BUT.
DAY IS ABOUT TO BREAK. THE TITANS SHOULD BE ACTIVE AGAIN SOON.
SO IF YOU'RE CONTENT TO SIT HERE DRINKING TEA BEYOND THE WALLS...
THAT MEANS YOU'VE KILLED ALL THE PURE TITANS ON THE ISLAND.
...ISN'T THAT RIGHT?
...AND WHAT IF WE DID?
WOULD YOU TRY TO INFORM MARLEY ?
NO...
IT'S AMAZ-ING.
I'M IN AWE.
...
WHAT'S THE SECOND REASON?

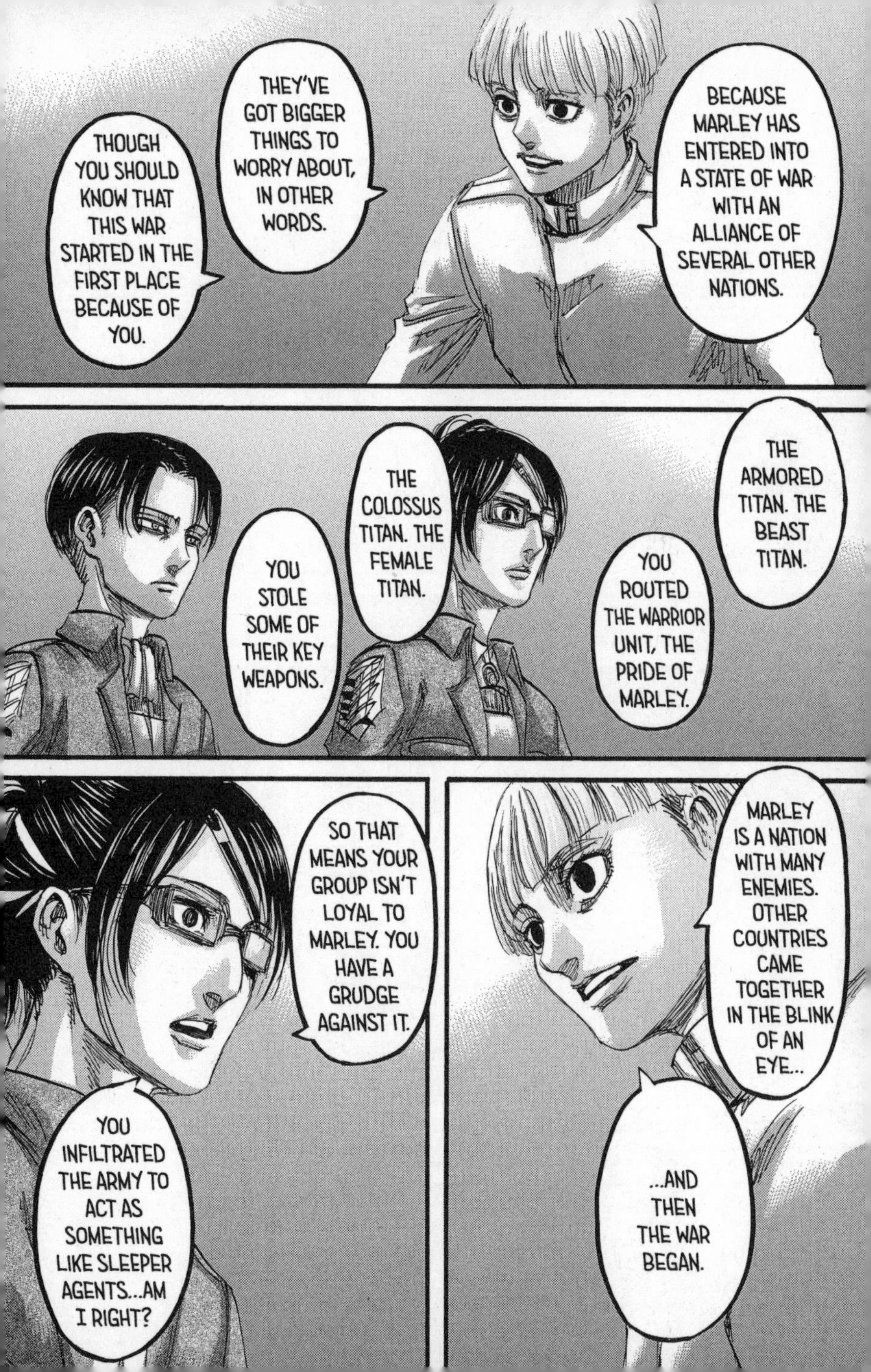
BECAUSE MARLEY HAS ENTERED INTO A STATE OF WAR WITH AN ALLIANCE OF SEVERAL OTHER NATIONS.
THEY'VE GOT BIGGER THINGS TO WORRY ABOUT, IN OTHER WORDS.
THOUGH YOU SHOULD KNOW THAT THIS WAR STARTED IN THE FIRST PLACE BECAUSE OF YOU.
THE ARMORED TITAN. THE BEAST TITAN.
YOU ROUTED THE WARRIOR UNIT, THE PRIDE OF MARLEY.
THE COLOSSUS TITAN. THE FEMALE TITAN.
YOU STOLE SOME OF THEIR KEY WEAPONS.
MARLEY IS A NATION WITH MANY ENEMIES. OTHER COUNTRIES CAME TOGETHER IN THE BLINK OF AN EYE...
...AND THEN THE WAR BEGAN.
SO THAT MEANS YOUR GROUP ISN'T LOYAL TO MARLEY. YOU HAVE A GRUDGE AGAINST IT.
YOU INFILTRATED THE ARMY TO ACT AS SOMETHING LIKE SLEEPER AGENTS...AM I RIGHT?

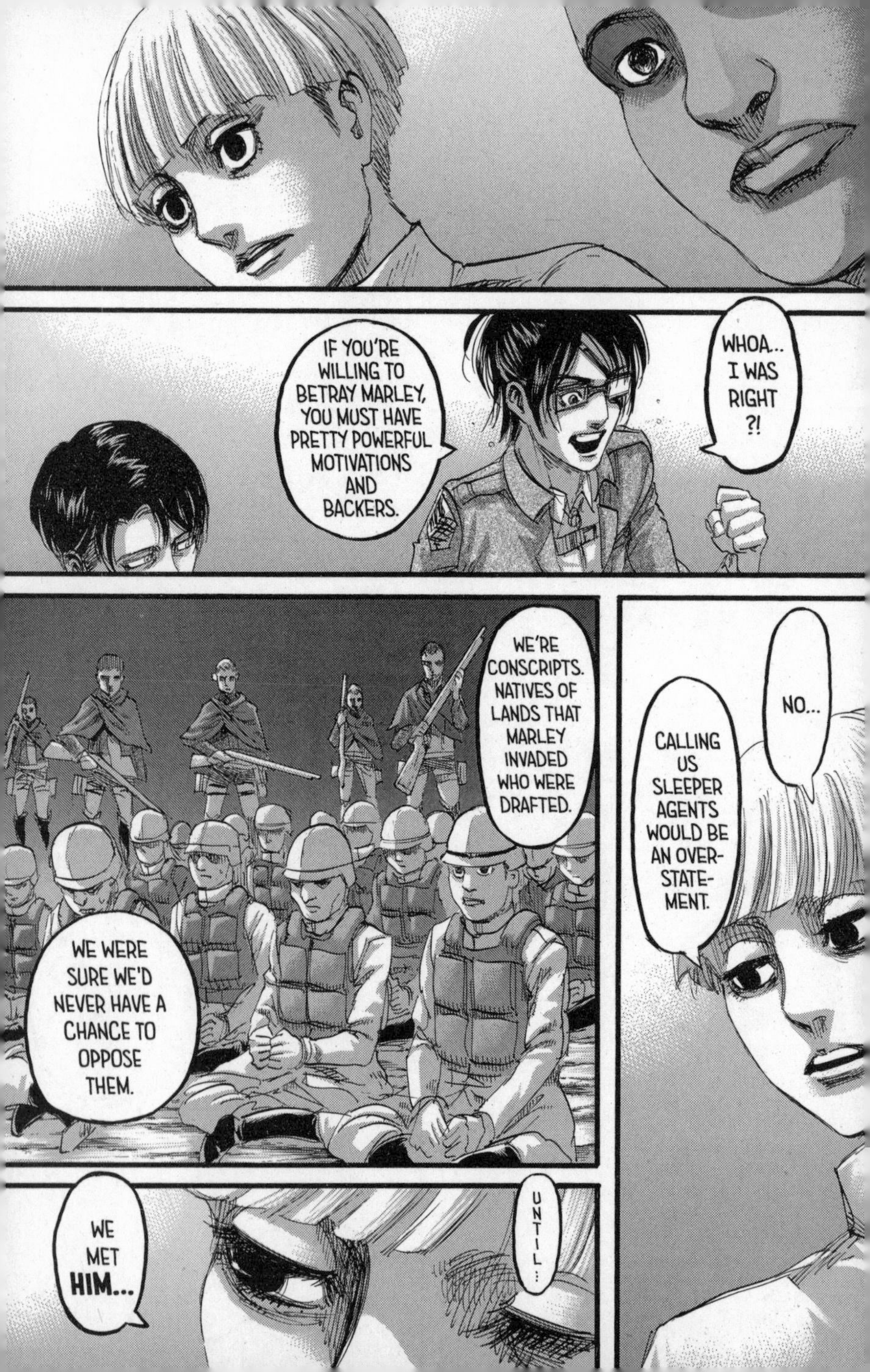
WHOA... I WAS RIGHT ?!
IF YOU'RE WILLING TO BETRAY MARLEY, YOU MUST HAVE PRETTY POWERFUL MOTIVATIONS AND BACKERS.
NO...
CALLING US SLEEPER AGENTS WOULD BE AN OVER-STATE-MENT.
WE'RE CONSCRIPTS. NATIVES OF LANDS THAT MARLEY INVADED WHO WERE DRAFTED.
WE WERE SURE WE'D NEVER HAVE A CHANCE TO OPPOSE THEM.
UNTIL...
WE MET **HIM...**

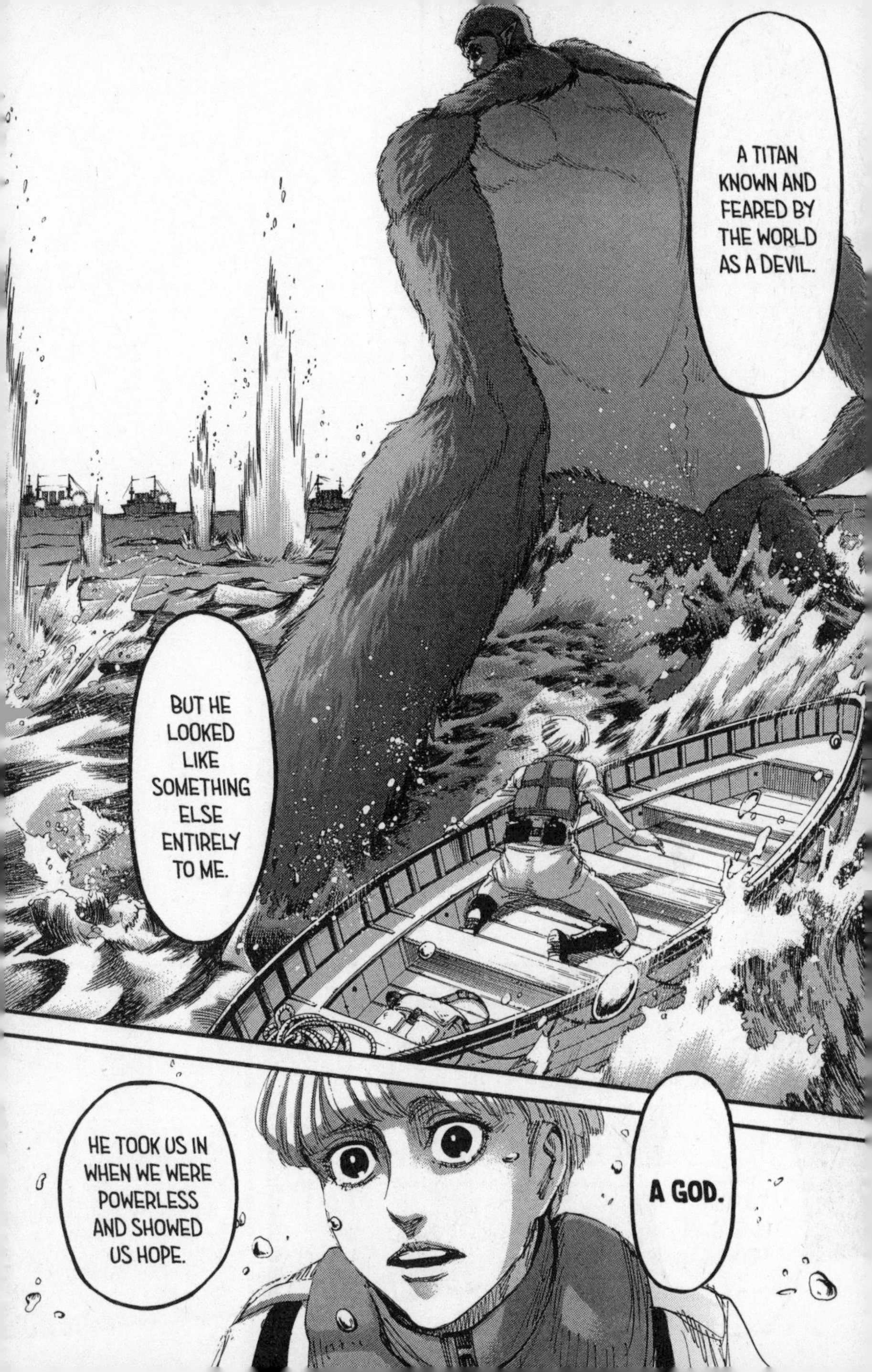
A TITAN KNOWN AND FEARED BY THE WORLD AS A DEVIL.
BUT HE LOOKED LIKE SOMETHING ELSE ENTIRELY TO ME.
A GOD.
HE TOOK US IN WHEN WE WERE POWERLESS AND SHOWED US HOPE.

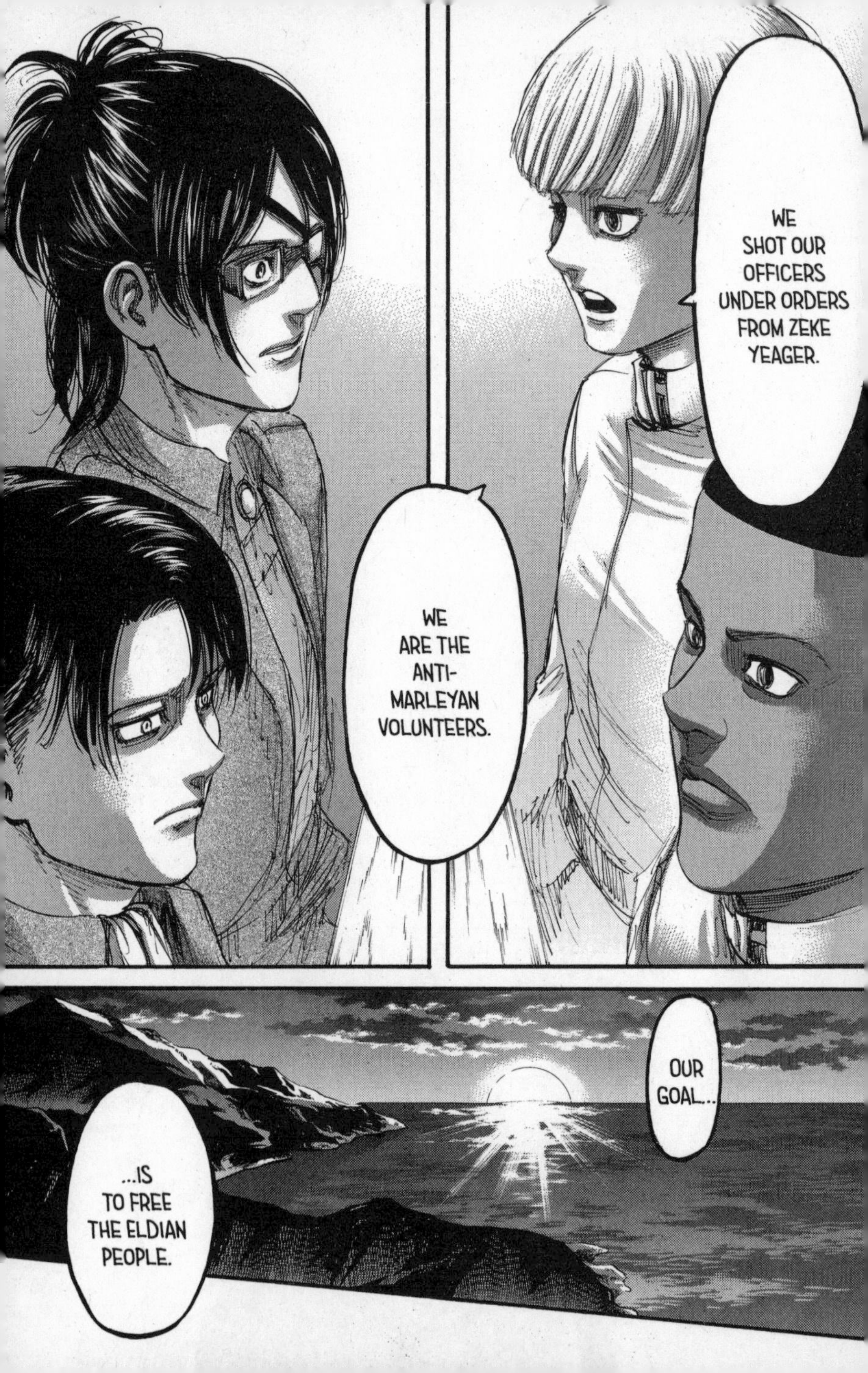
WE SHOT OUR OFFICERS UNDER ORDERS FROM ZEKE YEAGER.
WE ARE THE ANTI-MARLEYAN VOLUNTEERS.
OUR GOAL...
...IS TO FREE THE ELDIAN PEOPLE.

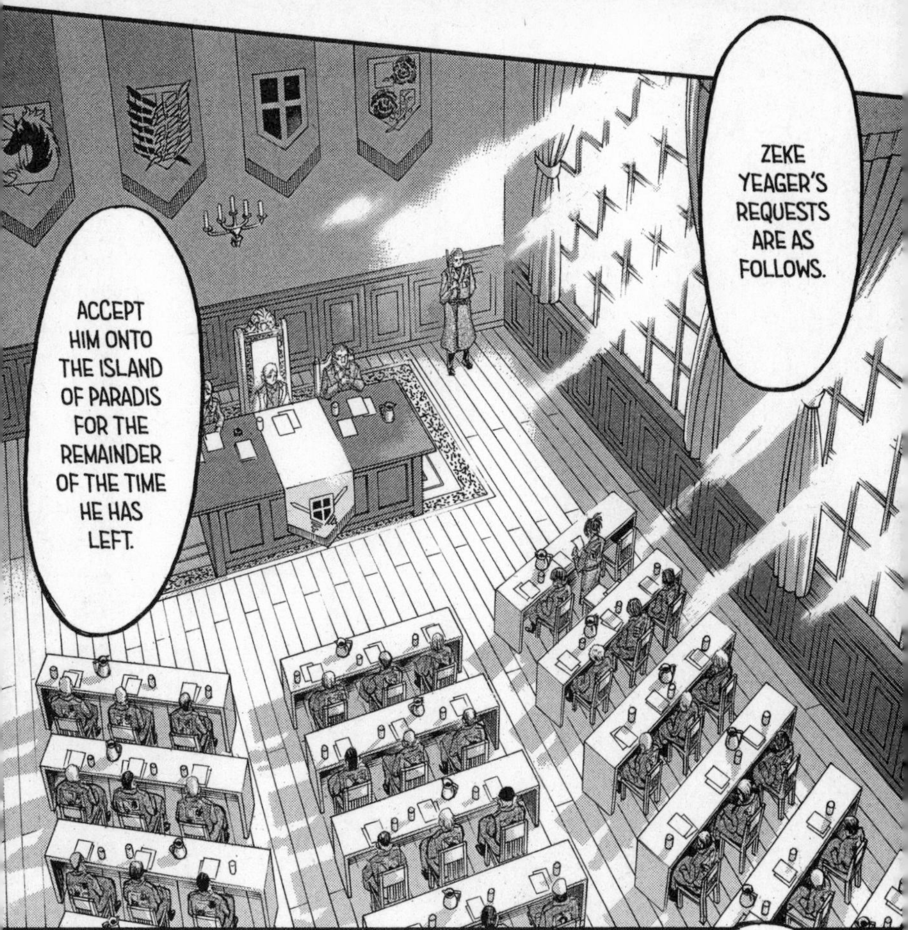
ZEKE YEAGER'S REQUESTS ARE AS FOLLOWS.
ACCEPT HIM ONTO THE ISLAND OF PARADIS FOR THE REMAINDER OF THE TIME HE HAS LEFT.
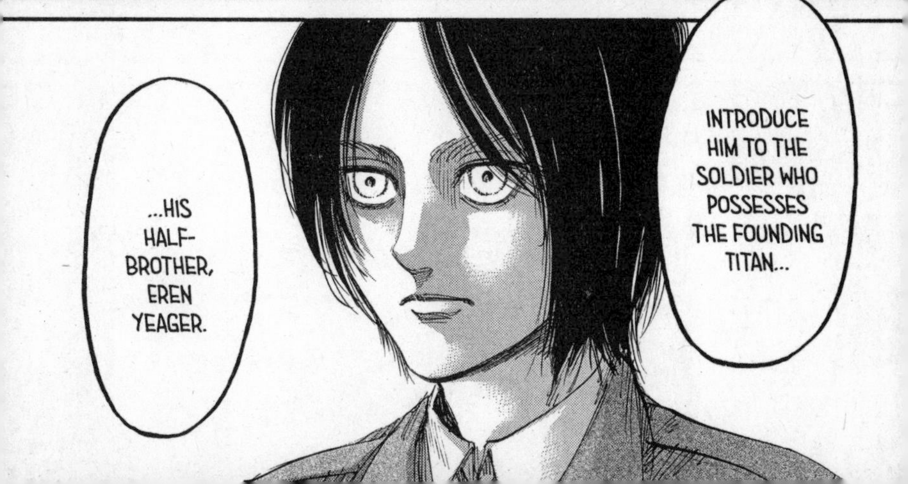
INTRODUCE HIM TO THE SOLDIER WHO POSSESSES THE FOUNDING TITAN...
...HIS HALF-BROTHER, EREN YEAGER.

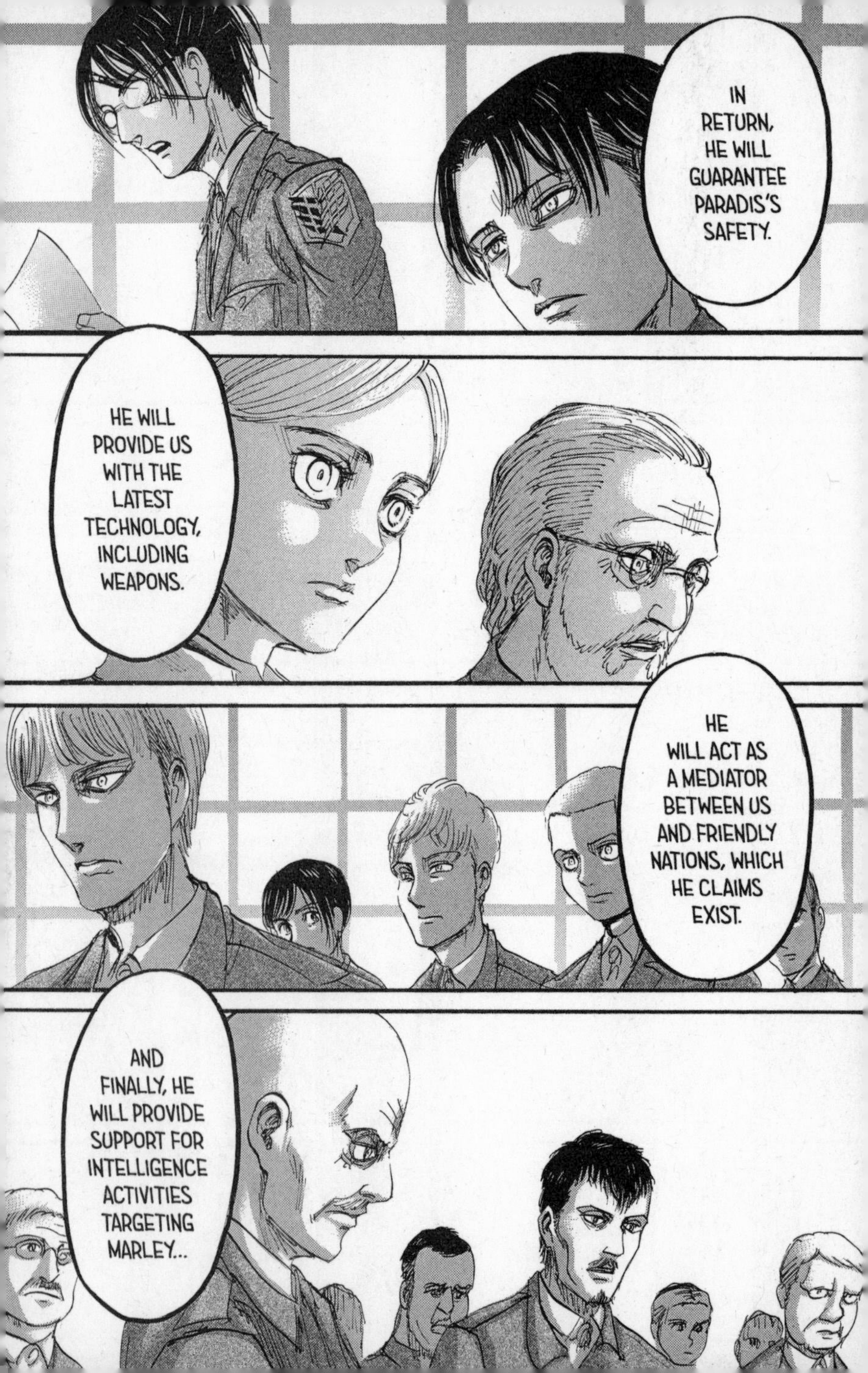
IN RETURN, HE WILL GUARANTEE PARADIS'S SAFETY.
HE WILL PROVIDE US WITH THE LATEST TECHNOLOGY, INCLUDING WEAPONS.
HE WILL ACT AS A MEDIATOR BETWEEN US AND FRIENDLY NATIONS, WHICH HE CLAIMS EXIST.
AND FINALLY, HE WILL PROVIDE SUPPORT FOR INTELLIGENCE ACTIVITIES TARGETING MARLEY...

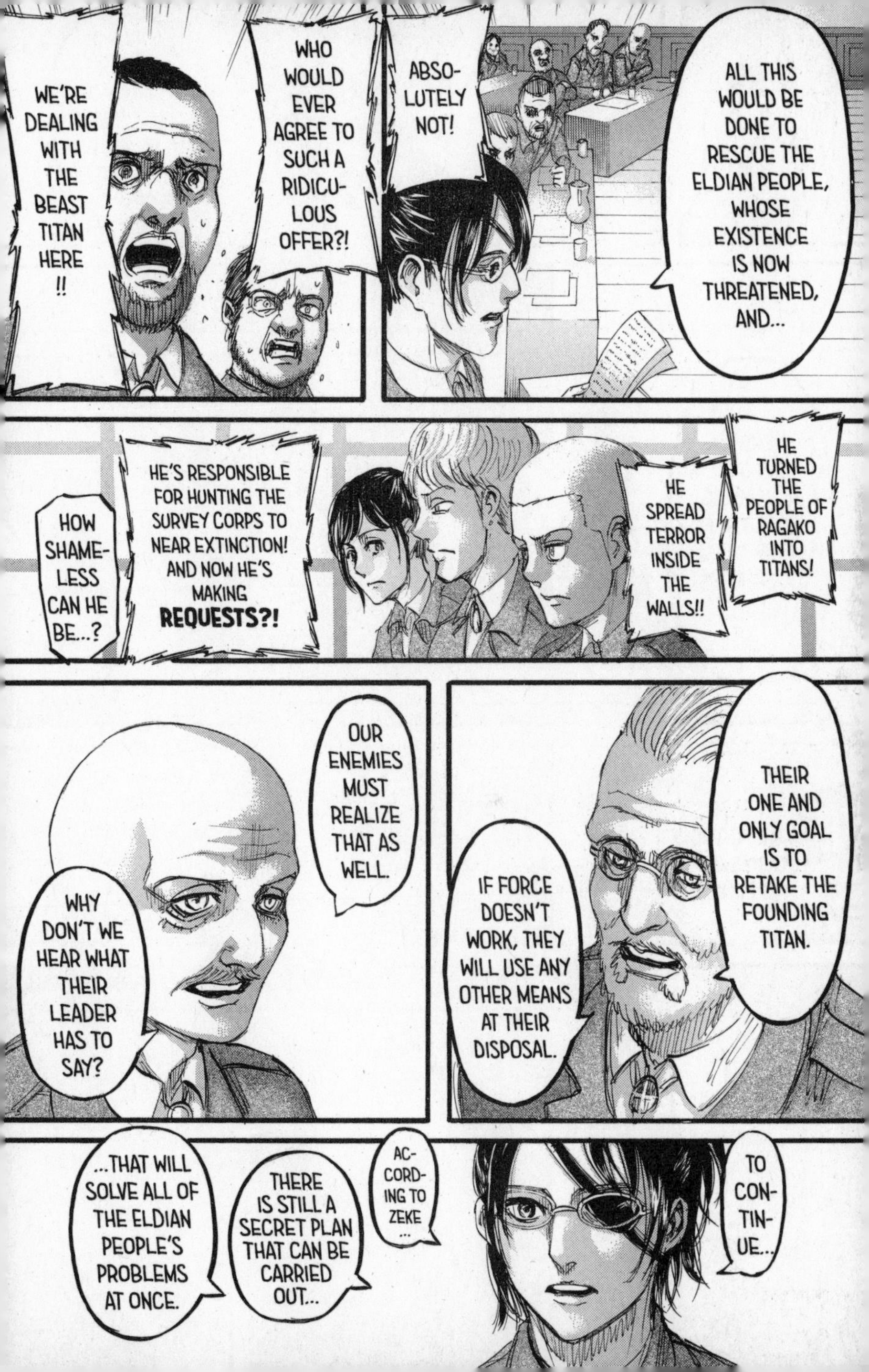
ALL THIS WOULD BE DONE TO RESCUE THE ELDIAN PEOPLE, WHOSE EXISTENCE IS NOW THREATENED, AND...
ABSOLUTELY NOT!
WHO WOULD EVER AGREE TO SUCH A RIDICULOUS OFFER?!
WE'RE DEALING WITH THE BEAST TITAN HERE!!
HE TURNED THE PEOPLE OF RAGAKO INTO TITANS!
HE SPREAD TERROR INSIDE THE WALLS!!
HE'S RESPONSIBLE FOR HUNTING THE SURVEY CORPS TO NEAR EXTINCTION! AND NOW HE'S MAKING **REQUESTS?!**
HOW SHAMELESS CAN HE BE...?
THEIR ONE AND ONLY GOAL IS TO RETAKE THE FOUNDING TITAN.
IF FORCE DOESN'T WORK, THEY WILL USE ANY OTHER MEANS AT THEIR DISPOSAL.
OUR ENEMIES MUST REALIZE THAT AS WELL.
WHY DON'T WE HEAR WHAT THEIR LEADER HAS TO SAY?
TO CONTINUE...
ACCORDING TO ZEKE...
THERE IS STILL A SECRET PLAN THAT CAN BE CARRIED OUT...
...THAT WILL SOLVE ALL OF THE ELDIAN PEOPLE'S PROBLEMS AT ONCE.

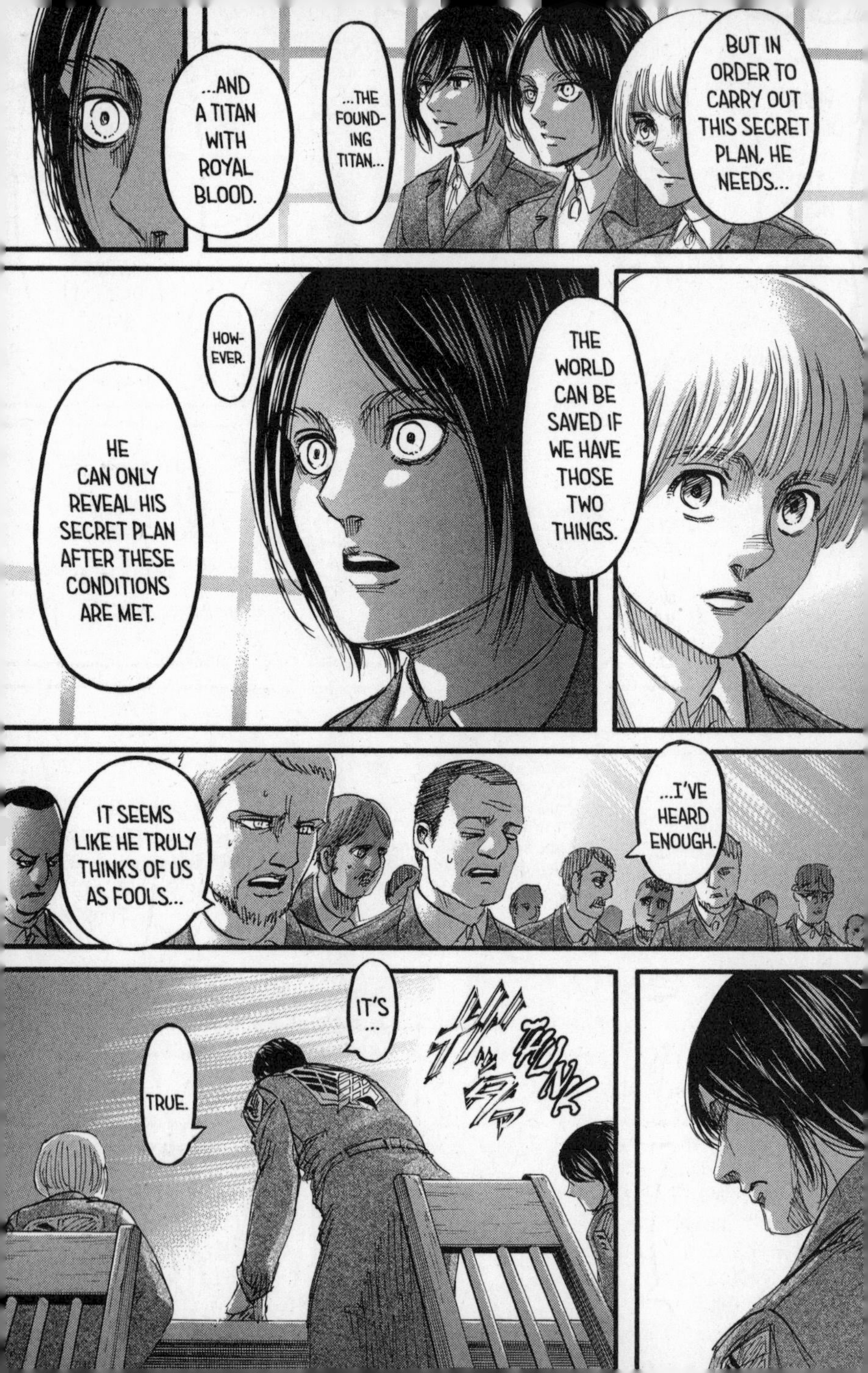
BUT IN ORDER TO CARRY OUT THIS SECRET PLAN, HE NEEDS...
...THE FOUNDING TITAN...
...AND A TITAN WITH ROYAL BLOOD.
THE WORLD CAN BE SAVED IF WE HAVE THOSE TWO THINGS.
HOWEVER.
HE CAN ONLY REVEAL HIS SECRET PLAN AFTER THESE CONDITIONS ARE MET.
...I'VE HEARD ENOUGH.
IT SEEMS LIKE HE TRULY THINKS OF US AS FOOLS...
THUNK
IT'S...
TRUE.

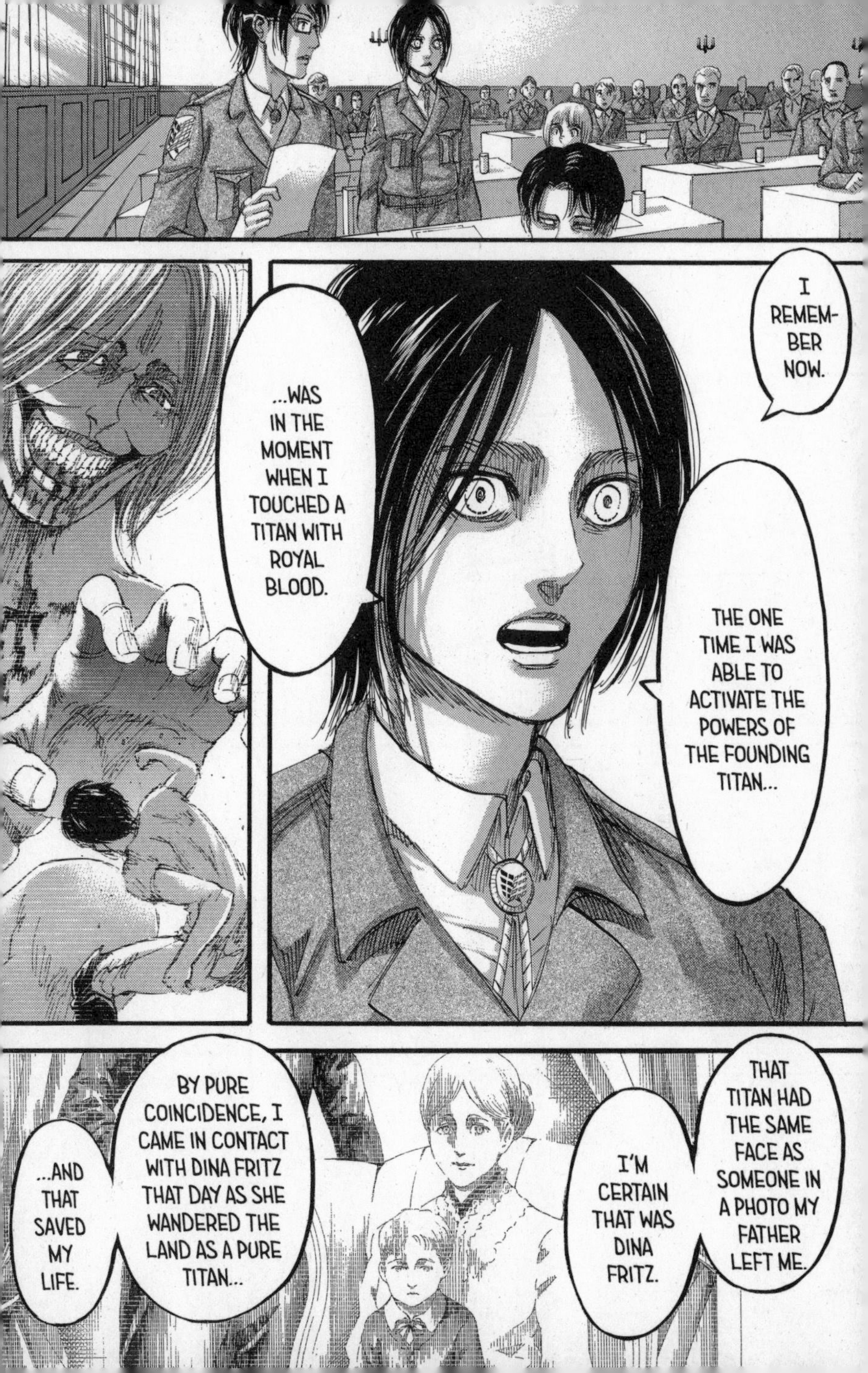
I REMEMBER NOW.
THE ONE TIME I WAS ABLE TO ACTIVATE THE POWERS OF THE FOUNDING TITAN...
...WAS IN THE MOMENT WHEN I TOUCHED A TITAN WITH ROYAL BLOOD.
THAT TITAN HAD THE SAME FACE AS SOMEONE IN A PHOTO MY FATHER LEFT ME.
I'M CERTAIN THAT WAS DINA FRITZ.
BY PURE COINCIDENCE, I CAME IN CONTACT WITH DINA FRITZ THAT DAY AS SHE WANDERED THE LAND AS A PURE TITAN...
...AND THAT SAVED MY LIFE.

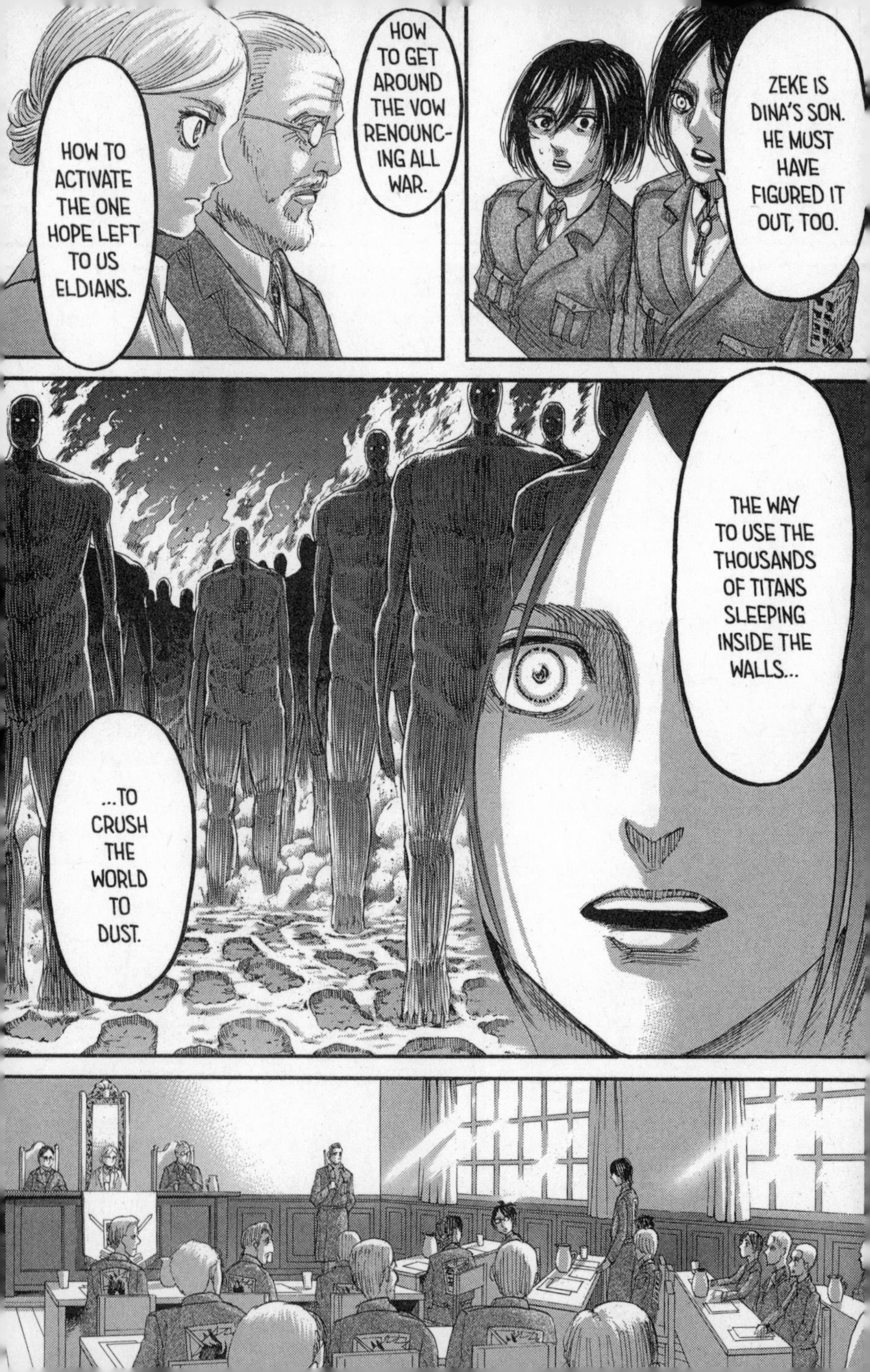
ZEKE IS DINA'S SON. HE MUST HAVE FIGURED IT OUT, TOO.
HOW TO GET AROUND THE VOW RENOUNC-ING ALL WAR.
HOW TO ACTIVATE THE ONE HOPE LEFT TO US ELDIANS.
THE WAY TO USE THE THOUSANDS OF TITANS SLEEPING INSIDE THE WALLS...
...TO CRUSH THE WORLD TO DUST.

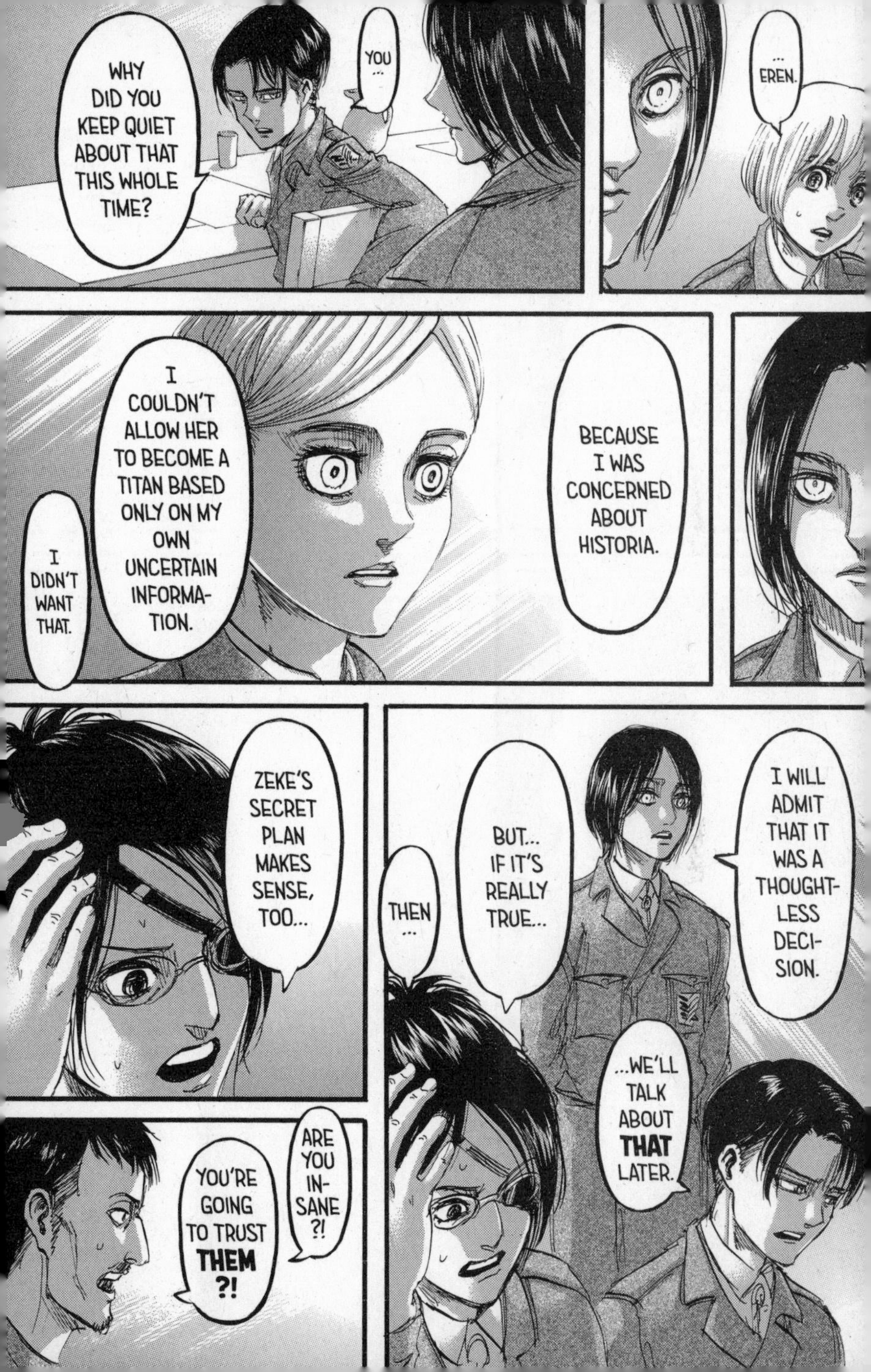
... EREN.
YOU ...
WHY DID YOU KEEP QUIET ABOUT THAT THIS WHOLE TIME?
BECAUSE I WAS CONCERNED ABOUT HISTORIA.
I COULDN'T ALLOW HER TO BECOME A TITAN BASED ONLY ON MY OWN UNCERTAIN INFORMATION.
I DIDN'T WANT THAT.
I WILL ADMIT THAT IT WAS A THOUGHTLESS DECISION.
BUT... IF IT'S REALLY TRUE...
THEN ...
...WE'LL TALK ABOUT **THAT** LATER.
ZEKE'S SECRET PLAN MAKES SENSE, TOO...
ARE YOU IN-SANE ?!
YOU'RE GOING TO TRUST **THEM ?!**

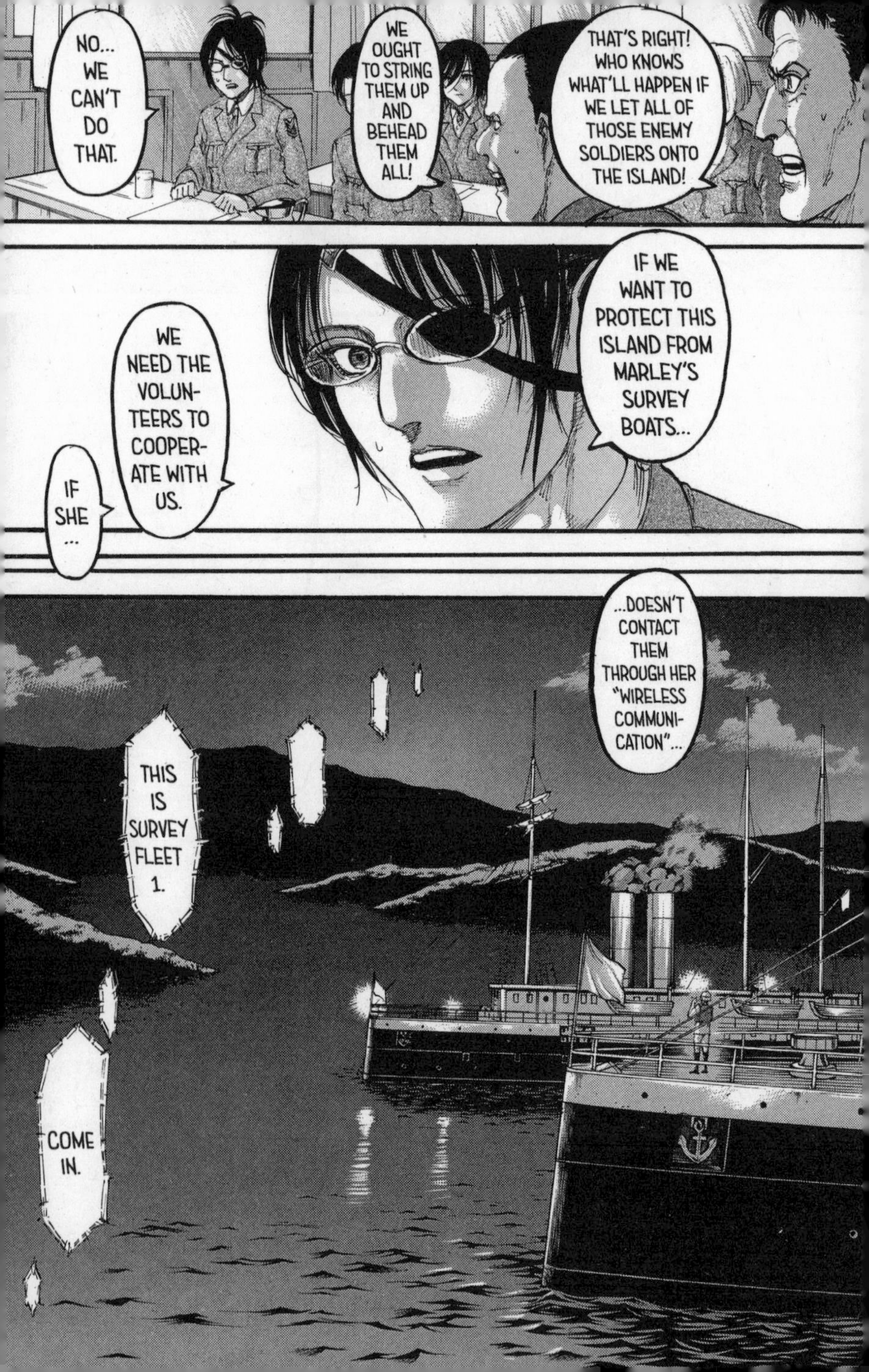
THAT'S RIGHT! WHO KNOWS WHAT'LL HAPPEN IF WE LET ALL OF THOSE ENEMY SOLDIERS ONTO THE ISLAND!
WE OUGHT TO STRING THEM UP AND BEHEAD THEM ALL!
NO... WE CAN'T DO THAT.
IF WE WANT TO PROTECT THIS ISLAND FROM MARLEY'S SURVEY BOATS...
WE NEED THE VOLUNTEERS TO COOPERATE WITH US.
IF SHE ...
...DOESN'T CONTACT THEM THROUGH HER "WIRELESS COMMUNICATION"...
THIS IS SURVEY FLEET 1.
COME IN.

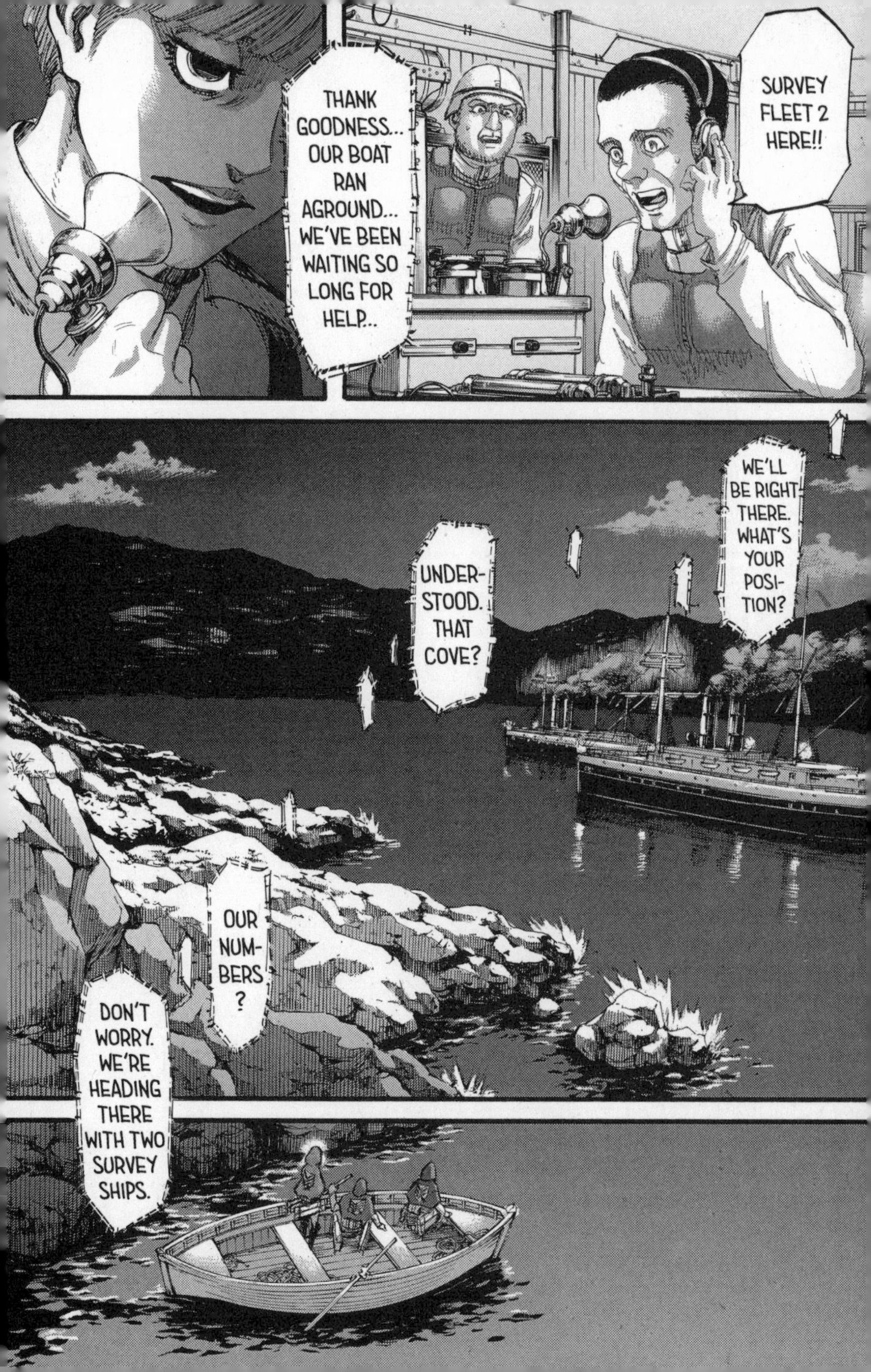
SURVEY FLEET 2 HERE!!
THANK GOODNESS... OUR BOAT RAN AGROUND... WE'VE BEEN WAITING SO LONG FOR HELP...
WE'LL BE RIGHT THERE. WHAT'S YOUR POSI-TION?
UNDER-STOOD. THAT COVE?
OUR NUM-BERS?
DON'T WORRY. WE'RE HEADING THERE WITH TWO SURVEY SHIPS.

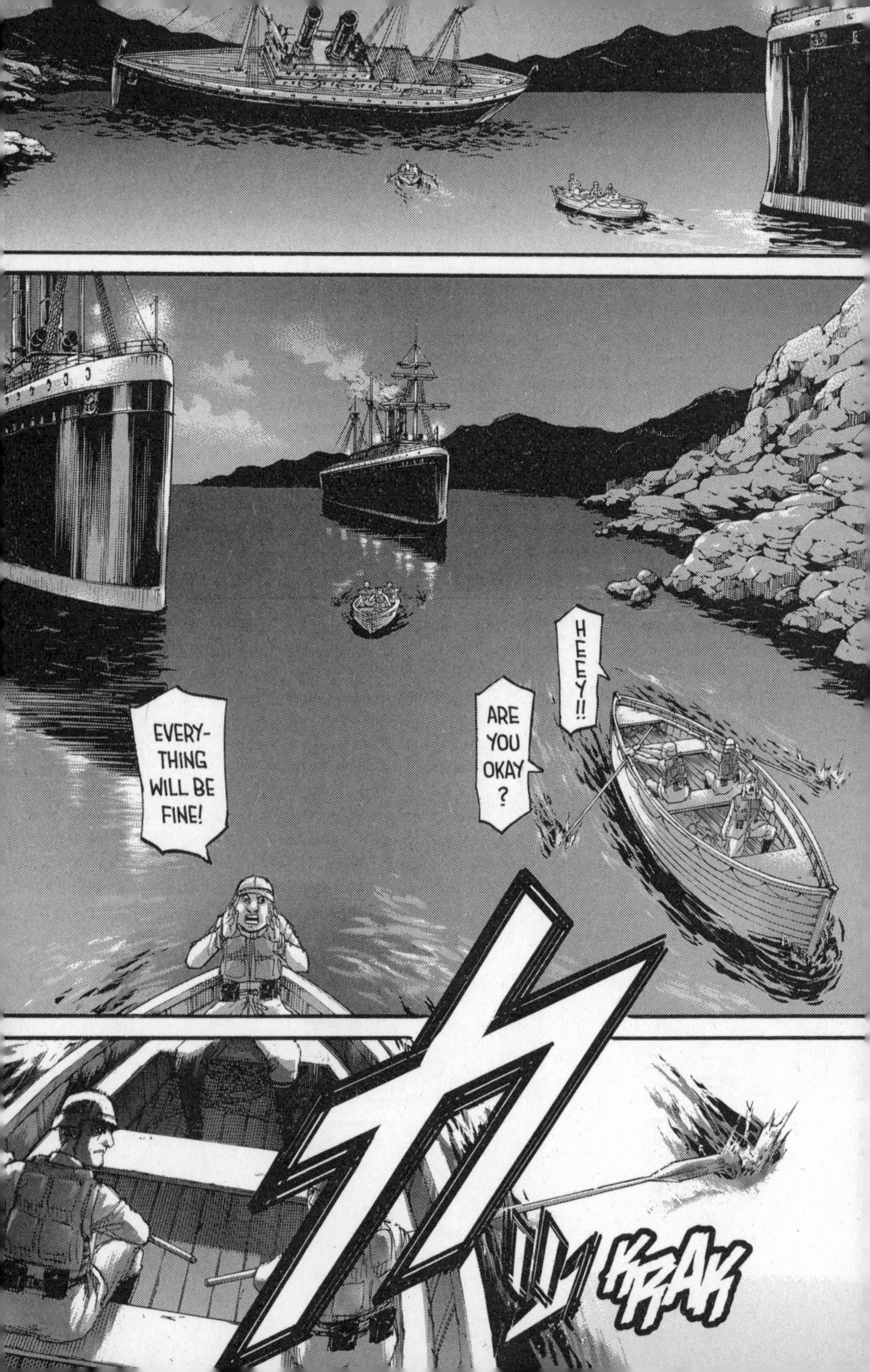
HEEEY!!
ARE YOU OKAY?
EVERYTHING WILL BE FINE!
KRAK

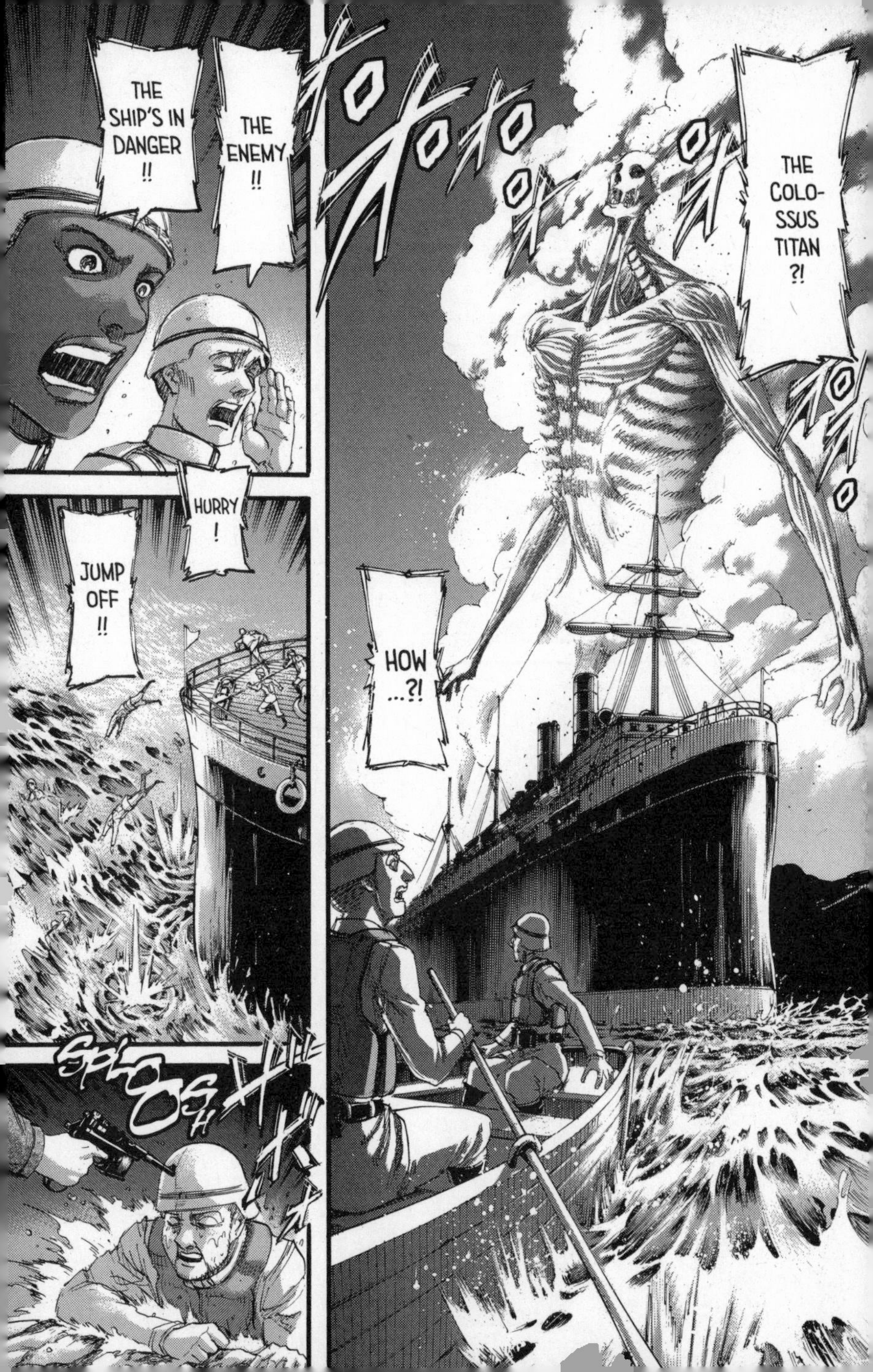
THE COLOSSUS TITAN ?!
HOW ...?!
THE ENEMY !!
THE SHIP'S IN DANGER !!
HURRY !
JUMP OFF !!
SPLOOSH

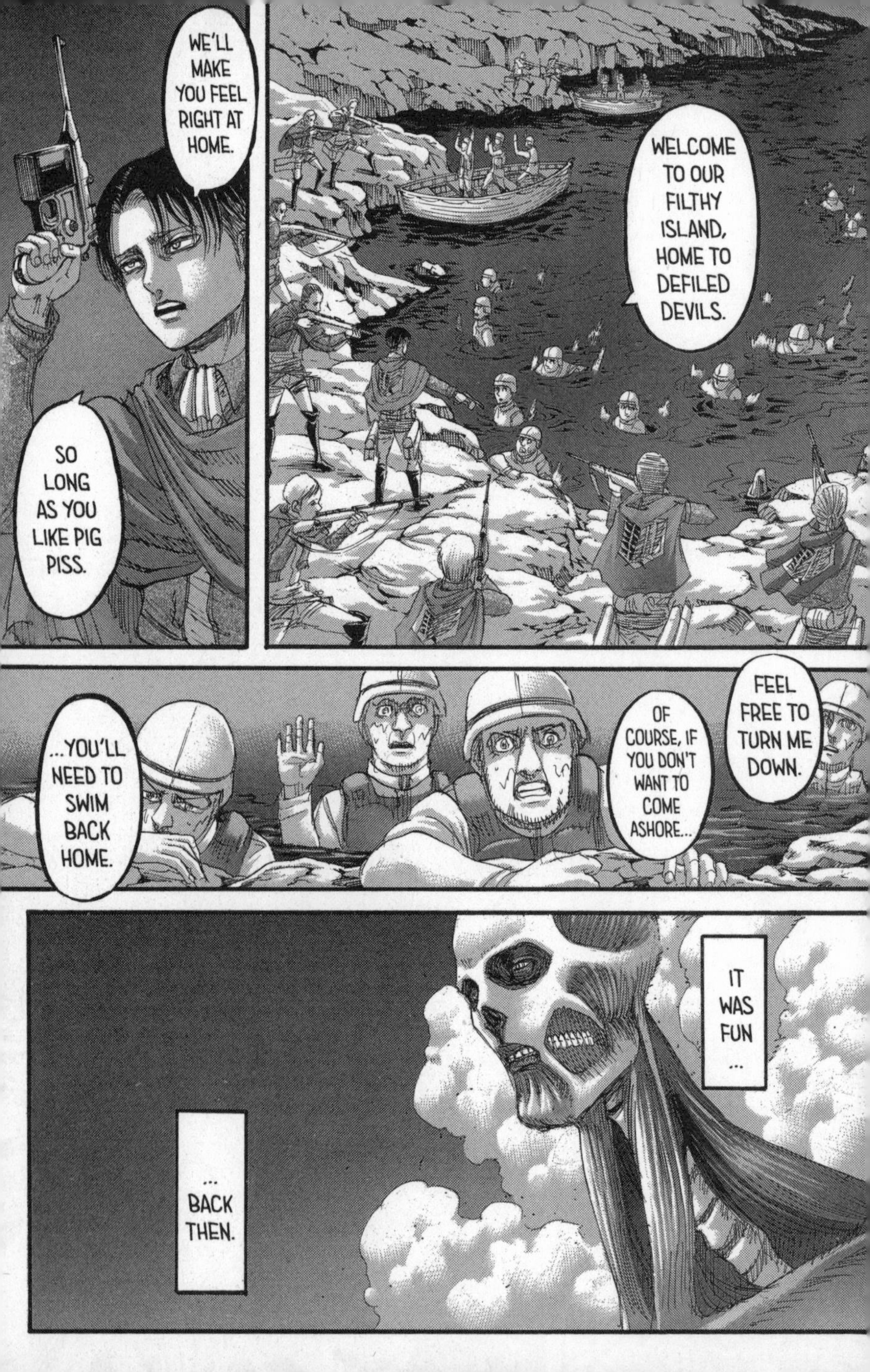
WELCOME TO OUR FILTHY ISLAND, HOME TO DEFILED DEVILS.
WE'LL MAKE YOU FEEL RIGHT AT HOME.
SO LONG AS YOU LIKE PIG PISS.
FEEL FREE TO TURN ME DOWN.
OF COURSE, IF YOU DON'T WANT TO COME ASHORE...
...YOU'LL NEED TO SWIM BACK HOME.
IT WAS FUN...
...BACK THEN.

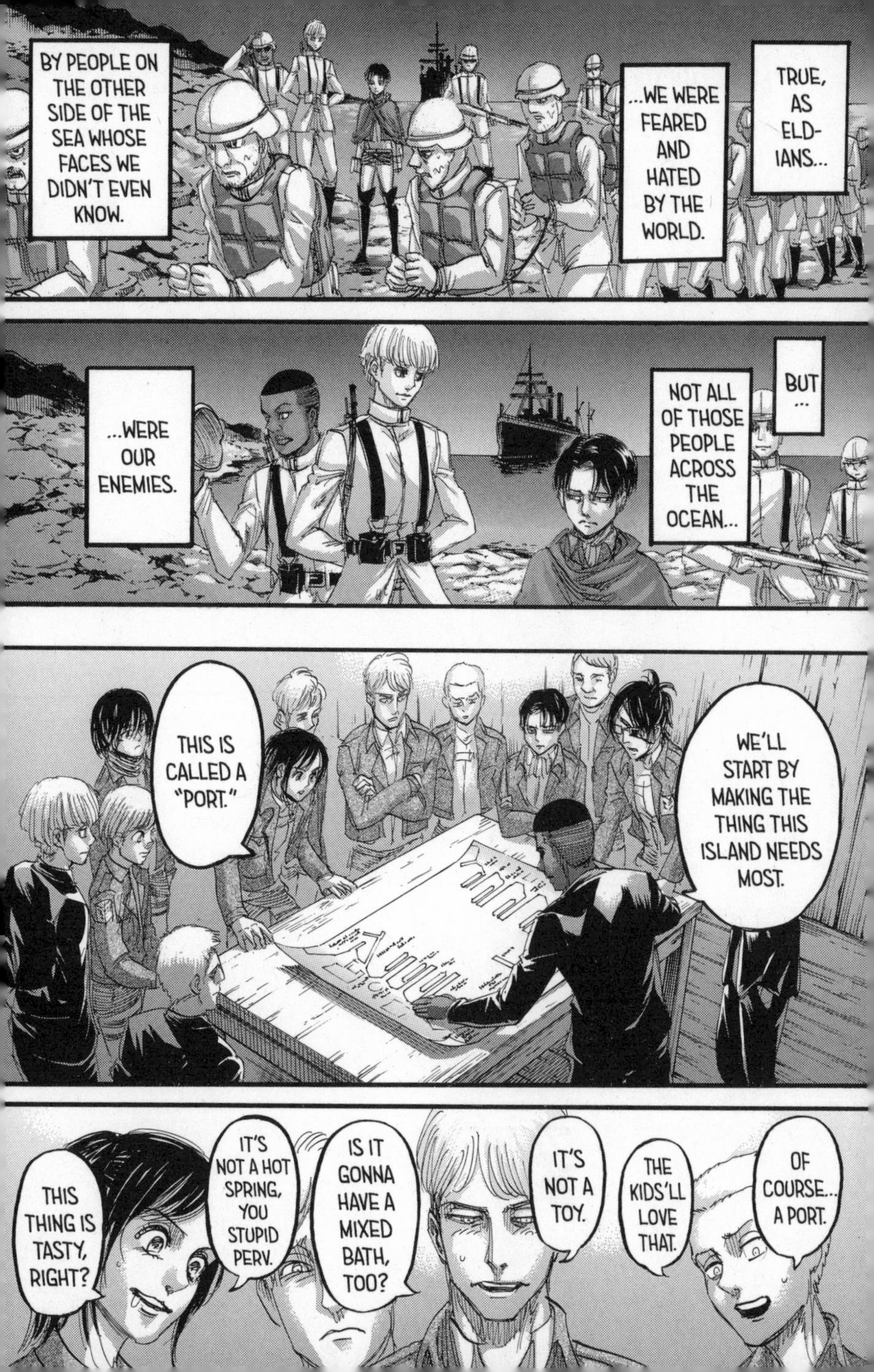
TRUE, AS ELDIANS...
...WE WERE FEARED AND HATED BY THE WORLD.
BY PEOPLE ON THE OTHER SIDE OF THE SEA WHOSE FACES WE DIDN'T EVEN KNOW.
BUT...
NOT ALL OF THOSE PEOPLE ACROSS THE OCEAN...
...WERE OUR ENEMIES.
WE'LL START BY MAKING THE THING THIS ISLAND NEEDS MOST.
THIS IS CALLED A "PORT."
OF COURSE... A PORT.
THE KIDS'LL LOVE THAT.
IT'S NOT A TOY.
IS IT GONNA HAVE A MIXED BATH, TOO?
IT'S NOT A HOT SPRING, YOU STUPID PERV.
THIS THING IS TASTY, RIGHT?

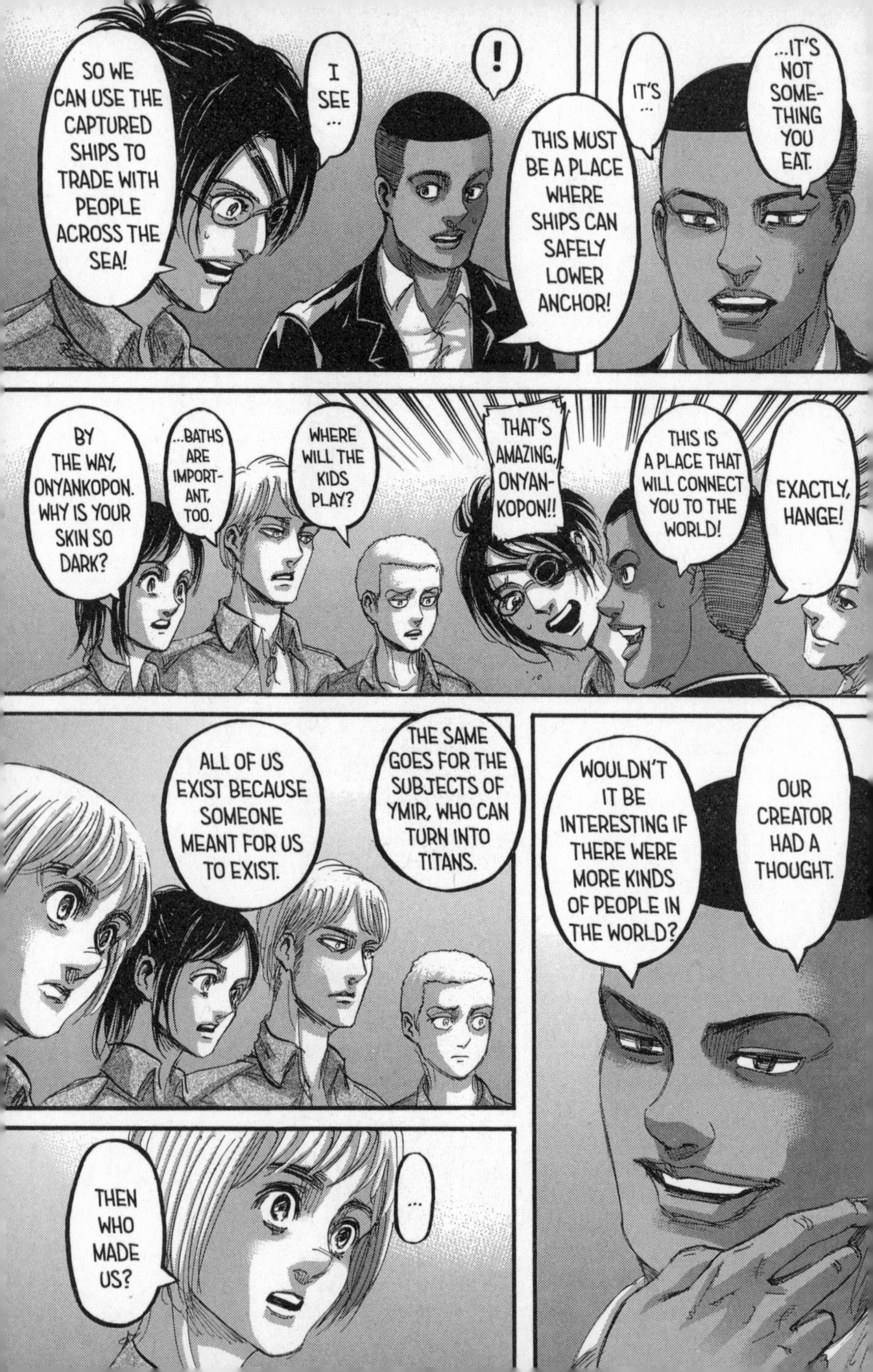
IT'S ...
...IT'S NOT SOME-THING YOU EAT.
!
THIS MUST BE A PLACE WHERE SHIPS CAN SAFELY LOWER ANCHOR!
I SEE ...
SO WE CAN USE THE CAPTURED SHIPS TO TRADE WITH PEOPLE ACROSS THE SEA!
EXACTLY, HANGE!
THIS IS A PLACE THAT WILL CONNECT YOU TO THE WORLD!
THAT'S AMAZING, ONYAN-KOPON!!
WHERE WILL THE KIDS PLAY?
...BATHS ARE IMPORT-ANT, TOO.
BY THE WAY, ONYANKOPON. WHY IS YOUR SKIN SO DARK?
OUR CREATOR HAD A THOUGHT.
WOULDN'T IT BE INTERESTING IF THERE WERE MORE KINDS OF PEOPLE IN THE WORLD?
ALL OF US EXIST BECAUSE SOMEONE MEANT FOR US TO EXIST.
THE SAME GOES FOR THE SUBJECTS OF YMIR, WHO CAN TURN INTO TITANS.
...
THEN WHO MADE US?

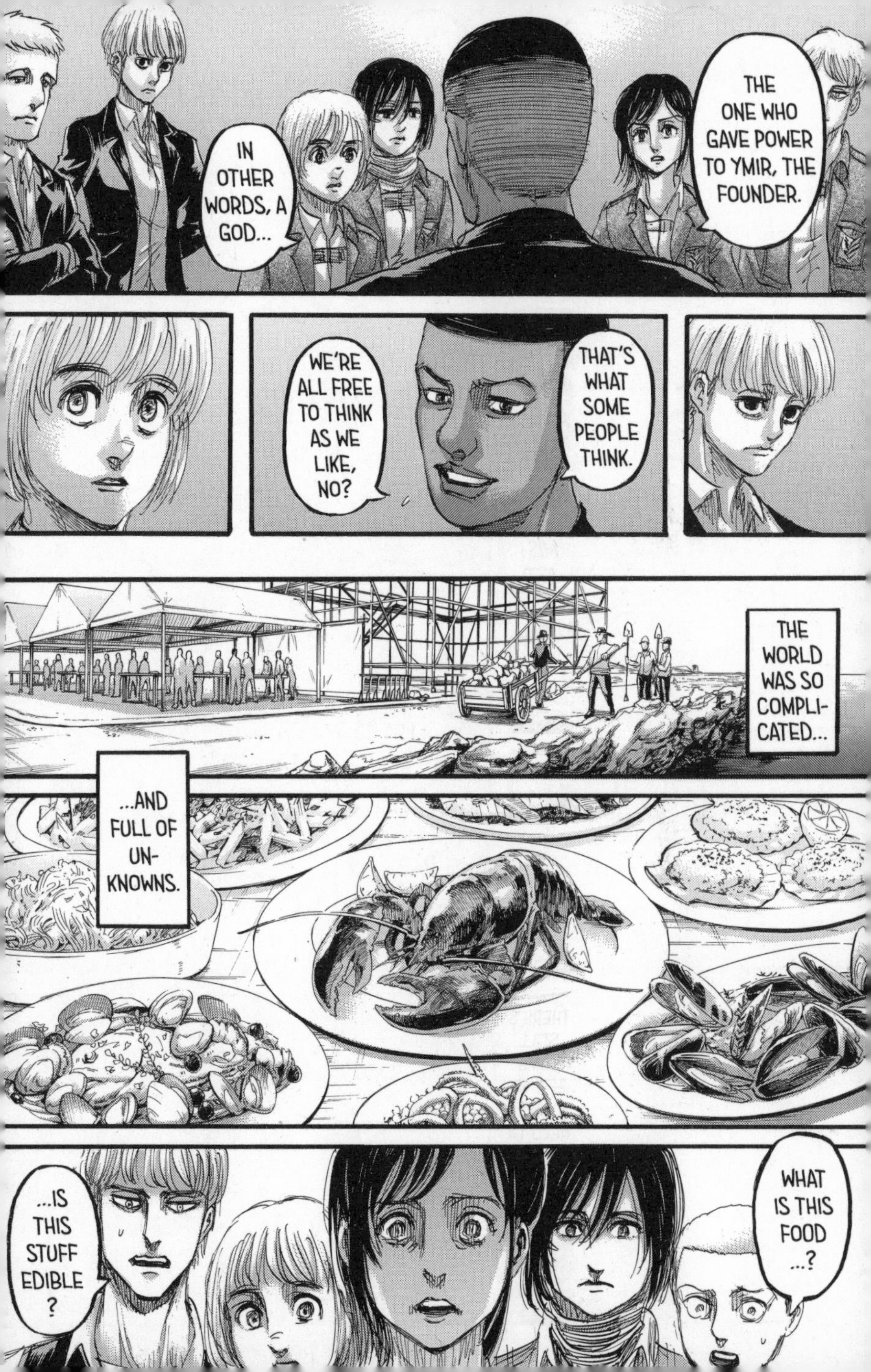
THE ONE WHO GAVE POWER TO YMIR, THE FOUNDER.
IN OTHER WORDS, A GOD...
THAT'S WHAT SOME PEOPLE THINK.
WE'RE ALL FREE TO THINK AS WE LIKE, NO?
THE WORLD WAS SO COMPLICATED...
...AND FULL OF UNKNOWNS.
WHAT IS THIS FOOD ...?
...IS THIS STUFF EDIBLE ?

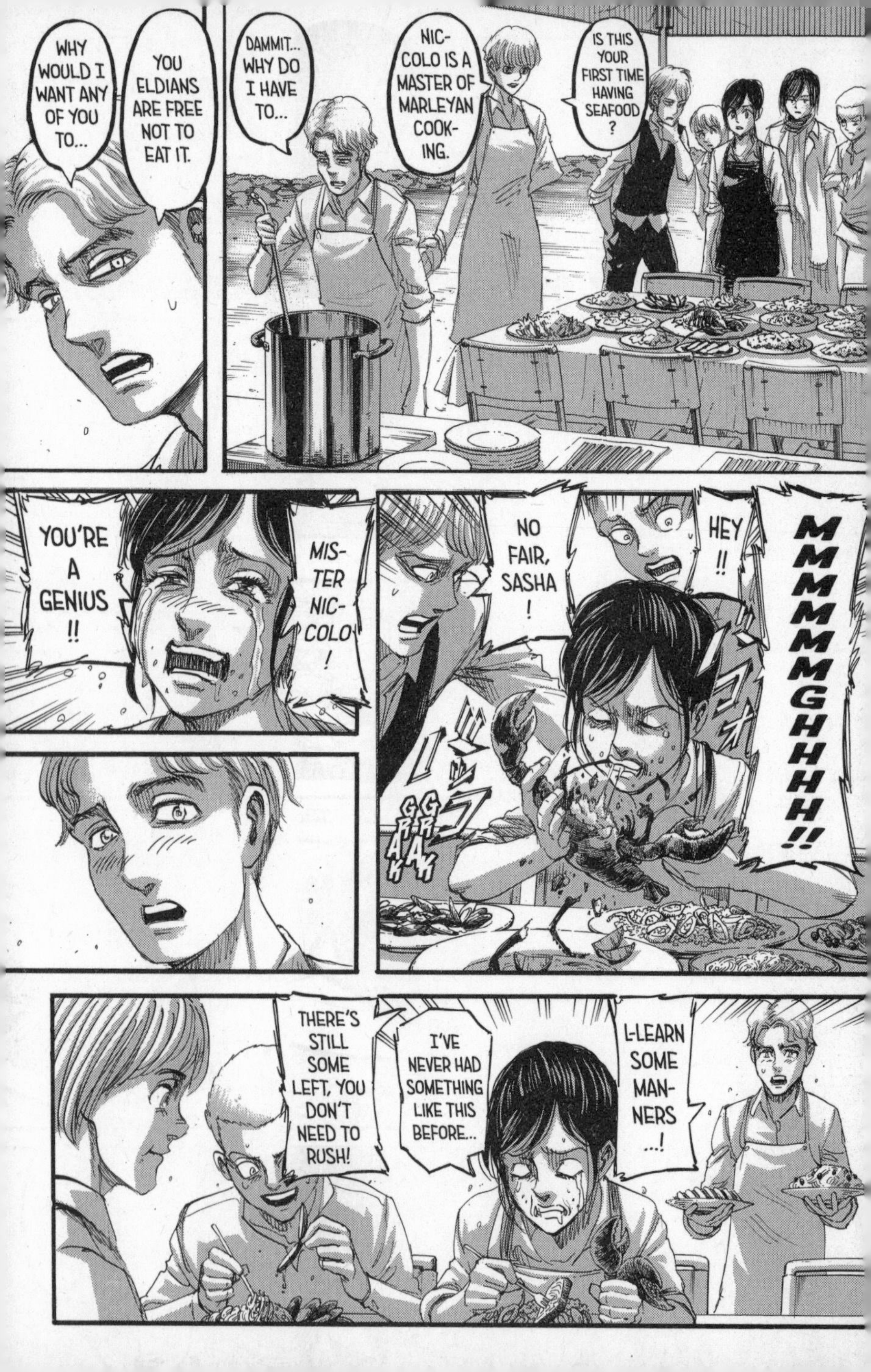
IS THIS YOUR FIRST TIME HAVING SEAFOOD?
NICCOLO IS A MASTER OF MARLEYAN COOKING.
DAMMIT... WHY DO I HAVE TO...
YOU ELDIANS ARE FREE NOT TO EAT IT.
WHY WOULD I WANT ANY OF YOU TO...
MMMMMMMGHHHHHH!!
HEY!!
NO FAIR, SASHA!
GGRRAAKK
MISTER NICCOLO!
YOU'RE A GENIUS!!
L-LEARN SOME MANNERS...!
I'VE NEVER HAD SOMETHING LIKE THIS BEFORE...
THERE'S STILL SOME LEFT, YOU DON'T NEED TO RUSH!

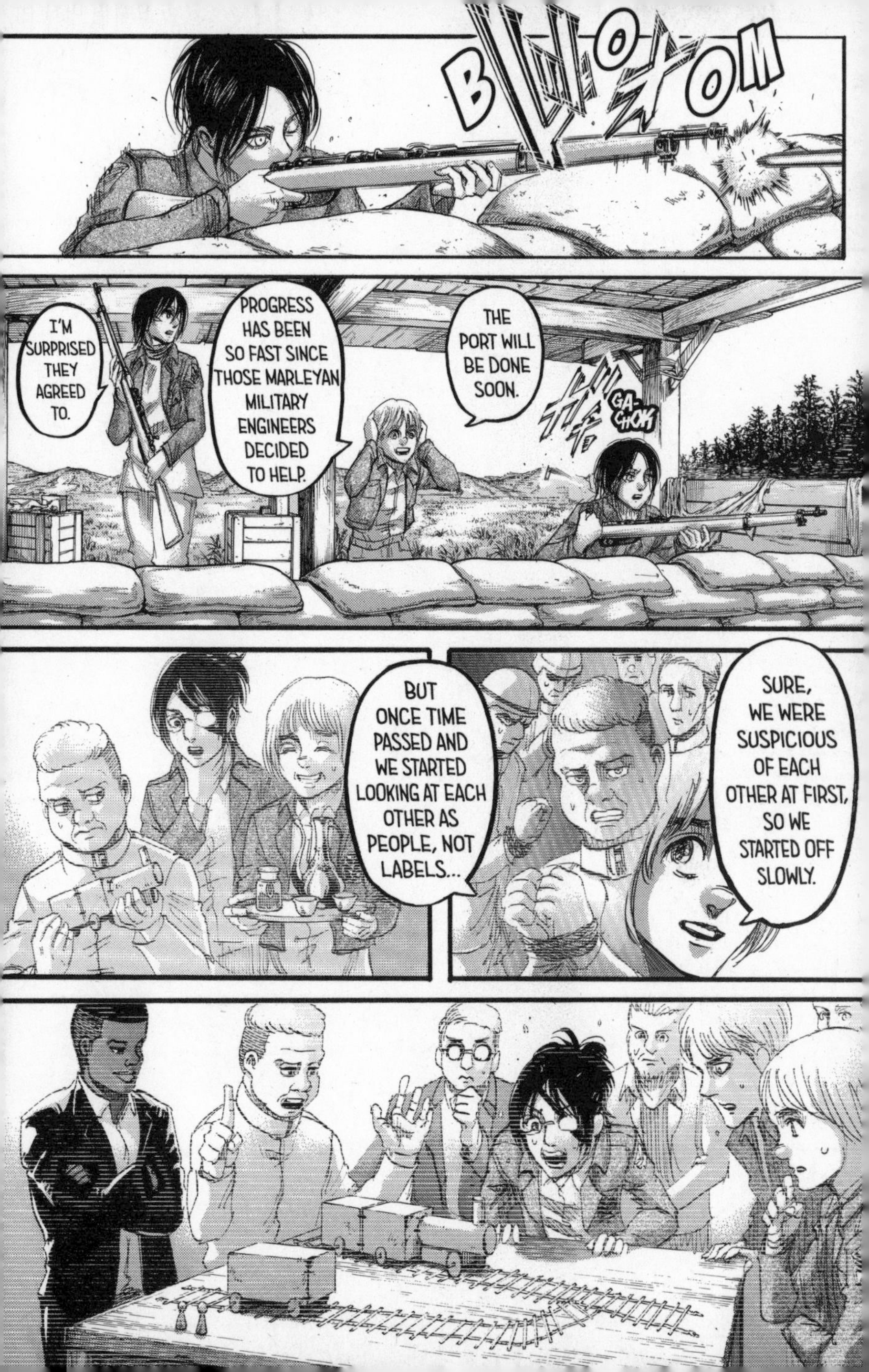
BOOM
GA-CHOK
THE PORT WILL BE DONE SOON.
PROGRESS HAS BEEN SO FAST SINCE THOSE MARLEYAN MILITARY ENGINEERS DECIDED TO HELP.
I'M SURPRISED THEY AGREED TO.
SURE, WE WERE SUSPICIOUS OF EACH OTHER AT FIRST, SO WE STARTED OFF SLOWLY.
BUT ONCE TIME PASSED AND WE STARTED LOOKING AT EACH OTHER AS PEOPLE, NOT LABELS...

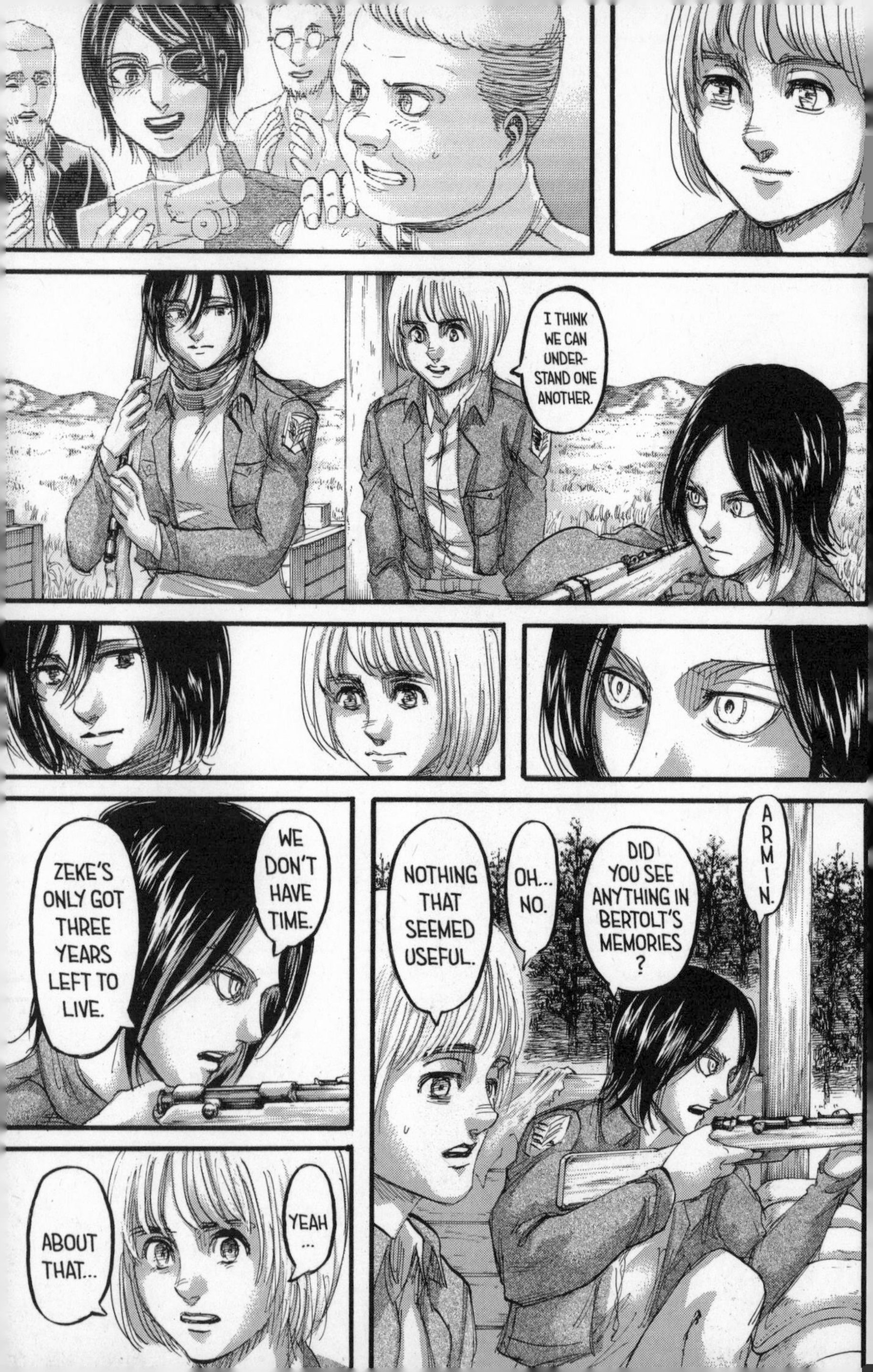
I THINK WE CAN UNDER-STAND ONE ANOTHER.
ARMIN.
DID YOU SEE ANYTHING IN BERTOLT'S MEMORIES?
OH... NO.
NOTHING THAT SEEMED USEFUL.
WE DON'T HAVE TIME.
ZEKE'S ONLY GOT THREE YEARS LEFT TO LIVE.
YEAH...
ABOUT THAT...

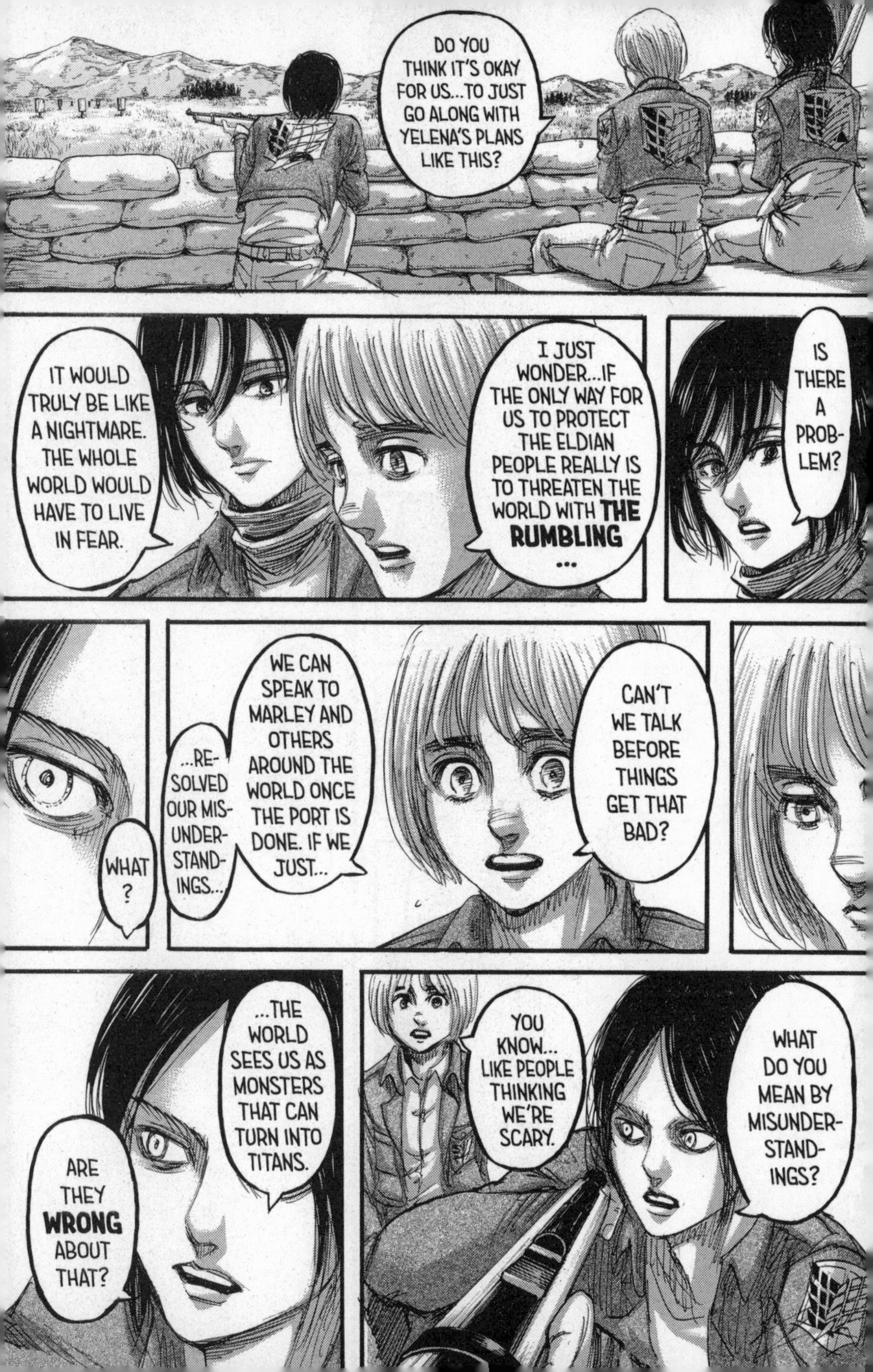
DO YOU THINK IT'S OKAY FOR US...TO JUST GO ALONG WITH YELENA'S PLANS LIKE THIS?
IS THERE A PROBLEM?
I JUST WONDER...IF THE ONLY WAY FOR US TO PROTECT THE ELDIAN PEOPLE REALLY IS TO THREATEN THE WORLD WITH **THE RUMBLING**...
IT WOULD TRULY BE LIKE A NIGHTMARE. THE WHOLE WORLD WOULD HAVE TO LIVE IN FEAR.
CAN'T WE TALK BEFORE THINGS GET THAT BAD?
WE CAN SPEAK TO MARLEY AND OTHERS AROUND THE WORLD ONCE THE PORT IS DONE. IF WE JUST...
...RESOLVED OUR MISUNDERSTANDINGS...
WHAT?
WHAT DO YOU MEAN BY MISUNDERSTANDINGS?
YOU KNOW... LIKE PEOPLE THINKING WE'RE SCARY.
...THE WORLD SEES US AS MONSTERS THAT CAN TURN INTO TITANS.
ARE THEY **WRONG** ABOUT THAT?

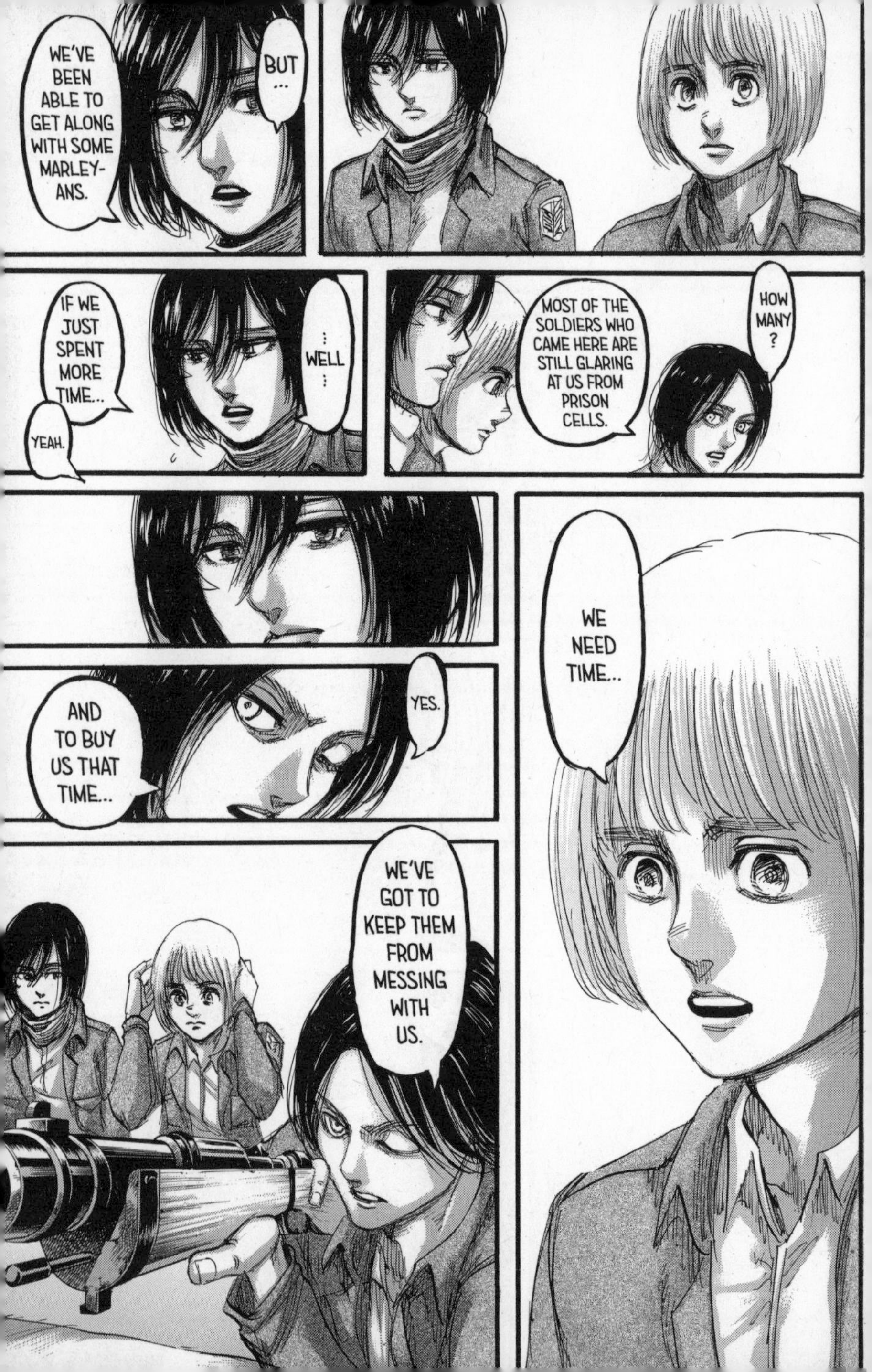
BUT ...
WE'VE BEEN ABLE TO GET ALONG WITH SOME MARLEY-ANS.
HOW MANY ?
MOST OF THE SOLDIERS WHO CAME HERE ARE STILL GLARING AT US FROM PRISON CELLS.
... WELL ...
IF WE JUST SPENT MORE TIME...
YEAH.
WE NEED TIME...
YES.
AND TO BUY US THAT TIME...
WE'VE GOT TO KEEP THEM FROM MESSING WITH US.

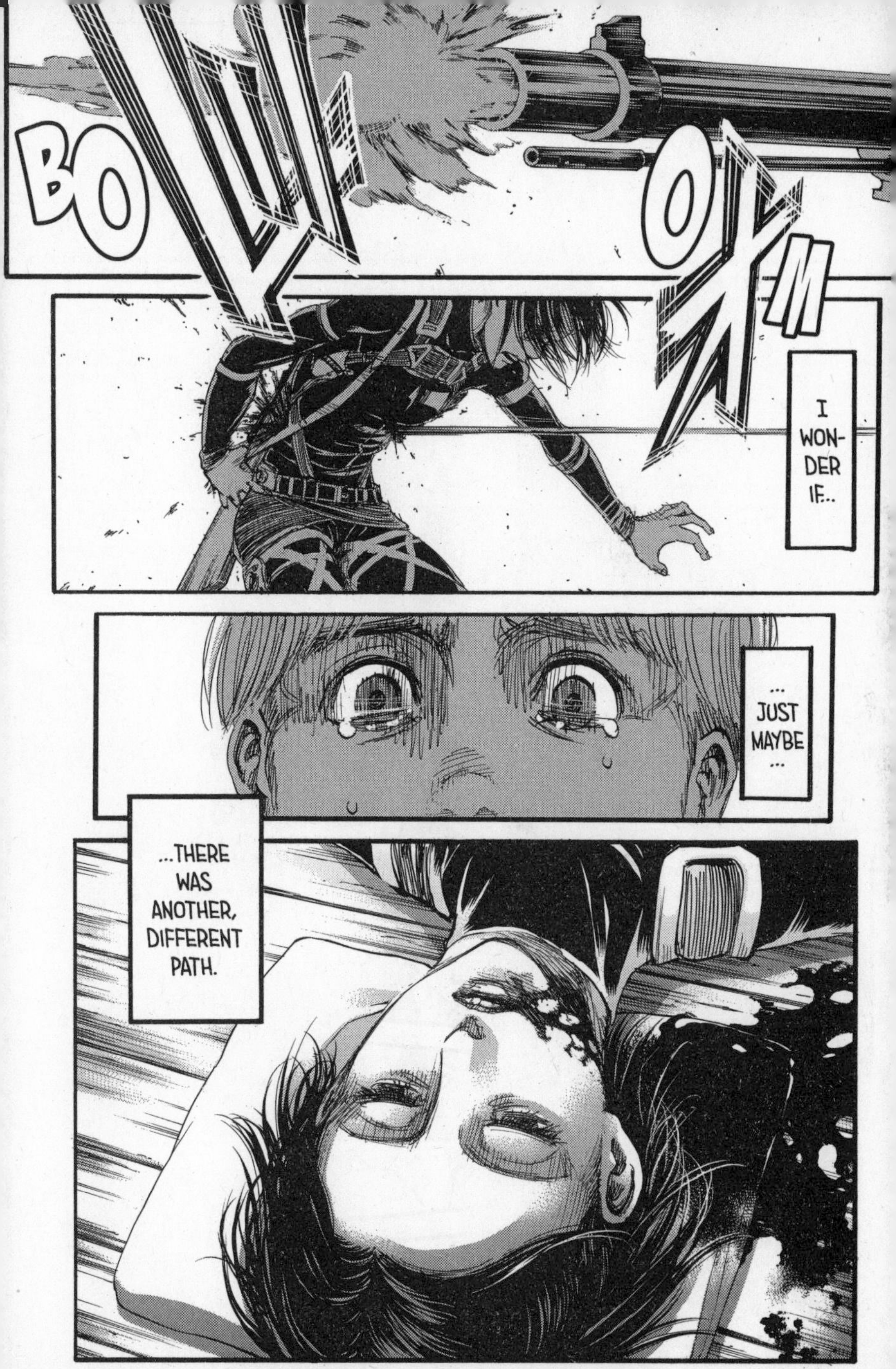
BOOM
I WON-DER IF..
...JUST MAYBE...
...THERE WAS ANOTHER, DIFFERENT PATH.

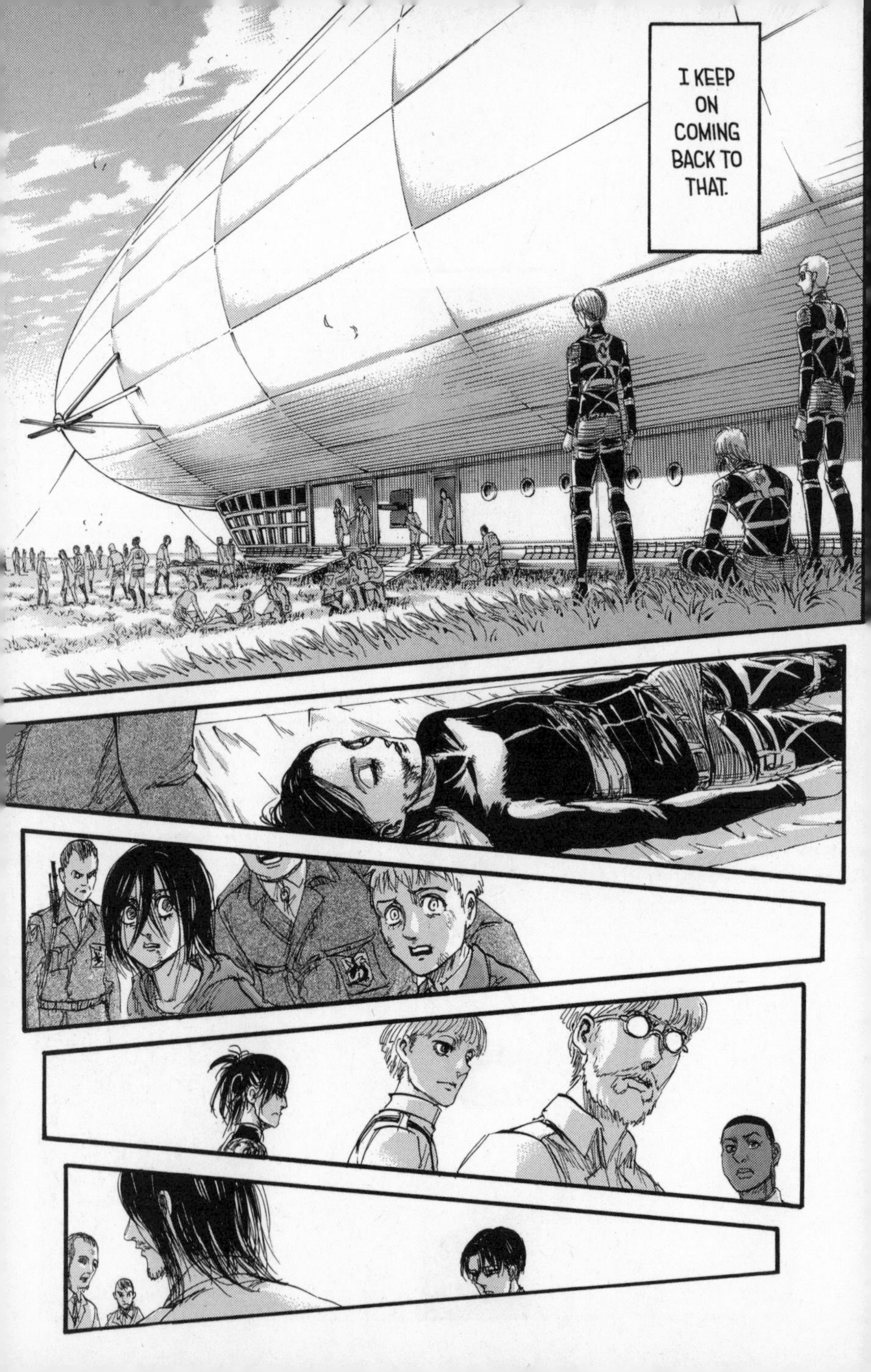
I KEEP ON COMING BACK TO THAT.

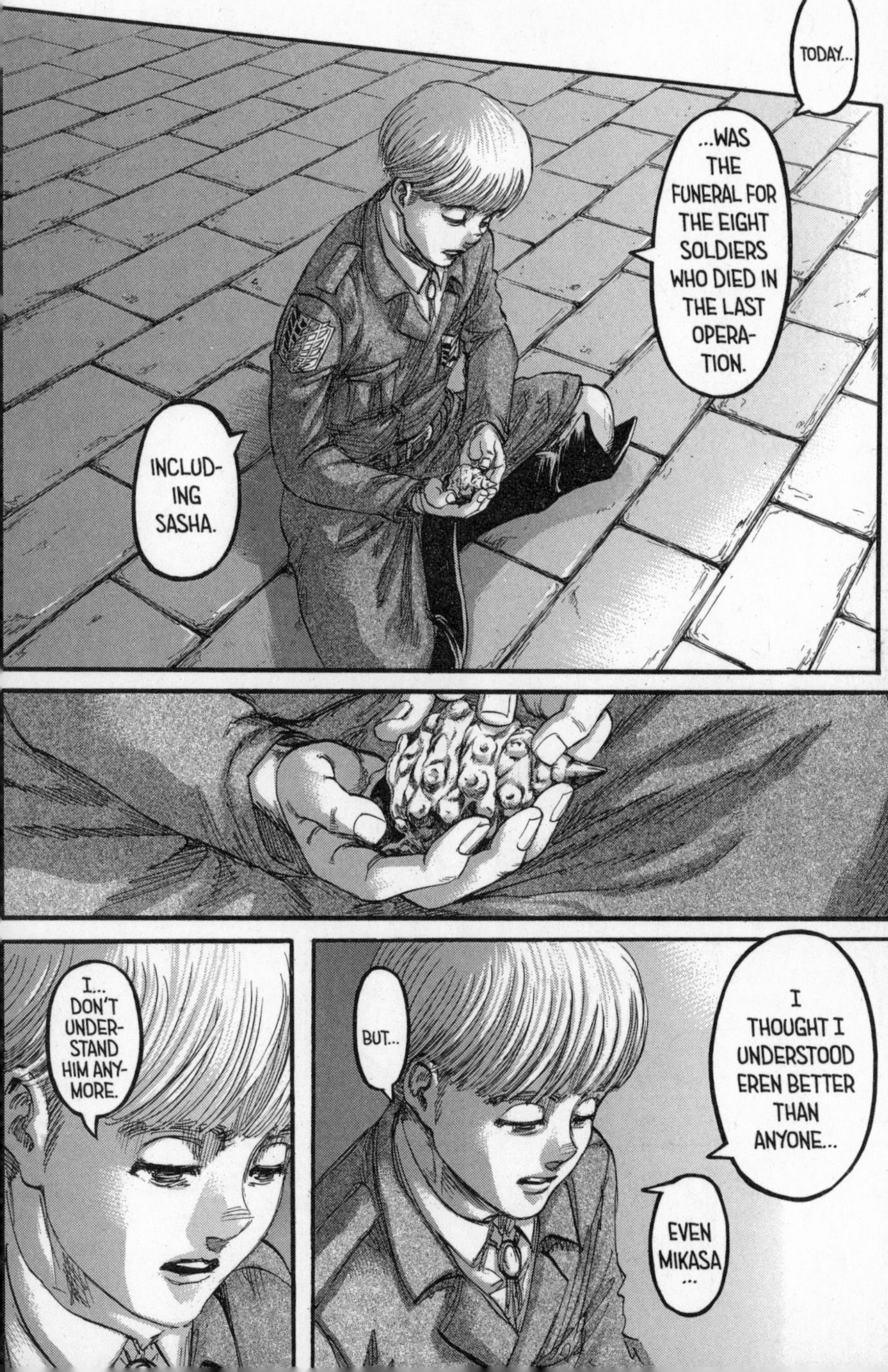
TODAY...
...WAS THE FUNERAL FOR THE EIGHT SOLDIERS WHO DIED IN THE LAST OPERA-TION.
INCLUD-ING SASHA.
I THOUGHT I UNDERSTOOD EREN BETTER THAN ANYONE...
EVEN MIKASA...
BUT...
I... DON'T UNDER-STAND HIM ANY-MORE.

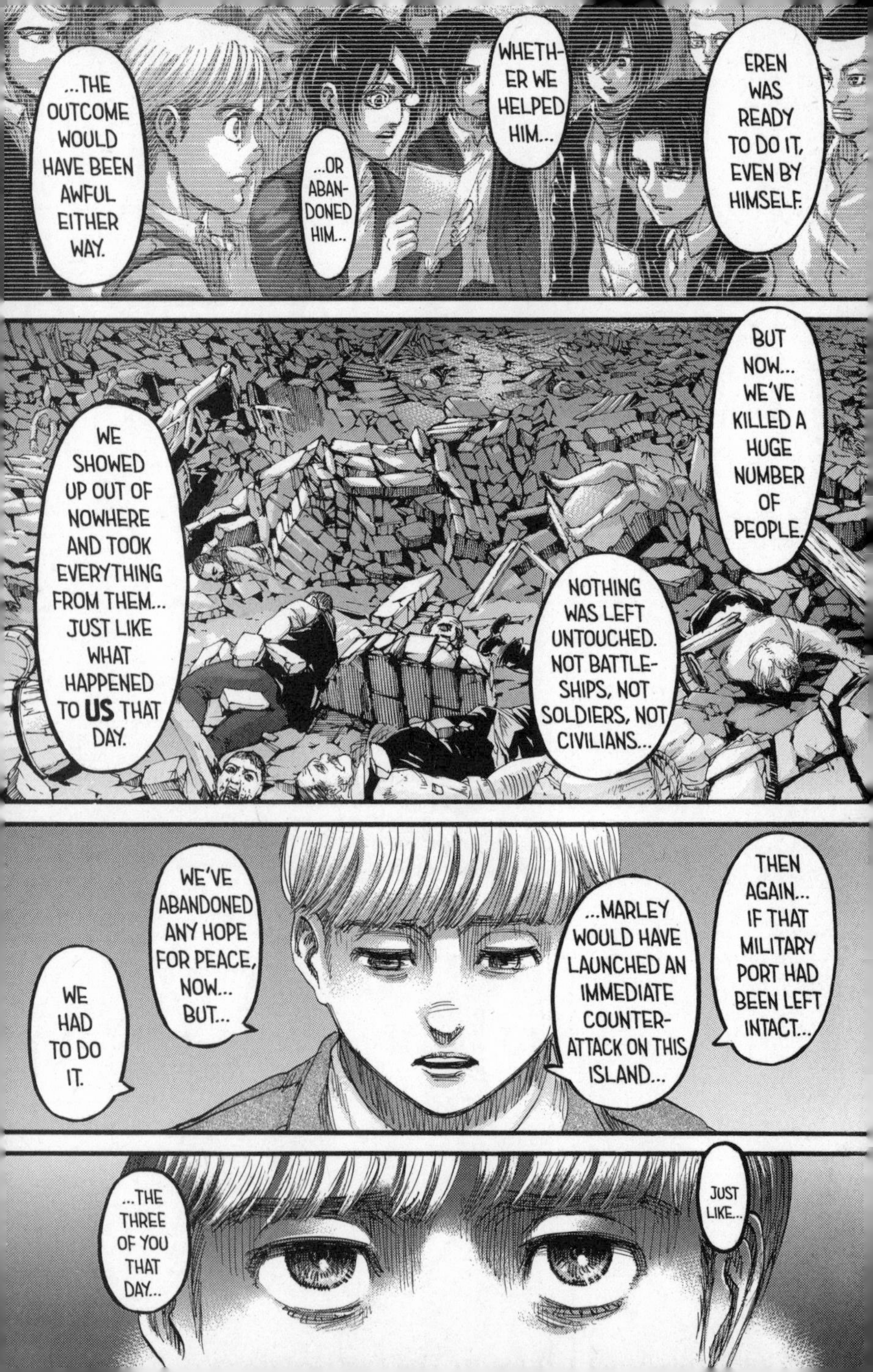
EREN WAS READY TO DO IT, EVEN BY HIMSELF.
WHETHER WE HELPED HIM...
...OR ABANDONED HIM...
...THE OUTCOME WOULD HAVE BEEN AWFUL EITHER WAY.
BUT NOW... WE'VE KILLED A HUGE NUMBER OF PEOPLE.
NOTHING WAS LEFT UNTOUCHED. NOT BATTLESHIPS, NOT SOLDIERS, NOT CIVILIANS...
WE SHOWED UP OUT OF NOWHERE AND TOOK EVERYTHING FROM THEM... JUST LIKE WHAT HAPPENED TO **US** THAT DAY.
THEN AGAIN... IF THAT MILITARY PORT HAD BEEN LEFT INTACT...
...MARLEY WOULD HAVE LAUNCHED AN IMMEDIATE COUNTERATTACK ON THIS ISLAND...
WE'VE ABANDONED ANY HOPE FOR PEACE, NOW... BUT...
WE HAD TO DO IT.
JUST LIKE...
...THE THREE OF YOU THAT DAY...

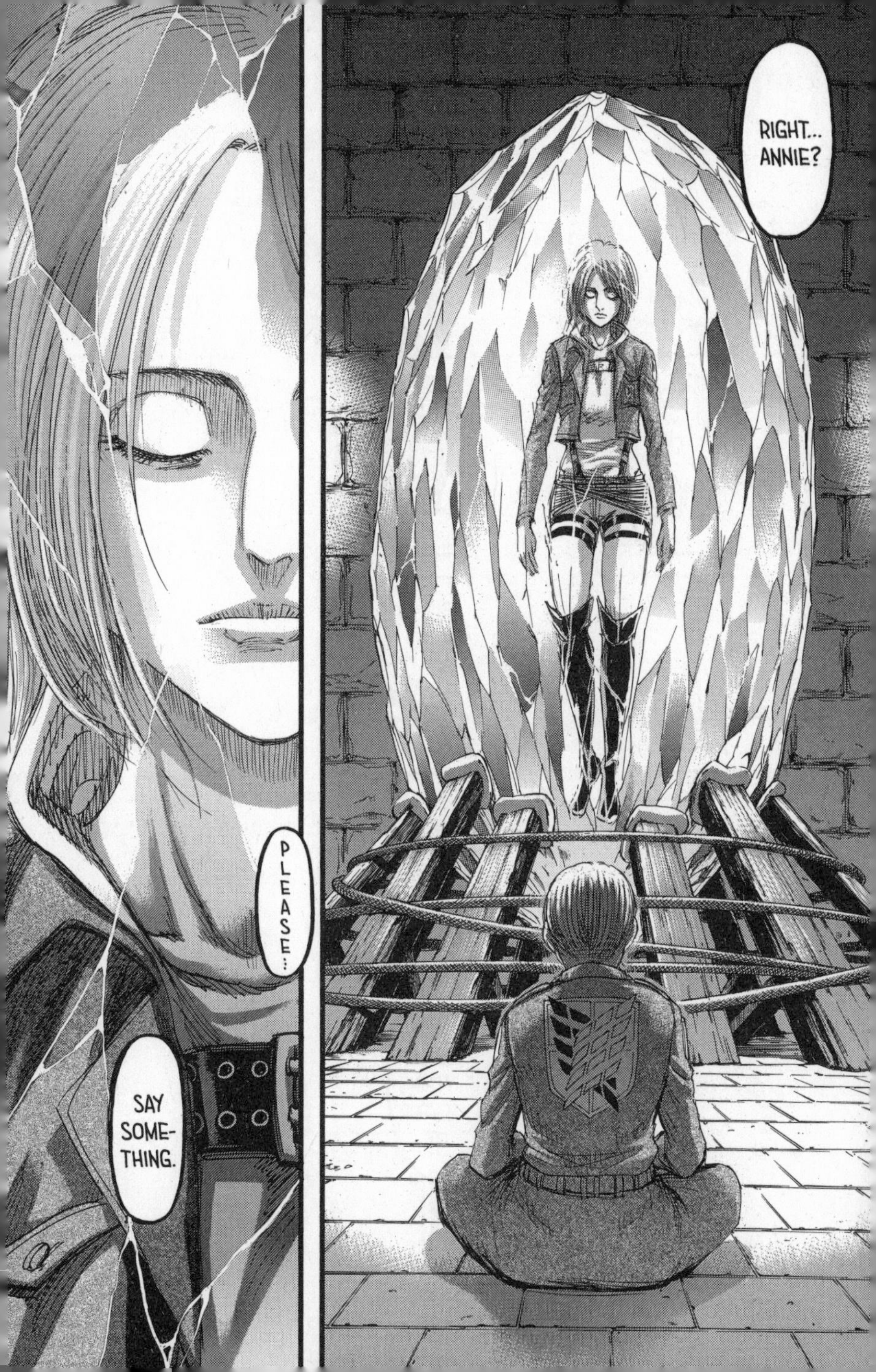
RIGHT... ANNIE?
PLEASE...
SAY SOMETHING.

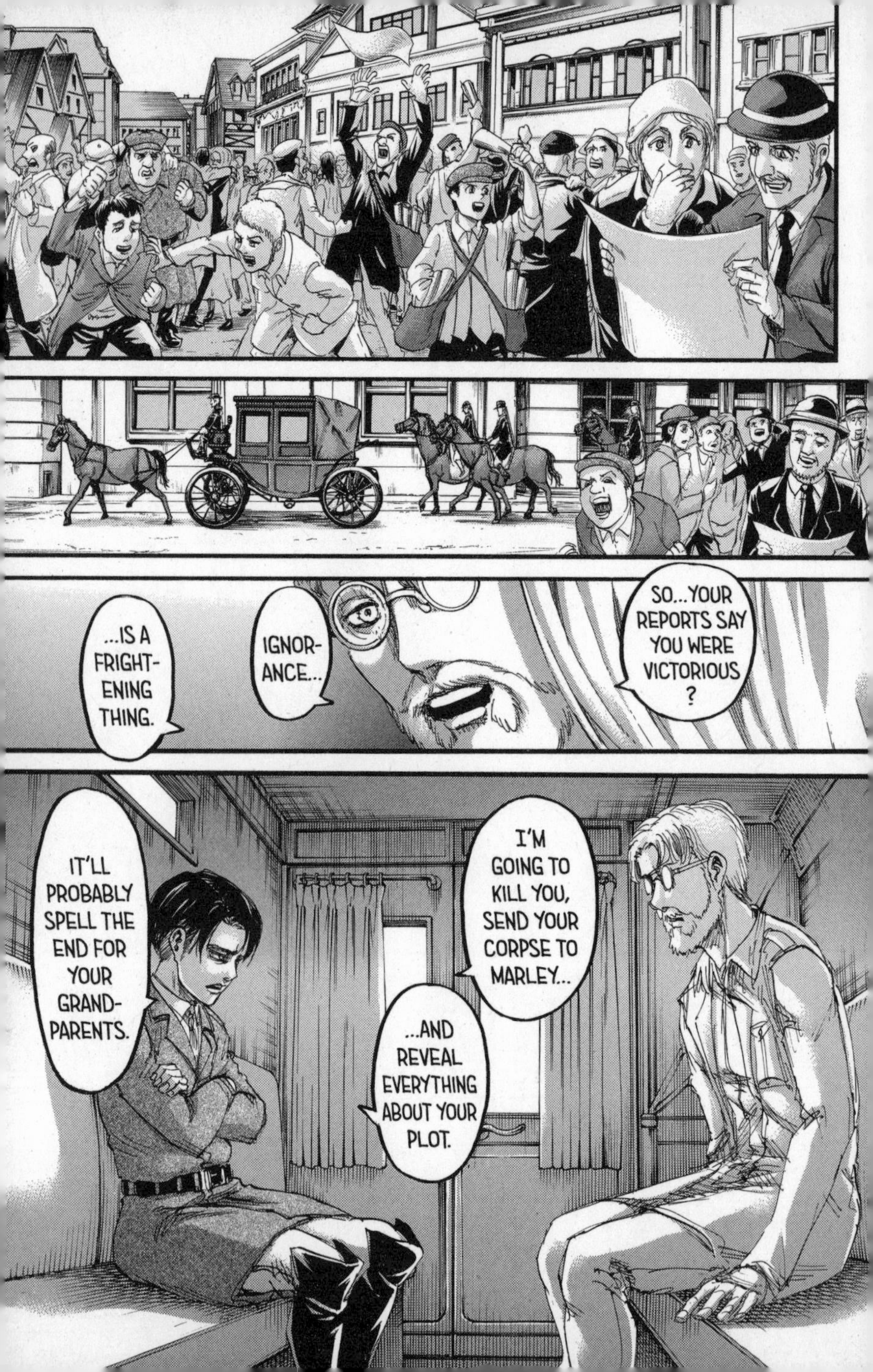
SO... YOUR REPORTS SAY YOU WERE VICTORIOUS?
IGNORANCE...
...IS A FRIGHTENING THING.
I'M GOING TO KILL YOU, SEND YOUR CORPSE TO MARLEY...
...AND REVEAL EVERYTHING ABOUT YOUR PLOT.
IT'LL PROBABLY SPELL THE END FOR YOUR GRANDPARENTS.

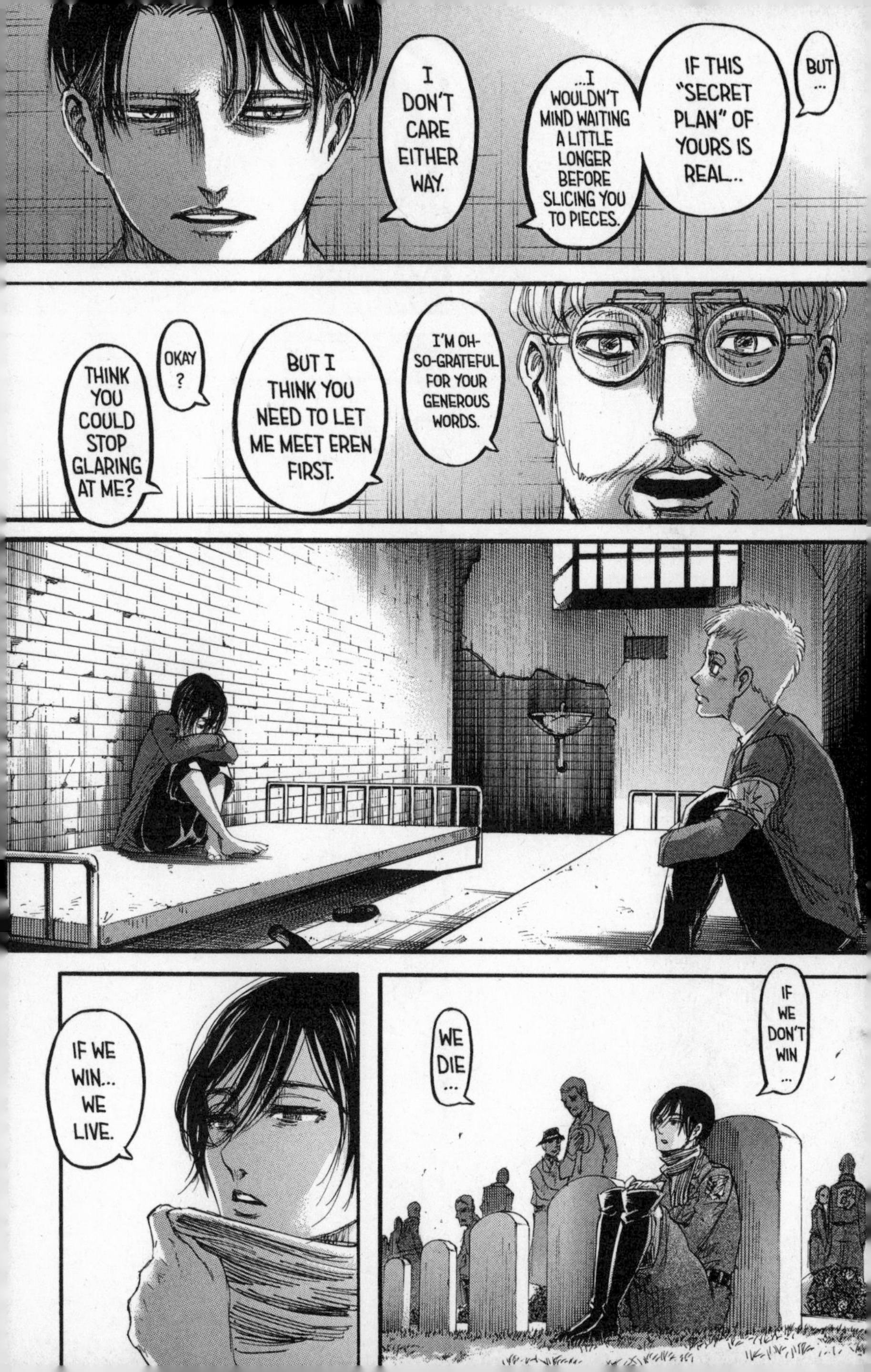
BUT ...
IF THIS "SECRET PLAN" OF YOURS IS REAL...
...I WOULDN'T MIND WAITING A LITTLE LONGER BEFORE SLICING YOU TO PIECES.
I DON'T CARE EITHER WAY.
I'M OH-SO-GRATEFUL FOR YOUR GENEROUS WORDS.
BUT I THINK YOU NEED TO LET ME MEET EREN FIRST.
OKAY ?
THINK YOU COULD STOP GLARING AT ME?
IF WE DON'T WIN ...
WE DIE ...
IF WE WIN... WE LIVE.

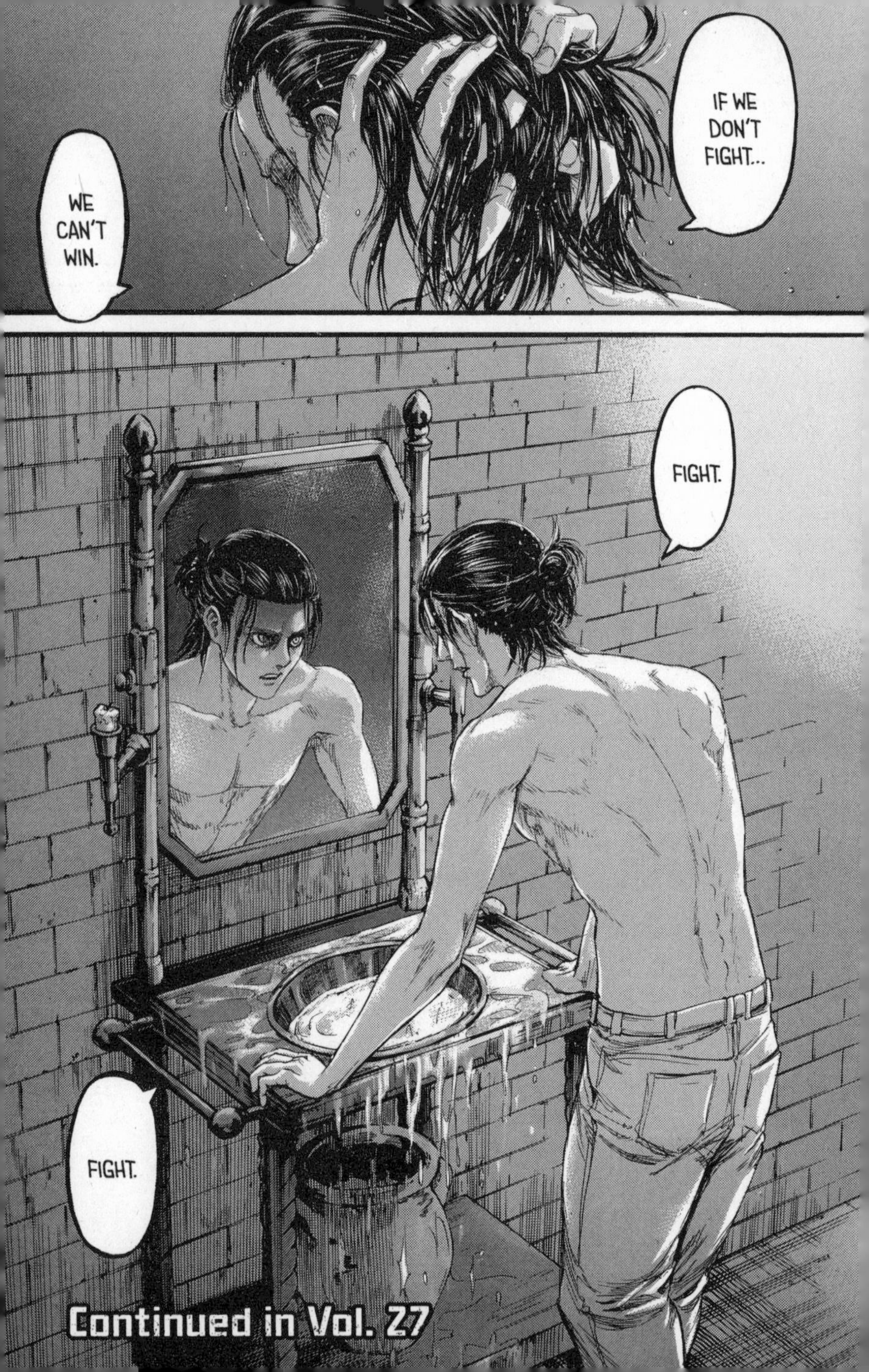
IF WE DON'T FIGHT...
WE CAN'T WIN.
FIGHT.
FIGHT.
Continued in Vol. 27

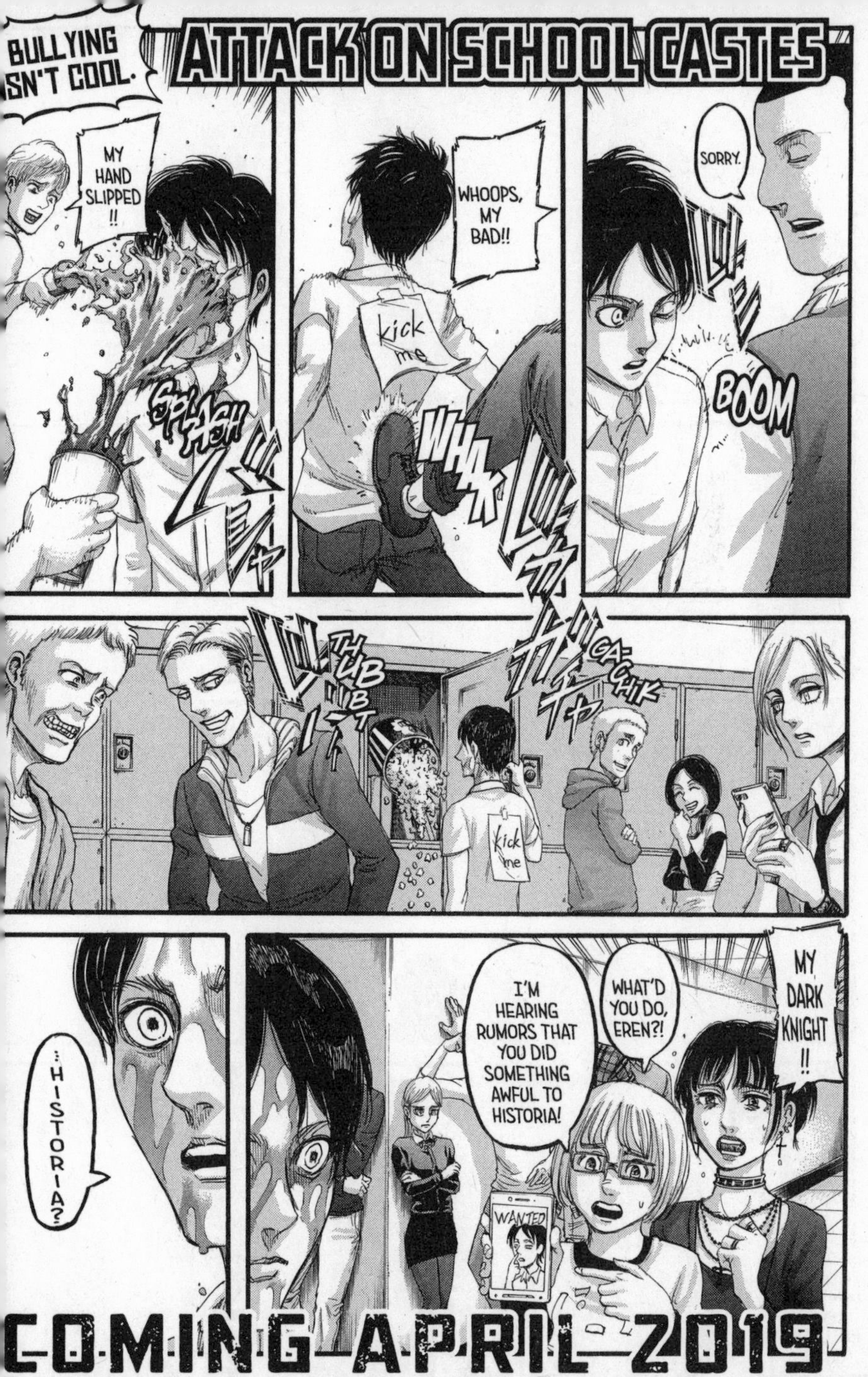
ATTACK ON SCHOOL CASTES
BULLYING ISN'T COOL.
SORRY.
BOOM
WHOOPS, MY BAD!!
kick me
WHAK
MY HAND SLIPPED!!
SPLASH
GACHIK
THUBBT
kick me
MY DARK KNIGHT!!
WHAT'D YOU DO, EREN?!
I'M HEARING RUMORS THAT YOU DID SOMETHING AWFUL TO HISTORIA!
WANTED
...HISTORIA?
COMING APRIL 2019

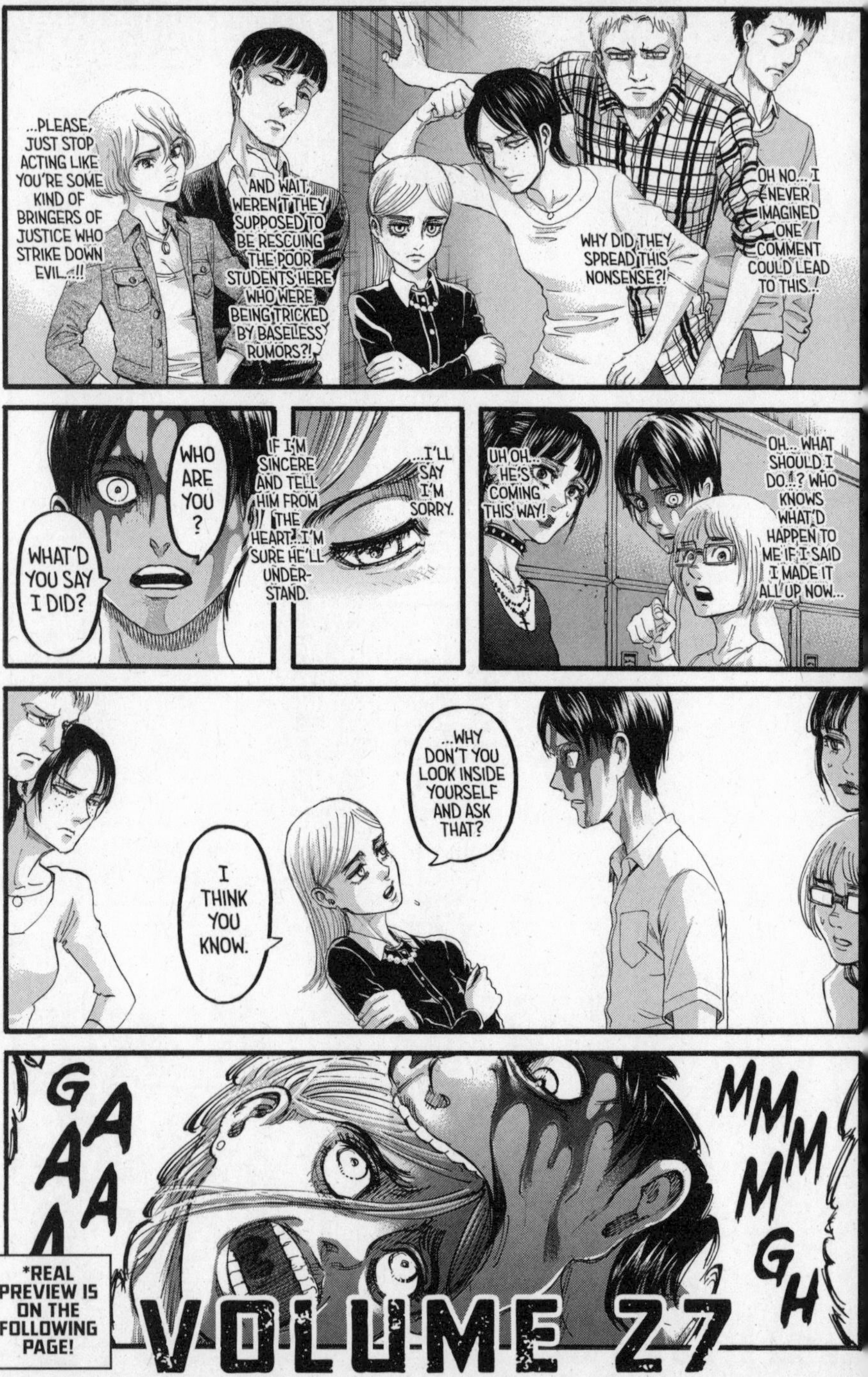
OH NO... I NEVER IMAGINED ONE COMMENT COULD LEAD TO THIS..
WHY DID THEY SPREAD THIS NONSENSE?!
AND WAIT, WEREN'T THEY SUPPOSED TO BE RESCUING THE POOR STUDENTS HERE WHO WERE BEING TRICKED BY BASELESS RUMORS?!
...PLEASE, JUST STOP ACTING LIKE YOU'RE SOME KIND OF BRINGERS OF JUSTICE WHO STRIKE DOWN EVIL...!!
OH... WHAT SHOULD I DO..? WHO KNOWS WHAT'D HAPPEN TO ME IF I SAID I MADE IT ALL UP NOW...
UH OH... HE'S COMING THIS WAY!
...I'LL SAY I'M SORRY.
IF I'M SINCERE AND TELL HIM FROM THE HEART, I'M SURE HE'LL UNDERSTAND.
WHO ARE YOU?
WHAT'D YOU SAY I DID?
...WHY DON'T YOU LOOK INSIDE YOURSELF AND ASK THAT?
I THINK YOU KNOW.
MMMMGH
GAAAA
*REAL PREVIEW IS ON THE FOLLOWING PAGE!
VOLUME 27

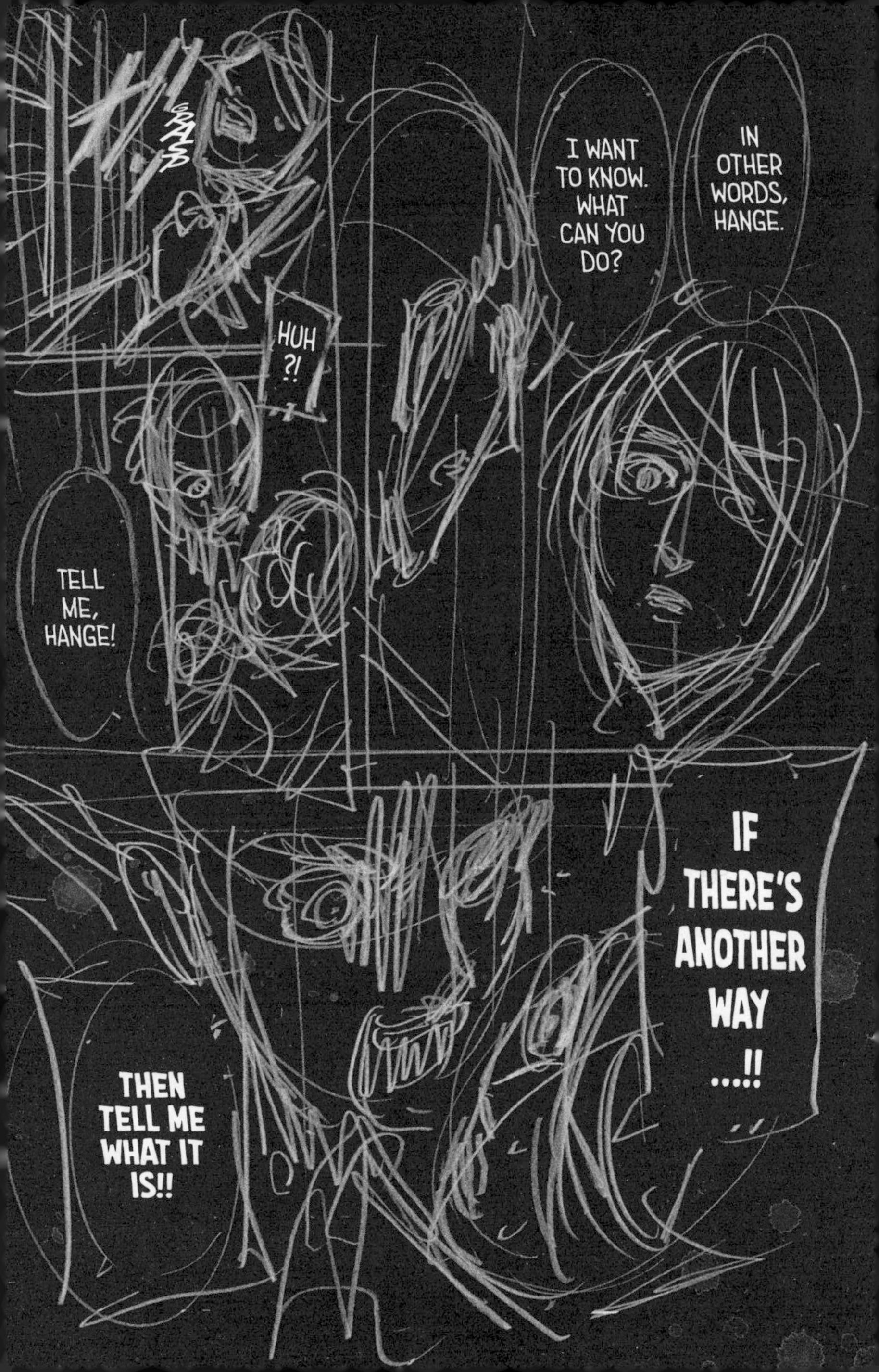
IN OTHER WORDS, HANGE.
I WANT TO KNOW. WHAT CAN YOU DO?
GRASP
HUH ?!
TELL ME, HANGE!
IF THERE'S ANOTHER WAY ...!!
THEN TELL ME WHAT IT IS!!

VOLUME 27 COMING 2019!

PEACE CANNOT BE ATTAINED THROUGH IDEALS ALONE.

JUST HOW MANY SACRIFICES HAVE BEEN MADE TO LAY THE FOUNDATION FOR PEACE...?

Attack on Titan 26 is a work of fiction. Names, characters, places, and incidents are the products of the author's imagination or are used fictitiously. Any resemblance to actual events, locales, or persons, living or dead, is entirely coincidental.

Published in the United States by Kodansha Comics, an imprint of Kodansha USA Publishing, LLC, New York.

Publication rights for this English edition arranged through Kodansha Ltd, Tokyo.

First published in Japan in 2018 by Kodansha Ltd., Tokyo as *Shingeki no kyojin*, volume 26.

ISBN 978-1-63236-6-542

Original cover design by Takashi Shimoyama (Red Rooster)

Printed in the United States of America.

www.kodanshacomics.com

9 8 7 6 5 4 3 2 1

Translation: Ko Ransom
Lettering: Steve Wands
Editing: Ben Applegate and Haruko Hashimoto
Kodansha Comics edition cover design by Phil Balsman